Traveling

Traveling

ON THE PATH OF *Joni Mitchell*

ANN POWERS

DEYST.

An Imprint of WILLIAM MORROW

DEYST.

HarperCollins books may be purchased for educational, business, or sales promotional use. For information, please email the Special Markets Department at SPsales@harpercollins.com.

FIRST EDITION

Designed by Alison Bloomer

Library of Congress Cataloging-in-Publication Data has been applied for.

ISBN 978-0-06-246372-2

24 25 26 27 28 LBC 5 4 3 2 1

To Eric and Bebe Weisbard, who always kept the light on as I wandered,
and to Jacob Ganz, who helped me become the kind of writer
who could risk a trip like this

contents

a note on naming

Joni Mitchell wanted to rethink the way music moved from her mouth to others' ears, to fill songs, even anthems, with the breath of the personal. Her art marks her as both a kind of seer and a friend. These roles require different titles. Throughout her life, she would be "Joni Mitchell" in public, "Joan" to close friends and "Joni" when the textual or musical encounter was public but felt more private— sometimes in interviews, very occasionally in hip-sounding ad copy, but most of all to her fans, in those moments when they spoke their love for her.

I feel comfortable calling Mitchell "Joni" as I consider both the revered figure she has become and the character she has crafted for herself in her music. But what of the artist who deserves serious critical attention? To call her "Joni" can, at times, feel somewhat trivializing. People often address creative women by their first names to make them approachable, cute, like your sister or your mom. Until Joni, no one called Shakespeare "Willy the Shake." (Well, except Lord Buckley, the jazz comic from whom she borrowed the term for "Talk To Me.") Yet when I put "Joni" aside and write "Mitchell," that can feel diminishing, too. Without "Joni," it's almost generic. It's a stage name, a divorced 1960s wife's name. It lacks her essence.

I decided the truest thing to do when it came to my slippery subject was to use "Joni" or "Mitchell" interchangeably, as the occasion demanded. This allowed for me to signal how I was thinking and feeling at different points, and also to make an argument Joni's own music makes. That the personal can be timeless. That the intimate speaks to the world.

Throughout these pages I call her by both or either name, following my intuition. Some aspects of her story feel more internal; others take place on bigger stages. I want to think about "Joni" and "Mitchell" in fruitful dialogue, the self-invented woman engaging with a masculinized inheritance. Women still wonder all the time if they should change their names. Sometimes the solution is to claim two.

Introduction

drawing the maps

I write this so many times in my head,
it's tattooed there, like a song.
What you are about to read is not a standard
account of the life and work of Joni Mitchell.
Instead, it's a tale of long journeying through
a life that changed popular music: of a
homesick wanderer forging ahead on routes
of her own invention, and of me on her trail,
heading toward the ringing of her voice.

I'm not a biographer, in the usual definition of that term; something in me instinctively opposes the idea that one person can sort through all the facts of another's life and come up with anything close to that stranger's true story. Instead, I'm a critic. A kind of mapmaker, as I see it, setting down lines meant to guide others along the trajectories of artists who are always one step ahead of me. In Mitchell I found an inexhaustible subject, one who never let me put down my pen and declare my maps complete.

As I tried to keep up, I had to embrace a new way of writing that made room for gaps, inconsistencies and contradictions, honoring those unstable elements as essential to a story well told. *I am on a lonely road, and I am traveling, traveling, traveling, traveling*, Mitchell sings in "All I Want," the opening track on her most revered album, *Blue*. I love that lyric because of the word she repeats at its end. Every "traveling" is different—determined, anxious, liberated, driven—as Joni extends her breath and clips it, finding a rhythm and immediately pushing away its constraints. So much ground covered in so little time. The line perfectly describes my experience writing this book. As I immersed myself in the landscapes and soundscapes where Mitchell landed and made her music, I had to keep uprooting myself, rejecting any settled stances about who this woman is and why her music is so special. I needed to keep moving because that's what she's always done.

What often happens to legends like Mitchell, not as people necessarily but as subjects of the world's impassioned interest, is that they get stuck within the edifice of fame. In some ways, they become monuments themselves—solid structures built from the aspects of themselves that others love most. Joni Mitchell the misunderstood musical genius, the emblematic free woman, the sad girl's or boy's best imaginary friend, has solidified into a series of qualities and traits rather than remaining a dynamic force running on both magic and flaws. She is: open tunings, confessional song-writing, jazz-rock. She is: a gamine old crone, a childless mother, a true blue lover leaving before the sun comes up. She is: always in her own category, so relatable, ultimately unknowable. In truth she's all of these things, but reducing her to any of them turns her into stone.

Mitchell's music chases and challenges society's assumptions about what a woman and an artist can be. Any singular view of her artistry, and her influence, diminishes it. I'm taking Mitchell's lead on this: "I feel sometimes like I'm a multiphrenic person," she once said, apparently inventing a term psychologists would later use to describe the condition of having "many selves and self-representations that conflict." Mitchell put it more plainly: "Will the real me stand up, you know."

My goal has been to follow Joni Mitchell as she's drifted and flown and to chart the rhythms of her inquiries. Her self-conception begins in movement: When asked to define herself, she rarely calls herself a musician first, saying that since she was a child she's been a dancer. And a painter. Shimmying with the boys and the bad girls in a Saskatoon dive, wrecking her stockings. Reaching her arms overhead to make brushstrokes on a canvas, opening up unimagined vistas with a smear of paint. A portrait hardens and becomes lifeless when its maker loses track of the breath, the living presence of her subject—a constantly shifting thing, blurry then focused then dissolving then clear, then different, the light has changed—and strives for something absolute. A mapmaker must be open to new routes. People are not definitive; neither is any one story. That is the point of Mitchell's songs. Life is stranger and bigger than that. And people, even geniuses, are smaller: human, always incomplete. Every legend is also one of us.

EMBARKING

Many years ago, I was standing in my front yard looking suspiciously at some gathering clouds when a New York editor called me and said, "I just really want to read you on Joni." My first reaction was to pull the phone away from my face and laugh. Of course the woman music critic should write about the woman demigod. Why didn't anyone ever say to me, "I really want to read you on the Beatles?" In fact, I knew why. With thirty years and tens of thousands of words behind me, I'd made contemplating what it means to be called a "woman in music" the heart of my work. Somewhere buried in a trunk at the back of my office closet is a clothbound notebook from my eighteenth year with *I LOVE WOMEN!* scrawled in blue ink halfway through and some gushing thoughts on Kate Bush, Chrissie Hynde, Debbie Harry, the artists of my New Wave generation; those renegades showed me that music could be the vehicle for my questions about what it means to move in a body gendered female through spaces dominated by men. Also in there is a typewritten talk I once gave on Joni Mitchell's *Blue.* I have, at times, given in to the inevitable, recognizing her brilliance. I just never lingered long in its proximity.

I took a breath, put the phone to my ear again. There was really nothing strange about someone thinking that a woman like me—white, raised middle-class, fancies herself a bohemian, loves a great ballad, grew up in the north but considers California a second home, can passably play the guitar—should be interested in Joni Mitchell. Yet my feelings about Mitchell and her music were more abstract than ardent. The fact is that I've always found her a daunting figure, difficult to identify with. Yes, I can hear the perfection in *Blue,* and the reach of *Hejira.* I recognize her innovations as a guitarist, her studio wizardry, the diamond shine of her voice. But at some point I got tired of hearing not only about how great Joni Mitchell is, but that she'd never been fully acknowledged as such.

As I saw it, she'd had more advantages than most. Her inestimable talent, of course, but also her prom queen looks, her close connections to powerful men like the Davids (Crosby, Geffen) and the canny charm that instantly won over the same people who often regarded her female peers as silly and excessive. The minute Mitchell stepped onto the musical stage she found critical approval and a devoted audience, and even when her career took inevitable downturns, she remained the spirit guide of so many listeners' hearts. I preferred underdogs. Even the rock and soul queens I loved best, like Janis Joplin and Aretha Franklin, were messier than Mitchell. Her svelte, swanlike cool felt so distant from my own way of being.

Hold on, I said to the editor, let me call you back in a minute. I needed time to walk around the block and fret a bit. To mull over the possibility of entering the Joni congregation. Devotees and scholars, mostly inseparable from one another, have documented her every guitar tuning, road trip and close encounter. Women and men alike have rhapsodized about her as both a soulmate and an unmatchable ideal. Joni conquered so many hearts and was called "genius" so many times that the slant rhyme between her name and that word is embedded in her story, its principal signpost. All the Joni worship freaked me out, frankly—it's so intense and uncompromising. To so many, she can do no wrong. I have never felt comfortable around the popular kids.

I took another breath. I did have to admit that there were times when Joni got to me, too. When I'd managed to push away all of this baggage and really listen to her music, I heard someone

I could recognize. A striver, restlessly curious. A soul acknowledging its own brokenness. A lady who loved a good joke. And certainly a brilliant musician, one who like most innovators could turn her shortcomings into strengths and process the dominant artistic conversations of her time through her own filters until they sounded unique. I'd spent enough time with Mitchell's full recorded catalog to know that she pulled this off many times—she didn't settle into her achievements, instead always wanting something different. Her songs themselves formed an argument against her being treated like a sacred cow. This made me wonder if I could find another Joni Mitchell, one less worshipped but better understood.

So I called back and said okay. I'd take a trip with Joni, make her life and work the center of my world for a while. Little did I know, as I set forth with her in mind, that this journey would take me into so many complicated spaces.

ECHOLOCATION

When it comes to art, I don't believe in anything timeless, but I do trust resonances, the echoes that intensify the impact of specific songs (or books, or paintings) in their moment and then carry them across the years. I fell in love with rock and roll as a kid because of the way the sound waves hit me, making me feel every inch of my body and the heat and freedom and joy people felt when it enraptured them. That's resonance in its most visceral form. I didn't want to be lifted into some celestial realm; I needed to know my own world better. Music always put me right in the middle of things. And the words of the songs I loved, which spoke so directly and demanded a response, enhanced the feeling that its present tense could be all-encompassing.

Later I came to realize that resonance is also a cultural thing. Great artists don't transcend their historical circumstances; they live deeply in specific times and places. They are also deeply themselves. Their gift is being able to figure out what elements from unsorted experience can make the jump beyond the moment they're generated, forming stories, sounds and images that vibrate and expand. A year or a century later, someone can encounter a great artist's work and recognize her own voice in its reverberations.

Joni Mitchell has a metaphor for this kind of connectivity. It came to her in the spring of 1976, when she was driving through the West and saw some military planes flying in formation, an encounter that could have only happened in the Space Age but which put her in mind of ancient things, of pilgrimage and prophecy. She used the image in her song "Amelia," invoking her favorite form of divination, the *I Ching*: in *the hexagram of the heavens*, she wrote, she saw *the strings of my guitar*. And then when she recorded the song she asked jazz guitarist Larry Carlton to put down swooping lines that reinforced her words, showing them to be about dreaming, about modernity, about the way people's lofty concepts of the universal are always grounded in what their own hands and minds can grasp.

That's resonance. It's personal; it's here and now; it's ancient. A hippie like Joni might say it's all about those vibes, linking total strangers by making them feel what they have in common in their bones. A vision experienced alone becomes a song that rings forth into the universe and survives there, its original meanings multiplying as it moves through time and space. I wanted to track these sound waves in Joni's story, navigating by echolocation.

To do this, I had to follow the molecules colliding and forming patterns within Mitchell's life and work. That meant staying light on my feet. Though this book proceeds chronologically,

I didn't write it that way. Instead of trudging along the timeline of her life from childhood to venerable old age, I sought out the turning points that shaped her and worked to understand how she made those turns central within her music. I started my explorations where I most easily found her, at the turn of the 1970s, when *Clouds* and *Blue* made Mitchell the avatar for a new kind of writerly openness. I learned as much as I could about the communities that formed her, as a folkie first and then as a California seeker reinventing that genre under the influence of Hollywood, jazz and the counterculture. Tracking down her friends and collaborators, I explored what it meant for her to deal with that quintessential problem for women working in creative fields: being female in scenes defined by men. Pushing up my sleeves in the Rock & Roll Hall of Fame archives and reading every early copy of *Rolling Stone* magazine helped me understand how she became the role model for a certain kind of liberated woman in the wake of a feminist movement she never endorsed.

Joni's resonances began filling my head as I continued to think, read, listen and write. I started to recognize how the matters that preoccupied her fit within the changing contexts through which she was living. Certain subjects emerged: childhood as an imaginary terrain where singer-songwriters could express their ideals and idiosyncrasies; sadness as a complicated form of women's liberation; side roads and retreats as the secret sources of an artist's strengths. And traveling, always traveling, the paradoxical grounding principle of her life.

By the time I hit the late 1970s, Joni was no longer an abstraction to me. The figure ossified by fame fell away bit by bit, and the full shape of a woman emerged. This Joni Mitchell was neither the abject bearer of women's sorrows nor a pop goddess beyond comprehension. She was a goofball, fast with a joke, a satirist casting a sharp eye on the haute-hippie pretensions that sometimes sucked her in. She threw herself into love affairs and spiritual pursuits with an openhearted enthusiasm that felt familiar. She's always said that at heart she's a real rock and roller, and her rebel spirit further won me over. I also valued her growing commitment to jazz, the dedication she brought to becoming the best musical collaborator and most inventive player and singer she could be. I became absorbed by the music and lore of the jazz-rock milieu where she then moved, invigorated by the curiosity that compelled her to push beyond easy definitions. That same spirit characterized her often undervalued 1980s work, and learning about her pursuit of new technologies and themes helped me better understand the sounds of that time, the era of my own youth.

The third act of Mitchell's life presented different narrative challenges. After age fifty, she retreated for long periods; she struggled with illness. Her reunion with Kilauren Gibb, the daughter she'd entrusted in adoption shortly after birth, answered some central questions about her life and work, but as an adoptive mother myself I felt hesitant to make any conjectures about this most intimate connection. Every adoption story is different, and I firmly believe it belongs only to those who've lived it. I would not pry; my resistance to doing so is one reason I'll never call myself a biographer. Eventually, though, I found I could follow Mitchell's signals as she moved into middle age and beyond. Learning to manage her new public identity as a mother, she found spiritual daughters, too, musicians and writers who craved her blessing. She played with her legacy in fascinating ways. And she began to build her archive just as doing so became a primary focus for musicians of her generation, and a matter of central importance within popular music itself.

Time went by and my Joni atlas grew. I took on a role that I'd never wanted: I became a kind of Joni expert. "Joni wrote about that," I'd pipe up in pop-trivia discussions. "Check out verse two of 'Cactus Tree.'" Or, "Joni used that synthesizer," "Joni played that club," "that guitarist toured with Joni in 1979." Friends tolerated my habitual flexing; they knew I'd been doing the work. But then they'd ask the inevitable question. "So, did you talk to her yet?" No, I'd say, and here's why.

I knew Joni Mitchell was a great interview—once she got going, she'd let it all hang out, when she wasn't lambasting her interlocutor for some opinion she found ridiculous. She once signed a contract to write an autobiography, but as of this writing she hasn't published one; instead, she laid it down through others' pens. A growing literature exists documenting her garrulous conversations. Its lodestone is Malka Marom's book-length collection of interviews *Joni Mitchell: In Her Own Words*. That collaboration with Mitchell's longtime friend, a fellow Canadian folk singer and public radio personality, is the most casually revealing document she has helped produce. And throughout her life, Mitchell welcomed many other writers into her home, their tape recorders discreetly activated.

These encounters became invaluable to me. Michelle Mercer's 2009 study of Mitchell's "blue period," *Will You Take Me As I Am*, was enriched by warm talk over white wine with Joni in her Sunshine Coast backyard. It did much to dispel widespread myths about her, including that she was ever glamorously aloof. David Yaffe's 2017 biography, *Reckless Daughter*, jumped off from a series of hours-long conversations punctuated by communication breakdowns; Yaffe emerged from those conflicts perhaps too eager to stay in Joni's good graces, but his book is powerful, especially when it comes to rich musical analysis, because it's grounded in that meaningful exchange. Marom's volume most convincingly conveys Mitchell's personality; teased and comforted and, occasionally, challenged by a genuine friend in discussions staged across several decades, Mitchell lets her thoughts detonate and scatter in revelatory ways, even if her streams of consciousness sometimes run over inconvenient truths. Waves of uncensored musings also characterize Mitchell's interviews in publications like *Rolling Stone* and *Vanity Fair* and preserved in anthologies edited by esteemed journalists like Barney Hoskyns and Susan Whitall. Sitting next to a bookshelf heaving with Joni's words, I never felt lacking for her insights.

In 2015, Mitchell suffered a debilitating aneurysm. For several years, it was unclear if she would ever speak in public again. I wrote much of this book during this time of her silence. When she finally did reemerge, at first as the honored guest at various tributes to her art, and then as a tentative but determined performer herself, I considered attempting a connection. I quickly decided against it, not only because her condition remained unclear but because, in truth, I feared what would happen if I sought her blessing.

Was I being cowardly? Perhaps. As someone who's spent years engaged in the weird dance between artists and their chroniclers, I knew that even a little intimacy can create the desire for more. The more beloved the artist, the more potent the craving. Despite her sometimes gleeful arrogance, maybe partly because of it, something about Joni Mitchell screams *to know her is to love her*—and to emphatically believe in her. Her supercharged appeal is a problem if clarity is your goal. It seduces. Mitchell's biographers know this; they have always wrestled with her potential disapproval. "I knew she would turn on me, that she would cast me out," Yaffe said in an interview after he'd published his book, and, indeed, she did reject him at certain points, though she would let him back in and cast him out again.

The problem he faced, now mine, is that, like anyone, Mitchell the woman has a firm idea of what her story means, even though over the years she's contradicted herself and filtered things through her own strong perspective. Memory is always tricky; its power lies in the conviction of the teller. And after decades of being mined and guarded like a treasure, Mitchell the legend (if not the woman; it's hard to tell) can't bear too much heavy questioning. "Joni Mitchell never lies," the rapper Q-Tip famously intoned in Janet Jackson's hit "Got 'Til It's Gone." That itself is a lie. We all fudge things, omit and embellish. I didn't want to reinforce a myth. I wanted to be able to raise the kinds of questions that could cause Mitchell to cast me out. So I chose to rely on the words she'd already offered and steer clear of the tenuous bond an interview creates.

Resonances don't register accurately if you're too close. I know what it's like to feel overly committed to an artist and lose critical perspective. It's a side effect of what Joni famously called the "star maker machinery," the process through which fame becomes grounded in the exchange of a celebrity's private life and inner thoughts for the price of a concert ticket, an album, a magazine. Fans think they know their favorite stars, and in a personal encounter the rush of instant familiarity can distort everything. Journalists are supposed to be different from fans, but we are people, full of the longing for acceptance. I don't want to seek Joni Mitchell's acceptance. I want to bring as wide a perspective as I can manage to her world, and I can do that only by maintaining some distance. In this way, I remain a witness, not a friend.

A PHASE

Others have not felt the same need for distance. The novelist Zadie Smith described the onset of her passion for Joni Mitchell almost as a physical affliction. "This is the effect that listening to Joni Mitchell has on me these days: uncontrollable tears," she wrote in the *New Yorker* in 2012. "An emotional overcoming, disconcertingly distant from happiness, more like joy—if joy is the recognition of an almost intolerable beauty. It's not a very civilized emotion." Smith's experience, no matter how intense, is typical for fans who become devoted to Joni. In her deeply subjective argument for Mitchell's inimitability, "The Joni Mitchell Problem," the essayist Meghan Daum recounts that after realizing her life goal of meeting Mitchell and making a chatty connection with her, she lost the singer's phone number. "After everything—after the dinner, after the art exhibit, after the decades spent with my own private Joni as she piloted me through the indignities of adolescence and the indecision of early adulthood and the parting clouds of middle adulthood—I let the woman herself slip away like a dream burned into abstraction by the glare of wakefulness." Her not-that-wakeful dream of Mitchell could not be disturbed by the reality of an actual person. To these famous fans, as for many people, introspective encounters with Mitchell's voice are so powerful and unique that they cannot be shared with others—even their source. Coming to love her is akin to achieving enlightenment: a shocking moment of insight that transforms the world.

Yet so many also talk about the experience as a phase. You know, like a "punk phase," when you had a Mohawk, or a "Dylan phase" that a cardboard box of bad undergrad poetry exposes. The Joni Mitchell phase is distinctive in its stunning impact and the feeling that lingers of being intertwined with her words and voice. The critic Ron Rosenbaum once wrote an ode to her song "Amelia" in which he described his relationship to it as a bout of musical addiction, "periods when I get tangled up . . . and play it over and over again for hours, sometimes days at a time." Even lifelong fans, like the musician Dan Bejar, use temporal language to describe listening to her: "I guess I'm going through something of a phase . . . that's lasted six or seven years now," he admitted a few years ago.

What other kinds of phases are life-changing? Puberty, for one thing. Menopause, for another. The experience of coming to love Joni Mitchell's music can feel almost biological, hitting in a hormonal wash, and often seems linked to gender. Women hear themselves in those songs, in solidarity with one another, as if no other musician of Mitchell's stature—including other women artists—could speak of womanhood at once so specifically and so universally. "All girls go through a Joni Mitchell phase," the singer-songwriter Tift Merritt once said. "If any girl tells you she never did, don't believe her." There's an essentialist sheen to such declarations, which imply that the only way to be truly feminine is to love Joni Mitchell. If you don't love her, are you not a real woman? I admit that the fact that I'd never fallen headlong for Joni made me wonder for a while if this was a problem I had. Maybe in my heart I'm a gay man? But gay men fall hard for Joni, too, or so the lore reveals. "You don't meet too many straight guys who love Joni Mitchell," Annette Bening, playing a lesbian, says to Mark Ruffalo, as her children's sperm-donating biological dad, who is screwing up her marriage by sleeping with her bisexual partner, in the movie *The Kids Are All Right*. It's a nice little encapsulation of the fluid nature of Joni's actual songwriting, but the joke is all about how Joni belongs to everyone as long as he's not a captain on the patriarchal home team.

The passionate assertion that women love Joni Mitchell the most—and must love her—reveals certain cultural presumptions about what a woman musician offers. (An aside: I have met cis-het men who are devoted to Mitchell, and they've told me that what she gave them was . . . a better understanding of the women in their lives.) Those presumptions may also have contributed to Mitchell's odd status as an outsider, though she's undeniably a central figure within popular music history. The musical canon has until very recently maintained a very solid glass ceiling, with even the most beloved women artists still treated as separate, even when equal to men. That's why, even though everybody agrees that Mitchell is likely the greatest singer-songwriter and also possibly the greatest guitarist, vocalist and producer of her time, she's also tagged "underappreciated." It's also why Mitchell fandom is identified as a "phase," even though it's hard to put borders around it. The paradox of the Joni Mitchell phase is that it beats time: it lasts forever.

GENIUS

Artists whose influence vibrates beyond a particular moment have a chance to enter the most elite category available: that of the genius. Talking to people about Joni Mitchell, I heard that word so often that its meaning was dulled. It's an accolade Mitchell's friends love to attach to her, especially the men; they usually say it with an oversized air of wonderment. David Crosby and James Taylor both invoked it when I talked to them. Graham Nash, who played the role of Mitchell's provisional husband during her first burst of fame, wrote in his memoir that "there was pure genius sitting in front of me" when, on the night they met, she played him fifteen of her songs before the first kiss. Her presence bewitched him into doing something he wasn't used to doing with a woman after midnight: taking her seriously.

Meeting Nash was an important step in Mitchell's rise to the throne as the queen of Laurel Canyon, a musical community scattered over the hills of West Los Angeles where men supported and competed with one another as they restyled the idea of the rock star, and women mostly took care of the babies and cooked the picnic meals the men consumed as they worked out harmonies in the backyard. Mitchell was not the only woman who focused on her art instead of making sandwiches—there was Carole King, who only entered the scene to work and then returned home to her daughters, and Cass Elliot, who managed to do both. But Mitchell understood that to not be banished to the kitchen, even temporarily, she needed to startle and amaze as only a uniquely gifted person can. The miracles are real—she did write "Woodstock" in an afternoon, did play her guitar in tunings no one had heard or even considered before, did devise melodies barely singable by others and execute them with ease. Yet like most miracles, Mitchell's can be explained. Her famous tunings, for example, still echoed what she'd learned from Black blues players like Elizabeth Cotten and Richie Havens. She had a lot of Joan Baez in her voice when she started out. She learned key lessons about songwriting from Leonard Cohen. She did have influences and peers.

Even in early interviews, Joni rarely acknowledged these sources, except to say that she was already moving on from them. Instead, she placed herself in the company of history's number ones: Picasso, Beethoven, Mozart. Also Bob Dylan. Let's think for just a minute about Dylan's genius, which most singer-songwriters sought to emulate in the late 1960s. He described it as a motivating impulse somewhat like the urge to vomit. It was a force that made him a channel not only for the moment he embodied but for all of American history. "It's like a ghost is writing a song," he'd say upon presenting the world with a classic like 1965's "Like a Rolling Stone." Imbued with the authority of his male voice, Dylan could invoke genius and stand for his time. Beethoven, history says, did that, too.

Could a woman do that? Dylan was able to share the spot-light and still own it. He could lock arms with the boys in his band, openly quote his sources, count himself among the greats from whom he borrowed so routinely that many (including Mitchell herself, though she later walked back her comment) have called him a plagiarist. He has long denied such charges, able to present himself as a conduit for history, because his place in it was secure. Joni stood on shakier ground. As a woman she wasn't granted the power to define anything beyond her own experience and its reso-nances; listeners may have heard themselves in her disclosures, but they remained specific and private. One early interviewer talked to Mitchell about her music as "like peeping in a window on someone and then discussing with her what you have seen." That's very dif-ferent from sitting down with Dylan and expounding on politics, mythology and the state of the world. A woman genius in those years was not perceived as engaging with the bigger picture. She simply made exquisite pictures of herself and her private life.

This is what often happens to women artists: for them, "genius" isolates and, at times, silences. The ones who figured out how to inhabit it had to take drastic measures. Think of Joni's role models: Georgia O'Keeffe in her desert, Emily Dickinson shut away upstairs. Only such singular figures embodied the highest apex of artistic expression. And often, they got stuck there, pitied as much as they were revered for their need to stand apart.

Joni Mitchell, I came to realize, was able to stand apart while continuing to move. She carried herself like no other. In many iconic photographs, and in her own paintings, her gaze challenges observers to approach, but with great care and no expectations. In the self-portrait adorning *Clouds* she holds a prairie lily like a gift, but her eyes are impassive and she does not smile; handing it over, it seems, she'll immediately walk away. For *Hejira*, she used collage techniques to alter Norman Seeff's photograph so that her body, below a face holding another cool gaze, opens up to reveal her soul: an empty highway stretching to infinity. Mitchell's self-portraits in song reinforce these images of self-containment: the lonely artist living in her paint box in "A Case of You"; the air-borne observer in "Both Sides Now," high enough to see the other side of the sky; the wanderer on the road, away from the horde, in "Woodstock." At first, I was intimidated by the self-sufficiency Mitchell projected through these images, and by how she so masterfully balanced it with longing, her openness to the touch of others. But I came to see it as revolutionary. So many songs sung by women seduce, cajole, plead, invite. Only a few artists—Billie Holiday, Édith Piaf—were able to create a space where they could simply commune with themselves. Joni's music showed how that space existed within herself, and then bore it onward with her.

She might not like it if I name it such but this is a feminist act. A man can hide within a crowd and reemerge more powerful. But a woman will be distracted by her surroundings, making sure everyone has one of those sandwiches, pressured to be pretty and to please. "I always smile when I'm nervous," Joni said in early interviews. She had to separate herself—metaphorically, sometimes literally—when she didn't want to just smile.

What she did so gracefully in her music and painting sometimes turned sour when she tried to talk about it. Mitchell's desire that others recognize her as a genius was inseparable from her need to distinguish herself from the people around her, especially other women. From the first time she articulated it, this exigency was both deeply felt and strategic. And it worked. "She is fulfilling something of a 'goddess' need in American rock, a woman who is more than a woman; a poet who expresses a full range of emotions without embarrassment," the critic Jacoba Atlas wrote of her in

1970. "Her legend is beginning to obscure her work; because she is virtually without competition (Joan Baez and Judy Collins don't have the output; Buffy Sainte-Marie doesn't have the immediate newness), she is without comparison." Mitchell accepted such problematic compliments.

Becoming exceptional was, for her, a form of self-protection, as the critic Lindsay Zoladz wrote in a 2017 essay on Mitchell and genius, claiming the term helped her resist dismissal and hone "a stainless steel bullshit detector." She saw what happened to women who didn't keep a tight rein on how the world regarded them. One of the few women singer-songwriters she named as an influence flopped, in fact, because she couldn't smell a threat. Laura Nyro had been David Geffen's primary passion project before he met Joni and became her guide through the music business. But he could never break Nyro to a larger audience. In Joni, he saw what Nyro could never be: a woman who could project power without terrifying people who weren't used to that.

Not long before Mitchell's breakthrough, Nyro held the spot she would soon occupy. She was an artist's artist, her songs covered by many of her peers, her potential dazzling. But Nyro, whose own recordings blended soul, pop and jazz with lush and nearly uncontained abandon, took up space in ways that many listeners found intimidating. She didn't cultivate the aura of aloofness that genius demands. It's intriguing to read accounts of Nyro's live performances around the time that Mitchell also gained public attention. Audiences were awed by her talent, but they also felt uncomfortable. "Laura Nyro Overwhelms," the headlines read. Nyro, who once said, "When I record, I'm not a human being, I'm not a woman," nonetheless displayed the excesses always associated with women. She was too public with her emotions, too wide with her swings. Her theatrics failed to impress the throng at the Monterey International Pop Festival; one year later, Mitchell released her first album and women's genius had a new sound, one to which more people could relate.

Seeing how Nyro became incomprehensible to so many, Mitchell worked harder to make her own status clear. She would stand alone because that was the safest place to be. When other women said she spoke for them, she acknowledged their love, but made sure to say that her songs really represented only her own emotions and experiences. This polite demurral was as strategic as it was sincere. Women artists have so often been reduced to ciphers for all of womankind, as if that category even really existed. As a painter, and one who loved figures more than abstraction, Mitchell would have encountered this prejudice early in her creative life. Male painters could draw the curve of a breast, just as novelists like Gustave Flaubert or John Cheever could write the inner life of a housewife, from a distance that allowed risk and even cruelty. They were never expected to represent a whole gender, even when depicting other men. But women got pushed into that "we."

I picked up the Margaret Atwood novel *Cat's Eye* from my shelf as I was thinking about Joni's genius and found a passage I remembered: the novel's difficult heroine, the painter Elaine, is asked by a journalist at her first retrospective why the female body so often looms large in her work. The interviewer was fishing for that universal, for the way Elaine's work stood for all of woman-kind. "I'm a painter. Painters paint women," she replies, exasper-ated. Critics have written about Mitchell and Atwood as prickly soul sisters; it was the stated assumption in this line of dialogue that got me. Painters paint women. Songwriters like James Tay-lor, who wrote "You Can Close Your Eyes" for Joni, or Graham Nash, who wrote "Our House" about her, feel confident describ-ing women's private moments, their longings, their oppression, their deaths. Taylor even closed in on the secret realm of another woman's suicide in his most famous song, "Fire and Rain": *Suzanne, the plans they made put an end to you.*

Men could be discreet by staying discrete, capturing one woman at a time with their brushstrokes, their words. But in the world where Joni emerged, women kept getting pushed into universals against their will. I think Joni perceived the separate sphere of the genius as a sanctuary from generic womanhood. From the beginning of her success, Joni always strove to describe less-than-ideal women, particularly herself, but others, too. Vain beauties and lost girls who might be small-minded or threatening or, though captivating, a little vapid. To be able to express such mixed feelings about other women in a song, Joni would have to be viewed as something other than a woman. In the years when she was first defining herself, people thought of "genius" as synonymous with "man." So it worked for her. It freed her from the femininity that threatened to hold her back.

Can you tell that I'm a little bit angry at Joni for trying to genius her way beyond gender? I have to acknowledge that her craving to be just herself (and, in that way, not just a woman) is the norm among artists, today as it was in her prime. Though this is changing in the new century, I can't count the times the musicians I've interviewed have cringed at any mention of feminism, much less female solidarity or even identification. Moving beyond such categories can, in fact, be a generative act. It's one that Mitchell has explored in her songs, even as she's spoken so profoundly about the particulars of her own experience in a female body. It's another aspect of her mobility, the way she always shifts perspectives, recognizing that many selves exist inside each of us. And it aligns her with her times: the moment she emerged, the time of songs like her "Cactus Tree"—with its hook, *she's so busy being free*—was one in which women across many fields were opening up new spaces, abandoning the stereotypes that had confined them and demanding wider definitions for themselves.

Here's how I think Joni Mitchell is indeed a genius. There's a way to think about the word that changes it from an exclusionary term to a gateway. It's the oldest definition, from the Latin: a guardian spirit associated with a time, place or community. This kind of genius doesn't float above things. She recognizes the circumstances that call for her to speak and makes them newly audible. In her music and through her presence, Mitchell tapped into the vitality of a space opening up, one that she in part created: a clearing in which women could fully be themselves and claim the power of that wholeness, while also acknowledging the risks and the pain of shaking off old ways. Not only women—people in general, because when one half of a binary changes shape, the whole structure softens, or shatters. In the time and place her music helped define, all kinds of people rethought themselves.

CONFESSION

Mitchell has been called "confessional" even more often than she's been called a genius. She's bristled every time. There's that famous quote in which she corrects those who would dwell on her biography: "If you see me in my songs and wonder about my life, then I'm not doing a good job. If you see yourself, then I'm doing what I was meant to do." That's a polite directive to fuck off with the gossip and look within. When Michelle Mercer asked her about being called "confessional," she offered a more controversial reply. "That's as close as someone could come to calling me a n———," she snapped.

It's never okay for a white person to use that vile epithet, but her blurting it out does reveal just how deeply she dislikes others telling her what to do. She'd once said to another writer asking a similar question that she preferred "penitent" to "confessional." Okay, that's basically a fancier synonym. It does exert more power—the penitent chooses to expose herself, while confessions are often coerced. For a moment, though, I'm going to argue for the confessional, not as a celebration of self-involvement but as both an excavation and a ritual exchange. And as a central aspect and cultural product of rock and roll. The critic M. L. Rosenthal connected it to poetry in 1959, just as rock and roll was giving America a fever of the personal. The women poets most often labeled this way, Sylvia Plath and Anne Sexton, were in many ways the literary equivalent of the rockers barnstorming through the teenage nation. Mitchell has always fought against an association with them, considering them needlessly provocative, yet if it's possible to separate those women from their suicides and the ensuing mythification of their lives, their poems can be reread as pulsing with the energy of electrified sound. Sexton even fronted a sort of jazz fusion band at one point. "It's better than a poem! Music beats us," she told a journalist once.

Music gives the confessional approach a better engine for its rituals of self-exposure than poetry can provide. That's because it's sung, it's rhythmic, it can get loud. David Shumway notes in his study of Mitchell as a confessional rock star that her music creates "an emotional immediacy that makes us believe we are experiencing truth rather than art." It breaks down distance with an irresistible magnetism. Joni felt this; she said, "I have a compulsion to be honest with my audience." Anne Sexton wrote in her poem "Music Swims Back To Me," "Music pours over the sense / and in a funny way / music sees more than I." Music is an electric shock that restores the mind instead of numbing it.

Acknowledging the potential shock of the confessional allows us to understand the singer-songwriter movement that Joni joined and led as radical and subversive, rather than in the way most people talk about it now, as "mellow." Is Taylor's "Fire and Rain," the ultimate soft-rock song, truly soft? It's about depression and suicide. Is Joni's *For the Roses* mellow? Its songs are about heroin addiction and sexual betrayal and episodes of mania. Mitchell may have been suspicious of Plath's and Sexton's posturing, as she called it, but she's always shared their mix of glamour and grit. Thin, nervous women, chic as hell—what they had to say isn't pretty. Sexton and Plath wrote about menstruation, childbirth, masturbation, cutting. Mitchell's blunt side exposed loneliness, neediness and the refusal to fill others' needs and an impulse toward independence that left damage in its wake.

"Thus the frightened little girl became a flamboyant and provocative woman; the timid child who skulked in closets burst forth as an exhibitionist," the poet Maxine Kumin said of Sexton, her close friend. Joni has said of the days when she was making *Blue* that she felt "like my guts were on the outside." Spiritual sisters, despite objections.

So I do want to revive the notion of the confessional artist but make it more dynamic. The intimacy of the relationship between a singer-songwriter and her audience is unrivaled within popular music. It resembles the transference of psychotherapy, or the grace that comes from fervent prayer: a mystical connection through which one being opens to another and their perspectives become indistinguishable. Who is speaking? Who is listening? The singer-songwriter's insights are just seeds until they grow within listeners' minds.

In 1970, the writer Jon Landau called the music of Mitchell and her fellow singer-songwriters "the new uterus of popular music." Wow, talk about a bloody metaphor. "I was in the womb all along," Anne Sexton wrote in 1968, at forty, contemplating her waning fertility. She wasn't just being cute and saying poems are babies. She was making the connection between going inside to create and literally getting visceral. Joni offered her own penitent's prayer, remembering what a middle school teacher who had similar sensibilities once told her: "I . . . would be punished by circumstance if I didn't write from my own blood."

Women learn young to mask their own blood. We pad our panties and hope it doesn't smell, shove bleached cotton up into ourselves and pray the dam doesn't break. The fear of women spilling over is fundamental within sexist society; applied to art, it morphs into the assumption that everything women create tumbles unprocessed from their innards, paired with the contradictory belief that women can't be trusted, are unreliable witnesses to their own lives. Confessional songwriting is often misunderstood as a soft art, wimpier than confrontational rock and roll. But Joni and the other women who were central to inventing the form found in this personal art a way to talk about things they were otherwise directed to tamp down. A famous early response Joni faced, sharing her music, came from one of the scene's young patriarchs, Kris Kristofferson, who said after hearing *Blue* (at least she said he said it), "Oh, Joni, save something for yourself." That Mitchell shared this comment with interviewers, making sure it became part of her lore, says a lot about how she understood the power of the confessional even as she pooh-poohed the term. What really bothered Kristofferson—and, according to her, men around her in general, who often felt uncomfortable with her acts of exposure—was that Joni didn't save *him* from parts of herself that he didn't want to acknowledge. Because showing those parts, voicing her confessions, revealed the sanitized version of things as a lie.

BEAUTY

Joni Mitchell is a beauty for the ages. Amazement at her model's bone structure and lithe bikini body greeted her from the first days of her career well into her peak years. She bewitched people, awed them, knocked them out. "They were glad to be sheep," an early reviewer wrote of her rapt audience. The same mood overtakes people today when they encounter Mitchell as a young woman inside the time machine of the Internet. A few years ago the filmmaker Martin Scorsese released a documentary about Bob Dylan's Rolling Thunder Revue tour, which she'd joined for sixteen dates in 1975. Soon, a clip went viral: it showed Joni at her old friend Gordon Lightfoot's house, teaching Dylan and Byrds guitarist Roger McGuinn her new song "Coyote." "Astonishing," people said, watching Joni unfurl its pulsing chords with jovial ease. "She leaves those boys in the dust." Performances like this one make me put aside all doubts about Joni's exceptional status. From the deftness of her fingers on the fretboard to the absolutely casual, slightly shy air with which she shares the song's loving and acerbic lyrics— inspired by the tour's official chronicler, the playwright Sam Shepard, as the boys clearly knew—it's a rare chance to witness a woman's spontaneous and total ownership of a room full of sheepishly awestruck men.

The online comments, though, quickly turned away from praising Joni's musical gifts and toward her pulchritude. *Good God, has there ever been a woman more beautiful?* The camera encourages this conflation of skill and sex appeal. It focuses briefly on her fingers shaping the strange changes of "Coyote" on the guitar, then pulls in on her face, cheekbones rouged in a perfect autumn shade, flaxen hair artfully arranged beneath a black beret. Forty-five years of women's liberation under the bridge since she made that clip, and Joni's beauty still rivals her music for attention.

I wonder if the astonishment men regularly expressed at the young Mitchell's musical prowess largely sprang from their inability to register that a woman could be both alluring and as—*more*—talented than they were. "She was like a storm," her early mentor and lover Leonard Cohen once said, trying to process the elemental combination she represented. The ad guys at her first record label capitalized on this charisma, promoting her as a "fragile, unique beauty" in antique dresses and presenting her to the editors in chief at *Glamour* and *Vogue*. One critic wrote in 1976: she is "the possessor of two of the finest instruments in popular music, a great set of pipes and those wonderful, vulnerable cheekbones." *Stop it with the cheekbones! Focus on the music,* feminists and other serious people said. But let's be honest: virtually no one did. One of Mitchell's biographers, Katherine Monk, called for "no judgment" regarding Joni's deployment of her assets. "That's the way the world worked in the 1960s," she wrote, as if it works differently today. It does not. Beauty still reads as virtue, as excellence. Any discussion of Joni Mitchell as singular among her musical peers must also acknowledge that in one crucial way, she was very much like nearly every pop star: she fit the physical requirements of fame.

It's embarrassing to admit it now, but her beauty is one thing that stopped what should have been my own youthful Joni Mitchell phase. I was an ordinary-looking kid. I gaped at Joni's golden visage, her lithe body unclothed in the gatefold photo of *For the Roses*, and felt that old surge of envy and exclusion the popular girls have raised in me since third grade. My musical heroines were lookers, too, but they messed with what genetics gave them. Remember, I was a New Waver. Women in that scene also possessed great cheekbones and doe eyes, but they came up in the wake of the women's movement and had been schooled in its critique of beauty standards. Debbie Harry smeared her lipstick and

ripped her dress; Kate Bush costumed herself as a lion or a bat and
grimaced as she danced. I could hang with those queens, in my
mind at least, because they sneered at the advantages they could
claim, even if they also benefited from them.

Beauty is real. Beauty is constructed. Beauty is the friend of
the fabulous and the enemy of the real. Like everyone else, sucking on its sugar, I believe it communicates some ultimate truth;
it's just a matter of whose beauty I can tolerate and experience as
a promise and not a threat. It took time and intensive listening to
recognize that even if she never smeared her makeup or snarled
into a microphone, Mitchell's music offered its own critique of
what she and her generation called "sex appeal."

Tracing her trajectories, I came to understand that beauty was
a problem for Joni, too. By the time she appeared nude in that
Joel Bernstein shot on her fifth album, the social battle over sex
appeal's value was fully raging. The action that ignited the second wave of women's liberation was a 1968 rally against the Miss
America Pageant where activists sang, "Ain't she sweet, making
profit off her meat." Two years later, Toni Morrison published
her debut novel *The Bluest Eye*, in which the white beauty ideal
coupled with sexual abuse drives a young Black girl mad. Despite
these protests, women's power even in progressive circles often
was attached to beauty. "Women? I guess they ought to exercise
Pussy Power?" the Black Panther Party leader Eldridge Cleaver
quipped around that time. Betty Friedan wasn't beautiful, and
wrote about the tyranny of cosmetics in *The Feminine Mystique*;
Gloria Steinem was beautiful, and put on giant sunglasses to al-
leviate the glare of others' eyes upon her. Trying to find her own
definition, the Black feminist pioneer Michele Wallace wore an
Afro to Black Power rallies, but worried that it would shrivel in
the rain. ("Despite Blackness," she wrote, "Black men still didn't

like short hair.") Joni did feel this conflict. "People's Parties," from 1974, tells of a "Photo Beauty" who's a little pathetic, but can still make her feel like an ugly duckling. *Cry for us all, Beauty*, she sings. She's making fun of the girl and protesting the concept.

The rock and roll scene that Mitchell inhabited had its own familiar forms of beauty worship, not that different from the ones her suburban mother had instilled in her. The only thing it did differently was emphasize that men can be objects of desire, as it staged a hot boy parade attended by a horde of screaming teenage girls. A few Black women and white brunettes did challenge the blonde norm: Tina Turner, Aretha Franklin, Janis Joplin and the de-debutanted Grace Slick were sensual powerhouses who would have likely never made the prom court. But all those fair ladies were still around. Joni was a queen in her scene; still, men ran the music industry, and they fought against any alterations of the beauty standard. "The groupies were generally better looking than the singers," Slick said about Laurel Canyon. Women's determination to assert themselves as artists had to be balanced by their efforts to direct and sustain the male gaze.

Joni had to feel this pressure. She made it to the cover of *Rolling Stone* as early as 1969, but earlier that year the magazine had turned away from artists long enough to devote an entire issue, later turned into a book, to the groupie phenomenon, focusing on the muses and helpmeets who'd devoted themselves to keeping male artists comfortable and satiated. No shade to dynamic and creative women like Pamela Des Barres and Christine Frka, who actually had their own band, the GTO's, and made art of the everyday as they turned their star consorts on to the fashion, literature, politics and even musical influences that infused their recordings. But the culture of classic rock inarguably valued women as companions first and artists second. Another *Rolling Stone* feature: the

"Beatle wives," the Fab Four's then-domestic partners and one sister, all Joni-style long-haired blondes, in clothes from the band's own Apple Boutique. That's the environment in which "the Beautiful People" became a feminized metonym for callously decadent wealth, those people at parties whom Joni simultaneously skewered and celebrated.

The singer-songwriter scene was the prettiest one of all. Inner beauty, the focus of the 1970s self-help movement, merely made model standards seem more natural. Joni's physicality had always seemed to me like an afterthought, something she didn't really have to tend. But as I got deeper into her songwriting, I could hear that she was fighting, too. Another beauty could always crowd her out.

It could have been Joni that Simone de Beauvoir was writing about in her 1949 proto-feminist manifesto *The Second Sex* when she observed the kept women of Parisian high society. "Even the most beautiful is never sure of tomorrow, for her weapons are magical, and magic is capricious." In her early songs, Joni is often waiting for men—the married flirt in "Conversation," the roving rogue in "Car on a Hill," the honey-dripping charmer of "See You Sometime." Later she became more interested in making them wait. But to quote another of her songs, it was always the same situation: *A pretty girl in your bathroom, checking out her sex appeal.*

Listening to this song as I pondered Joni's beauty, I was struck by the precarity of her position. No amount of primping can stop the face in the mirror from becoming an adversary. It's just a matter of time. What happens, I began to ask myself, when a beautiful woman sings of ugly things? When that ugliness surfaces within herself? In her songs Joni feels out of place among the Beautiful People, though in her glory days few may have noticed her sense of dislocation. She continually wondered if she could maintain the power others granted her even as they insisted it emanated from within. What is beauty? Real, constructed, deceptive, true: Mitchell wrote her way deep into this maze. Hers is a mind ill at ease in a body full of grace.

Beauty bites back. "Ah Joni," a fan once wrote to her in a letter, after devoting hundreds of words to an analysis of one of her songs, "you've got all Dostoevsky's brilliance, *plus* a beautiful ass."

A STORIED LIFE

Biography was invented to celebrate heroes—or, really, to organize such creatures into being. One living master of the form, Hermione Lee, calls it "a process of making up, or making over." Making up: composing, turning a person's disconnected experiences into a collection of verses and choruses that capture others' ears. Making over: as in a hairstyle, shaping what's available. Lee sees this process of restructuring as essential to getting a life to cohere on paper. Working against this is the messiness of memories, and of facts. "They do exist," Lee writes, "and lie around biographers in huge piles and boxes, waiting to be turned into story." Also lurking nearby, whether living or dead, is the biographer's subject, constantly objecting; that's how it feels, anyway. *You're getting it all wrong*, she hisses. *You're lost.* Her friends and enemies and others who've tried to speak her life shout their own objections in the distance. For every bit of essential guidance the biographer obtains, another leads her down a road that goes nowhere. It's in following those roads that the biographer becomes a mapmaker, charting a route through terrain that could be crossed in countless ways.

Today, biography often has another function: to render fully naked the already overexposed. In 1683 John Dryden called life writing the practice of presenting historical figures in their undress; now, that undress is more extreme than ever. "Masturbation, dental work, body odour, menstruation, gonorrhea, addictions and sexual preferences," as Lee writes, are the details that turn our favorite artists, athletes and politicians into characters worthy of the bestseller list. Readers crave these details, having already likely tasted them through mass-mediated gossip, reality television or even the subject's own social media feeds.

Mitchell's partly to blame for this, if only indirectly. Her breath on listeners' ears helped change the way people understand artists. She recalibrated music's frame, using care and craft to elevate the art of self-exposure. As she did so, she actually did save much for herself, choosing exactly which parts of her heartache and longing and desire to expose. Yet she managed to seem like she was giving everything. That made people want even more from her.

Joni herself soon grew impatient with what she and her fellow singer-songwriters had wrought. After *Blue*, she wanted to make music about new subjects, to be an observer and a collaborator and not just that woman looking you in the eye. Still writing from her own experience, she longed to be recognized for her thoughts about other things. Instead of a walking embodiment, she became a raconteur, and then a prophet, and sometimes a translator. Is this what an older woman had to do, fighting invisibility, no longer able to hold the gaze of the public merely by existing? I want to honor this Joni Mitchell, too, who reached for more, and was labeled "difficult" for doing so.

I came to love the pricklier Joni Mitchell. Over time, I realized that she was always there, waiting for me to understand. Even the Joni that people adore isn't really a role model. She's a morose girl who can't adjust her emotions properly. An anxious talker who needs a therapist. An unmoored soul who keeps leaving those who love her, because she fears they will leave her first. The unworthy Joni. All of her worries, her snark, her admissions

of weakness, her vanity, make her human, alive. Her torment-
ing concern about her place in the hierarchy of artists, her fear
of being alone, her need to push others away, her occasional but
significant bigotry and lapses of cultural judgment, her preoccupation with men, her competitiveness with women, her racial entitlement, her tendency to exaggerate, her unhealthy drive to just
keep working, her sad and serious doubts that anything she does
is worth it. Running down these ambiguities, I found the Joni who
can breathe into my ear.

This book is a record of deep research and of listening and
of many encounters with people who have encountered Mitchell,
as friend or lover, collaborator or competitor, embodiment of
a moment that has passed and inspiration whose presence feels
timeless. But it's really the story of an approach, or a series of
approaches, toward a subject that in many ways felt unapproach-
able. Joni Mitchell: aside from Aretha Franklin, the most critically
lauded woman in contemporary music; the most intensely embraced by her fans; the only popular musician who gets away with
being on a first-name basis with Ludwig B. and Willy the Shake.
A woman whose story everyone who cares about music knows,
because she told it so well herself in her songs. There is a clear
way up the mountain of Joni Mitchell's mythic life. I did not want
to take it, though.

Instead, I wanted to think about the byways, the roads where
she had wandered unnoticed. Turning down a main road, I wanted
to walk a little differently. I wanted to trace the shape of Mitchell's
art myself, through encounters that mostly remain unmapped. I
knew it would be difficult. Stars drown in the received wisdom of
those who uphold their greatness. This is an attempt at recovery.
Some, maybe Mitchell herself, may consider my charting revision-
ist. I have tried to resist or at least question common assumptions

about an artist whom so many believe they know so well. On occasion, I hope I've transgressed. That's what a self-made original like Mitchell would respect, I tell myself.

Joni Mitchell is a real person who recorded more than twenty albums over the course of nearly forty years, wrote at least a dozen songs that many people consider classics, changed rock guitar playing and pop songwriting and the way women talked in public about themselves. She is also an embodiment of freedom and singularity, of sorrow and of play. She is a touchstone connecting different musical styles and the people who created them. For some, she is a life force offering succor and inspiration. For others, a standard that will never be met. Joni Mitchell cannot be biographized because she is still living—literally, right now, but in another sense forever, through her defiantly fluid music. She cannot be captured wholly because, always moving beyond her own life story, she never rests. She has often been the object of others' obsessions, but as a subject, she cannot be owned. I can only follow her and call her name, again and again.

1

childish things

I begin my Joni Mitchell journey in the only place
that makes sense, sitting by my stereo, listening to her
music. Put the needle on the vinyl, press play and enter
the stream. Tune in to the first songs that made most
anyone think Joni Mitchell was an artist to discover—
the same songs that lead many listeners to her today.

"Both Sides Now," "The Circle Game" and, more
as an echo, "Urge for Going." What do they have in
common? Each conjures childhood from the viewpoint
of an adult, looking back on simpler beginnings
through the complexities of young womanhood.

Building a backstory, they establish a character, Joni Mitchell, by introducing her as a girl. This girl was a real person, one who'd lain on prairie grass and gazed at the wide sky, an explorer in her own backyard who soon knew she'd have to flee far beyond it. But she is also a device. Young Roberta Joan, the girl who walks behind Joni, her shadow. Something runs through these songs, the same thing that often draws listeners to Mitchell's music now: an instantly clear sense of self, made dynamic by unresolved yearning. The feeling, in real time, of growing up. I want to understand the girl they evoke, in the way that Mitchell herself did.

FIRST, THE FACTS. JONI WAS BORN ROBERTA JOAN ANDERSON IN 1943 TO MYRTLE AND Bill Anderson, a grocery store manager and a homemaker, and grew up mostly in Saskatoon, the chilly center of Canada's Prairie Provinces. The only child of somewhat distant parents, she was a popular kid who also spent a lot of time alone. She loved dress-up games and reading Rudyard Kipling stories and listening to the jazz her dad played on the gramophone. A normal kid, though dreamy. At nine, she contracted polio during one of that disease's epidemic surges and lost the ability to walk; she fought back and regained it. This experience pushed her toward becoming an artist instead of the athlete she'd assumed she would be, given her early fondness for outdoor fun, playing cowboy games and chasing after wild things. Remembering these years, she described herself in one song as a wild seed wanting the wind to carry her.

For a time, the Andersons lived in a house nestled into a cul-de-sac, and she would venture beyond the edge of the suburban development, letting herself get lost in the adjacent fields. This is where she would often place herself later, when she turned her recollections into the verses so many now know. Young Roberta Joan survived within Joni Mitchell as a figure in wide open space.

SKATING

Fast-forward for a moment to 1976. In my favorite photograph of Mitchell, that solitary girl reemerges. A woman glides toward the center of a vast expanse. Black skates, black tights, black coat and hat. Her skirt hangs past her knees, a flutter. She could be a crone. Yet her movement shows no signs of age, and her hair is blonde, streaming down her back. In another photograph taken the same day, she raises her arms, and the fur tassels on her coat look like feathers: she could be a bird. But she's bound to the ground, one leg lifted low, eyes cast toward the shaded ice. The image doesn't speak of freedom; it speaks of memory. Being alone in this space has taken the woman somewhere else, where she's been before. In this moment, she could be a child.

This was Joni Mitchell at the height of her womanly powers, returning to herself, Roberta Joan. How she got there: she exited a tour and the wilted five-year love affair with drummer John Geurin that the road was still enabling, landing in Madison, Wisconsin, in a hotel with her friend and documentarian, the photographer Joel Bernstein. At wits' end, she set a task for them—shoot some images for her next album, *Hejira*. She located those skates and they piled into a limo, hitting the lakeshore just as a storm was breaking. The photograph that made it to *Hejira*'s inner sleeve shows Joni flapping those wings, therianthropic, head cocked toward the future. The one I love evokes the self-containment and untested confidence of a happy childhood.

For the first ten years of her public life in music, leading up to this photograph that I read as both a preservation of innocence and an acknowledgment of its inevitable fading, Joni Mitchell had made growing up a focal point of her self-expression. Central to that process was an ongoing encounter with her younger self, the solitary prairie girl who ran free beyond her mother's door, and then, after polio taught her that freedom can and must also be internal, willed herself away from the home truths that had once comforted her. Actually, let's say not simply an "encounter" with that girl, but a construction of her. Growing up before and with her audience, through her songs, Joni Mitchell rewrote the story of her childhood, as we all do, in fragments, challenges and corrections. The actual circumstances of her youth made a difference, but perhaps not as much as what she did with them later, as a creative adult.

In 1976 Mitchell was about to release *Hejira*, a pilgrimage diary that would realize the full potential of popular music as a vehicle for considering the complexities of adult life. Yet for a moment, she grew girlish again. As she looked downward on that ice, was she remembering the Saskatchewan River instead of seeing that lake? Instead of all-black finery, was she imagining herself in white skates, red coat, mittens? "Perhaps the act of skating," the Alberta-based writer Marco Adria once wrote, "is as prototypically Canadian as any other physical action." Joni Mitchell grew up skating on flat waters. She's often written about rivers and lakes and ice. Think of the ice as memory. And of memory-building as a function of solitude, but a fragile one, easily intruded upon.

Perhaps with another turn of her blade, Mitchell imagined the lake to be something other than a river. Eyes cast downward, away, maybe she recalled her summer refuge: that field of burnt grass turned so blond by the sun that it's almost white, grass tall enough to hide a little human lying on her back and imagining a kingdom of make-believe in the clouds. Remembering the names she learned in school: feathery cirrus, marshmallow cumulus, stratus taking over the sky like a wall. *Wait, no, not marshmallow*, the Joni who wrote "Both Sides Now" in her early twenties might have thought so many years after the child Roberta Joan lay in that field. *Ice cream cone. Ice cream castle.* That song is about leaving innocence behind. But first the child in it gets to speak.

"When I was a kid," Joni Mitchell told the journalist Susan Gordon Lydon in 1969, "my mother used to take me out to the fields to teach me bird calls." The comment complements Lydon's description of Mitchell as she appeared that day in her Laurel Canyon bungalow: "Her face, lacking the forcefulness and luminescent quality it takes on when she performs, looks like a forthright farm girl's, with freckled pale skin, watery blue eyes, and prominent teeth and cheekbones. She speaks softly and gently, with great earnestness." The face Mitchell presented to the world in this early hippie heyday organically related to the straightforward yet high-flying voice she projected in her most popular songs. She was then, as she would call herself again decades later in the title of an album adorned with one of Bernstein's lake photographs, a prairie girl—her spirit aligned with nature and the flow of the seasons, her songwriting an extension of a young dreamer's act of throwing her arms out to embrace the world.

No voices can blame you for sun on your wings, she crooned in another of her childhood songs, the title track to her 1968 album debut *Song to a Seagull*, identifying with the bird in a way that lent her a certain fairy-tale glamour. Yet for all of her gold-washed memories, these songs often hint at discontent. She finished the verse with a swipe at her parents. *My gentle relations have names they must call me for loving the freedom of all flying things.*

The daughter whose mother taught her the vernacular of longspurs was one version of young Roberta Joan, ideal for public consumption in the country-loving twilight of a hippie revolution in retreat, and true to her earliest years, when her father, then in the military, kept the family moving from relatively large midwestern Canadian cities to tiny towns with quaint names like North Battleford. Country Joni is also lonesome Joni, taking comfort in the play of light on water on a pond, and the shapes of bugs, and the sound of wind, knowing that in another new town she'll have to make friends all over again. Cultivating independence helps an unmoored kid feel secure when everything changes. In the most romantic aspects of Mitchell's songwriting, young Roberta Joan is the free spirit every adult wants to remember and cultivate.

But there was another young Roberta Joan, more troubled and truer to her time. She was a suburban malcontent growing up amidst the unrest of the postwar years who considered her mother prim and clueless and her father ineffectual, two stumblers whose "judgment was so sucky all the time." Mitchell's biographer David Yaffe recounts an interview with her, then in her seventies, in which she expressed chilly contempt for Myrtle and Bill. "My parents are both color-blind while I am color acute," she told him. To their Roberta, these mundane relatively older parents were unsuited for nurturing the as-yet-unidentified genius in their midst. This primal discontent comes through in the undertones of songs like "Urge for Going" and becomes stingingly clear in the ones she wrote after beginning therapy later in life. "The Tea Leaf Prophecy," from 1988's *Chalk Mark in a Rain Storm*, tells of her mother going to a fortune-teller who predicts she'll be wed in a month—a true story and a genuine miracle, as she met Bill shortly after and the whirlwind grabbed them. It also contains a line delivered from mother to daughter that would zing off any psychoanalyst's couch: *Don't have kids when you get grown*, mother tells daughter, planting the weedy feeling of rejection in her. Malcontent Joni is always wrestling with this mother, alternately withholding and smothering.

"I WASN'T LONELY, BUT I WAS A LONE PERSON," A NEARLY FIFTY-YEAR-OLD MITCHELL told Brent Lannan, a reporter from her home province of Saskatchewan, reflecting on the seedling self beneath the many layers of experience that had made her the great artist she had become. This is the phrase that always enters my mind when I consider how, in her songs, Mitchell crafted a childhood she could celebrate. It comes across as a form of self-nurturing, a spirited pat on the back for that cowboy girl, whose pain she'd learned to view as a source of strength. *You are alone by choice, Roberta Joan. By nature.* The adult Mitchell collaged this creature together using her own memories, her friends' similar stories, and the preoccupations of her time.

What makes the story of Mitchell's childhood both distinctive and emblematic is the way it falls on a timeline of modernization and growth. Young Roberta Joan inhabited an edge: between towns growing into suburbs and the country postwar industry displaces; dividing the early twentieth-century country girl's trajectory toward marriage from that of the modern young woman who departs for the city and newly available roles; separating a parental generation raised on radio, patriotism and social conventions from children who will question everything they worked so hard to provide.

A grounding in solitude and the longing for escape unites the child songs of many of the friends and influences Mitchell would claim as she became an artist. Minnesota train watcher Bob Dylan,

North Carolina creek jumper James Taylor, North Ontario forest explorer Neil Young, Bronx alley creeper Laura Nyro: all of these stars of the singer-songwriter moment cultivated similar memories of discovering their interiority as tiny figures crossing fierce, enveloping landscapes. As Hayden Herrera, the biographer of another polio survivor–turned–artistic genius, Frida Kahlo, noted of that painter's tendency to dwell on the social deprivations of her childhood, "A lonely adult recalls earlier moments of loneliness." Those memories were tools that helped singer-songwriters like Mitchell connect to the ruling spirits of the coming "'Me' Decade": introspection, intimacy, individuality.

CHILD'S SONGS

In 1969, Joni Mitchell continued her explorations of young Roberta Joan's psyche by releasing an anthem for the blissed-out dreamers walking beside her in the secret gardens of their dream children's minds. "Songs to Aging Children Come" had been kicking around in her repertoire since her turtleneck days in the cafe scene connecting Detroit to Toronto to New York. Like many early Joni songs, it's a showcase for her flamboyant voice and poetic strivings, an incantatory description of the creative process as a dissembling spiritual experience. "The hallucinatory lyrics and helium-infused vocal warbling are matched by the far-out chord progressions," the musicologist Lloyd Whitesell has written of this song, noting "the unsettling effect of the far-flung harmonic path" forged by Mitchell's experiments with chromatic progression. "Songs to Aging Children Come" is ridiculous and awe-inspiring, like some scribbling in a college kid's tea-stained notebook that serves up genuine revelation amidst the doodles decorating it.

At twenty-five, Joni was dreaming of being both ancient and newborn, and believed somehow that her songs made her so. *Songs to aging children come,* she sings darkly in her lowest register. *I am one.* An aging child is a being distinct from the screaming teens whose energy had empowered rock and roll or the somber/suave/cynical adults for whom music-making or music-loving was a pleasant leisure-class pursuit. This spirit was new, the song suggested, yet imbued with ancient wisdom. Such a highly romantic view of youth as a state of free being has many sources. I hear the song and think of one of Joni's favorite books, which she'd loved since reading it at an inappropriate age: Friedrich Nietzsche's *Thus Spake Zarathustra*, with its central story of a soul transforming from a wise old camel to a fierce but threatened lion to a child—the one creature who can truly embrace new beginnings.

"Innocence is the child, and forgetfulness, a new beginning, a game, a self-rolling wheel, a first movement, a holy Yea." So spoke Zarathustra. A return to the child mind, his avowals attest, allows the human spirit to gain true freedom and self-determination. How many thousands of students and bohemians have underlined that "holy Yea" since Nietzsche's book was published in 1883 and surrounded it with exclamation marks? Joni read *Zarathustra* as a grade schooler—a curious kid, pulling something off the shelf in a part of the library where she shouldn't have gone, before a librarian shooed her away. So she could legitimately claim it for young Roberta Joan. But *Zarathustra* was also there when she set off on her artistic quest as an adult. She might have found a paperback edition laying on coffee tables in the homes friends occupied in Toronto's Yorkville and Greenwich Village and Laurel Canyon, stacked up next to D. T. Suzuki's *Living by Zen* and Kerouac's *The Dharma Bums*. Alongside the poets and painters of the time, singer-songwriters like her were attempting to enact what

Nietzsche's prophet described. "A man translates himself into a child asking for all there is in a language he has barely mastered," her brief lover and mentor Leonard Cohen wrote of prayer, a metaphor for art-making. Neil Young, Joni's friend and Canadian homie, put it less fancily. *I am a child*, he sang through his nose, like a choirboy. *I'll last a while.* These artists saw it as their duty to carry the child mind into their adult work.

The cult of the child was a strong force in the counterculture that coincided with the emergence of the singer-songwriter, connected to both hippie pastoralism and the rise of the pop-psychiatric industry of self-help, a force still drawing people back to their younger selves today. Adopting a child's perspective became almost a rite of passage for songwriters who wanted to earn accolades for being profound just as audiences decided en masse that it was possible for chaotic young people to be so. Bored with the educational vibe of the folk revival, connected to the teen scene of rock but trying to figure out how to indulge their wider poetic ambitions, singer-songwriters made self-development their métier.

Young waxed poetic about prepubescent fantasies not only in "I Am a Child" but in "Sugar Mountain," where *you can't be twenty*—calling bullshit on his self-infantilizing, Joni responded by writing a song in which the child survives in the adult, "The Circle Game." The melancholy she brought to her lyrics was in fact also present in the aching melody of Young's song, grounding his whimsical words. The happy-sad attitude infused the many songs that took up similar themes. Phil Ochs traced his arduous journey from the tube of his mother's birth canal through other narrowing passages in "Half a Century High." Cat Stevens, Beatles wannabe turned hot young sage, voiced the doubts of a boy leaving home for the first time in "Father and Son." Tom Rush, covering Murray McLauchlan, did the same in "Child's Song."

Janis Ian, barely out of her teens, mourned the dreamy days of youth in "When I Was a Child." Pop craftsman Neil Diamond showed his songwriterly side in "Shilo," which celebrated a boyhood imaginary friend. These are just the most obvious examples from a playlist that could run hours long.

Joni was coming across these aging children wherever she went. By the time she got to Laurel Canyon and started releasing her own albums, they'd proliferated, especially the male variety. She'd left older man Leonard behind in New York and partnered with a series of increasingly boyish catches: hairy David Crosby was soon dumped for wispy Graham Nash, who lost out to lanky James Taylor, known by the world as Sweet Baby James. He was later replaced (though only for an unhappy moment) by wide-eyed Jackson Browne. Joni's image as an aging child wasn't merely a product of sexist marketing: boys experienced and embraced the child cult, too. Browne (an actual wunderkind when he first started playing L.A.'s stages) found it more inspirational than most, going from "A Child in These Hills" to "I Thought I Was a Child" to the mournful and insightful "Daddy's Tune." These reflections became interwoven in his discography with songs about unexpectedly fathering a son, Ethan, at twenty-five, with his thengirlfriend Phyllis Major. In 1974, Ethan and Jackson appeared on the cover of *Rolling Stone*; "Boy Wonder Grows Up," the headline read. The headline attached to Cameron Crowe's profile inside the magazine reassured readers that their boy-man wouldn't lose touch with his inner juvenile. It read, "A Child's Garden of Jackson Browne."

Picture these boho babes with dewy eyes and glistening mops of hair, wearing playtime outfits of dungarees or cotton dresses, captured in photos doing playtime things—lying back in grassy fields, leaping about near the shore, blowing the tufts free on a

dandelion. Their songs harkened back to childhood but also replicated it, their cadences redolent of the nursery, their sing-along
harmonies sweet and high. Rock and roll had always messed with
childish things—*Eeny meenie and minie moe*, sang Fats Domino.
Country and soul music traded in testimonials to humble roots as
evidence of authenticity, like Dolly Parton's famous tale of the
patchwork jacket of her grade school days, "Coat of Many Colors,"
or Tina Turner's invocation of a rag doll in the song she made
famous, "River Deep-Mountain High." The countercultural version of the musical *bildungsroman* was something different: it was
a guide to retaining innocence by forming its affect into syllables,
images, memories rocked like a baby. The rock band these folkies
loved, the Beatles, set the standard with John Lennon's "Strawberry Fields Forever," which sonically replicated the woozy mix
of excitement, daydream drifting and dread that a kid can feel,
vulnerability shooting through a sense of adventure. In real life,
Strawberry Fields was an orphanage, but in the song it became a
place of healing.

    Nothing is real, and nothing to get hung about, Lennon sang as
the music flowed backward. It was also about an acid trip, where
if things went well the child mind could take over. In this forming child's garden of songs, the innocent self emerged to comfort
the adult singing and show listeners how to do the same. Writers
could revisit both their most treasured recollections and their most
painful sites of trauma. They could forgive others and themselves.
Judy Collins: *My father always promised us that we would live in
France.* Cat Stevens: *You're still young, that's your fault, there's so
much you have to know.* Neil Young: *You are a man, you understand,
you pick me up and lay me down again.* To reenter childhood as an
adult is to work toward reconciliation. Refuse to grow up the way
they wanted; you can fix it this time.

WARM FUZZIES

There were people out there who'd help uncover inner children, for a fee that might be covered under an insurance plan. Joni Mitchell introduced young Roberta Joan into her songs in the boom time of pop psychology. In the early 1960s one of its leading theorists, Eric Berne, offered the reading public a new way of talking about the psyche, calling it "transactional analysis." This system, which was not so much new as expertly mashed up from elements of game theory, cybernetics, affect theory and basic Freudian and Jungian principles, hit Americans in a new way when delivered by Berne, a ribald Canadian Jew who'd changed his name and moved to California to hock his theory among the affluent seekers just then loosening their neckties and apron strings. Noting that Berne's most popular book, *Games People Play*, had outsold racy volumes like Henry Miller's *Tropic of Cancer* and *The Works of the Marquis de Sade*, a journalist profiling him in 1967 attributed his success to his shit-talkingly vernacular way of helping people understand the voices in their own heads.

Instead of Freud's id, ego and superego, which Berne considered concepts too cerebral for practical application, he named three actual characters within each psyche. Child, Parent and Adult: the creative, impulsive original spirit; the internalized monitor and judge; and the rational actor who could respond to each and see reality. Berne's theories focused on the interactions among these inner selves, but only one really captured the popular imagination. That was the Child—the spirit of creativity and pleasure, but also of impulsiveness and chaos.

In 1963, Ohio-based psychiatrist W. Hugh Missildine published *Your Inner Child of the Past*, a bestseller to rival Berne's. It laid out the problems of this tiny psychic terror—"The child we once were can, and usually does, continue to balk or frustrate our adult satisfactions, to embarrass and exhaust us," an ad for the book read—but also presented it crying out for sympathy. By 1967, the inner child became a part of common parlance, name-checked as one to please in newspapers' travel columns and soup recipe roundups. That same year Thomas A. Harris resurfaced Berne's theories in his mega-seller *I'm OK—You're OK*, a highly read-able self-help guide that led to others, like Alvin Freed's *T.A. for Teens and Other Important People*, which employed language any elementary schooler could understand as it advised squabbling families to reconnect by doling out "warm fuzzies" instead of "cold pricklies."

Somewhere in a box of old papers I have my copy of that book, purchased by my mom, who dragged my dad, my brother and me to family therapy sessions where we had to try to generate some fuzzy feelings. In the awkward silence these sessions produced, I recall, I wondered why my parents were trying to conjure a kid spirit when I was right there. Furthermore, at precocious eleven, I wanted to be treated like a young woman. Like young Roberta Joan before me, I'd already made it to the adult section of the library, where I'd been reading Camus's *The Stranger* on furtive Wednes-day afternoons. Had I read the *New York Times* then, I would have vigorously agreed with Webster Schott's 1972 essay about Harris's still-influential book: "The kids read 'I'm OK, You're OK' to find out what in the world has happened to their parents."

The idea that a child mind holds a kind of wisdom adults struggle to access was powerful, especially amidst the rubble of the youthquake that was the counterculture. Psychotherapeu-tic exploration had always been a part of that scene. In group therapy retreats and emotionally draining "talk parties" in their own homes, the newly open-minded middle class formed great group-hug sprawls on the lawns of Northern California, sensually fingered rocks and old stuffed animals to reconnect with the polymorphous preschoolers they'd once been and screamed at one another in freeing primal tantrums that, in any grade school, would have been shut down in seconds flat. Inner children demanded acknowledgment and respect. It was easier to accept an inner child, often, than to enact the changes actual young people within the counterculture were demanding.

Singer-songwriters became central practitioners in this move to privatize the practice of empowering youth. Berne's original conception of the inner child identified that being as an artist, whose recovery of the gift of "awareness . . . living in the here and now" made creativity possible. Songwriters like Joni could draw a protective loop connecting themselves to listeners, echoing the dynamic of group therapy sessions. A literary and musical impulse became a therapeutic one. Songs from aging children guided listeners on their own healing journeys in league with, inspired by and often transcending the experience of therapy. This is one of Mitchell's most famous early lines: *I've looked at life from both sides now.* The inner child, avatar of direct experience and free imagination, can speak through and to the adult who reconsiders, mourns and embraces her within the golden circle of the song.

A LONELY GIRL

As I listen to Joni's songs that touch on childhood, the two kids who play hide-and-seek within them—the pretty, carefree waif picking off the petals on a flowering weed and the red-faced troublemaker yelling at her mother in the doorway—stop what they're doing and confront me. Yes, I recognize them. They live, in other versions, within me. There's the little Ann about whom I feel nostalgic and tender, who spent hours reading C. S. Lewis books in the crook of a backyard elm and dug for leprechaun gold in her mother's azalea beds. She comes alive again when I'm feeling at peace with my life, even a bit self-satisfied. Nostalgia paints her rosy picture. The other child within, though—the one with the bad haircut and snot on her upper lip, who hates her dumb elders and the mean kids who won't play with her and the minimum-security prison of her suburban surroundings—she stomps into my consciousness when I'm full of disappointment and self-doubt. She reminds me that the drifty days of childhood solitude often weren't golden-hued but tearstained, cloudy, dull. Miserable little Ann can take lovely little Ann down anytime. I want her around, because maybe she can help me understand my current miseries. But only my therapist can persuade me to give her a hug.

This is why the dissonance that dominates Joni's accounts of childhood interests me—it's something about her to which I can fully relate, as a product of the white middle-class, midcentury North American dream, with similar mixed-up feelings about the space my lucky circumstances granted me: seemingly infinite possibility that still so often felt like a trap. The coming-of-age story Mitchell's early songs put forward is a typical one for her time, and just a couple generations later, of mine, especially be-cause, like her, I am the only daughter of older parents who often doubted themselves. We children of postwar relative wealth and anxious white housewives' stay-at-home parenting were raised to believe that our little lives would keep getting bigger, as big as we could make them. The sky's the limit, kids! Yet when a girl like Joni (or me, even after feminism challenged norms) set her sights on goals different than her mother's or father's, she could be ac-cused of being ungrateful or, worse, unworthy, weird. A golden child, whose dreams align with those of her parents, is made of hope, but a weird child becomes a problem.

My father once cut back the branches on our backyard elm so that it stood bald and ugly in its spot next to our backyard's white picket fence, so that as I awkwardly lodged myself into the crook of its branches I was exposed, a fat dork left to entertain herself because no neighbor kids would have her over. When I tell this story, it always elicits a sympathetic sigh. An ugly inner child, effectively deployed, can sometimes soften people up. Yet despite nurturing ugly Ann for decades while despising her, I've also recently come to question her existence. A couple of years ago I found an old report card in my mother's department store Danish Modern dresser. It was from what I thought was one of my worst years, fourth grade, when I'd been christened a dog by some of the meanest boys in Our Lady of Fatima grade school. And yet, there was a comment in my teacher's neat script, denying that reality: "She is happy and talks a lot." A different Young Ann suddenly materialized, one I didn't remember. Which is the real one? How do they even know each other?

An adult who seeks her own childhood self will always be dissatisfied, whether she pursues that muse in a song or a shrink's office. To admit this is to suffer a loss that's hard to bear: the sacrifice of any coherent life story. Most people cling to both the loveliest memories of childhood and the most hideous ones because to admit that neither is definitive is to take the most painful, inevitable step of adulthood, into radical uncertainty. Mitchell's child songs transcend those most of her peers wrote because this is where she always means to dwell.

KIDS IN THE STREET

While young Roberta Joan was chasing winged marlins across Saskatoon's Aspen Parkland (or boys at the skating rink), Booker

T. Jones made his own forays through the yards of South Memphis. This was long before he became a soul producer and a pop innovator in scenes directly adjacent to Joni's folkish one. Jones had a paper route to keep him occupied while his mother and father worked at the local high school, a secretary and a math teacher. "I looked like a pregnant boy," the keyboardist and producer wrote in his memoir, remembering the two huge bags he hung over his eleven-year-old shoulders. Deliveries showed him the Memphis his middle-class parents tried to keep at arm's length: doors opened by little girls who said, "My mama say she not here," a shack where an old man who stank of kerosene lived and looked forward to their brief daily encounter, "sex workers, people with disabilities, addicts, homeless people and church faithful." Jones noticed it all, but the one window where he paused was at the house of pianist Phineas Newborn, Jr. There he'd fold papers and listen to Newborn practice, sometimes for an hour. It would throw off his whole afternoon.

Left to his own devices, Jones became a listener. "I began to absorb all sound," he wrote. "I heard rhythms in machines, in nature, in the wind." Only six years later he'd infuse what he'd soaked up into the organ parts he applied to some of soul music's most enduring hits, including his own instrumental classic "Green Onions." In these songs he evoked the sounds of his community struggling—the snarling dogs protecting derelict yards, the sound of police sirens, the jazz music that floated beyond the edges of Lincoln Park, breaking a boundary that the Black Memphians who congregated there weren't allowed, because of segregation, to cross.

Jones's childhood memories connect and contrast with those picturesquely filling the verses of the folkie poets coming out of Laurel Canyon. His path crossed theirs when he moved to Los

Angeles in 1969 as part of the circle around Oklahoma transplant Leon Russell, which included Jones's then-wife, Priscilla Coolidge. (Priscilla's sister Rita became lovers with Graham Nash after Joni left Nash for James Taylor.) Around that time Jones produced the first album by a hard to classify artist named Bill Withers, a former factory worker who should have been anointed a poet but, because he was Black and Southern and working-class, remained on some genre borderline. On that album is a song called "Grandma's Hands" that beautifully conveys a view of childhood with room for both nostalgia and painful realism. Withers sings of a now-dead grandmother who offered hugs and candy, but also held back a mother, her daughter, who might slap her children when she came to the end of her own rope. Unlike aging children like Joni, who played up the forlorn beauty of their green days and welcomed designations like "prairie girl," Withers had little to say when asked about his childhood in rural Slab Fork, West Virginia, except that he still enjoyed going back there and his mother was all right. He was vexed, though, by white journalists who might not necessarily consider his music to be the blues.

"I am the goddam blues," Withers once said. "Look at me. Shit. I'm from West Virginia, I'm the first man in my family not to work in the coal mines, my mother scrubbed floors on her knees for a living, and you're gonna tell me about the blues? Kiss my ass."

That flash of anger exposed the racial divide that always structures the story of popular music, even within this realm of childhood musings. Encounters with Black and Indigenous people play an important role in Mitchell's ongoing reconstruction of young Roberta Joan, especially in her later songs, after much inner work had given her tools to mine her subconscious. These figures are unsettling emissaries from the world beyond her restricted reach, embodying a vitality and grace that white suburban culture always

threatens to corrupt. "Harlem in Havana" has her sneaking into a
Black vaudeville troupe's tent show as a middle schooler and discovering transgressive desire. The flood of memories in "Song for
Sharon," dedicated to the best friend she left behind, is initiated
in part by a glimpse of New York construction workers that she
imagines as adult versions of "Little Indian kids" she'd once seen
climbing on a Canadian bridge. Most spectacularly, her song suite
"Paprika Plains" turns on a psychedelic memory of a group of Indigenous people gathered outside her town's general store. Tiny
Roberta Joan, witnessing this splendorous gathering, imprints the
memory through playacting: *I would tie on colored feathers and I'd
beat the drum like war.* The lyrics capture how memory traces solidify into stories. Three-foot-tall Joni took in the sight of these
thrillingly different neighbors and then drew it within her mind's
eye until it became indelible.

Placing her experiences of nonwhite others within the dreamy
consciousness of young Roberta Joan was a way for Mitchell to
imagine herself beyond the blandness of her own upbringing as
she perceived it. Yet it's worth saying that Black musicians like
Bill Withers wrote and spoke about their childhoods in ways that
challenged this romantic impulse. They didn't utterly contradict
the pastoral tendencies of inner-child music, but they demanded
acknowledgment of the inequities that many American children
faced.

Withers and many other Black artists whose work belongs in
the singer-songwriter canon never had the luxury to lull in childhood's magical sinecures. Some, like Withers, didn't even dare musical careers until trying something more practical, like mechanics.
Many others started pursuing musical careers in grade school, to
help their families transcend poverty, or simply because this path
offered a way beyond the segregated spaces of their daily lives. At

ten Aretha Franklin, in Detroit, was singing in her father's church, but not just as a worshipper, as an attraction. Chaka Khan, who in adulthood became a close friend of Mitchell's, started singing in bars at age eleven. Roberta Flack enrolled in Howard University at just fifteen. Stevie Wonder was signed to Motown Records at eleven and hit the road. "When you are traveling on the road," he told a reporter in 1973, "you have to learn to get to know yourself, always know where you are as a person, what your likes are. I had to learn this at a very young age, and fast."

Stevie Wonder was as engaged in inner exploration at the turn of the 1970s as anyone in Laurel Canyon, and the children to whom he gave voice in songs like "I Wish" or "Girl Blue" had magical elements; they were golden, playful, just beautiful. But they also faced pain and privation. "I Wish," the most nostalgic of his hits, begins with an image of a Christmas with no presents under the tree. The child's garden of singer-songwriter verses is more abundant when such songs, reminding us that an idyllic childhood is a luxury, are included. One whose tone makes me think of Mitchell's music was released by Jimi Hendrix, her fan and casual friend, in 1967. Hendrix, who faced horrifying poverty growing up in Seattle, struck a balance between dreaminess and hard truth in his ballad of dreams deferred, "Castles Made of Sand." In its final verse, Hendrix brings to life a desolate disabled girl who, mourning her inability to walk, decides to die. At the edge of the ocean—Hendrix's cool, watery guitar lines evoke Seattle's pearl gray Puget Sound—the girl hesitates. Something is coming into view. *Look, a golden-winged ship is passing my way,* Hendrix sings in her voice, his tone growing momentarily younger than his twenty-five years. Is it a rescue vessel or a feather-canyon illusion? "It really didn't have to stop, it just kept on going," Hendrix murmurs. He's also speaking for himself in that line, I think. The ship is the hope and the delusion of a child whose loneliness is reinforced by racism and other inequities—circumstances created by people in real life, not in some dreamtime.

THE CRIPPLER

To say that young Roberta Joan did not endure hardship would be a great oversight. She fell into the path of a viral disaster that struck in waves throughout the midtwentieth century, whose very mention terrified the parents of wandering summer children: polio.

Polio ran rampant through North America for sixty years before the vaccine devised by Dr. Jonas Salk got it under control. In Canada, multiple waves sickened approximately fifty thousand people, killing four thousand and rendering many more permanently disabled. Most were children. One was Mitchell, who contracted the illness around the time of her ninth birthday, in 1952.

Many who have written about Mitchell's life and work credit her affliction and determination to recover—which she did, mostly, in less than a year, though she retained nerve damage in her left hand that caused her to develop her famously original guitar-playing style—as a prime instigator of her artistry. Mitchell biographer David Yaffe considers her encounter with the disease her music's primal origin point. "The unique link between her inner life, her emotions, and her instrument—her whole body—was formed when she willed herself to stand up and walk," he wrote.

Yaffe's book takes its every cue from Mitchell herself, never arguing with her own myth-making, so this dramatic statement must have come from one primary source. Makes sense. By the time Yaffe, already utterly smitten, personally encountered Mitchell, she had been telling reporters about polio's impact on her life for decades, developing an account that grew more Dickensian as the years rolled by. "It was mystical to come back from that disease," she told the musician and writer Jim Irvin in 2005. She also shared a story with Irvin that she often told, about singing carols loudly in the direction of the droopy little Christmas tree her mother had set up in her room, crying into its branches that if she walked again she would somehow repay whatever blessing it could give her. After she did recover, she joined her school choir.

Mitchell's polio tales began as quick asides in her early interviews. One almost spun the experience as positive, noting that the illness had brought her closer to her mother, who homeschooled her for a few months after she left the hospital. She didn't write songs about her convalescence; the only musical gesture she made was an early cover version of Young's "Sugar Mountain," which quivers with the vulnerability of his own polio bout the same year as hers. Mitchell's answer song "The Circle Game" had applied a kind of whimsical stoicism to Young's theatrical vulnerability, a hot-towel-wrap remedy for his miserable mood. She sometimes said that her kinship with Young may be due to their complementary afflictions. "We were struck down by polio in the same epidemic: both in the back, in the precious spine, and in the right leg," she told *Musician*'s Vic Garbarini. "That's a great will-forger, you know."

Joni the willful victor over paralysis became a comical fatalist when she told Iain Blair of the *Chicago Tribune* in 1988 that she anticipated her frailness to eventually rob her of her feet: "I already have a cane collection. As soon as I go lame, which is inevitable, I'm going to start swinging it at people." (Chill of premonition: she did suffer from painful post-polio syndrome beginning not long after that, and her 2015 aneurysm would force her to have to learn to walk again.) In the 1990s she elaborated on her life as a sickly child in the most Gothic detail. Telling *Billboard*'s Timothy White that, due to the primitive conditions of her semi-rural preschool life—no running water, attacks of appendicitis and measles (two kinds!), "a life almost like [people on] the Russian tundra"—she was particularly susceptible to the virus commonly called "The Crippler."

On the day that it struck, Mitchell recalled, she dressed herself for school in pegged gray slacks, a gingham blouse and a blue sweater. "I looked in the mirror, and I don't know what I saw—dark circles under my eyes or a slight swelling of my face—but I said to myself, 'You look like a woman today.'" The next day, she collapsed.

The drama! There is no doubt that Mitchell, like thousands of children in the thrall of this baffling physical cataclysm, fundamentally changed as she fought the stealth enemy. Polio not only threatened sufferers' present lives and possible futures, it profoundly isolated them, not only in the moment, but through the stigma that faced "polios" after their recovery. Joni Mitchell's descent into polio and triumph over it changed her young life and later became part of the story of a lonely childhood that lent depth and supposed singularity to her music.

Reading Joni's polio panegyrics, I felt myself growing just slightly skeptical of the direct line she and her various biographers have drawn from childhood calamity to spectacularly high-achieving adulthood. Why? Partly because my detective's nose told me that the chronology isn't quite right. I was glad when I found one Mitchell scribe, Michelle Mercer, questioning the idea that polio did in young Roberta Joan and, from its ashes, Joni the artist rose. "With nothing but hobbled movement in a sea of grassy desolation, the story goes, she retreated into her imagination and an artist was born," Mercer writes. "But she'd already shown a talent for art before she contracted polio." Mercer puts more stock in the solitude reinforced by Mitchell's only-child status as the key to her gift for "building meaning from the smallest details and noting patterns in ephemeral events."

I believe young Roberta Joan would have grown up to be visionary Joni whether or not she'd spent a year paralyzed in bed. People who suffer don't have to become superheroes in response to their pain. Yet as I explored the history of polio in twentieth-century North America, I realized that this view of the disease as a seismic event, not only in individuals' lives but for an entire generation, is the dominant one. According to those who lived through it, polio helped make the baby boom the overachieving generation it was.

Marc Shell, a Canadian-born literary critic who contracted polio at age six, authored an epic cultural inquiry into the disease and its effects entitled *Polio and Its Aftermath: The Paralysis of Culture*. In it, he argues that the virus changed his generation's very idea of childhood. Suddenly, young people found among their number a certain group who were prematurely thrown into maturity. "The terrible suffering and the temperately triumphant sense of survivorship may be one reason that young polios so often seemed more grown up than others their age. It is as if they had already passed through that *midlife crisis*—a favorite term of the 1950s—which confers mature wisdom and tolerance." I read these words and think, that's another way to hear the phrase, *I've looked at life from both sides now*.

Polio was a strikingly common experience that rendered those it touched alien from the children they were just days before. Shell compares it to sexual trauma—sudden, unjust, changing everything. Those who recovered sufficiently, like Mitchell, bore its invisible scars. Polio's existence undid the idea of childhood as a safe space, making the inner child no longer a purely healing spirit but one who constantly reminds the adult of the harm that life might put in her way.

In stories of children whose idyllic solitude is broken by trauma, a sense of mission often surfaces as central within the healing process. This was true for many sickened by polio—as it was for Black youths trying to cope with racism like Booker T. Jones, who recognized music as a route to empowerment. Mitchell biographer Sheila Weller, whose sister contracted polio at seven, wrote in 2020 of the many "over-achievers" who endured the illness, identifying "Type-A" perfectionism as part of its "long and mostly unknown afterlife." She quotes numerous polios, including Mitchell, who've identified the struggle as formative, noting how many speak of their recovery as a kind of training regimen. "You always ask me why I'm so strong," her sister tells her. "It's because of the polio."

Polio didn't make Mitchell a musician, but it may have established the need to define herself, as she has for so long, as a genius. And because polio's struggle remains active in the background for life—present in Joni's numb left hand, and in the ghost pains she's endured since she hit her forties—it also teaches an artist's lesson: that meaningful struggles rarely completely resolve, instead resurfacing in different forms. I think of Joni picturing herself, so often in her songs, as someone engaged in a kind of race: running, skating, flying. Alone, competing against herself. "I run my own kind of marathon almost daily," one polio survivor once said. The artistic process also feels like this.

DREAMER

As she grew older, Joni herself became more urban, more sophisticated, more cosmopolitan. But she clung to a self that was solitary and innocent: *I came to the city and lived like Old Crusoe on an island of noise*, she sang in the title track from her first album. Old Crusoe is young Roberta Joan, a castaway in the mind of the adult invoking her, even though from preschool on Joni was actually a very social girl who loved dancing, was in the bowling club and lived closer to her town's bustling center than its outskirts.

From the first time I saw a picture of teenage Joni in a bouffant and a cute sweater set, surrounded by boys and laughing, I wanted to construct a child version of her that was more like me: not a nature-loving waif but a small ball of dissatisfaction and yearning who used her imagination to try and speed up the future's arrival. Another photo I tacked to my wall showed her in a sharpshooter outfit that was more costume than functional: spangled vest, play gun, her dungarees archly cuffed to show off dress boots. She looks about nine. Already understanding that she could escape the confines of circumstance by casting herself elsewhere.

I looked for the Roberta Joan who dreamed of cities, partly to dispel the tenacious myth of the prairie girl. I eventually found an ally in Mitchell herself, who countered her most famous child songs with a few like "Let the Wind Carry Me," which recounts her mom's disapproval of the tight skirt and green eyeshadow she donned in hopes of making an escape. In conversation she complicated her prairie girl self-construction by occasionally calling Saskatoon "extremely bigoted" and "very isolated, very unworldly." In 2018, when Saskatoon named a downtown promenade in her honor, the woman from the tourist bureau noted not that it traversed scenic meadows, but that it passed by young Joni's favorite public swimming pool, where she'd stay out of the water playing the jukebox in the rec area until her dimes ran out. City kid Roberta Joan had existed; I didn't have to make her up.

It was another aging child, a peer and former lover of Mitchell's, who steered me back to the prairie view. When I sat down with James Taylor in 2018, he was in an effusive mood, in Los Angeles to celebrate Mitchell's seventy-fifth birthday and play several of her songs at a tribute concert. He had many things to say about her—the good times they'd spent as the golden couple of 1970; the way her creativity always seemed sui generis to him; the feeling that they'd remained connected artistically despite the bitterness of their breakup in 1971. As we talked, he folded his long body into a curve, gazing at the table as if he was mentally drawing a map on it. I later discovered this was his default pose during interviews. He was demonstrating, I guess, the mode he feels is essential to creativity. Self-willed solitude.

I asked him what made Mitchell such an exceptional writer, able to balance thought and feeling with such delicacy. "I do have a theory about her growing up in Saskatchewan and having a lot of open and by our standards empty time, and enough quiet to have a rich internal life," he said. "I remember growing up in North Carolina and I think it's very connected to the way Joni must have grown up as a kid—there was a lot of time, a fair amount of boredom and sort of this internal imaginative life. I think it allowed her to become who she is." He smiled. "You work with what you've got, you know."

A child gazes into a big sky and she doesn't feel restored, but restless. Another plunges a tree branch into a creek to feel the current and wants to be swept away, not soothed by its burbling thrum. Aimless kids cut paths across landscapes adults find beautiful, and they might not dwell on the picturesque beauty but still feel potential opening up. "That must have been the case with Bob Dylan in Hibbing, Minnesota, or Neil Young in North Ontario, or any number of people who were somehow allowed enough time to form their own thought patterns," Taylor said. "There's an element of alienation, probably, in most of the people you'll see coming up with the kind of work that Joni does."

The psychoanalyst Adam Phillips once wrote that a child sees what she wants, not what is there. Adults walk alone through open spaces and feel like they're recapturing something. Children do the same, but know the limits of their small reach. In longing to be bigger, more powerful, *elsewhere*, they start creating themselves.

"I'm not saying that it's suffering, necessarily," Taylor said, "although it may be painful. I do think that artists somehow need to discover their own way through the maze, and they then offer a way that other people can use, too."

The child left to her own devices can begin to imagine getting somewhere, and that is the value, for the adult she becomes, of keeping her in mind. Taylor had just come from a rehearsal where he'd been singing "River," the legendary Mitchell song about dreaming of skating on flat frozen water back toward a more innocent time. The thoughts he shared with me suggested that it wasn't the river that he'd found himself contemplating, but the wish Joni had put into motion by envisioning it. The aspiration to skate away.

2

the humming of the wheels

The very first song Joni Mitchell claims to have written, called "Day After Day," is about leaving home, getting stuck, and desperately wanting to keep moving. She was twenty-one and unexpectedly pregnant, though it's unclear whether she knew that yet. The song, a blues, implies that she had her suspicions. One-way ticket to Toronto in her hand, she was headed to the Mariposa Folk Festival, her first big venture beyond the coffeehouses of Calgary where she'd begun to share her songs.

The baby's father, her fellow art student Brad MacMath, was sitting right there with her on the train whose hum Joni picked up in her song, but is absent in the lyrics, except as a source of anxiety and longing. More recognizable there is the influence of the Black artists beloved by the young folkies whom she'd begun to call friends. *Day after day*, it begins, *miles and miles of railroad track. Night after night, hummin' of the wheels.*

The woman Joni imagines in the song, a version of herself, once rode the rails but now sits alone in a room. A lover was supposed to follow her from a place whose markers are fading from her memory: *Lie awake and dream of days of auld lang syne, moonlight through the pine.* But like the reflected shimmer of night, he's fading. He doesn't show. Something is wrong, confining her: *Make a dollar, need it twice. Pray my darlin' comes before too late.* Given its place on the path of Mitchell's life, the song can be counted as confessional. But as with all of Mitchell's songwriting, it veers from introspection to an engagement with something larger: in this case, her generation's propensity to drift and the risks of that, for women in particular.

In 1964 Joni had just started her life as an explorer, but already she was dwelling on that itch to progress or escape, or both, and not only in the songs she wrote about the childhood she was leaving behind. The markers of her life at this point kept moving, and her songs captured that. "Urge for Going," "Born to Take the Highway," "Here Today and Gone Tomorrow." That train across Canada, some time in Calgary and Toronto, the sudden end of her affair with MacMath. A quickie marriage that took her to Detroit. The end of that union and her decision to entrust the daughter she bore in adoption, leaving her to wonder for years where that child herself had flown. A deeper immersion in her music, leading to career-cultivating side trips through the Midwest and New England and an eventual brief landing in New York. Idylls in London and South Florida. All of this happened before Joni Mitchell ever saw L.A.

From her teen years onward, Joni was propelled by a ruling tension between her need for grounding and solitude and her hankering for yet another port of call. I imagine her lugging a ukulele, and soon after a guitar, aboard the buses and trains of North America, or depositing her instrument carefully in the trunks of cars she shared with men named Eric, David, Patrick, Tom, all itinerant musicians like herself. Or driving her own vehicle from an army base to a church hall, happy to settle in for a week's run in a downtown strip of folk dives when a booker would give her that break. From 1963 to 1967, even for the two years when she was married to Chuck Mitchell and living in Detroit, Mitchell was a vagabond. It suited her. It also made for a strong persona and great songs.

Unlike some of her peers, she took each increasingly bigger step delicately, compelled to strive for a stable future as much as to live by the road's rules. Joni Mitchell in transition didn't simply fancy herself a free spirit; she worked to inhabit that archetype, though it sometimes contradicted her nature and the lessons of her upbringing and, in one central moment, her ability to care for another soul whose absent presence would stay with her from the moment she placed that baby in another family's care. Mitchell created herself through a determined kind of restlessness, presenting herself to her audiences and her friends as a makeshift homemaker who'd decorate her temporary lodgings with thrift-store tapestries and crystals, but who was happy to throw all that in a box when it was time to try another town. At twenty-two, she made a tape recording for her mother, a typically barbwired gift from a daughter looking in the rearview. Every one of its songs was about getting the hell away.

I like this picture of the young Joni, breaking free despite the hard decisions she had to make to do so. I can hardly resist romanticizing her as a femme Kerouac on her own road, continually casting her eyes past the suitcase packed at the foot of her latest bed (not to mention the hunky folk singer in it) and toward the door. In her early twenties, Joni insistently became her own person by setting forth in ways women have risked throughout modern history—leaving stifling small towns for the riskiness of the city, defying family expectations in hopes of encountering something, anything, new.

In the 1960s, such migrations became emblematic of women's liberation, chronicled in many novels, films and songs, not just Joni's. That wave extended into my own lifetime. I, too, left behind my boring hometown at the turn of my twenties with the fire of ambition in my belly, landing in San Francisco with the same lack of clear plans, looking for people who'd take my dares. She'd set out to conquer the coffeehouses; I pursued poetry and, a bit more avidly, poets. I forgot to call my parents for six months at a time. I know what it's like to be young and feel like you absolutely have to get to where things are happening. As I learned more about Joni's peregrinations, I thought about that compulsion, and how it can seem like the center keeps shifting further away, like the bright-burning heart of a fast-moving star. The thrill and terror of never having been more alone. One day I was climbing on the rocks at Ocean Beach, near the ruins of San Francisco's Sutro Baths, and I got stuck halfway down a cliff hanging over the crashing water. *If I fall*, I thought, *no one will know I was here and am gone*. In the story of Joni's early journeys, I feel that energy, the need to be seen and heard and to keep going because standing still might spell oblivion.

FIRST STEPS: OUT OF SASKATCHEWAN

Let's go back to where Joni's itinerant life began, to her dreaming days as a teen staying out too late for her parents' comfort. Before she left Saskatchewan, our heroine spent years planning her steps forward, her escape. I found evidence of this in a photograph of young Roberta Joan from around the time she started calling herself "Joni," the alter ego that would serve as a kind of passport. Joni and her friend Anne Bayin are perched on a flowery upholstered patio chair in a Saskatoon backyard. Joni is wearing a formfitting sundress, looking like she's at a garden party, ready to offer her guests lemonade. Anne, on the other hand, takes a rogue's pose. Her hip is cocked, her body enveloped in a baggy dark shawl-collared thing that might be a sweater and what seem to be trousers, though her legs are obscured. The girls are trying on each other's day-to-day identities: just before the camera lens snapped open, they'd swapped clothes. Anne looks uncomfortable in her pal's boyish outfit, but Joni is utterly poised. She could apparently imagine herself as either hausfrau or bohemian. Many years later, when she wrote the single woman's lament "Song for Sharon," she claimed she'd always dreamed of becoming a farmer's wife.

That shawl-collared smock is a signal: it's what an artist would wear. There's actually a picture of Joan Mitchell, the abstract-expressionist pioneer who shared the name Joni would soon obtain through marriage, wearing almost the same outfit that Joni lent Anne that day. Mitchell sits on a splattered tarp in her studio holding her poodle, the epitome of the bohemienne. Joni couldn't have known about this doppelgänger—or could she? She'd started taking art classes by then, and high school kids do have a way of sniffing out possible futures within the pages of magazines and library books. That other JM was living the life young

Roberta Joan (now Joni) could only dream about—drinking beer at the 7 Arts Coffee Gallery while Jack Kerouac read poetry in a voice loud enough to drown out the clinking glasses, talking existentialism and sex with men who almost took her seriously. In the 1950s, New York bohemianism offered one of the few examples of freedom to young women who wanted to work and still claim some kind of old-fashioned romance. Art, the Beats and jazz made the dreaming hearts of girls like Joni zing.

Mitchell has claimed that as a teen she hated Kerouac and his gang, thinking herself above them despite donning berets and dungarees in an attempt to enact "a satire on the Beats." (She also immediately despised Abstract Expressionists like Joan Mitchell, whose work she considered both sloppy and cold.) I have to call her on these remarks. A teen, no matter how sophisticated, wouldn't dress the part of someone she utterly disdained. And the Saskatoon version of the beatnik subculture was what she sought out in the dance halls and—her word—"brothels" she tried to get into on the weekends during those curfew-skirting years. Her later descriptions of what can only be called adolescent attempts at slumming reek of the enticing perfume of reefer and racial intermingling. Here is the seed of Mitchell's strong identification with Black men, which reached an apotheosis in the late 1970s, when she donned blackface and wore a "pimp" costume on the cover of her album *Don Juan's Reckless Daughter*. "I gravitated to the best dance halls from the age of 12 to the age of 16," she told reporter William Ruhlmann in 1995. "Like any young black trumpet player in the South, like John Handy or any New Orleans musician who knew he was a musician at an early age, somehow I was drawn to where the music was best, and it's always in the roughest areas." She did recognize, retrospectively, the privilege of her skin, explaining how she remained safe in these rough environs. "The street had a heart then, and a child, a baby, a clean-looking baby was not molested."

Her memory presents quite a florid scenario for a farm town where women couldn't even legally drink in bars until the 1960s. It isn't really possible to track Joni's alleged teenage peregrinations; the few high school friends who have given interviews tend to puff up her own mythologies. But say she did stumble into some rough places, as ambitious small-town kids sometimes do. Joni's teen adventures set a pattern she'd repeat into her adult years, of venturing forth and then collecting herself, of flirting with the wild side but never completely giving herself over to it. Her parents' influence remained powerful, despite the way she chafed against its restrictions, as did the conviction that drove this only child from her earliest dreaming days onward: that she was special and had an obligation, to herself and the cosmos, to make something major of herself.

The wild child had things to do besides dance all night with shady boys, as much as she loved to do that. When she was still in elementary school, meticulous Myrtle noticed Roberta Joan's bubbling interest in art and uncharacteristically allowed her to paint on her bedroom wall. Once she discovered this mode of self-expression, the child exhibited the focus of an artist—that is, the kind that made her doze off in class because she'd been up 'til three in the morning sketching and listening to rock and roll on the radio. In painting she found her primary expressive language, one she stayed with even when music took over her time. She would never abandon visual art, though for many years it was mostly a private outlet beyond the album covers she would sometimes illustrate herself; never learning musical notation, she came to think of songwriting and production as painterly processes, grounded in color and perspective as much as in rhythm and melody. To her these terms were synonymous. Not until the mid-1980s would she feel confident enough in her craft to stage regular gallery shows, but her unwavering insistence that in her deepest heart she was a painter is validated by many distinguishing qualities of her music: the impressionistic nature of her storytelling; her love of sound collage, evidenced by her pioneering use of tape loops and samples as well as musical pastiche; her attraction to jazz players like Wayne Shorter, who stress timbre and sonic space. In her first exploring years she turned to music for thrills and to writing for self-assertion (she had an English teacher who saw her potential), but painting gave her the model for unlocking creativity, and throughout her life, kept her in touch with its vernal burst. "The reason painters live, I think, to be quite old is because they're children, maybe more than any of the arts, that never grew up, never put their crayons away," she told a television interviewer in 1989.

Joni's absorption in the arts led to profligacy in all other things. She flunked twelfth grade and only recovered through the worried attentions of Myrtle and her teachers, who designed a special curriculum for her. She was still sneaking out to explore what nightlife she could find, and after hearing a folk trio in a local jazz spot—she liked their sense of humor more than their sound—she tried to talk her mom into buying her a guitar. She ended up with a baritone ukulele, which she'd cart around to the bonfire parties where the cool kids flocked after dark, singing out among friends for the first time.

Free spirits had long favored the uke, and despite her stated disinterest in beatnik culture, free was what Joni wanted to be. A staple instrument of colonial Hawaii, among mainlanders the ukulele became a children's toy with a sparkling aura of exoticism and a cheap solution for young adults unable to afford quality guitars. In 1920s Greenwich Village, a *Variety* columnist reminisced in 1960, the neighborhood was "a riot of batiks, Benda masks [those weird ceramic Harlequin masks later sold in college dorm-furniture marts], ukuleles, peasant blouses and 'how's your libido?'" And a soprano uke was the musical talisman Marilyn Monroe carried as the jazz musician Sugar Kane in 1959's *Some Like It Hot*. For Joni, drawing lines in her mind between Bohemia and Tinseltown, the uke was ideal. She could master it despite some lingering weakness in her left hand from the polio, and it sounded fine accompanying the ballads and blues in the Pete Seeger songbook she'd purchased along with it.

The uke was small enough to bring to the shores of Waskesiu Lake, the weekenders' destination just outside of town where young people would gather to drink beer in cans and sing the old folk ballads that were new to them—stories that would appeal to a teenage high romantic with a dramatic streak. Songs about lives lived a long throw from her own, in New Orleans brothels or ending on the gallows in eighteenth-century Scotland or running a moonshine still in the Reconstructionist South. As Sheila Weller notes in *Girls Like Us*, her classic book about Mitchell, Carole King and Carly Simon as embodiments of the countercultural "new woman," though the folk revival's earliest stars were mostly men like Woody Guthrie, Seeger and Lead Belly, the repertoire "kicked wide the door to *female* storytelling—and storytelling based on an exaggerated version of *real*, not imagined, experience (family treachery, mating and pregnancy, all larded with troubling consequences)." Jazzwomen like Abbey Lincoln and Nina Simone were doing the same thing, but their approaches, while appealing to a would-be sophisticate like Joni, were either too contemporary or too adult to seem attainable to her in 1962. Plucking out chords as best she could on her uke, Joni found her voice singing songs that felt like a lost legacy, songs that suggested ways out of the boredom of postwar middle-class affluence and into a wilder, weirder way of living.

Folk music didn't just speak to Joni Mitchell's soul; it offered her a way to be in with the "in" crowd, an early taste of a bigger world. Through a slightly older friend she got a job at a local coffeehouse and soon had secured a slot on its musical roster. The Louis Riel, flamboyantly named after the Indigenous resistance leader who'd gone on to found the province of Manitoba, boasted a calendar full of local folk ingenues alongside jazz guitarists, comedians and touring Americans like the Black balladeer Len Chandler. Joni gained a following among her own peers and was even featured on a local late-night television special. She still considered herself a painter and a poet as much as a singer, and she hadn't yet written a song of her own. But she was starting to ponder where music might take her that her other passions could not.

CALGARY TO MARIPOSA

She brought her uke with her when, after squeaking out of high school, Joni extended the line on her map six hundred kilometers west to Calgary. Enrolling in the Alberta College of Art and Design, she became a half-hearted if technically skilled student on the road toward a career in commercial draftsmanship. For money, she did some modeling for buyers in department stores, something she'd first tried in high school. Pretty soon she added instruments to her collection—a bigger baritone ukulele, a Martin tiple, which was the size of a travel guitar, and then an actual guitar. Painting remained her true passion, but music was gaining an edge, especially after she began working in a hot local coffeehouse with the multipurpose name the Depression. She became, as an article in the local paper put it, a "Two-Career Girl": "While

audiences assure her that she has considerable talent as an entertainer her instructor feels sure she can make a success drawing and
painting. Attractive, unattached and blessed with two talents, Joni
Anderson is now struggling with a choice that few 20-year-olds
have to make."

Looking back at her younger self, Mitchell would later describe her turn toward music as a rebellion against the stifling
curriculum her art teachers imposed. "It was stuck between auto
mechanics and cafeteria cooks in training," she said in a 1995 interview in the trade magazine *Goldmine*. She hated the aspects of
formal instruction that focused on the technical, but also had no
interest in what she perceived as a cold and violent turn in modern
art: the abstraction then popular in New York and among provincial Canadian academics. She wanted to be Vincent van Gogh, not
Jackson Pollock. Folk music was something she could enter into
on her own terms, and like her, its leading lights fetishized the
misty, supposedly more authentically expressive past.

She was also likely just looking for friends and a respite from
the solitude of the art studio. John Uren, the Depression's founder
and manager, remembered her as the kind of regular who'd show
up even when she wasn't working, eager to meet the many touring musicians passing through and join in whenever a spot opened
up onstage. "The thing about performing is that you're dealing
with live people, and when you get a warm response it becomes
addictive," he said in 2005. "Her art was solitary, her music was
communal."

This back-and-forth between music and art became one private route marked on her map. Another surfaced as she taught
herself guitar. The Espana SL-11 she'd bought was popular
among aspiring folk singers, but she wasn't able to learn the standard fingerings as easily as her friends did. Withering in her left

hand was polio's sad aftereffect. Mitchell found a way to not only overcome it but make it a kind of advantage.

Folk guitar might often sound staid to contemporary ears used to rock riffs and synthesizer flourishes, but virtuosity and experimentation were prized in the scene. The Black blues masters that folklorists like Alan Lomax and the Seegers introduced to white audiences used tunings and fingerpicking techniques they'd invented themselves. And Davey Graham, the English son of a Guyanese mother and Scottish father, released a jazz-rooted instrumental called "Anji" in 1962 that became a kind of litmus test for young players—as one critic has described it, "a portal from simple folk to new possibilities." Songs like that one circulated through the hootenannies where folk singers would swap knowledge and show off—this was a time when many would-be troubadours were absorbing jazz innovations alongside European balladry, and for Joni, who thought of the jazz trio Lambert, Hendricks, & Ross as "my Beatles," those connections must have been irresistible.

Young Joni being herself, already dead set on her own singularity, needed to find her own way into these experiments. Mitchell has often said that she found it in a Pete Seeger songbook called *How to Play Folk-Style Guitar*. "I went straight to the Cotten picking," she told the writer and acoustic guitar master Jeffrey Pepper Rodgers in a 1996 interview. "Your thumb went from the sixth string, fifth string, sixth string, fifth string. I couldn't do that, so I ended playing mostly the sixth string but banging it into the fifth string. So Elizabeth Cotten is definitely an influence; it's me not being able to play like her. If I could have I would have, but it's a good thing I couldn't, because it came out original."

Elizabeth Cotten was a self-taught rural Black woman who came to prominence in the American folk scene after being discovered by the woman whose house she kept, who happened to be Ruth Crawford Seeger, Pete's mom and the great doyenne of folk revivalism. Mostly because Cotten was so different from the earnest students who admired her—she was old, and from the South—she became known as a rustic oddity instead of the technical genius she was. As a child, she started playing music on her brother's banjo. Not wanting to tell her brother she was regularly swiping it, the left-handed Cotten taught herself to play it upside down, using her thumb to play the treble-string melodies and her fingers for the rumbling bass notes. Modifying the Cotten tuning to compensate for her polio-afflicted hand, Mitchell found a way to be her own kind of talent. Her guitar playing became the signature that her singing—strong, evocative, but in those first years clearly imitative of women stars of the folk scene, from Buffy Sainte-Marie to Judy Collins and Joan Baez—was not. The sound of the guitar is what makes Joni Mitchell's early recordings so haunting; it always seems to be a little off, like a lazy eye in a gorgeous face. Here is where young Joni first cultivated the tension inherent in everything she would later do, between glamour and eccentricity, the desire to draw people in and the urge to head off alone.

Another way to travel: her fingers pressed down on the fretboard and plucked patterns across the strings. Mitchell's exploratory playing was a way of making contact, being in dialogue with her predecessors and her peers. She noted how the different players she began to meet dropped a D or a G string to generate a noise that instantly registered as different—so many of those men, especially, who met her then would claim to be the one who first showed her how to grab the knob on her guitar head and twist it until the pitch of the strings changed. But Joni would not be one of those earnest white pretenders whose veneration for country blues risked outright imitation. In a strange way, as with her later forays into jazz fusion, she was able to hide her debts within the act of transformation. Even starting out, she wanted her music to be what the poet Godfrey John said of her slightly older contemporary and soon-to-be mentor, Buffy Sainte-Marie: "stamped with her own name." Bushwhacking along trails that already existed, young Joni rejected folk's preservationist tendencies and turned it into what, to her at least, felt like virgin territory.

"The moment I began to write I took the black blues tunings which were floating around," she said in *Goldmine*. "I had to simplify the shapes of the left hand, but I craved chordal movement that I couldn't get out of standard tuning without an extremely articulate left hand. So, to compensate for it, I found the tunings were a godsend. Not only that, but they made the guitar an unstable thing, but also an instrument of exploration, so that you could put the thing in a new tuning, you had to rediscover the neck, you'd need to search out the chordal movement, and you'd find five or six chords, and then there was the art of chaining them together in a creative manner. It was very exciting to discover my music. It still is, to this day."

I love the way she puts it: "It was very exciting to discover my music." I can just feel Joni at twenty, her right thumb slipping from the sixth string to the fifth, her left hand's fingers curling as best they could and then coming up over the fretboard to make a chord no one she knew had made before. Her chords formed a path, a patch of track she was laying down.

Elizabeth Cotten's most famous song was called "Freight Train," its round rhythms inspired by the wheels on the ones she'd see roll by her North Carolina window when she was a child. The patterns she created answered those she heard unfolding as those vehicles of transport, of possible escape, rolled past.

And she did venture beyond her home state, but only in her fifties, after raising a family and spending years working as a maid in other people's homes. She'd discovered her own music years before and buried it, letting it surface only for herself one day when she found a guitar laying around the Seeger family home, where she was again employed as a servant, no matter how often the kids said she was one of the family to them. Joni couldn't have related to the story behind the mix of volition and restraint in the Cotten style, the years of sacrificing for others and dreaming in quiet that it represented. Yet it laid something down for her, another version of that dilemma she did know well, her wish to be loved fighting her need to be free.

Folk music, as she discovered it in the clubs and legion halls and living rooms of Calgary, offered many variations on that tension. The folk revival is remembered for an earnestness veering into rigidity: these polite kids were suspicious of rock and roll, as proven by scene saint Seeger's objections to Bob Dylan's distorted sound at the 1965 Newport Folk Festival when he played with an electrified band. But wait—Dylan was one of those kids himself, and like Joni he'd been a teenage rock fan (and, in his case, player) before the most portable acoustic guitar became his thing. At the Depression, where she claimed a regular gig, and soon at other clubs with far-out names like the Fourth Dimension and the Yardbird Suite, Joni heard not only the gently florid ballads she herself favored, but jazz poetry, flamenco guitar, cowboy songs, civil rights anthems and dirty blues. One write-up of the Depression in the Mount Royal Junior College newspaper listed purveyors of all of those forms, with Joni singled out as having both a poignant repertoire and a charming demeanor. She was supposed to be the purity in the mix. But she was a sponge, soaking up particles from every surface.

It was in this spongelike state that she first heard Sainte-Marie, a woman not much older than herself who'd already proven that folk-rooted music could be all the things Mitchell would later demand—rhythm-driven and melodically free, artistically daring but also accessible, and rooted in an honest, even transgressive female perspective. Born in 1941, she was raised in New England in a family that felt unstable—she would say after stardom came that her mother had told her when she was very young that she was adopted and Indigenous, and that this disclosure made her feel lost and alone despite their bond. The feeling of being a changeling, of needing to flee toward an unknown home, permeated her life the way it permeates young Joni's fanciful songwriting. Her parents called her Beverly, a name she soon rejected. Like Roberta Joan, she often fled into wild patches near her home—though hers was just a trailer—but not merely to dream; she also sought to escape a place that, she later said, was harmful despite her mother's love. Music became another way for Sainte-Marie to establish her own space, through listening, and soon enough, singing. Rock and roll was her favorite. She loved to dance and taught herself guitar, playing in tunings of her own devising. As soon as she could, she fled Maine for college at UMass Amherst, joined the folk scene, and pretty soon was traveling to Canada, where she hoped to find traces of her Indigenous bloodline. She could never verify the identity of her birth parents, but was adopted into a Piapot Cree family in the custom of that First Nation in the early 1960s. By then she had also hit upon her musical approach, a blend of rock, blues and Indigenous sounds vibrating with the originality young Joni wanted more than anything.

Joni would have likely first heard Sainte-Marie during her final months in Calgary, upon the release of the young innovator's debut album, *It's My Way!* on Vanguard Records in 1964. That summer she and a few other Depression regulars, including Brad MacMath, took that three-day train ride to see the new star play as part of the Mariposa Folk Festival. Two years old and already both beloved and notorious among Canadian folk enthusiasts, the fest had been conceived by a woman, Ruth Jones, inspired to act by a motivational speaker who passed through her small Ontario town. It was booked by another woman, Estelle Klein, who'd been radicalized as a teen during summers spent at the Jewish Camp Naivelt. Mariposa's first two years accomplished Jones's stated goal of attracting more tourists to Orillia, a quiet lake community just north of Toronto, but by 1963 the gentle crowds had grown into a throng of twenty thousand dominated by teenagers on motorbikes.

On that train ride, gazing out the window as she leaned against MacMath's shoulder, Mitchell must have wondered what she was getting into. The papers had been full of reports declaring Mariposa a "disaster" plunging the folk revival into "mob rule." The fest was almost canceled when a local city council won an injunction that forced a last-minute relocation from the Orillia area to Maple Leaf Stadium in Toronto, where the crowds showed up at less than half capacity. Sainte-Marie herself almost missed her headlining spots, having to be retrieved from the airport after booking a ticket to fly to a powwow in Saskatchewan.

According to one interview he gave at the time, John Uren organized the pilgrimage to Mariposa as a fun field trip that might also promote the Calgary folk scene. There's no documentation of Joni's attendance at the festival that year, but a few things are known. She and Brad did get close to the action onstage—by pitching in on the stage crew. And she caught at least one of Sainte-Marie's sets, which electrified the crowd and helped establish her as a major folk star.

On the way to the fest, Joni had started writing that first song, a blues like one of Buffy's, a song of desolation and, in the very speaking of it, defiance. The voice in it belongs to a woman carried far from home by a lover and then abandoned. A train's wheels hum nearby, once her freedom, now her sorrow; Elizabeth Cotten's hand brushes across that verse. The defiance built into its rhythms says something will change soon. This girl will make a hard decision. She has followed not just a man, but a feeling that life can be bigger, and that feeling will carry her across another threshold soon.

A PAUSE

Just as the points on the map of Joni's life start connecting, carrying her somewhere, there's a blind spot. A presence in the shape of an absence. On that train ride she had likely known she was pregnant. In the fall of 1964 Joni had made it to Toronto and was graduating from church-hall gigs thrown together by friends to regular engagement in local nightclubs. Her college lover Brad MacMath hung out for a while but, he'd say years later, "we were not communicating," and pretty soon he left her in the bohemian enclave of Yorkville and headed off on his own quest. Joni made friends and tried to make money, but by winter something was getting in the way: her own body, and the condition she wasn't hiding but hadn't planned, either.

She gave birth to a daughter in February 1965. That fact alone didn't make her that different from other young hippie women in the neighborhood, whose openness to new ways of living made it a haven for single mothers and other outcasts from the norm. Sheila Weller's account of this period in Mitchell's life in *Girls Like Us* is the most complete rendered by her many biographers.

Shocked by how easily some girls even younger than her almost flaunted their freedom to have children and lovers and an unbound life, Mitchell, Weller writes, was torn up by going through this experience alone. "Yet despite the apparent melancholy, the poverty, the conspicuous pregnancy, and her aloneness (or perhaps because of these things), Joni exuded charisma," Weller writes. To the friends and acquaintances Weller sought out from that period, Mitchell seemed to be simultaneously stricken and doing just fine.

Such is the burden of the birth mother. I know the adoption triad intimately; I raised a child born of a woman even younger than Joni was when the baby she named Kelly Dale was born, in a different time and very different circumstances—an open adoption in which my kid's birth mom remains actively involved. Yet if I've learned anything in the twenty years since my child was born, it's that I had no real idea what her first mother was going through, even though we talked about it across many long nights. The experience of being a birth mother belongs to one person alone—like being an adoptive mother, it's incomprehensible within the norms of most people's parenting. And it changes over time. Sometimes from one day to another. I believe a birth mother is to herself many things at once—free and forever bound, divorced from shame and consumed by it, broken by longing for her lost one and determinedly stronger than anyone should be expected to be. But none of this is for me to really say. Nor is it for me to say what young Joni went through in February 1965.

A lot of talk has congealed around Joni Mitchell's motherhood. That she was callous to give up her daughter and that she had no other choice. That her birth mother status was highly unusual (in reality, Patti Smith, David Crosby and Maggie Roche are three other musicians around Joni's age whose first children were adopted by others). That she married Chuck Mitchell to form a proper family with the daughter then still in foster care, although, as Mitchell herself has intimated, she suspected from the start that would not be possible. That she never told anyone. That anyone would have known if they'd listened harder to her songs.

Mitchell did write one explicit song about Kelly Dale, called "Little Green," in which she laid out the whole story. Was it male cluelessness that caused most writers to not notice the true meaning of phrases like *you sign all the papers in the family name* when the song was released as part of Mitchell's confessional masterwork, *Blue*, in 1971? Or was the story of a broken bond between a woman and her child common enough in those times of changing family values that most assumed it was a character study? In some interviews from around that time, Mitchell said she had no children. Her friends knew, though, especially the women who were negotiating difficult mothering experiences of their own. Friends like Cass Elliot, raising her daughter in a chaotically communal situation while never acknowledging the father's name. And Judy Collins, who lost her son for two years in a custody battle at the height of her first success as a star carrying folk music onto the pop charts.

All I know is that this is Mitchell's story to tell, and that she chose to tell it much later, in the 1990s, when Kelly Dale (renamed Kilauren) found her and the pair reunited. In that moment of her becoming both grandmother to a boy she hadn't known existed and doyenne of an artistic legacy she was beginning to consider in full, Joni said more about the blind spot in her younger life. I'm choosing to follow her lead on this. Certainly Mitchell's loss as a birth mother affected the intensity of both her music and her ambition. As did her freedom as a birth mother. As did her guilt. Her hopes. Her remembering. Her forgetting. Her need to dwell on it.

Her need to never speak of it. This is her story to tell or not. This account will return to it later, when she finally did.

DETROIT: DOWN THE AISLE AND OUT THE DOOR

Music can be made and loved in solitude, and a romantic view of Mitchell's accelerating turn into songwriting at twenty-one might show her behind a creaky bedroom door in a cheap apartment, head bent over as she composes, murmuring her sorrow into the hollow body of her guitar. Becoming a different kind of vessel than what biology had presented, feeling the loss and turning it into transport. Yet Toronto's folk community was a tight one, and even in those foggy times, she took easily to collaboration. As young Joni's map expanded, conforming to the touring schedule of an emerging folk star, people's names began to mark her mileposts and temporary domiciles.

She had the baby and stayed in Toronto, but by then she'd left the notion of an art career mostly behind and adopted the suitcase rhythms of a musician. Even her choice of a mate for a scant two years kept her in motion, though she also made a home with him, a shelter that served as a way station for others making pencil marks on their own maps until those atlases were worn out with indentations—the touring life of repetitive places, new faces, circuits made in hopes of breaking out.

When she first left Saskatoon for Calgary, and even before that, ingenue Joni sought out folkish father figures to ease her separation from her parents and become her champions. Entrepreneurs and gatekeepers like John Uren at the Depression and Bernie Fiedler at Toronto's Riverboat, where Joni also waited tables when she wasn't singing, supported her without being immediately struck by her singularity, instead giving her the valuable chance to pay her dues. John and Marilyn McHugh, the fairy godparents of Yorkville, signed her up for extended engagements at their club the Penny Farthing. It was there that she met Chuck Mitchell, who was bringing in crowds with his repertoire of songs from English vaudeville, *The Threepenny Opera* and, sometimes, rising song-writers like Dino Valenti and Eric Andersen.

They were a pair, a marketable duo on parallel paths. Within months they married and resettled in Detroit. For a very short time, Kelly Dale lived with them, but as Mitchell later put it, "one month into the marriage, he chickened out, I chickened out." The trauma of adoption may have doomed this marriage; again, that's a story for Mitchell to tell. One thing is evident from the relatively ample coverage the Mitchells received from the regional press during their marriage—there was also the matter of rival drives for success.

Chuck and Joni were well matched in looks, self-regard and drive; their shared ambition helped them stand out from the crowd. The connections they made as they drove from Detroit to points east and south, as far as Florida, promised infinite expan-sion. Among their fellow musicians, Joni was getting most of the attention. Common accounts of Joni's early twenties often paint her as innocent, lonesome and ripped up by the tragedy of her broken-up motherhood. That Joni is a natural talent demurely waiting to be recognized. Truth is, though, she was as much a hustler as any young folkie who wanted a record contract and a chance to hang with the big names.

She and Chuck were a duo, but a tenuous one. Their musi-cal partnership splintered even before their marriage soured. A headline describing their occasional collaborations, published months after they wed, seems to predict the life span of their two-year, whirlwind marriage: "Two Single Acts Survive a Marriage."

Though they developed an act together that Joni always maintained she didn't much enjoy, often they'd play separate sets, even in different clubs. Chuck stuck to his repertoire of Brechtian show tunes and easy-listening folk, but Joni was looking into her small book of just-written originals. Their union made them a local "it" couple, and their fifth-floor walk-up, furnished by Joni in thrift-store finds, stained glass and her own artwork, became a hub for the local scene. Tom Rush, one of early folk's most prominent vocal stylists and leading men, remembers walking up all those stairs with an undiagnosed collapsed lung when he stayed with the Mitchells while touring in 1966; he ended up in the hospital and Joni subbed for him at the Chess Mate. "People complained," he laughed, remembering, when I met him fifty years later.

Looking backward at the Joni Anderson who'd just become Joni Mitchell is a little like trying to glance fresh at an inkblot image you've been studying for years, something that at first glance seemed like a rose or a bug or an airplane but that, with every *Yes, I see that!*, grows less open to interpretation. Joni Anderson was mostly unknown upon arriving in Toronto, and even after that, as she traveled within the Midwest and beyond. Her talents were still coalescing. But no one can really remember exactly what that looked or sounded like. When I asked people who knew her then about her forming days, they told me about the startling impact of her talent, but also her determination to come into focus as herself, to make an impression that couldn't be misinterpreted or dismissed.

I believe that there was no Joni Mitchell before she unleashed this need to stand out. She married Mitchell in hopes that they would raise Kelly Dale together; what she had when she walked away was a new life, but that newborn creature was herself. The sacrifice she made to give her daughter a more stable life was all about putting potential first—that unknown little one's and her own, separated yet forever intertwined. The terrifying uncertainty her decision manifested called for a conversion, an adherence to unshakable faith. Instead of God, Joni put that faith in her own soul, in its infinite capacity to grow and to lead her beyond the fatal confines of a normal life. I don't think she considered herself a genius at that point, but she started doing the work of genius: to create a space that only she could fill. For that she would have to see and learn so much more.

The Joni Anderson who sang on Thursday nights in a Calgary coffeehouse impressed, but could fade into the background. She might have still gone back to art school. She could have stayed in one place and raised her child. Joni Mitchell, having burned those roads behind her, knew something most people her age didn't know about commitment: its allure, but also its costs. An artist's firm conviction that she is meant for bigger things, combined with the luck of talent and charisma, can become a magnetic force that pulls the scattered lines of her life into a coherent shape and makes her story matter even before she's filled out its details.

In the period between taking Chuck Mitchell's name and leaving his bed, Joni Mitchell fully realized that she had what it took to succeed in a folk scene that, by 1965, had become a vehicle for pop stardom. Her voice was strong and clear; she could hit the high notes. She'd become a canny borrower of interesting techniques on guitar, and was starting to invent her own approach. And she looked the part. One of the first critics to review her club act, M.S. of the *Toronto Globe and Mail*, salivated a bit while adding this up: "Visually, Miss Mitchell was the epitome of what every producer of television beauty cream or shampoo ads must dream about: high cheek-bones; lustrous, blonde hair; full lips and bril-

liant smile." The leap Mitchell needed to become not just an ingenue but a legend happens in the review's next sentences: "Don't
just let the looks of this girl dazzle you. Listen to her."

DETROIT TO NEW YORK

By the time she started to realize that her marriage wasn't going to
last, something about the nascent being Joni Mitchell was bringing
to life started making people listen to her more intently. The songs
were part of it, but as Mitchell herself acidly acknowledged in a
1966 interview for the folk zine *Hoot*, her writing really wasn't that
original yet. In response to interviewer Anne Hershoran's comment that she was often compared to Joan Baez, the singer pointed
out that Baez herself had come to one of her first New York shows
and offered some backhanded praise: "She came down to the Gaslight and said that she liked my songs and everything . . . and that
I reminded her of Buffy Sainte-Marie!"

So she'd work on that, trading tips on open guitar tunings
with Rush and others who crashed at the Mitchell pad and gradu-
ally bringing her fae folkish wordplay into the mod urban present
tense where she really lived. (One younger woman Joni inspired,
Bonnie Raitt, recalls walking into a club where she was playing
after Mitchell, post-Chuck, had spent a fruitful couple of weeks in
London and having her head turned: "I saw Joni Mitchell, wearing
that little red satin pleated mini-skirt with her hair rolled up, and
that was it!") More than anything, Mitchell would compel herself
to keep moving, and make wanderlust her first great subject.

The twist she'd put into that first composition, "Day After
Day," became a trademark. At first the sadness in her song invokes the loneliness of women's blues, but then the listener realizes that this woman is a kind of stray, even when the lyrics claim

her lover is the one who left. The lonely places draw her spirit and that impulse makes her who she is.

She'd name it, this "urge for going," in the song that would reach more people than she could on her own. Tom Rush recorded it in 1966. Joni had cultivated his friendship as she toured the northeastern folk circuit with Chuck, from Detroit to Toronto and back but also to Boston, New York and all the little towns on the highways that got them there. I sought out Rush, still a folk-circuit favorite in his eighties, as one of those witnesses to Joni's ambition, her determination to become herself and, at the same time, bigger than that. He didn't hesitate to provide evidence.

"I remember thinking, here's a woman who really, really wants to be a big star," said Tom Rush, who was then one himself. "And she's gonna be a really, really big star. And it's not going to be enough."

Leaning back on a hotel-room couch one afternoon in Washington, D.C., Rush shared his thoughts on those first Joni years with the ease of someone who's been spinning insights into coffee-house gold for decades. He projected a certain dolefulness about his own choices, which involved both favoring cover songs over his own writing and scaling back just when he was hitting stardom in order to start a family in his native New Hampshire. Here was a man who'd chosen "enough" by stepping away from a burgeoning career in the late 1960s, and clearly he had mixed feelings about that. Like anyone reflecting on a legend, he engaged with Joni's story in ways useful for his own enrichment. Yet Rush was always a good friend and calm admirer of this bullet train of a woman, and his measured view of her resonated.

"I heard Joni at the Chess Mate in Detroit," recalled Rush, whose curly hair and rangy form as a young man made him just as much a "shampoo commercial" folk scene heartthrob as Joni ever was. "I was playing an engagement there. I didn't know who she was, but she asked the owner if she could do a guest set specifically so that I could hear some of her songs and maybe record them. Apparently she'd just started writing. She'd been doing standard folk fare with Chuck for quite a while, and he wasn't being supportive of her own stuff. He thought the money was in covering songs like 'Michael, Row the Boat Ashore.' Anyway, she got onstage and did four songs and I was floored. 'Urge for Going' was one of them. She came off and I asked her if she had any more songs, and she said, no, but give me a minute and I'll write some." Six weeks later she sent a tape with six tunes, including "Urge for Going."

Rush told me more about his encounters with Joni: how he'd taken her on a short tour in New England and the audiences embraced this "slip of a girl knocking you off your chair"; how during a 1967 uprising against aggressive policing he drove her from her Detroit apartment to safer ground, through streets burning on either side; how when they'd toured together she'd once whispered as he dozed on a couch that he could join her in her bed. He ruefully opted out. (She's never affirmed or denied this.)

I believed Rush, even as I thought about the other men who offered up similar stories about Joni during the years I was tracking her, eager to claim their spots on her map. Friends and lovers, fellow songwriters and producers, none as legendary as she. Over the years I talked to many, and their stories unfolded in sync: realizing her immense talent; considering her seductiveness and partaking or resisting; giving her a lift along the way. Women, too, had her demos in their purses and her friendship to enjoy, if not for as long as the men did. It's striking how many people played a role in the discovery of Joni Mitchell, as if she were a shoreline hidden and then reappearing in the mist, or an arrowhead picked up, admired, then left for the next beachcomber to run across.

Everyone who tells me such a story has to admit that Joni wasn't actually sitting around waiting for any of them. She secured Rush's attention with that special set at the Chess Mate. She made sure her tape made it into her hero Buffy Sainte-Marie's hands, a great hustle, since Sainte-Marie is the one who shared her music with Elliot Roberts, who would become her manager and help secure her stardom. Then one night she grabbed some time with Al Kooper, one of the hipster rogues she met after leaving Chuck for New York in 1967. She got him alone and played her songs for him. He roused Judy Collins with a three a.m. phone call and said, "Darlin', you gotta listen to this."

I wanted to hear Collins's side of this discovery tale. After Rush, she was the second major folk scene curator to take up the Joni cause. She's told the story a million times; why not once more?

"He put Joni on," Collins said, sitting in her chicly bohemian Upper West Side apartment one sunny afternoon in 2019. "He'd followed her home because she was good looking and she said she could write songs, so he figured he couldn't lose. Mind you, nobody knew about her except Tom Rush. She was playing basket shops in the Village, where the performers would send a basket out into the audience for money and half the time not get the basket back."

Judy, jarred out of her slumber but knowing that Kooper had a pretty good ear, stayed on the line as Joni played a song she'd recently written: "Both Sides Now."

"I thought, oh my God, what a song. I'd like to record it. I said, 'Let's talk tomorrow.'" The next day she called Jac Holzman, the head of Elektra Records and her producer, and told him the song would be her next hit.

In 1967, Collins was even more powerful than Rush when it came to showcasing the songs of a generation moving folk music toward the pop realm. He still got a little ruffled when I mentioned her. "Judy, Judy, Judy!" he said, only somewhat fondly. "Judy made some smart moves as the folk thing was fading. She put on a feather boa. Yep, she became a diva and started recording a lot of Leonard Cohen songs in a row; she put some distance between her and the fogies." He must have noticed my raised eyebrow; after all, Rush had turned to James Taylor and Jackson Browne the same way Judy took on Cohen, and both laid claim to Joni. "I guess I strapped on an electric guitar and tried to do that same thing," he admitted.

Collins's influence as a curator was vast, because her audience extended far beyond the folk scene. She rivaled Joan Baez as an artist who appealed across generations and to fans of pop queens like Barbra Streisand. Raised by a disc jockey father to appreciate all kinds of music, Collins heard something in "Both Sides Now" that Mitchell herself, then in the thick of the Greenwich Village folk world, might have hesitated to admit: the timelessness of a standard.

"My father was always bringing these musical soundtracks into the house," she said. "We'd listen and he'd explain—like with *South Pacific*, 'I'm Gonna Wash That Man Right Outa My Hair,' that's going to be a keeper, people are gonna sing that all the time. He would know exactly what the song was that was going to transcend the musical and wind up being the classic song. And I knew the same thing when I heard it."

After Judy fell in love with "Both Sides Now," she and Joni became friendly. She didn't even mind when Dave Van Ronk, an old-school Village bohemian who'd mentored Bob Dylan and many other ascendant folkies, recorded his own dusty-edged version of the song. Hers was so different, and she also recognized that "Joni was not stupid." It was in the younger singer's best interests for her songs to go wide. And Judy's folk bona fides were still in place; in fact, she'd recently joined the board of the Newport Folk Festival. That's how Joni, now fully separated from Chuck and freshly settled in New York, ended up on a stage with Leonard Cohen one afternoon in 1967—and then, for a brief period, in the arms of that famed Canadian poet, epicure and womanizer.

Mitchell's romantic dalliance with Cohen lasted maybe six months and seems typical of that freewheeling time; that same year she'd take up with David Crosby, who would prove far more influential to her career. But in so many tellings, including her own in songs like "The Gallery" and "Rainy Night House," it juts out like some kind of Plymouth Rock. Their infatuation has been rewritten, even partly by her, as an initiation, her entry into the first chamber of true greatness. Her biographer David Yaffe devotes a whole chapter to their connection while reducing Crosby, who actually produced her first album, to a parenthetical. Cohen's biographer, Sylvie Simmons, gives it only three paragraphs but cherry-picks the best details—that they painted each other's portraits, that Mitchell asked Cohen for a reading list that included Camus and the *I Ching*, which she used for years—and makes the most cogent observation about why this union feels so important: "For the first time the tables were turned: Leonard was the muse for a woman."

A review of Mitchell's first album in *Rolling Stone* didn't recognize that switch. Referencing the eponymous muse of his most famous love song, the writer, Les Brown, calls Mitchell "Leonard Cohen's 'Suzanne': she shows you where to look among the garbage and the flowers." But Cohen never wrote a love song that was clearly about Joni. She was the one who wrote reams about him: maybe half a dozen songs, depending how you read them, including one she never recorded, "The Wizard of Is," that directly rewrites "Suzanne." So it was she who made Cohen central in her narrative, reinforcing the connection in interviews where she called him a primary influence and one of her only deserving rivals. If overassociating a young woman artist with the powerful man she briefly knew is a sexist move, it's one that Mitchell herself found both useful and true.

She'd probably be horrified at a thought that occurs to me: that Judy Collins, as much as Cohen, shaped Joni's writerly voice on her first few albums. Collins was a mentor to Cohen before Mitchell met either of them, helping persuade him to turn from prose and poetry to writing and performing his own songs, and as one of the biggest drivers in the singer-songwriter scene evolving beyond the folk revival, her approval mattered. So did her vocal approach, which aimed to be both delicate and theatrical, shaped not only by her dad's Broadway leanings but by her own sense of rock and roll flair. Mitchell's early recordings get more interesting when they move away from the portentous folkisms she borrowed from Joan Baez and toward something similarly conversational, more like thinking out loud.

"It's all about the lyric, and the clarity," said Collins, who trained in operatic *bel canto* for decades—"it saves a voice." She continued, "I'm thinking of clarity and phrasing. What does a song say? What is a singer singing? If you can't understand, you're in trouble." Her crystalline diction contrasted with both the (often, ethnically) exaggerated vocal gestures of many folk singers and the smooshed-up blurts of mid-1960s rock stars. The singer-songwriters whose work she recorded, as they became stars themselves, also were known for this easy-to-follow singing style. Mitchell less than some, like James Taylor, for example, but just listen to a breakthrough composition like her "Cactus Tree" and hear the syllables ring.

Collins embraced, even relished, her role in bringing singer-songwriters' work to light. "I was not a writer myself at that time, so I had to pick the best of the best," she told me. "I must have seen, like through some sort of karmic kaleidoscope, that I had to have the best. I wasn't gonna sing anything that was under par. So that instinct was very refined."

That tastemaker role was formalized when Collins was invited by her friend and fellow folk-pop influencer Peter Yarrow to join the board of the Newport Folk Festival. She'd been playing the fest, then one of music's biggest star-making vehicles, since 1963, and had been there when Joan Baez introduced Bob Dylan and, two years later, when he shocked the crowd by plugging in with a rock band. Aware that Dylan's impact had made singer-songwriters the wave of the future—and that as that tide turned, the biggest pull came from those openly confessing their own life stories in their songs—she suggested an afternoon program highlighting such new talent. "I wanted Janis Ian, Tom Paxton, Joni and Leonard," she said. She faced a fight, especially from the Cambridge-based crowd still pulling from the ballad traditions Newport cofounder Pete Seeger always prioritized. When I remarked on this, Collins protested. "Pete was a writer! Woody Guthrie was a writer. The Boston crew, they had to have a traditional this and a workshop for that, and what's-his-name from 1830." She laughed, dismissing folk purism decades after it had dissolved partly due to her own efforts.

Collins prevailed. The afternoon session happened, and there, Joni met Leonard. There are famous photographs from that day taken by scene documentarian David Gahr: of Joni laughing like she'd just won a blue ribbon at the fair, and Leonard leaning into her, already beginning his seduction. There's also a shot of Joni and an unidentified man in a rain poncho listening intently to Collins as she shares something—advice? Instruction?—as Cohen poses strumming in the background, aware of the camera but listening, too. That photograph is less famous, but I prefer it. It speaks of a woman's authority and centrality instead of the erotic spark between a woman and a man.

After that day of showcases and poses, Collins took Mitchell further under her wing. "Joni and I, after we met, became very friendly," she recalled. "I'd go over to her place, it was a beautiful little tiny place with all these sparkling mirrors and lampshades and hanging crystals. This is before she moved to L.A. and became the Queen of Laurel Canyon." The two women shared not only musical ambition but the trauma of untethered motherhood: in 1965 Collins temporarily lost custody of her only son, Clark, to her ex-husband, who felt her career impeded her ability to parent. (Clark returned to her by 1968.) During their apartment lunches, Joni told Judy of her own loss of Kelly Dale. These heartfelt exchanges were intermingled with Joni sharing more of her songs.

Judy fully embraced this ambitious, vulnerable young woman, and was soon vying with other singers for her songs. "Michael from Mountains" was a natural for Judy, who was then dating a Welsh writer with that name. Best to her ears, still, was "Both Sides Now." She recorded it, and recorded it again. She knew her version could be a hit, with its distinctive woodwind-driven arrangement by Joshua Rifkin, but at first the mix was wrong. "It was played on a lot of radio stations, but it didn't take," she said. "So David Anderle"—one of Collins's main producers, who perhaps not coincidentally had a second career as a visual artist—said, "Let me give it a go. He remixed it and remixed it and remixed it and remixed it. And finally, he got a mix that worked and suddenly it got really big." Collins had her first Top 10 hit, and Mitchell gained new levels of buzz.

The connection between the two women intensified in the ensuing years, especially when both were romantically involved with members of the folk-rock supergroup Crosby, Stills, Nash & Young. (Collins's complicated relationship with Stephen Stills, whose alcoholism raged while hers festered, resulted in CS&N's biggest song—"Suite: Judy Blue Eyes.") Ultimately, though, the friendship sputtered out. "She began to get a little different," Collins explained. "I always thought, well, she lives in California. I mean, my New York friends stay friends for life, right? I was always sending her flowers and notes and she didn't answer them. And then once we were at a big festival together. And I said to her, are you still smoking? I'd recently quit. And I think she took great offense. I think I really nailed her. Her vulnerable part." Collins doesn't blame Mitchell, she said, for growing more distant after that.

As Collins shared this little story of a chilled connection—not with regret as much as to explain something to herself—I realized that Rush had said something similar, as had other folk scene fellow travelers who'd met, helped and even loved Joni as she made her way from hootenanny to basket shop tenement party. Mitchell moved on, and later, when someone ran their fingers along the lines of her maps and asked, *Is this where you started?*, she chose which signposts to remember. Remember Leonard Cohen, not David Blue, her other flamboyant curly haired companion from that period, who was big in '66 but never went much of anywhere, despite Joni's writing him checks and letting him crash in her apartment for years. Rank Bob Dylan, always, over Joan Baez, whom Joni felt was cold to her, and a somewhat embarrassing influence. Value men in general over women; it's easy to read of Mitchell's life and think she had no close female musician friends, since they almost never made it into her songs, though other women—childhood playmates, lovers' wives, the helpmates and muses in the scene who weren't also trying to become legendary—appear as decorative figures and objects of critique.

It's not that Joni had exactly forgotten her old friends: she mentioned them in interviews, sometimes showed up at their gigs, even placed the occasional phone call. But somewhere around 1967, the topography of the scene changed; it went 3D, and she was the one who ascended into rarer air. Like many artists who've been convinced their achievements are wholly singular, she liked the bird's-eye view, though it inevitably turned former equals and even mentors into specks.

In 1968, when "Both Sides Now" became Judy Collins's signature song, Joni wasn't yet the one who flew away. She made herself part of as many circles as possible.

FLORIDA

By the time she and Leonard Cohen were mostly done with each other, perpetual motion had overtaken Mitchell's life. Chuck was nothing, a smudge on a memory. Her family, still in the provinces, heard from her rarely, though sometimes she'd send her mother a hand-labeled tape of her new songs. Canada still dominated her touring schedule, but the U.S. was starting to take over, with Los Angeles on the horizon. She even hopped the pond to London for a couple of weeks. Forward, forward. And everywhere she went she found new friends eager to declare her the Next Big Thing, hungrily reaching for the songs she held before them and then scattering them along the road, recording them and playing them in their own sets. Her reputation began to precede her.

She claimed every opportunity, exceeding expectations, moving on toward the next barrier she could leap.

This is the best-known story of the fledgling Joni, a legend in waiting, singled out almost before she even had a community to call her own. The greatness she later secured crowds out any idea that she once might have been a beginner. Becoming legendary is a strange process of both expansion and reduction—the knotty totality of a person is smoothed out into one official portrait, and in a way, the legend becomes a former person, at least in the public view. She's now a vessel, an embodiment, an interface. Even more endangered is any clear memory of that person as they were before this process of abstraction began.

The more people told me Joni Mitchell astounded them from the jump, the more they wondered at her instant brilliance, the more I wanted them to take a breath and tell me about her detours. Her rise was momentous, but not without a few unwieldy turns. What I hear in her music always makes me want to search out the turns she took that don't fit as well into that story of inherent unassailable greatness. Dropping the needle on her earliest recordings, I hear a dazzling voice and a dramatic sensibility, but I also can sense a young woman almost desperately cultivating an old soul. The Joni I hear is the one who was still learning how to play her instruments and sneaking looks at her friends' fingers as they ran across the fretboards of their guitars. She sometimes resented those folkie gods and goddesses who became her advocates, and felt their attentions as patronizing. And as much as she wanted to be great or at least famous, there were times when she did enjoy herself. I want to retrace her footsteps and highlight her idylls instead of the strictly upward path. That's where I want to leave her within this chapter reinscribing her maps.

Joni actually played around a lot in those greenish-golden times. Consider her sojourn to England with Joe Boyd, arranged to help her secure an overseas publishing deal. Boyd, a friend and maybe more, spirited her away from Newport, where he was working with English folkies the Incredible String Band, and he came away with stories like everybody else's, of her blowing the minds of his friends in bands like Fairport Convention. But she also just goofed around, went shopping on Carnaby Street. The mod look suited her skinny frame, and she came back to the States with a suitcase full of the miniskirts that Bonnie Raitt admired. In the midst of being special, she did ordinary things.

It's difficult to tell the tale of ordinary Joni strictly from the vantage point of New York. There's just too much game there, all that energy spent on feeling immortally important. And once she hit Los Angeles in late 1967, with a devoted new manager, Elliot Roberts, openly declaring her the next Bob Dylan, the ambition engine went even more hotly into overdrive. But I can see a fainter line on Joni's map: it veers in another direction before she takes over Laurel Canyon. There's a summer on the other southern coast. A respite from her future, though it gets tied up in that future again.

Coconut Grove, Florida, became a folk mecca in the early 1960s in the most all-American way: through the efforts of a few vagabond impresarios cultivating a trend. It's the oldest continually inhabited neighborhood in Miami, annexed to the city in 1925 after a century growing up in black and white. South Florida tourism originated in the Grove, built on the sweat of Bahamian immigrant workers (who established their own neighborhood, called Kebo) and the internationalism of its rising merchant class. As Miami grew up to be both a gateway to postcolonial trade and a playground for northeasterners craving sun and salt breezes, Coconut Grove remained the funky older sibling of the pastel city to the north.

The twentieth century commenced and planned communities like the Spanish-style Coral Gables sprang up nearby. Coconut Grove remained Miami's own New Orleans, its tolerant, party-loving heart. It survived a devastating hurricane in 1926 and its residents rebuilt their wooden houses, boat docks and shanty bars. The kind of relaxed hospitality that develops in neighborhoods centered on nightlife typified the Grove, where crash pads for musicians and actors were everywhere and the neighbors let you pick mangoes from their trees. Black bars like the Tiki Club and the Poinciana and gay enclaves like the Candlelight Inn dotted the avenues; by the time the folk revival had young people turning storefronts into coffeehouses, the Grove was ready. And so were the singer-songwriters of Greenwich Village, eager to hop down the coast and shed their sweaters for the winter. One of those early Grove adopters was Joni.

Folk came to the Grove around 1962, when Vince Martin, a member of the scene's early sensations the Tarriers, arrived with some cash from a hit single and a plan to start a sportfishing business. That didn't go too well, but he met another musician, Bobby Ingram, whose give-it-a-shot spirit made him an excellent partner for new ventures. It was Ingram who told me the story of folk music in the Grove, and of Joni's idyll there, not long after Martin's death in 2018 and before his own the following year.

I found Ingram through a website advertising a late-career comeback he enjoyed after helping organize a fiftieth-anniversary reunion show celebrating the Flick, one of the Grove's favorite folk revival spots. He'd released a new album and started sharing his stories with local Miami newspapers; most mentioned Mitchell in passing. Ingram, I knew, probably had his own well-rehearsed Joni story, but I wanted to hear something else from him. I wanted to get a sense of this unique environment where the names getting big up north—not only Joni, but Odetta and her cult-hero guitarist Bruce Langhorne, Paul Simon and Art Garfunkel, Richie Havens, John Sebastian and, most important for Joni, David Crosby—came for the gigs and the chance to jump in the ocean after a show. Doing so felt like a way into something not often talked about: young Joni's pursuit of pleasure and cultivation of joy.

Bobby Ingram helped me find this byway. Driving up to the ramshackle house where his daughter, Bryn, had directed me on a winter day, I looked up at the thick weave of palm trees encroaching on the bungalow and thought, *This would have been a great neighborhood for a young up-and-comer to hide for a while in 1967.* Bryn welcomed me in through a storm-sturdy wooden door and past a living room with rattan furniture and framed photographs of her brother, Liam, as a child playing in the surf and her mom, Gay, in a wet suit, cuddling a dolphin. Liam and Gay were both gone by now, the son in an Alaskan car accident in 2005 and the mother after a brief illness in 2012. She'd been an Olympic-caliber swimmer and an anticaptivity activist, and Bobby's last wife and one true love. Bobby himself sat in the enclosed porch off the living room, surrounded by papers and knickknacks. White thatchy hair, rumpled plaid shirt, big smile; he was settled into the remembering phase of his life.

Bobby told me about an open-ended young adulthood that eventually placed him within Joni's musical world, in the thick of it but always somehow a little bit off to the side. Ingram was close with Crosby, the one name always mentioned when Joni's time in the Grove comes up. He was there when David first heard and "discovered" her playing at the Gaslight on Grand Avenue in

September 1967. And he saw her depart Crosby's yacht, the *Mayan*, in 1970, on a dock in Panama. Between those two dates the folk scene in Coconut Grove served as both incubator and retreat for a young woman who needed a breather now and then.

As we talked, Bobby apologized for the occasional clanging outside. The Grove was still what it used to be in pockets like his little street, but just across the way huge mansions were being constructed and the palm canopy eliminated tree by tree. "The Grove was unique. The Grove was wood; the Gables was stucco and tile roofs, Spanish. That is the Gables by design. But the Grove is a free for all."

Bobby's life was a free-for-all, too, directed by twists of fate and his willingness to leap. At fourteen the native New York City kid was hit by a car and sent to Florida to recover in a balmier climate. His father, a musician, accompanied him and soon found work. Already infatuated with the radio, Bobby suddenly was immersed in a much bigger sound world, finding everything from country to soul to Caribbean calypso music on the Miami radio dial. This music fed his desire to ramble. He joined the navy, working on submarines and oil rigs and eventually landing back in Florida on vacation.

That's when he met Vince Martin, who was singing in a little bar called Drum Beaters, right near the Playboy Club. Impressed by Martin's swagger as he crooned folk songs and demanded that the yammering audience listen to him, Ingram chatted him up after his set. Pretty soon they started talking about opening a coffeehouse close to the University of Miami campus, one like those Martin regularly played in New York.

"So one night, he and I went to the Grove," he said. "I'd been there, on the outskirts, to the beatnik bars on 27th avenue. That was 1961. The Black neighborhood was to the west; the whites around were mostly elites from New York." It really did feel like Greenwich Village South; a coffeehouse, they just knew, would fly. In fact, Martin and Ingram's first coffeehouse venture was a bust, but with a little extra investment they got it going.

As soon as the Coffee House (what a name, Ingram said with a laugh) became fully operational, "the folkies came out of the woodwork." Within a year another folk venue opened, then another. Ingram started playing there himself. He was soon asked to join the Balladeers, a touring band led by the jazz percussionist Les Baxter. Why the hell not? He leapt again.

Groups like the Balladeers all had rotating casts. One young singer-songwriter who passed through the Balladeers was California native David Crosby, who, like Bobby, was adventuring around the country back then.

Bobby and David became fast friends on the road, despite the soon-to-be rock star's occasional volatility. "David and I were very close, but sometimes it was wham bam get out of the dressing room before he hits you again," Bobby recalled. "David was a little bit outsized. He was bigger than his shorts." Bobby wasn't that wild, and by this time his first wife was pregnant; he left the Balladeers and ended up back in the Grove. He found it rife with potential and interesting weirdos. The main one was a guy named Fred Neil who loved sea creatures and hated the little bit of fame that was coming his way up in the Village, where he and Vince Martin often performed together. Neil had been a songwriter at New York's hit factory the Brill Building but had gone full-blown hippie. "I remember going to Vince's house and listening to the Bulgarian folk choir," Bobby said. "Fred Neil insisted on that. It was on the record player at Vince's house on Aviation Avenue, and we were just learning how to be stoned and listen to music."

The sounds in Coconut Grove were coming from everywhere and going everywhere in 1966, and the clubs had plenty of work for up-and-comers from the North. One night Bobby stopped by his crowd's favorite eatery, Dean's Waffle Shop, and there was Vince in a booth with a girl. "Vince had been going to Detroit and there was a scene that crossed the border at the Detroit-Windsor Junction," Bobby told me. "He was bringing musicians down from there. We'd spend hours in Dean's Waffle Shop drinking endless cups of coffee and playing that word game, Botticelli. I'm sitting there with Karen, my then-wife, and there was this sweet blonde girl sitting at the table with Vince. She was down as kind of an accessory to her husband, Chuck, at the time. I knew there was tension between her and Chuck, because of what happened later."

At this point Bobby admitted that he wasn't free of the influence of the Joni myth. Sheila Weller had put his name into her book *Girls Like Us*, which includes a couple of pages on David meeting Joni when he came to see another singer-songwriter, Estrella Berosini, at the Grove Gaslight. Bobby, who wasn't paying a ton of attention to Joni back when, had gobbled up Weller's account of his own scene. Wanting to extend his own authority about Joni's evolution via her relationship with his friend David, he'd boned up on others' accounts, absorbing their conviction that she was a knockout no one could resist.

This part of our conversation didn't really interest me. By 2019 Crosby had been dining out on his tale of being run over by Mitchell's charisma at the Gaslight for so many years he could have opened his own Joni-themed restaurant. More intriguing to me was Bobby's description of the musical openness of that time and place. He had his hand in several clubs; at one, a Jewish guy played flamenco guitar, while at another Richie Havens played his open-tuned blues and at another Tom Rush fought off the girls, so many of them that his engagements were known as "a rush on Rush." The guy who'd opened the Gaslight, Sam Hood—whose sister Bobby had dated in high school—was married to a folk singer who later became the revolutionary women's music activist Alix Dobkin. At the Flick there was a San Francisco vibe due to the Tiffany lamps and a modest light show. It was a classy joint. "But things were going on," Bobby confided. "The kitchen staff was sniffing all the nitrous oxide out of the whipped cream cans. We were a mad bunch back then."

As Bobby's tales spiraled around me, I thought about what I already knew about Joni's time in Coconut Grove. She returned often after the first foray with Chuck, settling in alone for the summer of 1967. In a way it must have been comforting, to be so far from New York's careerism and gossip, yet so close to the friends who'd come down to play for a week or two and show her a new tuning or listen to the songs she'd just written. And then she met David. That meant sex and being adored, and a new angle on her future. But not right away. They enjoyed the weather first.

Raised in California, Crosby had first come to the Grove during his own folkie apprenticeship, when he was grabbing all sorts of opportunities—briefly singing in a duo with Terry Callier, a jazz-loving Black folkie from Chicago, and hanging around the Village before Joni ever got there. He loved the small-town vibe, and the easy hedonism. "Back then it was just us on bikes, whizzing through the beautiful jasmine-scented night in love with life, smoking pot, happier than clams," he wrote in his memoir *Long Time Gone*. That summer feeling brought him back in 1967. By then he'd already graduated from folk chorale member to rock star as a member of the Byrds. His excesses, or maybe his arrogance, or maybe his insistence that his weird, jazzy, drug-infused songs be taken seriously, got him booted from that group. In Florida he could be a working-class musician again.

"There were several coffee houses where we could work," he told me in an interview not long after I'd spent that afternoon with Bobby. "That's what drew me, anyway. I rode a Greyhound bus down from New York." He didn't have to mention that he boarded that bus in fancy boots and his signature cape, because that's all part of the legend. As was every detail of the story as he told it to me, just another journalist, for the millionth time: how Joni sucked him in "like falling into a cement mixer," how he immediately knew she was more talented than Dylan or Cohen or even himself, how he fell in love with her artistry and her femininity all at once.

Bobby put things more bluntly. "David lived in what we would call a state of intense hornage," he said. "We were all that way, but David was a little more obvious." If Crosby wanted a woman, "he'd grab a guitar and sit down right in front of you and sing right in your face. And if that didn't work, he'd try something else." Bobby laughed and said that while he was happy to claim the bit of fame Weller's book offered by naming him as the one who'd hooked David up with Joni, he doubted he would have actually done it. "I called him and said, knowing your intentions, I probably would have been reluctant to introduce you. And he said fuck you, because that's how he and I communicate."

Ingram's read on the David and Joni relationship puts her back in that state of forward motion where her legend lives, but gently. "He was her escape," he said of David's role in her life. "Her lifeboat." As he said that, I silently noted that here was another guy letting what he read as Joni's overweening ambition crowd out other reasons she might have liked the lover she said reminded her of the cartoon character Yosemite Sam. Crosby's own memoir quotes Joni saying that yes, he certainly aided her rise to prominence, but the best things about time with him in Florida were the swims and the jokes and the way he seemed to have diamonds in his eyes when he laughed. Pleasure first! The leg up could come later.

I like the idea of this time, this place, this man as Joni's life-boat. A means to float awhile and take the measure of her potential, maybe even relishing a chance to pause its relentless flow. I know it was also carrying her forward, forward: that Florida summer, she'd already partnered with her manager, Roberts, and he'd developed a whole Dylan strategy for her, a way, as he once said, "of people being guided by your music and using it as the soundtrack to their lives." Strong personal connections like her new intimacy with Crosby would only enhance that plan, which Roberts thought would best be realized in Los Angeles, where a new scene was brewing. These thoughts likely never left her, no matter how many times she put her feet in the sand of the opposite coast.

But she took the long way. She paused. And later, she'd return to the Grove, after Crosby had produced her first album and she'd left him as a lover for his bandmate Graham Nash and as a protegé for the young mogul David Geffen, adopting her own strategies musically. Crosby was not just a boat in some metaphorical way, after all; he was a sailor, and in 1970 he took his beloved Bluenose schooner the *Mayan* through the Panama Canal. On board were Joni and Graham, her close friend, the actor Ronee Blakley, and a couple of other wayfarers. Bobby and Gay joined the trip halfway.

It was another case of Bobby and Joni crossing paths, like little skiffs. She grew weary of the salt life halfway through the journey and departed as he and Gay boarded. "There were two bunks on the *Mayan*," he said. "David had the owner's state room on the starboard side, then there was the centerboard bunk, and port side there was a double. So Joni and Graham gave that one up on the day Gay and I came aboard and they moved to the roof. Unfortunately the roof they moved to was over our heads, and they were saying goodbye rather eagerly, pretty much all night."

The time she did spend on board still shines like a crystalline memory, a moment of rest as she barreled on. The journey, Crosby writes in his memoir, was one of the most Edenic experiences of his life. "Absolutely amazing, sailing through a three-tiered rainforest, a jungle two hundred feet high, with parrots and monkeys and alligators and all that stuff." And there was music. Graham, Joni and David all had their guitars bungeed up over their heads in the bunks. They would play together in the Caribbean sunshine and find corners where they could write, too. "There's a fern that falls off a royal poinciana tree," Bobby Ingram told me. "And then it dries out and it has a lot of seeds in it; it's a perfect maraca. We had a few of those on the boat."

I don't know why Joni left this idyll early, after the journey through the canal. Maybe the close quarters were just too much. So different from the Grove itself, where privacy came easy, just a few steps down the beach. Or maybe she just needed to get back onto routes she could choose, to get to drawing those lines on her maps again. Bobby remembers the last time he saw her on that trip, a first glimpse into her next chapter. "I've got a photograph of Joni on a field dock," he said. "We were tied up getting fuel. She's sitting there in some bright shirt, and she's playing her guitar. And we were sailing off."

She'd find her own damn way to Los Angeles, reconnecting with David and engaging the help of Elliot Roberts and her new agent, David Geffen, to guide her toward a more linear path. Her unspoken goal to become more than just another girl singer with an ex-husband and a little dream would solidify into a strategy. Entering a circle of songwriters who understood that she was serious about becoming great, she would hang out for a while. She'd even make a home or two in the hills above Hollywood. Yet the searcher inside her kept looking around. The central lessons of her first traveling years continued to serve her: that risk is real, but can pay off; that grief never fully fades, but a clear mind and a curious heart make you stronger than its pull.

I hold the stories of Mitchell's early migrations close. They establish a through line that helps make sense of all her work. It's not the usual kind; it curves and gets tangled. But it clarifies so much of what comes later. Not only the many creative manifestations of her restlessness, but the connections her songs make between loneliness and self-preservation, sorrow and hope, the whir of wheels turning and the unceasing rush of blood that keeps a person alive. When Joni Anderson set out from Saskatchewan, she didn't know that the journey would be, throughout her life, her destination.

3

the boys

Joni did wander back toward David, but as she kept moving he wasn't necessarily the main thing on her mind. Her manager, Elliot Roberts, had already primed her for a transition to Los Angeles, securing a record deal for her at the Warner Bros. imprint Reprise Records via the influential executive Mo Ostin, who was transforming Frank Sinatra's label into a mod haven with artists like Jimi Hendrix and the Kinks. She'd informed Roberts of her Florida liaison, according to him, with a giddy phone call: "Listen, I'm fucking a Byrd."

When she arrived in Hollywood, soon to make her way to the Laurel Canyon hills, where her reputation would be secured, she resumed the romance. As was already her way, she blended interpersonal connections with creative work and was less committed to being one man's old lady than to finding her place within a whole coterie of charming, ambitious men—and a few accepted women—inhabiting the cottages dotting the Canyon's winding roads, little hobbit homes ideal for cultivating artisanal careers that fit within music's fantasy factory.

Young girls are coming to the Canyon, sang the Mamas & the Papas, the Canyon's pop ambassadors, in 1967. The girls turned heads and made for a pretty chorus, but the boys, like predatory head Papa John Phillips, were the ones who commandeered the scene. And the boys loved Joni from the start, even as they kept their circles tight and their creative camaraderie closed to most women. From the moment she landed in California, she became the exception that both challenged and reinforced the scene's homosocial rule: a woman who would neither compromise nor slink off to a separate sphere, whose instantly apparent gifts men felt as a challenge instead of a threat.

Men on the rock scene in 1967 didn't really have the skills to recognize women as more powerful than they were. Certainly not beyond the intimate confines of romance—and so many of the era's most popular songs were just men venting about what women might do to them, how they lost control in their presence but would regain control, dammit, *don't you love her madly, a squirming dog who's just had her day, please don't let on that you knew me when I was hungry and it was your world*. These songs ensured that women knew that the rock world had a place for them, and they'd better stay in it.

Joni knew that place and could occupy it when necessary. The albums she made in her first Canyon years are aggressively feminine in tone, built around her aerial soprano and lyrics that leaned flowery even when she was talking about breaking hearts and getting free. She bought her own Canyon hobbit house with money from the first, *Song to a Seagull*, and made it a haven where her friends were welcome and her pies sat on the windowsill. The guys on the scene all had ladies installed to run their domestic lives; like most working women after her, she didn't mind managing the second shift. Joni soon broke with the promiscuous Crosby in favor of a boy who was a bit girlish, Graham Nash. "Just sit there and look groovy," she directed him when the *New York Times* came to call. She'd take care of the rest.

But when she played, she made sure the boys listened. That was a nonnegotiable from the beginning. It's arguable, in fact, that she infiltrated her particular boy gang precisely for that purpose. With them gathered around her, she'd be noticed. And she had noticed that they'd be happy to serve that purpose for her. Crosby, Nash and the rest recognized almost immediately that to be near Joni Mitchell was to make music in her shadow. The odd thing was that the shadow remained invisible to outsiders for so many years.

The boys welcomed her as their equal. As much, anyway, as any man did in those days, when even the biggest women rock stars had better also be somebody's old lady or at least a surrogate mama—the ones who brought the food to the endless party, if not the drugs. "My house is a very free house," Mamas & the Papas member Cass Elliot, major rock star and Laurel Canyon hostess with the mostest, told an interviewer in 1968. "It's not a crash pad and people don't come without calling. But on an afternoon, especially on weekends, I always get a lot of delicatessen food in, because I know David is going to come over for a swim and things are going to happen. Music happens in my house and that pleases me."

With David Crosby in her pool, probably naked, Cass felt happily in charge of something. Joni's trick and what made her different was that she extended her hospitality only so far. Though she could cook and knit and loved home decoration, she wasn't going to stay in the frau position, as she called it. She'd eat from the deli tray another woman had painstakingly assembled and sing her own compositions. "Joni Mitchell has written many songs sitting in my living room," Cass continued. "Christmas Day when we were all having dinner, she was writing songs." Joni was like that proverbial girl in the playground pickup game who cheers on the boys, but then grabs the ball and throws it in a perfect spiral toward the basket. And then passes the ball back. And then grabs it again. She built her reputation, the shadow she cast, one beautiful arc at a time.

LIONS AND LAMBS

When David Crosby and I sat down across a table on a winter's day in Washington, D.C., in 2019, he was midtour, a little shaky from a recent fall and in mild atonement mode. The man who once zoomed around Laurel Canyon on his motorcycle in a velvet cape wore an old gray T-shirt and had a medical tube in his arm. But he could still hit the perfect middle note: he'd put together a new band with three musicians young enough to be the oldest of his grandchildren, two of them women, and was enjoying musical revelations he hadn't expected at seventy-seven. Back when he was a badass in the Byrds and then Crosby, Stills, Nash & Young, it was all about dick energy: the rivalry, the homoerotic edge. "We were wrong," he'd been saying lately. "Having women in bands is a great idea." He finally recognized the missed opportunities of the past.

It's kind of a drag, Crosby agreed, that the woman he could have had in his band was Mitchell. When I met him, he spoke of her in hushed tones, saying, "She was the best singer-songwriter of our times." His voice rose a little when he said that, as if I might be surprised. But every one of Mitchell's old lovers and running buddies crows about this revelation now. As I moved through the list—paramours Crosby, Graham Nash, and James Taylor, pals including the drummer Russ Kunkel and the producer/musician/ manager Peter Asher—I soon discovered that humility is one source by which old men recharge themselves.

Crosby wasn't humble when Mitchell met him, that's for sure. The romance was fleeting; the friendship endured. "I had dinner with her a while ago, like a month ago," he said. What did they talk about? "Everything. The state of her body. The state of her mind. The state of her art. I apologized to her for a couple of things." Crosby didn't need to tell me why he'd asked Mitchell for forgiveness; I'd read his memoirs, and her many interviews. When they first met, he led her on a little bit, acting the sweetheart under the humid moon; even then he was figuring out how to in- stall other women on his yacht. Not that she was fooled. Then in California, he turned her into his protégée—his find. She went along with the act. Late at night after parties he'd trot her out like some kind of hallucinatory angel, after getting the gathered crowd high on mind-blowing sinsemilla—even he later agreed that he was playing the sideshow barker to the hilt. Beyond his cashing in on her talent even as he genuinely helped her, there are the sins of omission or inaction or plain male cluelessness he committed as they went from lovers to collaborators to compadres riding rock's fame train. Taking the sole producer credit on her first album because it needed a man's name, after all, and his was bigger than hers. Living out the orgy dream supposedly owed a rock star—in the Northern California home where he eventually retreated, he had one room that was just a big pit filled with mattresses—while she pursued freedom her own way, as a neat serial monogamist, only to be shamed by the media as everybody's old lady. Calling her his band's "mascot," and thinking saying that was being nice.

The biggest thing Crosby may have had to answer for, however, was also his most significant gift to Mitchell. He was the one who led her into the boys' club that would change her life.

Mitchell and Crosby were united by each other's charisma and talent, by a love of jazz and fantasy novels, and also by some unhappy life experiences. Mitchell had escaped the mental grip of ex-husband Chuck and the overwhelming if fleeting influence of folk festival holy man Leonard Cohen; in Florida she'd worked through some lonely times and toward a new beginning. Crosby had endured a much more visible artistic breakup, with the Byrds; he was tossed out of L.A.'s own version of the Beatles for being— depends on who you ask—either erratic and arrogant or musically overambitious. So they were both brokenhearted in complicated ways. Also, though few knew it, Crosby had fathered a son in 1962, three years before Joni gave birth to her daughter. Both children were in closed adoptions—for all intents and purposes, lost.

So here were these self-starters, wild cards, dragging some pain and guilt into the fire of their ambitions. Intimate competitors. "I had to accept the fact that she was better than I was and was always going to be better than I was and treat it as a target to try and hope for," Crosby told me. "I just worked my butt off trying to be as good as she was." That was good training for Mitchell, to have someone more like a brother than a would-be father figure challenging her every day.

But Crosby was also in the middle of something else. Stephen Stills had been down in the Grove, stinging from the conflicts within his own band, Buffalo Springfield, which he'd leave behind within a year. Late nights on the boat, they'd write together. Crosby also knew that Graham Nash, the hippie-est of the post-Beatles bunch he'd met when the Byrds toured England, was leaning away from his pop group the Hollies and toward something new. Later, when Graham met Joni at Crosby's suggestion while both were on tour in Ottawa in 1968, Mitchell became another reason Nash needed to relocate to L.A. And Neil Young, Joni's old friend from the Canadian hootenanny scene, was hanging around, too. Though he and Stills had clashed in Springfield, Joni's familiar face might eventually have helped bring him back into the circle and expand the CS&N trio to a foursome—acronymically, CSNY, one of the most successful supergroups in rock.

According to legend, Crosby, Stills and Nash came together in Joni's woodsy little Laurel Canyon kitchen. (Like most legends, this one has its naysayers: Stephen Stills claims that the three men first harmonized at Cass Elliot's house a few miles away, partly because he was intimidated by Mitchell and didn't feel comfortable singing at her place.) The uncanny blend of Stills's earthy baritone, Crosby's elastic tenor and Nash's high keen was so shockingly perfect, Crosby would tell *Rolling Stone* writer Ben Fong-Torres in 1970, "the feeling of that was, man, like havin' someone give you head all of a sudden in a sound sleep. It was like waking up on acid." The sound soon became the Canyon's latest drug. And Joni's voice was always in the mix, if not literally, then as a major influence. "We listened to each other all the time," Crosby told me. "And more than that, we sang with each other."

So here was Joni Mitchell in her first L.A. incarnation. Her own woman, always, but also the muse of Crosby, Stills and Nash. Her association with the band helped establish her as an American rock star and became a pretty chain around her neck. She was one of the boys, with everything that position promised and took away.

What does it mean to be one of the boys? For Graham Nash, it meant that Mitchell "would have picked up a basketball and shot hoops" if the moment required it. Also that she would stay up all night sharing songs, with no child around to distract her, and no compunction to interrupt herself and refill anybody's cup of mushroom tea. Nash has been calling Mitchell one of the boys for decades, seeing that role as indivisible from the one she had in his life after she and Crosby parted: ideal woman. It was all wrapped up in one big exchange of energy. "The feeling between them was very high, almost amorous, you know?" Mitchell would later tell CS&N biographer David Zimmer. "Part of the thrill for me being around them was seeing how they were exciting themselves, mutually."

Trying to understand why, throughout her career, Mitchell has chosen boys' clubs instead of the company of women, I thought about surveying the various fields where tomboy infiltration was the historical norm. Then I realized that to do so would be to confront most organized realms of public endeavor. Sports, obviously. Science. Big business. The military. "What isn't a boys' club besides needlepoint and nursery school?" a canny woman once asked. And in the late 1960s, despite the personal revolution that was supposed to be making everybody more androgynous— one memorable cartoon in *Rolling Stone* showed a couple, one with long locks and one with a greaser's ducktail, stripping off their glad rags to reveal that the "boy" was a "girl" and the "girl" a "boy"—in the Canyon the needle hadn't moved that far from the norm.

Yet something about the worlds of artistic endeavor often changes the way men act out dominance and the way women experience it. As Mitchell would write a few years later in "The Boho Dance," one of her musical satires of the scene—with a little swipe at her fave bad boy Bobby Dylan too—bohemians are subterranean by their own design. They duck norms. Boho dudes fancied themselves explorers of their own forbidden femininity: "sensitive guy" was a role to investigate, along with "cowboy" and "pirate" and "poet." A lot of them were really just exploring women. Here's Crosby, very stoned, sharing his big vision with Neil Young, who was trying out a new movie camera, in 1972: "On one side you've got a set of values that's doom, death, degradation and despair, being dealt out from the bottom of the deck by a gray-faced man who hates you; and on the other side you've got a girl running through a field of flowers, man, and half-naked and high and laughing in the sunshine." This variety of "honoring the feminine" gave women symbolic power—but that was all.

Amidst the frolicking freaks, Mitchell presented herself differently. She sincerely believed that in the space of art-making, gender divisions dissolved. But while Crosby's vision reflected the counterculture's faith in a "natural" world where men and women were complementary, but not interchangeable, Mitchell was an old-school bohemienne, a woman whose life depended on donning the smock of the artist in order to transcend the norms that would entrap her.

Mitchell spoke about this with the feminist historian Alice Echols in 1994. Agreeing that art creates what Echols calls "a kind of liberated zone" beyond gender constrictions, the artist told a childhood tomboy tale. That cowboy girl Roberta Joan resurfaced.

As a kid, she said, she never enjoyed playing with girls, who were incessantly competitive and wrapped up in superficial things. So for Christmas one year, she asked for a Roy Rogers outfit, wanting in on the neighborhood boys' Western games instead of the movie star or nursemaid ones granted her as a daughter. But once her dismayed parents relented and she arrived at the playground in red shirt and gold star, she was still rejected: the prince of the gang told her that her drag wasn't a magic cloak, that she could only be Roy's wife, Dale, who "stays home and cooks." Chagrined, she retreated and sought out new friends, finally meeting a couple of music nerds, who transported her via piano rhapsodies to a place where "there was no role playing, so play was able to happen."

THE SECRET

Reading Mitchell's exchange with Echols, I recalled something the poet Diane di Prima had once said, remembering her own betrothal to the creative process: "I opened the door and let my rough-and-tumble self out." If only the men around her had wanted her to do that. They thought they did, at times, but then they'd say stuff that made the reality clear. Possibly the same year prepubescent Mitchell was discovering her rough self—1954— the poet Allen Ginsberg dreamed that his mentor, the novelist John Clellon Holmes, wrote him a letter announcing that "the social organization which is most true of itself to the artist is the boy gang." The young women of the newly christened Beat Generation couldn't join that boy gang with a simple costume change, although they tried, in their solid black tights and their blue jeans with leather sandals, long earrings offsetting their pixie cuts.

Joyce Johnson—writer, urban adventurer, close friend of di Prima, lover of messy men, including Jack Kerouac—put Ginsberg's channeling of Holmes at the conceptual center of her memoir about Beat women, *Minor Characters*. Like Mitchell's lyrics, Johnson's stories of accommodating rogues and fickle friends while pursuing her own muse form a kind of inner seam that makes the masculine myth reversible—showing how, so often in these disappointingly old-fashioned undergrounds, freedom-seeking women ended up spending their energies helping men achieve that state. Her memoir centers on her affair with Kerouac, who could never rest in her arms; sometimes after sex, he'd sleep in an unheated back room in her flat. "At night when the cold air came with a rush into the little room where Jack was sleeping, and seeped under the edges of the closed door, I could imagine myself in a place without walls, an immense campground where, lying wrapped in blankets, I could feel in my own warmth absolute proof of my existence," she writes of that time. Though she recalls him fondly, Johnson also remembers how Kerouac wrote about the female body then: "that lumpy roll of flesh with the juicy hole." There she is, caught between a life in the open and another one confined by hate.

I turned to Beat women to better understand Mitchell's position in her boy gang partly because she had gone through her Beat phase in high school—the beret quickly following the Roy Rogers hat—but mostly because the Canyon hippie boys stood upon ground the Beats' boots first trampled. They just wore sandals instead. Johnson writes of going to the same folk clubs that would later draw Joni to New York, of hearing the same origin myths of American art. The folk revival's Woody Guthrie–style ideal was smelly and rawboned, distinctly male. And the jazz that Johnson, a native Manhattanite, loved offered a different, citified side of the same romance, also mythologizing boys' games—cutting contests and frantic bebop showdowns in cigarette smoke-dank rooms.

"I know some very good women musicians but—I'm just out of place with them. . . . I have something that has been embedded in me through good strong men," Mary Lou Williams, one of jazz's most innovative mid-century composers, once told an interviewer. Often being strong meant behaving recklessly, and women were expected to hold their own—but also know to step back and provide support. "When one of the boys needed a steadying belt, he knew my purse always contained a pint of cognac or Scotch," wrote the famously game jazz singer Anita O'Day in her memoir of life on the road. The addiction that became the fight of her life descended while she was being one of the boys.

Whether jazz or folk was her jam, the Beat-era woman knew when to be tough and when to do the other thing required: disappear into a mist of mystery. Di Prima recalled the ideal Beat girl, soon to be a folk star: "Mary Travers, 1953, a hint of butch in her collar, scarf around her neck, her head held just a bit too high, and her large dog, entering a MacDougal Street restaurant, breathless, looking around from the doorway. Her quick exit. As if whatever she wanted wasn't there." (Travers later became a central figure in the folk revival as part of the trio Peter, Paul and Mary.) If the Beat male soul flourished in fresh air, the Beat woman thrived in the opposite atmosphere. "One prerequisite of beauty then was the Secret. To look somehow as if you carried a secret. A sorrow you could not tell." Doesn't it sound like di Prima is talking about Joni Mitchell?

Often the Beat girl's Secret is a pregnancy that ends with her heading alone to some shady New Jersey doctor's office for an abortion, cash in hand but no consort along for the ride, or raising a child who changes her life in ways the men around her can't fathom. Or entrusting the baby in adoption, as Mitchell did.

"We lived outside, as if," wrote Hettie Jones, another central

Beat woman and wife of the poet LeRoi Jones, who also fathered
one of Diane di Prima's five children. What a great way of describing the lives of women who didn't yet have the language or social
support for expressing their defiance. By the time Mitchell was old
enough to try to navigate her identical situation, women living
"outside, as if" still struggled against the tide of conformity that
defined gender relations in even the most supposedly progressive
scenes. Jazz, poetry and city life in general offered contact with
like-minded others and the chance to live with men in ways that
occasionally felt new. Yet as Mitchell learned, those guys did have
their own version of the Secret—something she could never really
touch. Johnson named it: "I learned myself by the age of sixteen
that just as girls guarded their virginity, boys guarded something
less tangible which they called Themselves. They seemed to believe they had a mission in life, from which they could easily be
deflected by being exposed to too much emotion." Emotion: the
feminine wile. Virginity can only be lost once, but a Himself, properly maintained, can last forever. Likewise, a Secret can do untold
damage; manhood comes with its own protective shield against
such things. Hey anybody, wanna play some basketball?

When a woman becomes a boys' girl, it seems, she's grabbing
a chance. But does she also make a sacrifice? To be the one woman
in a club, or one of only a few, reinscribes men's power. The one
recalibrates her being so that she can become attuned to the cus-
toms and beliefs that would otherwise exclude her. In the process,
she inevitably compartmentalizes her experience of herself "as a
woman." This can feel like a free choice, but it has a cost: her very
self, at least part of it, becomes the Secret.

Beat culture set the template for the rock counterculture, and
most women who hung out there experienced something like this.
"I didn't feel like a woman amongst a group of men recording,"

Carly Simon said about making her breakthrough album—*No Secrets* was the title, in fact—in London with an all-male band; yet she also revealed that while on the road she prepared their avocado-sandwich lunches. She had to be the helpmeet when necessary. Carole King, remembering her tours with James Taylor and his superstar group of session musicians, firmly suppressed her womanhood: "I've always enjoyed being a sideman. For the record, it is 'sideman' regardless of gender." But she was the one who had to arrange her touring life to accommodate the needs of her two young daughters, instead of just waving goodbye to a wife. Cass Elliot wrested control of her artistic life back from John Phillips after the Mamas & the Papas broke up, telling a *Rolling Stone* interviewer she was determined to tell her own story; she still chose all male songwriters (with one important exception—her sister, Leah Kunkel) to provide material for her debut solo album.

Were these women in denial? They didn't necessarily earn more power when *not* perceived as one of the guys. Michelle Phillips was drafted into the Mamas & the Papas after meeting twenty-seven-year-old John as a teen. She wasn't that keen on singing professionally; she preferred modeling. "I was working for *Vogue* and *Seventeen* and *Bazaar* and Saks Fifth Avenue," she told me during an interview in her comfortable L.A. home one November afternoon in 2018. "I was making a lot of money. And John said, I promise you, you'll make more money singing than you do modeling. And so, just out of total greed, I decided to give it a chance."

"Do you think he was being controlling?" I asked her.

"Well, if I look back on it, yes, he was being controlling," she replied. "But at the time, I just thought, well, you know? Let's give it a shot."

John Phillips had realized that as the folk revival became a pop phenomenon, it needed women's voices. But not, it seemed, too much of women's consciousness. The good old-fashioned folk circles that launched the careers of strong personalities like Joan Baez and Judy Collins still had little room for women writing their own songs. As the people's music, folk was meant to emanate from communal sources; yet many of its male stars, from Woody Guthrie to Pete Seeger to Bob Dylan, always included originals in their repertoires. Furthermore, those romanticized communal spaces were themselves male-dominated: the factory floor, the hobo train car, the ship deck. Women could claim hearth songs and lullabies, at least, but then came rock—an explosion that fully pushed them to the side as all-male bands became the standard. The women who'd gained some legitimacy in early 1960s girl groups or as pop balladeers and R&B queens found themselves diminished within the post-Beatles paradigm.

Women were allowed in sometimes, if they could modulate their presence. When John Phillips put together the Mamas & the Papas, he recruited Elliot, an aspiring Broadway star and one of the biggest, baddest soloists he knew. But, Michelle Phillips told me, he required Cass to tamp down her power and merge her voice with Michelle's. "John would finally say to her, if you're not going to blend with Michelle, we'll just have Michelle do this by herself," she recalled. "Cass and I learned to blend together, and that's what made the sound."

Contained and modulated female voices, nearly always wrapped up in male ones, helped the folk-pop sound forge a deeper connection to the boyish paradigm of post-Beatles rock. Not only the Mamas & the Papas, but Peter, Paul and Mary; Sonny & Cher; Ian & Sylvia; and the Jefferson Airplane all featured powerhouse women singers—but rarely did those voices rise alone. (Grace Slick of the Airplane had her moments, and since Sonny could barely sing, Cher did, too.) Cass and Michelle's blend was brassy and matched that of John and Denny Doherty. Women singing together felt old hat, too much like those girl groups, then fading in influence. In the soul realm, women still held their own, with the undeniable Aretha Franklin clearing space and the rock boys taking notes from Tina Turner. In Black culture, women gained expressive power in the church, which fed directly into secular music. But rock's ideal women were almost always white and, in the absence of any meaningful opportunity to play into each other's strengths, half boy.

HELLO, LADIES

Why would a woman want to be the odd one out in a boys' world? Well, power, obviously. The power of having been designated the exception. I have experienced this myself many times as a music writer coming up in various rock undergrounds. What I learned as one of the boys was not that men act like dogs around women, ogling and pinching (I went through puberty at eleven, and already knew that), but that they get a thrill from criticizing us. They love to be able to inform a woman they've decided to respect that other women are not worthy. *If only there were more like you.* The biggest cost of becoming a boys' girl isn't the risk of being somehow violated, but the requirement that you give up your alliances with these now-competitors. You are expected to recognize yourself as better, or at least fundamentally unique.

Mitchell fell for this. She had women friends, but did not forge close ties with other women artists. With only one or two exceptions—Buffy Sainte-Marie, who helped her early on, and Laura Nyro, who shared a powerful male ally in David Geffen— once she hit the Canyon, Mitchell would name only men as peers and influences. And in her songs, especially on her third album *Ladies of the Canyon*, she was a flat-out mean girl.

That album depicts the Laurel Canyon scene in all its macramé glory. But the fondly rendered travelogues it features eventually reveal themselves as whimsically cruel toward the wispy wives and hangers-on mentioned in its title. "Conversation": a song about a wife who is destroying her man's soul, and Mitchell's earnest attempts to rescue him. *She only brings him out to show her friends/I want to free him.* "The Arrangement": written for but not used in an Elia Kazan melodrama, a lament for a man whose conventional life—and wife—have stunted his growth. *And the wife, she keeps the keys.* "Blue Boy": an account of how a man's surrender to a woman's will turns them both to stone. Even that deadly femme is a coquette. *Shyly from a feather fan, she'll glance for him.*

And then there's the album's title track. A supposed celebration of three real women in the Canyon scene—the musician and circus performer Estrella Berosini, the underground comix artist Trina Robbins and Annie Burden, wife of album cover designer Gary Burden—it has Mitchell putting on her frilliest Waltz of the Flowers voice to celebrate these spirits "coloring up the sunshine hours" of her summery L.A. life. She paints them as a rococo triptych in mended glad rags, caring for cats and kids, drifting around like hearth spirits. Estrella's songs are *tiny hammers*. Trina does create a *pattern all her own* in her drawing book, but Mitchell portrays her as more seamstress than artist. *She may bake some brownies today*, Mitchell sings of mama Annie, sounding like the second soprano in a Saskatoon church choir. It's all very sweet, but so homely, unheroic. Contrast this song with "Cactus Tree," the defining self-portrait from Joni's debut—a depiction of feminine freedom as prickly, self-sustaining and irresistibly undomesticated.

"Ladies of the Canyon" is a quietly caustic encomium that exposes the reality of its time and place. Laurel Canyon was like many countercultural scenes that hadn't quite felt the effects of the then-forming women's movement. Women found it difficult to assert themselves. "It was hard, it was really hard," said Leah Kunkel, Cass Elliot's sister and a strikingly gifted music producer and singer-songwriter in her own right, who came into the Canyon scene when she followed Cass from the East Coast to L.A. fresh out of high school. Kunkel was a student at CalArts, in the music department, when Cass introduced her to Monkees member Peter Tork; the two dated for a while as Leah played the hootenanny nights and open mics at clubs like the Unicorn and the Troubadour. Then she met drummer Russ Kunkel, who'd go on to be a real Canyon insider, playing with most of the scene's luminaries, including Joni. The Kunkels had a son, Nathaniel, when Leah was just twenty. That put her in the Ladies of the Canyon category, even as she found ways around that role, beyond the scene, forging other connections that helped her have a flourishing musical career.

I found out about Kunkel from that songwriting credit on her more famous sister's solo debut. She gave me insight into what Canyon life was like for women who had as much potential as the boys did, but weren't designated exceptional. She's rarely mentioned in histories of Los Angeles singer-songwriters, though she released four albums and sang on many classics of the genre by Jackson Browne, James Taylor, Art Garfunkel and others. Kunkel does credit Mitchell for partially opening the door for women singer-songwriters. But like many of her friends, she'd been marked as a wife before she could walk through it. "I definitely had two different lives," she said. She never abandoned her work as a singer-songwriter, cultivating her own creative circle down the hill in Hollywood, becoming close to Stephen Bishop, Jules Shear and Jennifer Warnes. But Leah's days were taken up with "preschool and health foods and dentist appointments"—even more so when, after Cass's death in 1974, she adopted her daughter, Owen. While she raised the kids, she says, Russ conducted his boy's life apart from the home they'd made. She managed to make a couple of solo albums during her marriage, but they didn't chart, and instead she became a highly in-demand session singer. After she and Russ divorced, she formed an all-woman trio called the Coyote Sisters—an antidote to the lack of support she'd found within the Canyon crowd. Eventually, she put music fully on the back burner and became an attorney, continuing to release music but no longer chasing the pop dream.

Mitchell's self-styled independent woman stance didn't offer Kunkel a model she could use. She could better relate to another rare star in Canyon circles: Carole King. King had two daughters and, like Kunkel, a studio-musician spouse, bassist Charles Larkey. But she also had money of her own. With the savings and status she'd earned as a professional songwriter in her early years, writing hits for groups like the Shirelles with her first husband, Gerry Goffin, King could afford a nanny and not be scorned for hiring one. Goffin, living nearby and going through his own dark period of drugs and mental instability, made her first years in California difficult. King had her own approach to keeping the feminine Secret; though her history was well-known, she still managed to compartmentalize her family life. When she married the much younger Larkey in 1970, that allowed her to better integrate her worlds, because he was in her band. But that marriage broke up in part because King found herself unable to balance all the demands placed upon her.

Another problem for women in the Canyon was that the young girls that John Phillips so poetically celebrated in that Mamas & the Papas hit often came in hopes of nailing their very own sensitive singer-songwriter. "John Phillips fucked every single girl who came to the Canyon," Michelle Phillips said of her long-deceased ex, who, like David Crosby, was a notorious sybarite. "But, you know, young girls are attracted to music and musicians. You couldn't look out the window without seeing them walking up and down." In the L.A. scene, groupies—women who made a vocation of taking care of male musicians—often became celebrities themselves. Groupies weren't boys' girls in the same way Mitchell was—they never compartmentalized their femininity, and even if they did have some artistic ambition, they always valued their star-fucks above all. What they did share with someone like Mitchell was a commitment to mobility. A supergroupie always had many men in her back pocket.

As glamorized as they were, groupies proved a problem for Mitchell and other women who wanted to be taken seriously as artists, because they were also reviled. They embodied the shame as well as the glory of femininity; to be called a "groupie" when you weren't one was to lose whatever status you were fighting to maintain. In theory, the hippie world appreciated sex, even fetishized it as a force that could change lives. New values prioritizing erotic freedom, promoted across the spectrum from pockets of the feminist movement to hedonistic ventures like Hugh Hefner's growing *Playboy* empire, should have made a space for women who openly enjoyed making sexual conquests. Yet the old hierarchies snuck back in. A woman who consorted with an already-partnered powerful man could be banished to the lower order of the slut or the homewrecker if she demanded too much. And even a wife or serious girlfriend who intruded on the sacred space of the all-male band might be derided as a nuisance. Free women like Joni upset the whole order by doing what they wanted and still demanding respect.

In songs that questioned the value of wives and girlfriends while longing for the intimacy of spiritual marriage, Mitchell tried to think her way around and through sexism rather than confronting it head-on. (She would do that later, occasionally, in songs like "Don't Interrupt the Sorrow" and "Not to Blame.") Such versatility is what's expected of the boys' girl. Mitchell may have been Crosby's lady and then Nash's, but she knew better than to settle too firmly into the role of domestic partner. A deft woman can act like a wife in one moment, a sister in another, a flirty temptress in a third. Maybe even sometimes an equal. She travels among men who see her in different ways, or at least in the usual ways at different times. I believe that the men around Joni genuinely saw her as far beyond women like Kunkel or Phillips or possibly even King, whom they deeply esteemed, and that she also loudly and constantly insisted on this status. Yet has anyone ever asked why, when Crosby, Stills and Nash sat in her kitchen that day and first sang together, she wasn't asked to join the band?

HER HOUSE

When I met Graham Nash, a few weeks before I sat down with David Crosby, I asked him if he and Mitchell had ever collaborated during their time as a couple. "The only time I ever remember playing piano and singing with Joni was at the Philadelphia Music Academy, when we played 'Our House' together with four hands," he said. "Which was interesting." That probably would have been in 1971, after they broke up. Instead of trying to collaborate, and out of respect for—or intimidated by?—her huge talent, he'd kept his distance creatively during their coupled time. "Being a writer myself, I knew it's very different when you're alone in a room or whether there's somebody else sitting in the corner. I realized that, and tried to give her as much space as possible. And fortunately David and Stephen and I were in the studio twenty hours a day."

As her boys' gang established its foundation, Joni was left to reflect upon the dynamics of the creative intimacies that both welcomed and excluded her. *Willy is my child, he is my father*, she sings in a pensive love song she wrote for Nash. The line has struck many as deeply insightful, capturing something basic about heterosexual relationships, especially as they were changing during the hippie era, with everyone loving on their inner children and contemplating all kinds of archetypes. I have to admit I've always found it kind of creepy. I never got the daddy thing as a way of relating to men, nor have I much enjoyed men's childishness. But then, I'm a generation younger than Mitchell, and entered my dating years armed with feminist handbooks on how to cultivate equal romantic partnerships. Mitchell didn't have that luxury. Exploring what a man could be to her, she looked to the familiar touchstones of the nuclear family.

When they were intertwined, David really had been something like a brother. He had no interest in having authority over her, nor in being held down. In addition, he liked threesomes—even wrote one of his most notorious songs, "Triad," about that—and though it's almost certain nothing intimate ever happened along those lines within Joni's boys' club, he would have probably been open to it. Nash, sweet Willy to his friends, was another matter altogether: like Mitchell herself, he was a refugee from social convention rather than an outlaw. He's the one who happily moved into her hobbit cottage and called it "our house," the paramour willing to be a prop during her interviews, to sit there and look groovy.

Entering into a groovy partnership often worked in a woman's favor in the Canyon, even as being perceived as just a wife guaranteed exclusion. This was Hollywood, after all, or just next door, and high-profile romances added something to a star's portfolio. Plus, they really were a bunch of workaholics, Joni most of all. Office romances happened. In fact, it's difficult to think of a woman artist in late-'60s California rock who wasn't part of a power couple. Joni and David, Joni and Graham. Grace Slick and Paul Kantner. Bonnie and Delaney Bramlett. Michelle and John Phillips. Linda Ronstadt and J. D. Souther. Also Souther and Judee Sill, a gifted songwriter who died young of a drug overdose after her career was derailed, in part, by her inability to negotiate the Laurel Canyon boys' club. Judy Collins and Stephen Stills. Carole King had her work husband, James Taylor, alongside her actual husband, Charles Larkey. The rock mags treated these couples like latter-day Bogarts and Bacalls, interviewing them in their homes, describing their furnishings in detail. *Rolling Stone* became the official magazine of the rock elite in part by devoting a serious chunk of every issue to the comings and goings of these serial monogamists. Journalists treated the few women who did remain mostly alone—like Cass Elliot, who never revealed the father of her daughter, or Janis Joplin—as freaks or lonely hearts. Undomesticated men sometimes also posed a problem. David Crosby was simultaneously mocked and pitied after his serious girlfriend Christine Hinton died in a 1969 car crash and he really started going wild.

WHY SO MANY COUPLINGS, BEYOND THEIR USEFULNESS IN PROMOTING CAREERS? OBVI-
ous reasons. People living music 24/7 need to do things in bed
sometimes. Creative energy is volatile and sparks other kinds of
sparks. But also, if a woman was clearly with somebody, she became less distracting; the general dynamic of men getting off on
one another's energy could remain intact. And she also became
a kind of role model for their own explorations of the feminine.
Those high harmonies, those bared souls. The emerging ideal of
the sensitive male created a need in the Canyon men; they realized they had something to learn from the women whom they
admired. Something emotional, at least.

So the soft boys needed the ladies around to educate them and
to be receptive to their new explorations of emotion. Plus, it helped
them keep things straight. Laurel Canyon was a very heterosexual
scene, much more so than the freakier rock worlds of San Francisco and New York or even the Sunset Strip just below it. The
teasing homosociality that the Beatles and the Stones played with
didn't have a place there. David Geffen, Mitchell's agent, was gay,
but firmly in the closet. The repression of queer presence worked
hand in hand with all the straight coupling to reinforce that hippie
presumption Crosby expressed when enthusing about naked hippie chicks in the sunshine: that the best way to live well and make
art is to return to the natural. Define "the natural"? In the '60s it
was the well-cultivated feeling that everything was just flowing.
Weed, not white powder. Denim and gingham, not patent leather
or glitter. California, not New York. Confessional songwriting,
not dirty-ass rock and roll. In a way it was a weird throwback all
the way to the nineteenth century, when virtue shone from within.

Joni had that natural beauty, and though she certainly loved
her boots and short skirts, she looked sublime in granny gowns.
Beat women had worn jeans and cut their hair short, but in the

Canyon, women were back to being ladies again. Mitchell adapted to the new fashions. The sporty little racing-stripe mini she'd worn to charm the crowds (and Leonard Cohen) at the Newport Folk Festival in 1967 gave way to long ruffled skirts, millions of necklaces and gauzy tops with princess sleeves. "We female folksingers dressed like a combination of gypsies and princesses," Judy Collins told Sheila Weller in 2017. "I wore Mexican wedding dresses, and I decorated them with flowers. I was very romantic-looking. It was so important to us to be feminine—but in an ironclad way." Mitchell played the part. Her music was the silver dagger in her own right hand, allowing her to be a lady and still govern her own destiny.

She wielded it in many ways, including as a tool of seduction. In *Girls Like Us*, Weller describes this as an act of feminist empowerment. True, but it's an older trick than that. The way Joni's romantic partners talk about it recalls stories of queens and consorts, Maid Marian and Scheherazade. So many men in Mitchell's early life treasure a story of hearing her sing—only for them—and being erotically disassembled by the experience. None tells the story with more brio than Graham Nash.

Nash was a recently divorced rock star when he first met Mitchell at that party in Ottawa, where his band the Hollies was touring and she had a folk club gig. He tells the story well, and has done so many times in the decades since he and Mitchell's two-year love affair ended. He has, in fact, become a semiprofessional tender of the Mitchell flame. It's fairly impossible to gain new insight about Mitchell from a conversation with Nash at this point, but I appreciated that he spun out the old tales with grace and wit.

"Whenever Joni entered the room, you knew it," he told me. "There was something about her, even from the first night

I met her. We had done a show and afterward there was a reception. You've got a cheap plastic cup with some awful wine in it and you're trying to remember the promoter's wife's name, that kind of stuff. My manager, Robin Britten, was rabidly on my ear, talking, talking. And I said, Robin, would you stop talking, I'm trying to catch the eye of this beautiful woman in the corner of the room! He said, if you'd just listen to me, that's Joni Mitchell. She's a friend of David Crosby's. And David told her, if I was ever around, you two should meet.

"She had what looked like a giant Bible. She was wearing a pale blue satin dress; she looked astoundingly beautiful. It wasn't a Bible; it was a music box. It would have played beautifully, but it had one note that creaked—" Here Nash demonstrated with a high squeal. "We laughed about that. And we became friends instantly."

How many real-life women of the modern era would come to a low-rent Canadian backstage party armed with a genuine magical talisman? Joni Mitchell was not playing when it came to enchantment.

The scene continued. Nash tells the next chapter better in his memoir than he did to me, so I'll quote him. "She invited me back to the place where she was staying, the [Château] Laurier, a beautiful old French Gothic hotel in the heart of town," he writes. "Flames licked at logs in the fireplace, incense burned in ashtrays, candles were lit strategically, and beautiful scarves had been draped over the lamps. It was a seduction scene extraordinaire.

"That was all a healthy man needed, but Joni wasn't done, not by a long shot. She picked up her guitar, sat in front of the fireplace, and *started to play songs* . . . she played fifteen of the greatest songs I'd ever heard in my life, and I'm *dying*." Overwhelmed "not only as a man but as a musician," Nash fell in love on the spot.

This story walked right out of one of the Arthurian romances Mitchell probably had placed on a bookshelf near her fire-hazard candles. I had those dusty old volumes, too, and in my youth they guided me. Fancying myself a huntress in pursuit of my creative writing program classmates, I developed similar strategies, though as we know my allure was nowhere near the level of Mitchell's. Free verse and tarot decks were the bait in my lair. Part of the fun of the whole experience—really, as much as the often-disappointing sex—was the sport of it: setting up the environment, imagining how the evening would go, going so deep into my own scripts that they became improvisation. Isn't it the artist's dream, that her creation comes to life so vividly that it can encompass her, and draw others in, too? In the thick of it with guys like Nash, Mitchell was also always seducing herself. As for the sex—that was her entitlement as much as any man's.

But back to Graham Nash. What they shared was imagination, and the deep desire to reconstruct themselves. He came in ready to learn. When Nash met Mitchell he was already hoping to flee the Hollies, something Crosby knew from hanging out with him in London back when he was in the Byrds. Nash looked to Crosby and Stills as examples and enablers as he cultivated seriousness. "Stephen was writing all this [political] stuff," he told me. "David was writing songs about Robert Kennedy. Each song had a reason to live, instead of just 'Moon-June-screw me in the back of the car,' which I was used to writing for years. These guys, including Joan, were writing real songs that changed your mind."

In Mitchell, Nash saw someone whose very being pointed toward the future. "Her existence, and her embodying and expressing her existence, in those songs, was political," he said. Her demand for self-definition, rendered in gracefully feminine ways, was a slap-kiss in the face of the Man. Yet she also could offer him the comforts of home that he craved. Unlike Crosby, who genuinely pursued unconventional relationships—though always as the alpha male—Nash wanted what made Mitchell most comfortable, too: domestic bliss. Their time together marked a particular chapter in the CSNY boys' club, when a lot of things seemed possible, including fairly standard-issue happiness.

They got together for real a few months after the Ontario idyll. Nash had arrived at Crosby's place, intending to stay. He had a cold. Mitchell took him in like the helpmeet she could be, and he never left. She has described their match as deeply comfortable, much less of a pain in the ass than her alliance with Crosby. For him, it was a new high. "That was an incredible time for me, probably the most intensely creative, free, and special time I've ever experienced. Not only was I in love with Joni but I was in love with David and Stephen and I was in love with the music and I'd taken a giant chance."

What more could a man want than intimacy with a woman who also could hang with his boys? They tried it out. With Crosby, Mitchell had experienced a powerful meeting of minds and career ambitions. With Nash, she learned day-to-day survival with a male peer. It wasn't easy. They fought over the piano. She'd whip something up for journalists who came by, but beyond that neither she nor Nash really enjoyed cooking. "Soup and salad and that was it," he wrote in his memoir. He was gone a lot anyway, recording or touring with his bandmates, which gave her the solitude to create. Still, her love of setting a scene, which led her to adorn the little house she owned with her favorite stained glass and wildflowers and an antique clock, produced genuine domesticity. It started to feel, to her, a bit too much like homemaking. That tension would eventually drive her from him, in the sadness and frustration that would echo through her great album *Blue*.

Adding to her doubts about Nash's grip was the fact that he just had to immortalize their retreat into the domestic in a song that to this day defines Mitchell's Canyon years for millions of people. It may seem uncharitable to say a bad word about "Our House," one of the sweetest and most beloved sing-alongs of that confusing hippie time. I have no doubt that Nash still feels every word of it as his and Joni's truth, something worth preserving eternally, though their romance lasted only a few seasons. But his loving ballad isn't exactly liberating. He lights the fire. She puts flowers in a vase that she bought, okay. But what does he really offer her? Sunlight shining through the window: a perspective? A chance to be calm, as a woman should be? She, on the other hand, offers him her most precious commodity: her songs. *Play your love songs all night long for me, only for me*, Nash sings.

I have always found "Our House" slightly disturbing, if irresistible. It wasn't their house, after all. It was hers. She'd purchased it with that first record advance. Am I being unfair to one of the few men in her life who was consistently kind to her? He didn't cheat, didn't threaten her, didn't leave her alone with a baby. Nash is a self-described simple man, a pop songwriter who has never done anything but kneel at the altar of Mitchell's genius. He provided her with a foundation that she needed during her time in the CSNY boys' club. Isn't that what your parents want for you: a good foundation?

Is that what she wanted? Perhaps not. Her eye was still on the horizon, always. "He was madly in love with her, and she liked him and thought he was an okay guy," an anonymous friend told one of Nash's biographers. But back to the fairy tale. Undoubtedly they both felt its enchantment. And it was useful, maybe more so to Nash in the end. She even broke up with him in an impossibly poetic way: sending him a telegram from Greece, which he received while laying down a new floor in her kitchen. It read, *If you hold sand too tightly in your hand it will run through your fingers*. Who doesn't want their story to have an ending for the ages? Nash tells it all the time.

NOBODY'S OLD LADY

The history of boys' girls is mostly one of women claiming power that also at least partially erases them. To be the only one of your kind puts you on a bottom rung; the standards of excellence among your peers will always honor the norm, not you, the exception. Also, you'll always be suspect—mistrusted by the peers who had to find other ways toward fulfillment and underestimated by the gatekeepers who let you in provisionally. This explains why the stories of "women in" science/art/sports/business so often have to be recovered: forming at the edge of the picture, they're easily cut out of the frame.

Not so for Joni Mitchell. She possessed a stronger will than most. The critic Lindsay Zoladz asked in 2017, "Why is Joni Mitchell the token female musician that even the most macho rock guys are comfortable calling 'great'?" Good question, and not easy to unravel. The boys, when asked, simply say it's a fact that her talent exceeds others'. "It's a matter of degree," Crosby told me. Her female peers, some of them stung by Mitchell's lack of interest in them, tend to be less effusive or more offhand about her chops. "I wasn't in the same league as Aretha Franklin, Joni Mitchell, or Barbra Streisand (whom I considered *real* singers)," Carole King wrote in her memoir. No problem, she'd find another way.

King's way was to downplay her sexuality image-wise, even when she let it ring out in songs like "I Feel the Earth Move." Other women in and around Laurel Canyon performed similar balancing acts. An intriguing report by *Los Angeles Times* writer Barbara Rowes from a few years after the Canyon scene's peak, 1973, quotes a wide array of women artists on how they negotiated rock's double standard. Jackie DeShannon, whose songwriting career predated Mitchell's arrival, noted that "you had to have double the guts and 20 times the talent" as a woman artist, partly because before the women's liberation movement women fans were assumed to consider performers of their own gender more threatening—"A rival for her escort," DeShannon said— than relatable. Karen Carpenter said she dealt with this problem of being perceived as an antagonist by "not being a bossy chick" onstage or off. Claudia Lennear, one of an elite group of Black women session singers in Los Angeles, laid out her strict rules about dating the men in her bands: "I'd have to be stupid to take them up on it," she said. (She did claim David Bowie as "a very, very close friend," but has remained discreet about their relationship.) Christine McVie, then married to her Fleetwood Mac bandmate John McVie, took that strictly business approach farther, avoiding "male groupies" by going "back to the hotel for a hot bath" after a show. This portrait of the female rocker as a practical semi-Puritan may not have been wholly honest, but it illustrates what Mitchell faced in her ascendant years. Her own game plan resembled what Rowes's subjects articulated. She didn't openly party, kept her love affairs contained as a self-professed "serial monogamist," and even when singing about freedom, projected a gravity that could seem almost prudish at times.

Above all, from the moment she entered the L.A. scene, Joni Mitchell argued for her own singular status as a songwriter and singer. And her boy gang backed her up. Nobody bothered to resist what was presented to them as obvious. Mitchell was stringently demanding about her artistic process and, whenever anyone questioned it, her reputation. The payback she and Geffen demanded for CSNY taking her countercultural anthem "Woodstock," its inclusion in a film that's still shown in art houses on the regular, is an example. Her reclamation happened swiftly and was guaranteed to pay off grandly. And "Woodstock" is about the only case of her almost losing something important from these years.

Like many successful people, Mitchell complained about her newfound fame. "Lately, life has been constantly filled with interruptions. I don't have five hours to myself," she told Ben Fong-Torres in the first profile *Rolling Stone* published about her, in 1969. That afternoon, Fong-Torres noted, Mitchell was making the crust for a rhubarb pie and Nash was lingering near the kitchen. But the profile doesn't overdomesticate Mitchell, instead focusing on her songwriting process and her plans to mount an art show, write a movie and publish a book.

From that 1969 cover story onward, Mitchell fashioned herself as something of a rock Garbo, serious and glamorous, accepting the place in the spotlight she felt was hers by right but never craved. This was, of course, typical of musicians with countercultural aspirations—believing their mere existence was a challenge to the status quo, they inhabited fame as if it were ordinary life and did business with people whom they could believe didn't embody the Man. Execs like Geffen and Roberts, A&M Records publicity director Derek Taylor (who started with the Beatles) and Dunhill Records founder Lou Adler dressed, smoked and partied with the same enthusiasm as did their clients, maintaining the illusion that being in it for love meant you weren't also in it for money.

From this mix of social, creative and business connections arose a controversy whose centrality in the Joni Mitchell myth has always felt odd to me. It involves that glorified tabloid *Rolling*

Stone, which was also one of the greatest products of New Journalism and a prime inventor of my own lifelong preoccupation, rock criticism. As I got more into the matter of Joni as one of the boys, I knew I'd have to look into the story of near libel that appears in so many accounts of her life as proof that she was and remains deeply underestimated, shrunken in others' eyes by her status as a woman. That just didn't sound right to me, considering how much glory her boys and everyone else I talked with constantly poured on her. So I found a complete run of back issues and did some digging to find out the truth. It felt like a necessary move to fully understand how Joni experienced herself as a Canyon celebrity and a boys' girl.

The official organ of a counterculture that eschewed such categories, Jann Wenner's magazine emerged from the roots of the underground press in San Francisco and always treated musicians more like fascinating friends than journalistic subjects. In its early years, *Rolling Stone* had a strange relationship with the L.A. scene; rooted in the wilder and more overtly political Bay Area underground, Wenner and his staff treated Southern California like the suburbs. "Los Angeles is a relaxed and relaxing city, veined with canyons where musicians and artists live," wrote L.A. correspondent Jerry Hopkins in 1968. "It is also 'uptight plastic America,' crawling with buyers and peddlers of flesh and the masters of artificiality." It was Hopkins who created the "joke" that made Mitchell hate *Rolling Stone*, turning her against Wenner for a decade and causing an uproar within—and about—her boy gang.

In 1972 Hopkins and some other staffers created a graphic titled "Hollywood's Hot 100," charting the "very incestuous" rock scene in and around Hollywood using exploding stars, graphic squares, crudely drawn guitars, hearts and lipstick smudges. Mitchell's name was marked by the latter. *Kiss kiss, kiss kiss*, read the words around it, with lines extending to those men whose hearts she'd supposedly crushed: Nash, Crosby and James Taylor. The chart uniquely sexualized Mitchell by framing her name with a smudgy lipstick print, and classified nearly all of the few women included by their romances as much as their music. Joni was singled out, but also reduced to the status of other women on the scene. On the rarely seen other half of the two-page spread, Rita Coolidge's name also blossomed with broken hearts (including one for Graham Nash, by then her ex) and the unbroken heart-line connecting Carole King and Charles Larkey extended to make it seem at first glance like she was dating her whole band. The chart illustrates how sexism was embedded in *Rolling Stone*'s definition of irreverence: women got a ribbing for their sexual exploits but were only considered worth including if they'd made a match that impressed. Otherwise they were relegated to the corners.

This was the second time *Rolling Stone* had made a joke like this at Mitchell's expense. In a four-page feature on the previous year in music published in February 1971, next to a photo of her with Stills at Big Sur, the magazine named Mitchell "Old Lady of the Year" for her "friendships with David Crosby, Steve Stills, Graham Nash, Neil Young, James Taylor, et al." (Kind of a fudge: Mitchell never dated Stills or Young.) "Old Man of the Year" was mass murderer Charles Manson, "for his friendships with [his accomplices] Patti Krenwinkel, Susan Atkins, Linda Kasabian, et al."

Reading these ridiculous swipes decades later, I thought it was obvious that the most distasteful thing about them is the Manson comparison. And I noticed that within many of the features that dared to insult Joni, others were targeted more cruelly, particularly Cass Elliot, whose name appeared in that 1971 year-end wrap-up next to the cover of the album *Songs of the Humpbacked Whale*—a cheap shot about her weight. But Mitchell's mistreatment in *Roll-*

ing Stone has swelled to epic proportions within her legend, even as the context containing it has been forgotten. I think this was due to her special position. Unlike many women in the scene, she felt empowered to call out her own mistreatment. With the boys ready to rush to her defense, she didn't settle for the kind of quotidian trivialization that undermined many of her women peers.

Here's what I discovered when I actually went back and read through the magazine during the years of Joni's boy-gang membership, the time of her rise within the rock world. For one: she wasn't even the worst-treated member of the club. Stephen Stills won that prize handily, consistently ribbed in *Rolling Stone*'s news-and-buzz section (later called "Random Notes") as a drug-addled baby who couldn't even hold it together to be a proper rock star. In the same awards spread as Mitchell's "Old Lady" snub, he won "Bust of the Year" for a police incident that "involved nude chickies and crawling around on the floor." Later that year, a one-line item notes that Stills's tour with the band Manassas had been delayed because of lost luggage. "All together now, *awwww*," the anonymous writer sneered.

Crosby, an acknowledged power player whom it benefited *Rolling Stone* to treat well, was less persecuted—though his promiscuities were parodied when the magazine declared him so sex crazed that one year he qualified, by himself, as a "Couple of the Year." Nash was mostly singled out as a nice guy and an overly tender soul, but aside from Neil Young, respected for his freaky independence, Mitchell's boys were generally treated as irritating if talented prima donnas. Lenny Kaye's assessment of Nash's 1971 solo debut *Songs for Beginners* typifies the backhanded love they received from *Stone*: "While it may never be my favorite album," he wrote, "I'm not going to cringe whenever my upstairs neighbors put it on as part of their continuous CSNY festival."

Mitchell's defenders have cited her treatment as an example of *Rolling Stone*'s descent into the realm of gossip rags. But it was *always* a gossip rag. I read every "Random Notes" section from 1967 to 1974, and it's one long parade of the mundane (which recording session is happening where) and the colorfully personal. Everything from Randy Newman's tonsillectomy to the changing colors of Todd Rundgren's hair is considered news. Donny Osmond's pubescent voice change, the ongoing feud between Paul McCartney and John Lennon and their wives, and Sammy Davis Jr.'s plans to move to the Bahamas is covered. And the romance! Every wedding, birth and new "woosome twosome" is noted with congratulations in order. Amidst the great longform reporting on everything from cults to political conventions, and the career-making reviews, *RS* used gossip not just as filler, but as a main ingredient.

Within this deliberately cheeky atmosphere, Mitchell was treated with great admiration and respect, consistently lauded in her first years of success as one of the most strikingly sophisticated artists of the time. True, Les Brown's review of her first album did begin with a description of her as "a penny yellow blonde with a vanilla voice," but it also cites "flashes of brilliance" that occur "so regularly that a higher consistency is achieved" and concludes by applauding her "full sense of composed music and written words." Record reviews editor Jon Landau singled her out in his 1970 year-end essay: "Joni Mitchell's developed the ability to express the mood of frustrated intellect in a time when thought is so undervalued to an ever-expanding degree." Gary Von Tersch compared her favorably to Judy Collins in a negative review of Judy's 1970 album *Whales & Nightingales*, writing that Collins "totally lacks . . . the poetry and vision of Joni Mitchell." This pattern of elevating Mitchell over others only intensified over the years. Landau declared Mitchell's *Court and Spark* "the first great pop album of 1974" right next to his assessment of Carly Simon's *Hotcakes*, which, he wrote, "contains more fun than profundity." In fact the only true swipe at Mitchell the artist was a snide aside about her work's lack of seriousness in a Langdon Winner review of CSNY's *Deja Vu* album. Amidst all the praise, Winner's remark stands out like an old man's sneering leer during a coronation.

So, over the course of half a decade, a few insensitive jokes about her love life—that's the sum of Mitchell's supposedly horrific treatment in *Rolling Stone*. Other women suffered much worse. Joan Baez got the Stephen Stills treatment, consistently poked fun at and addressed as the diminutive "Joanie." Janis Joplin's talents were described in mostly sexual terms. Cass Elliot was described as a "groupie," though also admired for her ability to recognize and promote gifted artists—including Mitchell. Profiling Linda Ronstadt in 1971, *Stone* staffer Fong-Torres described her as "sexy, sexual or just plain sex." Mitchell's ire did not rise because she was treated differently than other women. She was mad because she very occasionally received the same insults or questionable praise that they did.

Mitchell's frustration in those days was directed as much toward her own record label as toward any media outlet, and for good reason. Music advertising and promotion in the free love era was sex-soaked and often gleefully sexist. Ads for stereo components showed lingerie-clad babes breathlessly surrendering to average guys, overwhelmed by the size of their subwoofers. Album covers with titles like *Pass the Butter* and *Mom's Apple Pie* showed stylized depictions of women's genitalia, enticingly displayed. Recording artists—men and women both—had to decide how much objectification they could take. Here's a list of men who posed seminaked on album covers or in magazines in the 1970s: the Allman Brothers, the Rolling Stones, Grand Funk (repeatedly), Al Green,

Dr. Hook. The guys often played sexual display for a lark. Women knew that such antics could backfire on them, though they dared it anyway; Ronstadt, for instance, frolicked in hot pants with pigs on the cover of 1970's *Silk Purse*.

At Reprise, Mitchell would not surrender one iota of her sexual self-possession to the men in the promotions department. She fought back at every turn. Around the same time *Rolling Stone* was treating her like everybody else, to her chagrin, the label took out a series of ads whose copy lines played around with sexual innuendo as a way of explaining why Mitchell was slow to release new music. "Joni Mitchell is 90% Virgin," one read. "Joni Mitchell Takes Forever," said the next; and then, "Joni Mitchell Finally Comes Across." Each orgasm-teasing tagline was accompanied by a couple of mildly lascivious paragraphs sparkling with lines like "Janis is dandy. Joni just feels better." The ads also offered readers posters of the "pretty" Joni for a quarter. It's all a little distasteful. For Mitchell, the campaign was rage-inducing.

Looking through her then–label head Mo Ostin's papers at the Rock & Roll Hall of Fame library, I discovered the correspondence around this incident. It escalated quickly. In one memo, Ostin noted that Mitchell can be a "funny" lady who's "fussy about advertising copy"; in another, he suggested that all copy be eliminated from future Mitchell ads—just tasteful pictures from then on. There was also a copy of a qualified apology addressed to Mitchell's Lookout Mountain address from Creative Services department head Stan Cornyn, the mind behind the campaign.

In the letter, dated February 11, 1969, Cornyn insists "It was in no way my intent to embarrass you," before arguing, "it is my believe [*sic*] that the ad is an enormously effective one from the advertising standpoint, particularly since I wrote it myself." He continues: "As evidence of its effectiveness, today we received over

150 requests for Joni Mitchell posters." Offering to withdraw the offensive material from the public eye, he repeats, "I want you to understand that it's an enormously effective ad."

Cornyn was legendary for his innovative ad campaigns, but this one really just followed along with the era's mood. Two years before, Dave Van Ronk's record label, Verve, had promoted that relatively unsexy folk singer's latest release with a similar tagline: "Dave Van Ronk Goes All the Way." Elsewhere in the magazines in which the Mitchell campaign appeared, ads for other albums featured images of women in bondage or sucking suggestively on bananas and wishbones. One ad for 8-track tapes promoted the groupie ideal with a photo of a lion-maned, lip-glossed young woman practically tonguing a tape, and the tagline, "Get even closer to them." Mitchell's line "We've got to get ourselves back to the garden" was a tagline of the insouciant late 1960s, but so was "Sex sells." And according to men in suits like Stan Cornyn, rock stars were its ideal salespeople.

Saying no to such shenanigans, Mitchell demanded what few others had the confidence to even consider. She would not be objectified—instead, she would make herself the subject of her own erotic pursuits. I could find no reply to Cornyn's letter, but evidence of Mitchell's power became clear as the paper trail unfolded. In 1978, by which time she was on Geffen's subsidiary Asylum, that label's national manager wrote to an associate, "Joni, as you probably know, is an extremely important artist for us not only because of the potential sales she can generate, but because of her universal acceptance by those in the underground and folk bag." Her arrogance had served her well; now she was pure prestige. Mitchell had managed what few women could: she moved through her time with the boys and came out her own woman.

LA RONDE

Love and sex and pretty pictures for the papers—this is what people talk about when it comes to Mitchell and her boy gang, but
that was all extra. Music was the point, and the prize. I need to talk
about the music Joni made with, about, for, and despite the boys.

Coming to Los Angeles to reach the audience she knew she
deserved, Mitchell primarily sought not lovers, but peers. Someone who could give her a look of recognition when she turned a
chord progression she'd heard on a Tim Hardin recording into
something completely different. Somebody who'd come into a recording session and hit the harmony she heard in her head. Someone else to listen to the mix, so she could shore up arguments and
not be dominated by any one opinion. As she knew from every
scene she'd ever walked through, if Mitchell didn't become one of
the guys, she'd still be surrounded by men. All the studio players.
The recording engineers and producers. David Geffen and Elliot
Roberts, doing her business, and Mo Ostin at her label. Almost
everybody in her sights, except for the few women with ambitions like her own, feeling like the spotlight was on them just for
existing.

The boys around Mitchell felt her unflagging commitment to
her work. The way she'd pull out her guitar and turn away at a
holiday dinner or even in the thick of a make-out session. Some,
like Stephen Stills, would admit that her talent scared them. But
most wanted to solve the puzzles her songs laid out. Nash may
have found it romantic to hear her tinkling away at the piano in
their Lookout Mountain house, but he was also listening like a
hawk.

He recalls one such moment in his memoir: "Once, I heard her
playing in a gorgeous new configuration. After she was finished
and had gone into the kitchen, I picked up her guitar and the notes

that cascaded out were like shooting stars; they astounded me. I figured out a couple of ways to play interesting sounds with it, and then I finished 'Lady of the Island' using Joni's special tuning."

That nice guy Graham. He stole her tuning! Maybe that's one of the reasons why she was, in Crosby's words, "a very turbulent girl": the boys were always at her shoulder trying to figure out her tricks. Nash probably ran into the kitchen immediately and said, *Hey, Joni, I wrote a song for you!* Did she throw a salad fork at him? At least he wrote her a sexy lyric to go with his borrowing, all about her burnished golden limbs.

It was okay. I mean, she was taking from them, too. Mitchell needed to figure out how to put some rock and roll into her swoon, and that she got from the boys. You can see and hear how they shaped one another's sound in a recording of folk-rock pioneer Dino Valenti's anthem "Get Together" at the Big Sur Folk Festival in 1969. Her moment onstage with CS&N (plus Lovin' Spoonful frontman John Sebastian) was clearly something of a showcase for her, and it worked: *Rolling Stone* later singled her out as one of the festival's most exciting surprises. (That review included a photograph of her leaning against Crosby, cool in a cowboy hat.) There's a hint of her future composition "Big Yellow Taxi" in the strum. Mitchell took the lead vocal.

Watching the performance now, I can see her pulling back on the phrases, her timing making the melody almost seem like a counterpoint. Stills played off of this by driving things forward with hard little riffs and some vocal embellishments borrowed from Cuban music, which he loved. Nash, Crosby and Sebastian, handclapping a bouncing rhythm, took a minute to get the harmonies right. But they were solid by the second chorus. Joni had laid it all out for them, dropping into little diminished fifths at the end of the verses, pointing Crosby toward some unexpected middle notes.

The boys pushed her forward. She pulled them back, her singing saying, *Try a different route*.

In her face in that clip I see something that isn't usually there, won't be there until she assembles her big bands a few years later: relaxation. These guys got her. She'd been around one or two men who could sing the way she could—had heard Tim Hardin continually expanding his soul thing and Tim Buckley getting ever more ethereal and funkier as his music got weirder. But nobody was seeking exactly the combination she wanted, mixing the airy space of Joan Baez's folk ballads with the old-fashioned pop sweets ("musical-y," she'd once called the tone) of the Beatles, and adding the push of heavier rock and roll.

CSNY *were* that combination. Crosby, like her, loved jazz and had even sung in a duo with the Black troubadour Terry Callier for a while. Stills was a rocker who dipped his feet into the Latin diaspora; he'd been raised that way in Florida and other points south. And Nash had come up in the song factory of the British Invasion. Neil Young was in and out of the picture, a self-styled loner, but when he was around, he made Mitchell feel even more comfortable, because of their old Canadian connection and a prickly love of new musical things that complemented her own. She could learn from these guys.

The songs Mitchell wrote then, and the ones the boys wrote back, form an infinite round, with each final chord seeming to echo into the next one's opening measures. All the romance stuff pales in comparison to what these friends accomplished musically, writing hits that defined the turn of the 1970s on the folk-rock scene. Each song amplifies their intimate connections, their occasionally feverish competitiveness and their conviction that, individually and together, they were better than anybody else. And each sold the story of their mutual, complicated love.

Over the next few years, the Laurel Canyon circle expanded, and she nurtured new collaborations, moving others to the back burner as she entertained new possibilities. Taking control as a producer was a big part of this process. Crosby's spare production on *Song to a Seagull* had served its purpose, isolating her voice as if it were a sapphire in a floating ring setting, but she was driven toward wider vistas. Reprise brought in Paul Rothchild to help on *Clouds*—he'd done groundbreaking work helping organize another garrulous personality, Doors front man Jim Morrison, on that band's hit records—but it was a bad match. Rothchild stepped out at some point to tend to some Doors business, and Mitchell persuaded engineer Henry Lewy to finish the album with her alone. From then on they were a team, with Lewy becoming a more crucial and long-standing collaborator than any of her more glamorous friends. "Henry Lewy and I have had a working relationship made in heaven, where there's no ego in play and it's just pure joyous child's play, mutually supportive," she told Malka Marom in the mid-1970s. He would never be credited as a coproducer, she wasn't sharing the captain's chair anymore, though a memo from Ostin shows he was paid a one percent royalty on *Clouds* and *Blue*. His input was central as she organically grew her sound, adding lush multitracked harmonies and other Beatlesesque flourishes to *Ladies of the Canyon* and tentatively exploring the rhythmic palettes of jazz and global music.

Not just in the lyrics, but in their bones, the songs were all about relationships. When Nash huffed in a 1971 interview that people were just listening to the Canyon songs for the gossip, he definitely protested too much. They brought it all on themselves, name-checking and borrowing from one another constantly. Here's a little playlist tracing some ways that Joni and the boys made music together, from song to song, even when they didn't admit it. It's a product of my imagination, not reflecting strict chronology; one listener's guide to a fine group romance.

Start with a track from Mitchell's second album, *Clouds*, inspired by the New York lover-mentor she'd left as well as the one who greeted her in California. "That Song About the Midway" is a slightly bitter kiss goodbye to a dazzling egotist. Cohen and Crosby both fit the bill. Its haunting qualities come from her use of the Mixolydian mode, often used in the blues. Crosby heard something in this, and he wrote "Guinnevere," which appears on CS&N's debut album, also from 1969. That song introduces the "magic tuning" David discovered while trying to figure out what Joni was up to on guitar. Its lyrics describe three women, his polyamorous dream; one is clearly Joni. Nash came up with his own Renaissance Faire fancy, perhaps in response—"Lady of the Island." This is the one Nash wrote on Joni's open-tuned guitar. Its blue wash of psychedelic rock shows up in Joni's "The Arrangement," from *Ladies of the Canyon*. It's influenced by Debussy in the way Nash's songs were then redolent of classical guitar compositions. The assertive moodiness suggests her doubts about the common-law marriage she'd eased into with Nash.

He replied, or so I hear, with "Our House." Just as "The Arrangement" argues against old-fashioned house and home, his song, of course, draws things back into the domestic sphere. Musically, it's Willy reminding everybody in the circle that they all still love the Beatles. Parlor piano for the longhairs, major chords for happy people. Joni wasn't having any of that, though, so she offered him "Willy," also on *Ladies of the Canyon*. She bursts his bubble with her melancholy. Their romance was getting rocky. Time for Neil Young to walk into the room with the song he wrote for Willy after the breakup, "Only Love Can Break Your

Heart." It's a weird one, though. It offers up more parlor piano, but with the keys a little wobbly. Its lyrics advise self-preservation in the face of potential love disaster. The effect is soothing, but a little bitter.

Where was Stephen Stills while all this was happening? On his own trip, but still tuned in. He joined into the writers' round with an epic flavored by all the other songs I've mentioned so far:

"Suite: Judy Blue Eyes." A rock and roll plea if there ever was one, directed at Judy Collins, who'd electrified his life but then chose New York and psychoanalysis over California and her dashing, drug-addled love. As Willy had with Joni, in the lyrics Stephen begs Judy to put aside her own things, just be his lady and change his life. The *Don Quixote* of baby boomer romance, "Suite" is four songs in one—something the Beatles were doing, but so was Joni in some of her more sweeping songs, like "The Dawntreader," from her first album. (That one's about David, of course.) Stephen was clearly listening to her experiments.

But now it was time for Joni to make a break from her boys and their edifying, tenacious influence. She said farewell in the sweetest way, with "Big Yellow Taxi." Is there a more CSNY song not by CSNY? And you know what, trying on their poppier, even danceable style more deliberately gave Joni a song that would become a major fan favorite, covered and interpolated by other artists for decades to come. It's best known for its environmentalist lyrics and a chorus that offers exactly the kind of melody that you wake up in the morning hearing and then can't get out of your head. "Taxi" is a much bigger turning point for Joni than most fans usually recognize. Here is where the African diaspora rhythms that take over her work around 1975 first get her dancing; here's where she throws in those old swing-era harmonies and pushes her phrasing up to double speed. Doing her own take on the CSNY thing, she discovered the template for her jazz era, soon to come.

IT'S FITTING THAT THIS SONG SHOULD END OUR PLAYLIST; IT REPRESENTS THE FULL fruit of Joni's musical interaction with her boy gang, in which she shows she can play every part they offer—rocker, wit, dreamer, weirdo—and do so laughing.

You might be wondering why I didn't include "Woodstock" on my playlist. That song deserves its own place in the story of Joni Mitchell's interactions with her boys. It has long played a central and complicated role in her legend. Written in a Manhattan hotel after she turned on the television to watch reports of CSNY playing the biggest festival of the rock era, "Woodstock" has been held up as an example of how sexism kept women from the countercultural action and how they used their creativity to triumph anyway. The story I heard for years was about a damsel mistaken for being in distress: the band had decided that she was too delicate to dive with them into the crowds at Yasgur's farm and sequestered her away seemingly against her will. The truth had more to do with pure business than misplaced gallantry. Mitchell was scheduled to appear on the *Dick Cavett Show* the next day, and Geffen, her agent, considered that more important than a trek into the chaos of what then looked like a somewhat disastrously overextended freak fest.

Watch the *Cavett* clip sometime to see how Mitchell kept her chin up even when she felt she was being screwed. The knowledge that Geffen was wrong is etched into her steely smile. She could have gone to Woodstock. There, right next to her, sat Crosby and Stills, helicoptered in and full of wild tales about what Crosby gleefully told Cavett was "the biggest batch of gypsies you ever saw." Mitchell knew she'd been persuaded to sit out a historical watershed. But the set of her jaw said she also knew she had more to show for her absence than the Woodstock mud that remained stuck to Stills's blue jeans.

Writing a song about what the TV showed her in that midtown hotel room, Mitchell actually had a far more relatable experience than the boys, with their helicopter entitlement, had enjoyed. As most North Americans had for the moon landing and the Vietnam War, she'd flipped a switch and electronically connected with rock's gathering of the tribes. The often-praised eeriness of her "Woodstock" generates itself within those cathode-ray beams. Her song is in the past tense, her lyrics' language anachronistically medieval: *Can I walk beside you?* she sings to the pilgrim she finds on the road. *I feel to be a cog in something turning.* Yet "Woodstock" also feels very turn-of-the-'70s, in the way Mitchell transforms the pilgrimage at its center into a psychedelic trip: a journey not in devotion to a God, but in search of self. Mitchell's idea of psychedelia is deeply psychological and, as always with her, medium cool. When the song's narrator and her new companion arrive in Woodstock, they are overtaken by a vision of bomber planes becoming butterflies. The image invokes an acid high, but also a cinematic screen dream. With "Woodstock," Mitchell offered all of the millions of her generation who didn't make it to the farm a vision they could enter, and an assurance that the garden you need to get back to grows in your own head.

Stephen Stills heard it right away, the way this song's dream would infiltrate others' waking lives. Nash noted the moment in his memoir. CSNY had just returned from the festival. "She played it for us before we even got settled," he writes. "I noticed Stephen listening intently with that strange look in his eyes." Stills asked Mitchell for the song, and the right to "change it a little," as soon as she finished singing. The muscles in her back tightened, Nash said, but "because Joni was one of the lads, to say nothing of being my girlfriend, she merely shrugged and said, 'Sure.'"

And so CSNY turned Mitchell's pre-Raphaelite fever dream into a blues stomper built around a backbeat. It was the lead single from their smash album *Déjà Vu* and went to number eleven on the charts. Geffen, ever the fixer, made sure Mitchell made as much bank as possible from this borrowing, insisting that Michael Wadleigh, the director of the soon-to-be-released Woodstock concert film, use CSNY's version of the song under the closing credits. The royalties would roll in. Mitchell's own version, resolutely ethereal, appears on *Ladies of the Canyon* alongside her other mordant accounts of the ups and downs of Canyon life.

David Crosby eventually came around to her approach. On *Here If You Listen*, the album he was promoting when I met him, he'd rerecorded it, foregrounding his women bandmates' voices in an arrangement more indebted to Joni than to Stills. "We put it in the set one night and when we hit that first four-part harmony the audience started applauding right in the middle of the song," he said. "We looked at each other and said, we know what this is." The power of Joni, meeting them on the road.

4

the sorrow

Mitchell moved on from the boys, and she didn't. She remained in Laurel Canyon until 1971, when she sold the "Our House" house and took a lonely sabbatical in British Columbia, fixing up a coastal retreat there, before returning to Hollywood—but this time, to Bel-Air. Before that she jumped over to Europe for the famous season that produced songs like "Carey," about a redheaded American lover she met in Greece, and "California," which shows her longing for a welcome party back on the Sunset Strip.

Much has been written about these years she spent as a gadabout, mostly about the love affairs she cultivated with that red rogue Carey Raditz and with James Taylor, who joined her on the Mediterranean shore and then in London for a few gigs and a blossoming romance. *Ladies of the Canyon*, made under Nash's wing, came out during this time and shows his English influence, but right at that moment she was severing their bond. Soon that immortal telegram came to Willy from the far shore, and he felt the fine sand grains of her goodbye running through his fingers.

Joni was more interested in Taylor's fingers by then. I mean that lasciviously, but also musically. Mitchell's romantic life, especially in this period, has been fetishized in myriad ways, as emblematic of a free woman's self-development but also as pure titillation, a pretty woman kissing pretty men. What I want to focus on is the way James Taylor's fingers moved across the fretboard of his guitar, and how Joni learned from his intricate techniques, as he learned from her unusual tunings, and each learned from the other how to bare their souls with grace and precision instead of just letting it all hang out. And I also want to consider how they got better at expressing their feelings, not within their love affair but to their audiences. The essential subject that Taylor and Mitchell explored together, and then separately during their own tumultuous breakup, was the gradient sound of sadness: how it could be expressed gently with careful breaths and quiet musical phrasings, or swell toward something that feels universal on a high note or with the crash of a minor chord.

Joni's intimacies and her internal struggles over them matter as raw material, but her art comes alive through the hard work of refining those feelings so that they reflect and commune with a listener's own. In the early years of the 1970s she focused her energies on understanding what it means to be blue—what that term signified within her own vocabulary, but also as a musical legacy leading her toward the blues and jazz, and as a color key unlocking untold stories of deprivation, need and loneliness, especially ones told by women.

One of the most resonant lines she would ever write reveals the delicacy of this process. It comes in the middle of "River," the heartbroken Christmas carol from her fourth album, *Blue*. Her lament is a touchstone for so many people that it's become not just a standard, but a chromosome within pop's DNA. Songs like this—the Beatles' "Yesterday," Leonard Cohen's "Hallelujah," the Dolly Parton–penned, Whitney Houston–propelled "I Will Always Love You"—break away from themselves while remaining intact. Interpretations and interpolations of such songs, references to and misreadings of them, produce daughter cells that both replicate and dilute the original.

Put down this book for four minutes right now, and listen to "River." You know it: Joni's piano chiming "Jingle Bells" and then turning that chestnut's knee-jerk nostalgia mournful; her lyric doing the same thing, calling in winter's hope and its bare clarity. *It's coming on Christmas, they're cutting down trees . . .*

"River" is the kind of pop song that serves a cultural need. An argument for loneliness, it gives the listener permission to openly mope. Organized cheer can be oppressive, especially in winter's darkest days. This carol eradicates the cinnamon scent of happy holidays with a shot of freezing air; a nonjoiner can hum it to herself when everybody else is holly jolly–ing. Over the years, its uses have extended beyond the season. It's a staple at public memorial services and in private mourning sessions, and within Hollywood rom-coms like *Love, Actually*, in which the "cold English wife" played by Emma Thompson declares that Mitchell's music taught her how to feel. The realization that you've lost something, the admission that you'll never get it back: these are just some of the emotional crises "River" has come to represent. Joni Mitchell didn't necessarily mean to surrender this divulgence of her own alienation to the entire world, but the world took it, and now it flows like the water underneath a stream's gelid surface, moving where it is pulled.

At its source, though, "River" was something specific, and when Mitchell released it in 1971, new. Its core of cool, formed by the limpid melody and floating rhythm and a chorus built around the hushed word "wish," prevents full immersion in any one emotion. This makes it a quintessential Mitchell song: an inquiry, as she also famously described her open-tuning chords. For a woman to make such a scrupulous investigation of her own sense of stymied dislocation in the world was daring; Nina Simone had done it, as had Billie Holiday, but the rock world had little room for this. "River" resists catharsis, even resolution. It takes up the problem of sadness, instead of creating a comfortable place for it.

I'm so hard to handle, Joni sings, and then comes that line. She pulls in her breath in the middle of the phrase as if she knows it's a risk to say it. *I'm selfish and I'm sad*. It's the kind of thing a woman says in real life. "I'm selfish" is what you tell a lover to get them to not walk out the door. "I'm sad" is the cry you sound in the silence after it's shut. There's so much in that word combination. Does being selfish guarantee Mitchell will be sad? It is sad to be selfish? Selfish to be sad? The rest of "River" undulates around this uncertainty.

Mitchell's delivery, powered by the breath in and the breath out, makes you think about how "selfish" so often passes judgment on "sad," especially when applied to a woman. A woman needs to hold her sorrow in place as in a picture frame, containing it so that it kindles just enough sympathy in others, but never letting it push beyond its justified edges. That would be selfish. Tantrums, crying jags the children might hear, days spent in bed, suicide. Sadness from women, when not picturesque, disrupts in dangerous ways.

What makes "River" so powerful is how it makes us think about being sad: about the crises sorrow perpetuates, the urgency with which it takes over and the energy it takes to fight back. To be selfish and sad is to demand the right to negative emotions while recognizing the harm they do to oneself and others. The song's tight circle of a melody and the way Mitchell sings it embody an inner battle for composure. Her voice surges, then pulls sternly back. The piano lines are grounded in simple chord changes, with every right-hand flourish slightly restrained by a stern quarter note from the left hand.

"River" captures what it feels like to be sad, but also to question one's right to be sad, to long for and simultaneously worry about the urge to get lost in the sorrow. It's also about wanting to get away from others who see you as sad, and from the circumstances reinforcing your sorrow. It's this Mitchell song that most directly captures the mood of the epigrammatic writing of her literary twin, Joan Didion, the queen of migraines and malaise. It especially recalls Didion's classic 1970 novel of women's fatal sadness, *Play It as It Lays*. In sparse prose, that book relates the story of Maria Wyeth, the female Hamlet of swinging '60s Hollywood, driven to quiet madness by her inability to act when life throws disaster in her wake. "I have trouble with *as it was*," Wyeth famously says, sharing confidences about a lost/abandoned daughter and a bad marriage and dead parents and a friend's suicide (which she assisted) from some anonymous clinic for the mentally broken down. This broken beauty inhabits sadness because she can't do anything else; she can't even tell a story straight. But in that, she's an ordinary woman (qualifying terms: white, heterosexual, wealthy, desired) of her time.

In those days sadness unto death, or at least unto inertia, was a cultural marker that made the isolation of middle-class white women within suburban homes seem glamorous instead of pathetic. It made their husbands feel needed without really asking them to solve anything. Popular culture offered a steady supply of midcentury modern neurasthenics and hysterics. I'm thinking about the death-driven heroines of suburbanite novels by John Updike and Richard Yates (and that boy's girl Didion), and of Peggy Lee singing "Is That All There Is?" in her Valium alto, and of Marilyn Monroe overdosing in her Brentwood bungalow. In these songs and films and lives, sadness was a form of protest that negated the self. A river you can skate away on doesn't really get you anywhere, does it? Except alone, for a few precious moments, in the cold.

"River" expresses an attraction to the void, but Joni wanted to be sad and to stay alive, moving through it. In another song on *Blue*—"Little Green," the one about the daughter Joni had left behind, trusting that the baby would be better without her— Mitchell uses the word "sad" again, but she finds a way out of it this time. *You sign all the papers in the family name,* she sings. *You're sad and you're sorry, but you're not ashamed.* At first her singing recalls what she does on "River." "Sad" feels like a breath in; "sorry," a breath out. But then "not ashamed" comes in a burst of air, burying the others. In this lament for her Kelly Dale, Mitchell confines sadness to the deep layers of her consciousness. "Sorry" says goodbye to the pain, and "not ashamed" is what Joni will embody after doing so. But in "River" there's no such resolution. "Selfish" and "sad" circle around each other. How, the song asks, can a woman survive the grief her life creates without denying it? How can she be sad and be a good person, a good woman, too?

The sadness in "River" or *Play It as It Lays* is the kind you can't clean up. It stays in the water. The women's liberation movement identified it clearly but couldn't eradicate it, though it did give some women a way to imagine themselves beyond it. Still, even today women (many of them white, heterosexual, middle-class, desired) are writing novels with antiheroines who stay in bed for a year, and essay collections with titles like *So Sad Today*. These contemporary takes on the subject frame it in relation to the self-fictionalization that happens online and the perilous recalibrations of now-ubiquitous psych meds. Time has shown that liberation is a repetitive process. "I think of how sadness can be an inheritance, a feminist inheritance," the theorist Sara Ahmed wrote in her 2017 book *Living a Feminist Life*. She also called complaint a pedagogy: a way of teaching about the ways of the world. The feminist encounter with sadness, like Mitchell's music, recognizes the persistence of the problem of *as it was*.

SAD LIBERATION

The reclamation of sadness by women was a hallmark of early second-wave feminism, if a controversial one. All over the movement and beyond it, women rewrote the tales of feminine suffering their parents and teachers and doctors and husbands had so often told them. Exorcism was often the point. Get rid of those old stories about women collapsing into gloom. Let Ophelia float downstream—goodbye. "This above all, to refuse to be a victim," wrote Margaret Atwood in her 1972 novel *Surfacing*. "Unless I can do that I can do nothing."

Betty Friedan reported the need to shout that refusal in one of the founding documents of the women's liberation movement, 1963's *The Feminine Mystique*. For the book she'd interviewed her former Smith College classmates, now firmly settled into comfortable housewife lives. Their sadness was a sickness. "It was in these women that I first began to notice the tell-tale signs of the problem that has no name," she wrote in one of the book's many editions. "Their voices were dull and flat, or nervous and jittery; they were listless and bored, or frantically 'busy' around the house or community. They talked about 'fulfillment' in the wife-and-mother terms of the mystique, but they were desperately eager to talk about this other 'problem,' with which they seemed very familiar indeed."

Friedan's male peers in taking on the suburban blight also identified this sickness, but they weren't very sympathetic to its invalids. The awful climaxes of Updike's *Rabbit, Run* and Yates's *Revolutionary Road* center on women so perverted by ennui they do away with their own children. (One, during a self-induced abortion, also accidentally does away with herself.) These anti-heroines scatter destruction in their wake. Male writers of the postwar middle class regarded the women they killed off in their stories as perpetrators, not just victims. Women were behind what Yates identified, in suburban life, as "an outright betrayal of our best and bravest revolutionary spirit"—they generated the "lust for conformity" that the postwar consumer culture made epidemic. Friedan's insight was that women were not villains but victims. The movement that arose partly in response to her book insisted that women could walk beyond that victimhood.

But it wasn't always easy to give up the old anomie, and the allure that went with it. In 1973 Erica Jong wrote in her bestselling sex novel, *Fear of Flying*: "We had more in our lives than just men; we had our work, travel, friends. Then why did our lives seem to come down to a long succession of sad songs about men?" Joni often asked that question in her music, showing herself agonizing over a married guy in "Conversation" or worrying herself into a state as she flies away from a different lover on "This Flight Tonight." At that moment, she sang, she'd like to turn the plane around. Why, she wondered, did she still care so much about some man's feelings in the very moment when she was making her own life bigger?

I could have used an answer to that question in my green years as a hungry romantic. Those pretty neurasthenics men invented were all up in my head, but in my own life, I soon realized being a sad girl was just embarrassing. Snot and smeared makeup and not much sympathy from the boys I was trying to lure. Mitchell's early songs bear brilliant traces of such excess: in her keening, she sometimes sounds utterly ridiculous. *Here is a shell for you*, she sings in the title track, "Blue," hitting that clammy metaphor hard with an extra-wobbly high note. And you can just see it, Joni walking on the beach alone some morning, mooning over an undeserving dude, and seeing a perfectly intact remnant of a limpet, shoving it in her pocket to bestow upon him later. He'll pick it up from the table at the club and examine it as if it could potentially be a snack. Then he'll put it in his denim jacket pocket to go through the wash later.

Here are some highlights from my own reel of melancholic displays. One time in high school my little weirdo gang was in my friend Nora's basement and the boys started bellowing a drinking song they'd learned in youth orchestra, and for some reason I decided this was the time to sing the mournful folk ballad "The Water Is Wide" a cappella all the way through. Maybe I started first, actually, and they were trying to drown me out. Justifiably, to be honest. My boyfriend, who was in that acute stage of high school romance where you're really in love and also really trying to get someone to sleep with you, tried to get them to stop. They wouldn't. "Just sing it to me," he said. I gave up and stormed off instead.

A few years later I was on a date with another very sweet musician, a country guitar player who'd actually told me he liked girls with glasses (that never happened!), and after dinner, back at my place, I put on a Nick Drake record. English hippie troubadour, dead at twenty-six, the male equivalent of drowned Ophelia. Saddest of the sad. After telling my new prospect to sit down and listen, I started weeping inconsolably. I told him it was an existential crisis, but really I just wanted to be on a date with a different guy who was a very messed-up person and also a drunk. Faking despair to get rid of a dude: brilliant. It did work.

Also around that time I had a brief dalliance with a guitar player whose moaning vocals turned his band's punk breakdowns into something I heard as heartbroken and deep. He was seriously just passing through, and after our weird night together, I got his address in Los Angeles so I could send him a "spiritual enhancement kit" I'd made from powders I'd bought at the local botanica. I was trying to play the role of some kind of high priestess of sadness, as if I could cure his malaise by showing him how well I understood mine. The powders must have all sloshed together into a brown dust pile, since I sent them in a big plastic bag. Anyway, I never heard from him again.

These stories do not make me uniquely ridiculous. Most women have similar ones. We all want to be as sexy as Maria Wyeth, but most of us are more like Lili Taylor in the proto-'90s teen movie *Say Anything*, the frumpy friend in the lumpy sweater writing songs about an oblivious fool who is truly not worth it. (In this decade, it's Olivia Rodrigo topping the pop charts with lines like, "Just watch as I crucify myself for some weird second-string loser who's not worth mentioning.") In those same years I was taking women's studies classes, devouring feminist literature. But sadness was rarely on the syllabus. In the 1980s—as it does today, in the mainstream—feminism mostly aligned itself with go-getterism. We can bring home the bacon and fry it up in a pan! All that positive energy didn't eliminate the anguish. Instead, it reinforced the shame around it.

I reached out to Alice Echols, a Joni chronicler and a prime historian of second-wave feminism, to help me understand why the movement made so little space to acknowledge what had been a defining quality of conventional femininity. "Sadness felt like a capitulation, especially because the dominant cultural message was that feminists were sad and lonely and thwarted and frustrated and deeply unhappy. So owning up to it was hard," she replied. Many women's libbers, Echols explained, led lives made precarious by their rejection of husbands and hearth. They didn't have much money, weren't even noticed by many in straight society, and, even if by choice, often lived their lives mostly alone. They really struggled. "I do think that the disparity between what they were trying to bring about and what happened was just too great for some to manage," Echols observed, noting that some feminist stars, like Shulamith Firestone, died impoverished. Echols wasn't saying that these women had made wrong choices—just difficult and sometimes impossible ones. Though they won a lot, they paid a lot, too.

Mitchell's music demands the integration of sadness into a free woman's range of emotions, in defiance of go-getterism. It reminds women that liberation is very difficult to fully achieve, both within society and internally. *Don't interrupt the sorrow!* she sang in the closest thing to a feminist anthem that she ever wrote. In fact, that's the song's title line—so important is the message that along with rage and joy comes confusion and insecurity and the acknowledgment that liberation can almost never be fully achieved, especially from the strictures in a woman's own psyche. She rarely wrote in such declarative language, but she did continually challenge anyone—liberationist or ladies' man—who would say that women should keep their feelings of dissatisfaction and insecurity to themselves.

RUST ON THE RAZOR

The musical form that most deftly integrates sadness and other emotions—joy, defiance, humor—is, of course, the blues. Coming up in the folk revival, Mitchell had ample time to study its legacies. Her very earliest songs show its influence, though she quickly headed down other paths. Many white folk singers considered the blues a direct route into the African-American experience, grounded in gritty details, subversiveness and sex. The few performers of color in the folk scene—old folks like the Reverend Gary Davis, and younger ones like Richie Havens and Odetta—were granted authority in this space, but that didn't stop every white guy with a hangover from eagerly invading it.

While a certain strain of blues, redolent of the country, attracted the white college crowd in Toronto and Greenwich Village, another was getting a revamp from Black women innovators like Abbey Lincoln and Nina Simone. Mitchell would eventually declare her kinship with Simone, the classically trained jazz revolutionary whose songs brought fire to the fight for civil rights. Joni claimed that Simone was her fan, running up to her at the Beverly Center and enveloping her in a hug while shouting the name of her mid-1980s song about white hypocrisy in the face of African hunger: "Ethiopia!" This story is worth repeating because it shows that Mitchell recognized the kinship she and Simone shared, in their defiant insistence that sad songs should rip off the Band-Aid of sentimentality.

The uncompromising Simone was a galvanizing force whose music inspired the women who would invent Black feminism at the same time that white feminists were struggling with sadness in their own ways: writers like Toni Morrison, Maya Angelou, Angela Davis, Ntozake Shange. What these women heard in the blues of Ma Rainey and Bessie Smith was the decision to speak sadness unflinchingly. Their work showed how the structures of slavery, never dismantled, had made the particulars of Black women's grief and vexation both ever-present and incomprehensible to many white people. Black feminists of the 1960s and 1970s heard a deep pragmatism in the blues: the determination to make the hurt obvious. Rainey sang in a low, slow moan about sweet rough men and her own aching feet. She and her sisters carved out a space for that pain. Suddenly, everybody could hear it.

Writing about that same pain in her 1969 memoir, *I Know Why the Caged Bird Sings*, Maya Angelou ran her thumb against that sharp edge of the blues and considered its absorption into white culture. "If growing up is painful for the Southern Black girl, being aware of her displacement is the rust on the razor that threatens the throat," she wrote. "It is an unnecessary insult." The blues queens had reckoned with the advent of white women torch singers taking their songs, then white boys claiming them as rock and roll, then folk singers treating them like sacred texts but only sometimes crediting the source. Inheritors like Angelou, who was also a singer, returned the blues to its rightful place.

Within this canon, the work that reminds me the most of Mitchell's dissection of sadness is Ntozake Shange's choreopoem *for colored girls who have considered suicide/when the rainbow is enuf*, which was first produced in 1975 and became, for a generation of Black sad girls, the river that carried them through their own pain. In the play, a cast of seven actors representing the every-women who live *outside Chicago/outside Detroit/outside Houston* share the stories that real women often kept to themselves: of joy and dancing and sexual power in counterpoint with horrific abuse and violation.

One segment of Shange's choreopoem, "no more love poems #1," is a deconstruction of a love triangle that includes a passage spoken by a wronged woman to her man, but also to America. *I had convinced myself colored girls had no right to sorrow/& I lived & loved that way & kept sorrow on the curb,* Shange writes. The poem documents the harm this repression causes—*I cdnt stand it I cdnt stand being sorry & colored at the same time.* Shange's conclusion: it's both necessary and redundant for modern Black women to wail and weep. Mourning lives inside them, even as they battle fiercely to escape it.

Don't interrupt the sorrow. The audiences who embraced Shange and told her she was singing their lives after performances in countless school auditoriums, community centers and make-shift basement theaters knew that here, more than any white kids' song circle, was where the blues needed to go.

MELANCHOLIA

Mitchell could never be called a blueswoman, and that was okay with her. She had her own models for sad success, looking to Europe like the traveler she was. "If you are sad, then you should feel sad," Mitchell told a reporter in 1969. "The French are good at that. They show what they feel and in that way purge themselves of it. My next album will be even sadder. It gets into the pain of the heart."

Though most listeners identify Mitchell's early albums as folk, the influence of European pop is present, too. Everyone in Laurel Canyon loved the Beatles especially, but I also hear the gossamer chic of rock-era chanteuses like Françoise Hardy and Marianne Faithfull in Joni songs like "Marcie" and "Michael from Mountains." These accounts of lost-and-found love employ circular melodies and unusual guitar fingerings to unmoor the stories Mitchell tells; they remain unresolved. It's as if Mitchell had completely internalized the mood of the Beatles' "Norwegian Wood (This Bird Has Flown)," the ultimate existentialist rock ballad, in which maybe nothing happens and maybe the world is on fire. Somewhere between the casual and the cataclysmic, melancholy gains a different allure. It oscillates and vacillates, as the scholar Anne Hilker puts it in her essential essay on Mitchell and that psychological condition, "Dreams and False Alarms." This foundational wavering manifests musically as a kind of Eurotrash languor.

Judy Collins was the master of this affect. Her version of "Both Sides Now," which propelled Mitchell toward stardom, also invoked "Norwegian Wood," and the Pop Art take on pre-Raphaelite dreaminess that Hardy and Faithfull cultivated. Producer Mark Abramson set Collins's airy voice against the tinkle of an electric keyboard, producing an effect similar to that achieved by Andrew Loog Oldham on Faithfull's hit "As Tears Go By." *I sit and watch the children play*, Faithfull sings, calm as a statue within the swirling arrangement. There are so many kinds of sad songs, but the eeriest are the pretty ones, signaling innocence, death before aging. Ophelia resurfacing, her body entangled in water lilies. In the 1960s, fine-boned ingenues with hair the color of wheat sang these songs and people swooned.

Collins, her voice clear as a brook, brought an unworried calm to "Both Sides Now" that made its core of disillusionment shimmer like possibility. That's what Faithfull had done on "As Tears Go By," a cool account of spiritual malaise (or maybe heroin addiction) written by her thoughtless lover Mick Jagger. As did Hardy on her first hit "Tous Les Garçons Et Les Filles," her spacey alto slowing down the merry-go-round melody of that song about feeling shut out of love. In New York, the German model Nico recovered from her bondage adventures in the Velvet Underground by going Eurosad on her solo debut *Chelsea Girl*, intoning a childlike *la, la, la, la* in the middle of her recording of "These Days," written by the teenage Jackson Browne, whom she'd seduced without ever telling him one personal detail about her life. These recordings do what youthful melancholy does when deliberately cultivated: they create distance, allowing a young person to ease into the sweet oblivion of nostalgia without having to suffer the ache of being on the other end of time lost.

When I listen to this music by women who possibly inspired Joni, I think of a painting that preoccupied me in my years of women's studies classes and problematic boyfriends, when I was trying to conquer sadness by actively pursuing it. It's by the English academic painter John William Waterhouse, from 1888, and depicts the Lady of Shalott, the Rapunzel of the Arthurian legend cycle. The Lady is confined to a tower where she can only look at the outside world through a mirror; she makes tapestries showing what she sees. One day, she notices a beautiful boy in the glass— the Arthurian hippie hero Lancelot. Drawn by desire though she knows it will kill her, she escapes from the tower in a small boat. She has no oar. In the painting the Lady sits nestled in her tapestries, a look of pain and determination on her face. She is dropping the chain that ties the boat to its mooring. The river will take her toward Lancelot, but also toward death.

At twenty-three I bought a print of this painting in a San Francisco art museum gift store and tacked it above the entryway to the flat where I lived with my four roommates and two oven mice. Each day, arriving home from my record store–clerk shift, I'd gaze at it, thinking, *She is brave enough to row right into death. She's actually already dead.* I wanted to be that brave, but not in a suicidal sense. What I saw her risking was surrender to heartbreak's undertow. You know that desire will continually and repeatedly slay you, but you just have to keep going, the river pulls you with your memento mori gathered around you. And you drown, yet stay alive through it in some ceaseless version of the end.

There's something of this fatal loneliness in Mitchell's own rendition of "Both Sides Now," on her second album, *Clouds*. But like someone looking at her own life through a mirror, Mitchell also keeps her distance. She seems to be trying on sadness, playing the part. She's like a little girl who's seen her mother cry and is imagining what those tears feel like. Despite the grief she'd experienced, the loss of her daughter and the many miles she'd gone from her home, she kept her sadness light enough to carry. Unlike the Lady of Shalott, she would not let the drift of sadness sink her; she would find an oar, take control and speak. She would make *Blue*.

HER KIND OF BLUE

Accounts abound of the recording sessions at A&M Studios on North La Brea Avenue in January 1971, and of the months before, when Mitchell started sharing the songs that would eventually add up to her fourth album, *Blue*. Whole books have been written about her retreat and return, the break she took from the Canyon before she recorded the album, when she wandered from

Greek hippie communes to Paris hotel rooms collecting the sex
and laughs and loneliness from which the songs would come. It's
her legendary period. But the creative process is as mundane as it
is miraculous. It's dribs and drabs and then a rush and then back
to staring at the ceiling, wondering if the rush will come back.
No single personal or artistic choice changes everything. Instead,
little things turn struggle into flow.

Blue is about working through something—a heartache, people say. But it's just as much a document of the process of sharing
that heartache, an inquiry into personal storytelling itself. Until
Blue, Mitchell was getting there, but she hadn't wholly figured out
what she alone could say. That's because what each person alone
can say is, in its pure state, incommunicable. Stories are what get
made in conversation and left behind as their tellers keep living
and evolving.

Though pristine, Mitchell's songs here don't feel perfect. As
Sylvia Plath said, a woman perfected is marble-white, dead. Joni
felt unnervingly alive when she made *Blue*—the lyrics in its very
first song say so—and she wanted to share that feeling. She also
had this idea that she couldn't help but be honest. She turned her
convictions into the basis of her craft. Honesty, everyone knows,
is an impossible ideal, at best provisional. So *Blue* always feels
exquisitely unfinished. Its inexhaustible immediacy proves that no
artwork ever truly solidifies; it changes every time someone new
encounters it. That's its rare quality, also immanent in the brushstrokes of the Japanese *shan shui* master Sesshū and the voice of
Billie Holiday: Their makers' mark is inscribed so delicately in
these works, yet so unmistakably, that they feel immortal in a
unique way. They are monuments that breathe.

Every time I listen to *Blue*, I feel like I'm there with Mitchell and her small occasional band as they make their choices and

take their risks. Little things, turning struggle into flow: maybe the brush hitting Russ Kunkel's drum, or James Taylor idly strumming a chord progression he'd just laid down on the album he was making across the way. Sometimes, certainly, it was Joni alone, trying out a new way to hit a low note, or to sing the word "California." This is what people mean when they call *Blue* "personal." More than many pop albums made in its era of recording-studio innovation, it's very obviously made by people in a particular room, note by note. Mainly one person, who put her process up front in a way that no one had done, exactly, before.

Over decades, even as *Blue* continually restored itself and redrew its borders through others' encounters with it, the album's reputation solidified. It became a classic—the most beloved Joni album, the most written about, the one that encapsulates the essence of her talent. Or so people say, putting pins in it. Over time, enough people put enough pins in the same spot and the music that means so many different things to different people gained an official story.

This one:

The *Blue* album, there's hardly a dishonest note in the vocals. At that period of my life, I had no personal defenses. I felt like a cellophane wrapper on a pack of cigarettes. I felt like I had absolutely no secrets from the world and I couldn't pretend in my life to be strong. Or to be happy. But the advantage of it in the music was that there were no defenses there either.

Mitchell said this in 1979 to Cameron Crowe, a *Rolling Stone* writer she particularly trusted. As usual, her gift for choosing exactly the right image to put the listener deep inside a story blew everything else out of the room. It's virtually impossible to find

an account of *Blue* from the last fifty years that doesn't include
that quote. And of course. *Blue* has a particular effect on people;
it softens our defenses. So cellophane makes sense: there's pathos
in its thin plasticity. Zadie Smith, writing an essay to help her
understand why, though she mostly loved only soul music, *Blue*
got to her, made this point as well as anybody: "I can't listen to
Joni Mitchell in a room with other people, or on an iPod, walking
the streets. Too risky. I can never guarantee that I'm going to be
able to get through the song without being made transparent—to
anybody and everything, to the whole world. A mortifying sense
of porousness. Although it's comforting to learn that the feeling I have listening to these songs is the same feeling the artist
had while creating them." Then she reiterated the words about
cellophane.

Mitchell herself clung to the image, repeating it to Vic Garbarini in *Musician* magazine in 1983, and Amanda Ghost on the BBC
in 2007. Hell, she'd used the line "I felt like cellophane" as part of
her in-concert banter even earlier, in 1974, explaining a completely
different kind of song from a completely different album—the
acerbic "People's Parties" from the poppy *Court and Spark*. She
knew a great metaphor when she'd hit on one, even if it had first
occurred to her because she needed another cigarette, and looking
down, she simply reflected upon the wrapper that she held in her
hand.

Here's the problem with "cellophane" as the main explanation
for the greatness of *Blue*: it gets to an essence by downplaying the
long process that distilled it. Think about what it takes to make
any memorable work, not to mention a masterpiece. If you've ever
tried, you know the best part is that seeming magic when, for a
moment, what is on the inside of your brain overcomes the barrier
of your hesitation and actually emerges on the page or the canvas,

almost whole. When *you* become transparent! It really feels that way. Who can blame Mitchell for wanting to dwell on that experience? But as others have grabbed at the cellophane to understand the power of *Blue*, so many fingers on that one image transformed it into something other than a metaphor. It's become the immutable fact about the album's impact and staying power.

I want to make a different choice in trying to understand *Blue*. I want to honor the craft of it, the thinking, the substance. The solid work that made Mitchell able to communicate this idea she had about becoming transparent. I think that work started years before Mitchell wrote the songs that would become the album, back when she first heard Miles Davis play his horn.

I'll start with something else Mitchell said to an inquiring writer about *Blue*. She was talking to the jazz critic Michelle Mercer, whose thoughtful book on the *Blue* period was inspired by conversations the two had one summer at Mitchell's Sunshine Coast retreat. Mercer writes, "Joni also resents being reduced to a musical memoirist because it puts the art behind the feeling, when in her work feeling is a construct of art." And then she quotes Mitchell on the title track of *Blue*: "I think the first few notes on 'Blue' sound like a muted trumpet tone. Just the opening part, it's very influenced by Miles."

What if *Blue* were framed not as a direct outpouring of emotion but as a response to another artist's careful distillation of similar impulses and moods? As not only the apex of Mitchell's confessional period, but also the beginning of the jazz phase that continued throughout the 1970s? "On *Blue*," Mercer writes, "Mitchell began to integrate the music she loved into the music she made." Mitchell is never one to go for the obvious connection, and if anyone asked her, she'd probably say, *No, I prefer Miles's Sketches of Spain*. But the line from one *Blue* to another draws itself anyway. Put that trumpet mute in the place where cellophane resides, and the masterpiece makes sense in a different way.

Miles Davis recorded *Kind of Blue* in 1959, in two sessions, with a band that didn't live much beyond those weeks in the studio. Its members spanned the range of jazz expressiveness: earthy pleasure in the horn of Cannonball Adderley; austere introversion from the fingers of pianist Bill Evans; edgy experimentalism in the cascades of notes let forth by tenor sax player John Coltrane. Plus a rhythm section that didn't just hold the bottom; Paul Chambers and Jimmy Cobb could float.

Davis enlisted these men to do what Mitchell later did on *Blue*—make room for a clear idea. He was already one of the world's most popular jazz musicians and an embodiment, really *the* embodiment, of postwar cool. The critic Gary Giddins captured the trumpeter's allure when he wrote, long after that moment, "Miles was the first subject of a *Playboy* interview. Miles didn't need a last name. Miles was an idiom unto himself." Not unlike Joni, who became an idiom—the singer-songwriter mode, embodied—after releasing the album whose cover resembled the jazz sleeves she'd loved since high school, when a boy had placed them in her arms as she stood at her locker one afternoon back in Saskatoon.

Kind of Blue announced what it would accomplish—something Davis had been headed toward for a while—from the first two dozen bars of its first track, "So What," which used only two chords. This was "modal jazz," based around the use of different scales, or sets of notes connected to a fundamental frequency, instead of chord progressions, clusters of notes that are more highly structured. Explanations of modal music can get as complicated as you want, touching upon ancient Greek philosophy, classical impressionism, Middle Eastern drones and the twelve-bar blues. Or, keep it simple, the way jazz teachers explain modes to students: "few chords, lots of space."

The modal approach on *Kind of Blue* distinguished it from the sometimes frenetic, always multilayered sound of hard bop, which dominated jazz at the turn of the 1960s. Some thought it a step back. But within its less cluttered atmosphere, players could explore voicings that, to their own ears, often came closer to the core of thinking and feeling. Admirers of *Kind of Blue*—and they are legion; it's the bestselling jazz recording of all time—have described this accomplishment in different ways. Ashley Kahn, who wrote a book on the album, says the approaches of Davis and Evans, his main compositional collaborator in the sessions, were "all about pruning away excess and distilling emotion." Giddins describes it as a revolutionary blend of experimentation and accessibility—Zen or James Joyce, but for everyone. Darius Brubeck, jazz educator and the son of another cool jazz legend, Dave Brubeck, notes that "*Kind of Blue* was not so much a revolution as a realization, a supreme realization of supreme simplicity." Any of these assessments could apply to Mitchell's *Blue* as well. They illuminate the complex contours of crumpled cellophane.

When I spoke to him about the *Blue* sessions, James Taylor, who played on three songs on the album, made an interesting analogy. We were talking about Mitchell's choice to use a dulcimer instead of a guitar. "Like a Japanese calligrapher, or those traditional monochromatic paintings, the limitation is something to push against, to push off," he said. This struck me for one particular reason. In the liner notes Davis asked him to write for *Kind of Blue*, Evans (sort of the James Taylor of his time: tall, handsome, bookish, addiction-prone) began with this allusion:

"There is a Japanese visual art in which the artist is forced to be spontaneous. He must paint on a thin stretched parchment with a special brush and black water paint in such a way that an unnatural or interrupted stroke will destroy the line or break through the parchment. Erasures or changes are impossible. These artists must practice a particular discipline, that of allowing the idea to express itself in communication with their hands in such a direct way that deliberation cannot interfere."

What Davis gave his players, Evans explained, was the parchment and instructions for the practice: uninterrupted strokes. On *Blue*, Mitchell issued herself the same mandate. What is cellophane, anyway? A framing material that seems to not exist. In these songs she would create structures with enough space to communicate the experience of thoughts forming. As early as her first album, Mitchell (like Davis before her) was already using a polymodal compositional approach, moving from scale to scale within songs as a way of letting seemingly oppositional tones and moods arise within the same phrases. She made this fundamental difference in her music more evident on *Blue* by putting aside her folkie theatricality and her Beatlesque rock edge. Mitchell's approach on *Blue* seems simple to the careless ear; that's why its radicalism is often overlooked. It is not raw. Rawness is the worst state to be in when creating something, because an unthinking person quickly sinks into bad habits. Though she brought raw feelings into the room, the fundamental challenge this music made to rock and folk norms required her and her collaborators to be deeply mindful, to play with care and continually surprise themselves.

"I had a drum kit in the studio," Russ Kunkel told me about his time in Studio C, which resulted in credits for him on three *Blue* tracks. "But if I played it at all, I played it like a percussion instrument, not like a drum kit." He was following Mitchell's lead. Her dulcimer, with its four strings played in open tuning, was the folkie equivalent of Davis's muted trumpet—an instrument whose limits demanded inventiveness. Davis used mutes to create a restrained sound that resembled a torch singer's. On the dulcimer, Mitchell learned a "slap technique" from its maker, Joellen Lapidus: she would strum and dampen the strings almost at the same time, to create an effect that evoked a drum. This innovation led Kunkel into new places.

"For me it was heaven sent," he said of the dulcimer. "It has a choral structure, but it's also like playing a shaker at the same time, because it's percussive on the strings, right? So she became the click." Mitchell was the heartbeat he could follow and parry with. "I would have to be mindful to stay out of the same frequency range she was in, so I would pick lower instruments or I would play little things on the floor toms or I would play with my hands, or I'd use a percussion instrument."

Taylor found the same freedom working with her, adding his guitar parts to "California," "Carey," "All I Want" and "A Case of You." "I said it probably too many times that Joni is like, you tap the tree, and you know, it's like maple syrup," he told me. "This stuff, this nectar comes out of the most unusual places."

Sweet Baby James. He was the one who could be so hard to handle. Younger than her, and dangerous in a few ways: he liked drugs too much, didn't like L.A. enough and kept his eye out for other women all the time. But in the one way that really mattered to Mitchell—musically—none of her other early lovers suited her more perfectly than Taylor. He, too, played the guitar in a way all his own, running counterpoints across the bass strings, getting away from standard chords. And also like Mitchell, he was writing songs that felt like thoughts just rolling out, but which were as carefully composed and deeply connected to myth and legend as the blues songs that ran through his head the way jazz ran through hers.

Old love, new love. Always bringing problems. The whole cellophane thing—the vulnerability, the raw electric nerve connecting Joni's soul to those songs—is supposedly rooted in all this romantic trauma, along with the pressures of new stardom and the aftereffects of one bad acid trip. Many of the album's most ardent fans feel that the sadness messy love generates is *Blue*'s main point. However . . . as Kunkel said to me: "She had broken up with Graham, she had already started seeing James. Who wouldn't be happy?" We both laughed. In 1970 Taylor was even more highly certified as a dreamboat than Nash, and better for Mitchell in other ways. He didn't want to get married, and neither did Joni; that's why she'd left Nash in the first place. And they harmonized perfectly together. When they were inside the songs, his sense of time and hers perfectly matched.

PEOPLE NOTICED HOW WELL PAIRED THEY WERE. MITCHELL AND TAYLOR SANG BACK-ground harmonies on the version of "Will You Love Me Tomorrow" that Carole King included on *Tapestry*, which she was recording down the hall from them during the *Blue* sessions. She writes in her memoir, "Though James and Joni are singing on separate mics, their closeness is almost a physical presence." One profile of Taylor from around the same time described them together on the set of the movie *Two-Lane Blacktop*, which features Taylor in a starring role. "In Tucumcari, Joni knitted the vest James now wears constantly and played her guitar in a field of tall grass near the set. Technicians heard strains of her soft guitar music when the wind was blowing toward them." Like probably every interviewer before me, I asked Taylor about that vest, transformed into a sweater in the last verse of the first song on *Blue*, "All I Want." He turned the familiar question into a chance to praise his long-ago lover's ingenuity. "If she'd had steel wool she could have knitted me a car," he said with a grin.

So maybe Joni and James were good when she made *Blue*. Or maybe they weren't. Maybe he was using heroin. Maybe he wasn't. According to the gossip that would become historical record, Taylor in his twenties was one of those icy-hot guys, like Miles, in fact, who always needed to make sure that he could get another woman if need be; like Bill Evans, he was also an off-again, mostly on-again junkie. When they were making *Blue*, the emotional shutdown that is addiction's prime cause and most devastating side effect had already started pulling James and Joni apart. She'd write a great song about it, "Cold Blue Steel and Sweet Fire," and put it on her next album, *For the Roses*, made when their romance was definitely no more.

But if you are a lover of *Blue*, I want you to do something right now. Forget all that. Stop fantasizing about these two gorgeous avatars of the sexual revolution. Resist the rush you get imagining Joni's pain. Where songs start is not that important. When Evans wrote "Peace Piece," which became the launching point for *Kind of Blue*'s final track, "Flamenco Sketches," he was spiraling into a drug dependency that would grip him for the rest of his life. He was exhausted. But even though jazz lovers know that, few talk about "Peace Piece" in terms of Evans's personal struggle, his haunted head as he sat up all night barely moving his fingers across the song's two chords. On the contrary, "Peace Piece" is held up as a balm whose ingredients are spiritual serenity and intellectual rigor. The key to what Evans created, as we now hear it, is not his pain but his engagement with the process of sitting with that pain until it offered self-awareness. Discipline even in the midst of crisis allowed for the miracle of "Peace Piece." Why not acknowledge that the same is true of *Blue*?

It's been difficult for some reason. Ideology, I guess. Mitchell herself has said that she bled these songs onto the pages, and that's what everyone has chosen to remember. The master herself has come to think of *Blue* primarily as a wound. That's just how people stuck on the gender binary talk about creativity. Women bleed. Men forge through. But in fact, art of this caliber is always made through both the cut and the suture.

Back to James and Joni for a moment: what shows through on *Blue* is what they learned from each other as players. Taylor loved the acoustic blues he'd heard as a kid in North Carolina, and was a jazz fan, though he was more into the swinging eclecticism of Ray Charles than post-bop. He admired Miles Davis, and his way of leaving space in his phrasing—that indeterminate drawl—recalls the dropped time (some have called it "junkie time") of *Kind of Blue*. Then there were his guitar innovations. Though he wasn't devoted to open tunings the way Mitchell was, he'd developed a fingerpicking style that allowed him to sustain notes and smoothly move from chord to chord, a technique inspired by what he'd learned on the instruments he picked up as a child, the cello and the piano.

That Mitchell was involved with Taylor at the time of *Blue* makes a difference, but not because of their kisses or their quarrels or their mutual slights. The crucial turn they made together was a musical one. As rock and even folk was growing more ornate, these two went where Miles and his band had gone a decade earlier, toward supreme simplicity. Neither stayed there. *Blue* was a kind of oasis where they could linger in its light.

The most famous description of *Kind of Blue* came from the English critic Kenneth Tynan's nine-year-old daughter. One night Tynan was listening to the album in his study and, walking past, she identified the artist. "How do you know?" her father asked.

"Because he sounds like a little boy who's been locked out and is trying to get in."

This story resonates in good and bad ways. It plays into some tenacious stereotypes of the Black musical genius as childlike, and gently banishes jazz to culture's unlit backyard. Yet the child's observation does somehow describe both the act of creation that *Kind of Blue* set in vinyl and one common experience of spending time with it. Denied nearly any guidance from their leader—no charts, no rehearsals—Davis's band members each found themselves on the outside of their own preconceptions and used whatever ingenuity and strengths they could muster to get back in. But no one forced anything. Instead, each picked the lock in his own way. Spending time with the album, even sixty-plus years after its release, the fan does the same. Putting aside old habits and associations, the listener reenters the process of listening.

Blue offers a similar reentry: into the process of love. Mitchell's lyrics would seem, on the surface, to be the most conventional element in *Blue*. They chase romance down vivid but not unfamiliar paths, from the lonely road to the warm bedroom to the riverbank and the bar. Plenty of bards have been here before. What makes *Blue*'s poetry distinctive is the unfolding, or to use a word Joni does in "All I Want," the unraveling. These lines, like the improvisations in a jazz quintet, reject resolution. They run on, or end abruptly; they slip from heavy metaphor to plain talk. The musicologist David Ake has described Bill Evans's piano playing as a long trail of themes and variations, each line seeming to generate itself out of the previous one. Mitchell's lyrics on *Blue* do something similar. Every song turns around at some point and contradicts itself. A jaunty melody masks the bitter taste of grief; a hopeful declaration ricochets into self-doubt. The lyrics were not improvised, but as in a great jazz run, they expose the erratic essence of emotional experience and honor the heroism inherent in the simple human act of making sense of oneself.

She started with "All I Want," a run-on sentence that takes her right into the arms of paradox: *I hate you some, I hate you some, I love you some, I love you when I forget about me*. She never genuinely forgets herself, though. She's always adding up the memories that haunt her, the ones she enjoys, the ones she suppresses, observing herself as she builds these revelations and alibis. There's "My Old Man," for Graham, a little bitter at the core. There's "A Case of You" for her long-gone older lover, Leonard Cohen, but also possibly for Graham and, I think, for James, a song about stamina: *I could drink a case of you, darlin'*, she brags, trumpeting a ridiculous high note, *and still be on my feet*. There's "Little Green," for her daughter Kelly Dale—such an obvious confession, and no one got its meaning at the time. There's "Carey," for Raditz, enjoyed and left behind in Greece. You can hear Mitchell happily handing off their story to him.

And then the title track, for James. But also for Miles, maybe. *Here is a shell for you*—I've always considered that line embarrassingly faux-naïf. But what if it's an instruction for the listener? Here is a frame, fill it in with your own colors. *Inside you'll hear a sigh, a foggy lullaby*. That's a jazz lyric. Juliette Gréco, Miles Davis's lover during an idyll he spent in Europe as a young man, described him this way: "There was such an unusual harmony between the man, the instrument and the sound—it was pretty shattering." *Blue* is Mitchell exploring the same harmony, between her psyche, her voice and her songs. The listener finds her own space within this flux, her own story. The one that echoes later.

It's interesting to think about why people decide some works of art can change their lives. What do we ask of those who make them? From some, authority: the ability to command a room, or a genre, to bend it to their will. On the bandstand, Miles Davis would often turn away from the audience, to focus on the band— but fans embraced this aloof stance as a sign he was leading them into the future. From others, sacrifice. Fifty years on, can we see Mitchell's downcast eyes on the cover of *Blue*, her turn inward, as a sign not merely of a woman's sadness, but of self-possession. With *Blue*, Mitchell fully realized her authority; she rewrote the stories of her own life, not only in words, but by finding music that would make each word sound differently. That's why, every time a listener turns to *Blue*, the path of desire and disappointment and slowly accruing wisdom the songs lay out appears in slightly different form. The songs remain in that present tense in which they were created. Maybe it's impossible to know what happened when Joni Mitchell made *Blue* because every time the record plays, it's still happening.

5

freedom through fusion

After *Blue*, Joni was wrung out. The meticulous Japanese brush techniques she'd employed on it exhausted her; they left her with a cramp in her psyche. She started to think about using other muscles. In late 1971, she took a break. Traveled a bit, again; went to Hawaii. Then she headed to the Sunshine Coast north of Vancouver to build her rustic house and, as she told journalist Penny Valentine, "lead a kind of 'Heidi' existence, you know, with goats and an orchard."

She swam in Halfmoon Bay, fell asleep listening to the creatures outside her door, and eventually started writing more songs.

These new ones echoed the *Blue* material in many ways—semi-autobiographical, still pretty sad. Many were about James Taylor, now fully her ex and heading toward a new chapter with another woman, Carly Simon, also a singer-songwriter telling truths about gendered love's complexities. Joni wrote "Lesson in Survival" across the miles to him, and "Cold Blue Steel and Sweet Fire," about the drugs that had come between them. On "See You Sometime," she fondly recalled his signature suspenders. Taylor was set to marry Simon on November 3, 1972, just before the release of the album containing those songs, *For the Roses*. Joni was processing such things. Her bookshelves in British Columbia held a row of self-help manuals, and she spent time learning a newish avocation: photography. In her writing she continued to expose herself, but then turned her lens outward, remaining in the frame but placing herself in larger contexts. Inventing the selfie, you might say. This trick altered her sense of being in ways she'd already started exploring in playful songs like "Carey." She increasingly positioned herself as a character in scenes she built with poetic attention to detail, the way the filmmakers who were also her peers, like Robert Altman or Martin Scorsese, were doing in their revolutionary work. And like those auteurs, she needed a full cast of collaborators—ones who weren't necessarily vying for their own spotlights and were willing to support her in populating these wider milieus.

The hippie dream had atomized, breaking down into more personal quests. Some countercultural types fled to rural outposts as Joni herself had, while others pursued identity-driven politics under the banners of women's liberation, gay pride and Black power. Meanwhile, aspirations that had once seemed utopian became fodder for new forms of consumerism. Suburban spouse-swapping, *Joy of Sex*–style manuals and art-house porn flicks domesticated the ideal of free love. Cocaine—the productivity drug—gained a foothold over psychedelics as the hedonist's indulgence of choice. For businessmen like Joni's mentors David Geffen and Elliot Roberts, who brought her to their newly founded Asylum Records, the art of the deal kept getting higher-stakes, making musicians like her into paper millionaires. These developments felt risky for a woman whose ideal audience remained "thirty or forty people" in a smoky club. She started looking around for scenes that still seemed to value that quality of intimacy. At the same time, she enjoyed her lifestyle, her two houses, her swimming pool. She also thought it might be cool if she could have a real Top 40 moment.

After not too long up north, she'd had enough rest and restoration. Back in L.A., she crashed at Geffen's place and momentarily reunited with the boys, strictly for fun—and maybe a little coin. Geffen had been goading her for a hit single, and one night she huddled with Nash, Crosby and Young with the intent of giving him one. She only half liked the result, but it did put her on the charts. As importantly, the song was a signpost for her audience as she headed beyond her home base of folk and into a new quarter populated by sounds she'd always loved but, until now, hadn't given herself full permission to claim: jazz.

Appearing in the middle of side two of *For the Roses*, "You Turn Me On, I'm a Radio" calls itself a country song—*I'm a little bit corny*, Joni sings in the chorus, referring to that Nashville sound—and maybe it sounded that way when she and the boys were working it out. She even recorded a loping demo version with Young and a couple of the guys who played on his 1972 country classic, *Harvest*. But aside from Nash on harmonica, the band heard on the hit single wasn't made up of her old friends, or Nashville cats, or even country rockers. Stars of the Los Angeles recording session scene, Joni's collaborators were eclectic by necessity and expert in combining elements purists might prefer were kept apart. Joni herself provided strums and a multitracked vocal chorus that uncannily replicates a pedal steel guitar. Russ Kunkel maintained a gentle drumbeat. Beneath that and dancing around Nash's harmonica parts was jazzman Wilton Felder's bass, adding just the tiniest bit of grease, and Motown favorite Bobbye Hall's bubbling and sassy percussion, answering Joni's vocals the way Aretha Franklin's sisters would reply to her soul shouts.

With this ensemble, Mitchell created a prime example of a style becoming common in myriad musical realms in the 1970s. Rooted in jazz, it broke down distinctions between musical genres—and, at the same time, found commonalities among them. This method applied the countercultural principle of mind expansion to musical practice, offering new routes to freedom that came from mixing elements previously kept stringently separate. Some called it fusion. Others despised that term, but it captures what Mitchell was up to: rearranging her brain, opening up her circles, carrying her suitcase into new haunts, ready to learn. And ready to do so in the company of others as she led her band.

JAZZ IS

It's common for Joni chroniclers to call the phase she eased into after *For the Roses* her jazz era. I've done that myself. But even Mitchell's biggest fans—even her jazz collaborators—still can't totally agree whether her 1970s music actually fits within the art form's lineage. She herself maintains that most of the records she's released since 1972 do not, entirely. Joni turned to jazz, she's often said, because the Laurel Canyon—connected masters who'd played on her earlier albums couldn't keep up with her latest experiments. But she was dipping in, not wholly converting. Pretty typical is a remark she made to critic Robert Hilburn in 2008: "Some people thought I was trying to do jazz and not quite getting it, but I wasn't. The only thing I have in common with jazz is sometimes experimental rhythms, and these wide harmonies that are outside the rules of jazz."

To which I say: Joni, for once you've underestimated yourself. In her mind, jazz was charts, rules, a certain education in the standard compositions and techniques. She couldn't claim such expertise. I know that feeling well. As the kind of music writer who craves variety, I've sometimes taken on jazz assignments, but I've never felt fully confident doing so. Here was a point in my Joni chase where I felt like she turned around and looked at me for a minute, saying, *Yeah, I totally know where you're coming from*. I was stuck in the jazz conundrum that Joni eventually solved for herself by simply refusing to dwell in it, as she's so often done with externally imposed definitions and limitations. The conundrum is this: jazz is both the freest form of popular music and the one most heavily policed. It's always belonged to both brothels and concert halls, been celebrated as high art and dismissed as rowdy entertainment, served as a conduit for Black Americans to infiltrate the cultural mainstream and a separate sphere where they could nurture their own language and challenge the white exploiters who wanted to profit from it. As it developed, it also became the provenance of white experts who earned their rights through grueling apprenticeship, attending the best schools, poring over other players' recordings, memorizing their fingerings and breath patterns until their expertise became lethal. Needless to say, most of these jazz sages have been male. Women approaching the repertoire have had to prove themselves with extra mettle, and one who didn't even know how to read charts—like Joni, like me—why should she even try?

The question of who knows enough to talk about jazz is also tied tight to another one—who controls jazz, who owns it—and that's a political matter as well as a musicological one. In the fusion era, controversies ignited as white rockers adopted elements of the music to great commercial success. Were they colonizers? I knew that my own whiteness meant that I'd have to take care even approaching the question of whether Mitchell counts as a jazz musician, or if fusion, where she would belong if she did, is too compromised to count as jazz. I quickly realized that her occasional rejection of the genre as a home base wasn't just another instance of her resisting categorization. It reflected her own doubts about whether she ever belonged in this particular club.

I began to think that Mitchell might have felt as confused as I did about how a nonexpert could fit within jazz, even on its edges. As she moved away from her old modes of musical practice, she started to expand her own sense of self, too, identifying with Black men, especially, in ways that eventually became troubling. But she also kept her gimlet eye cast on the divisions she couldn't breach. From *For the Roses* onward, she became preoccupied with troubled borderlines, where unexpected alliances formed and people could transform themselves, but where custom and the law might clamp down at any moment, reasserting old divisions. She immersed herself within the supposedly liberated social milieus of 1970s Hollywood and Manhattan and found hypocrites and lost people among the sophisticates and gurus. She became fascinated with the postcolonial collisions between white elites and the Black, brown and Indigenous people they romanticized and exploited, and considered—clumsily, at times—her own role in these exchanges. Aware of her own precarity on the margin between youthful beauty and funky middle age, she considered her choice to remain unsettled as a single woman and a traveler unwilling, unable, to settle down. The fusion sounds she created with her collaborators continually complicated the stories she wanted to tell within music that refused to fit any easy definitions.

The musicologist Kevin Fellezs borrows a phrase from literary theorist Isobel Armstrong, "the broken middle," to describe how fusion always remains within a "precarious but potentially productive moment of becoming"—not quite jazz, not quite rock, not quite funk, not able to elude any of these categories and become something totally new. I love this metaphor. It applies not only to music but to everything within 1970s culture that surrounded and fed the era's jazz conundrum: the movement of women, queer people and people of color from the margins of progressive discourse to their own definitions of the center; the class tensions defining a time when the economy boomed but felt alarmingly unstable; the dissolution of old mores and social anchors with no clear new model for success. In the song "Don Juan's Reckless Daughter," Joni names this agitation: "restless multiplicity." The broken middle is what she's talking about—a time and place when every possibility leads to conflict and every conflict gives birth to a different future.

It's easy to make a mess when you're trying new things. Mitchell did it when she went so far as to assume a Black male persona whom she called Art Nouveau when she was making *Don Juan's Reckless Daughter*—the most shocking move in her long career, and one for which she's never apologized. (More on this later!) I can't ignore the economic and political factors that allowed white artists in the 1970s to sell millions of albums and play to thousands of fans while Black risk-takers often labored in small clubs for fifty dollars a night. In most other ways, though, I admire her audaciousness, as did her Black collaborators and fans. She was shaking up her formulas. The late great music writer Greg Tate, whose dedication to Black innovation was matched by his disdain for any outwardly imposed limitations, later concocted one that suits what she was pouring into the test tube. "As in quantum physics, there is a wave/particle paradox evident in jazz," he wrote in 2002. The conservative view that jazz means harmonic improvisation applied to a narrow repertoire is one side of the paradox; the other way to look at jazz, Tate wrote, is looser. He calls it "the exploration of sound, timbre, technology and expressive musical effects." Tate's definition of jazz is generous but musically exacting, his embrace of fusion delighting in multiplicity. By the way, he was a huge Joni Mitchell fan. I kept his words in mind as I followed Joni through the 1970s, locating her music in that broken middle where more than one definition always fits.

FUSION'S BIG BANG

Jazz fusion's origins are enigmatic. Depending on how wide you make that frame, it could have originated in 1963, when the Black guitarist Wes Montgomery made an album with strings and his producer Orrin Keepnews slapped the title *Fusion!* on it. Or in 1965, when the white guitarist Larry Coryell formed a band called the Free Spirits to imagine "what it would be like if John Coltrane met George Harrison." Maybe 1966 was the year, and San Francisco the place—Sly Stone put together his big band there, supplementing its basic funk lineup with Cynthia Robinson's trumpet and jazz-trained Jerry Martini's saxophone. Or maybe it started the way Joni heard it, inside a corny country song, when the vibraphonist Gary Burton integrated rural and urban elements on his groundbreaking *Duster*. That same year, 1967, the singer Flora Purim and percussionist Airto Moreira left Rio for New York, bringing their own recombinations, samba rhythms meeting the wilder beats of rural Brazil. Fusion was happening everywhere before the name became widespread.

Joni's path crossed those of these pioneers many times as she traveled from the coffeehouse to the Sunset Strip. Montgomery suffered a fatal heart attack in 1968, but won a posthumous Grammy for jazz instrumental album that year, the same one her *Clouds* won in the Folk category. The Free Spirits played on the Greenwich Village strip where Joni had gained an audience in the mid-1960s, and she shared a bill with Sly and the Family Stone at the Isle of Wight in 1970. In 1967, Joni's pal from the Village Al Kooper formed Blood, Sweat & Tears, a horn-powered band that would soon open up the Top 40 to the poppier side of fusion. Two of her friends on the singer-songwriter circuit, Laura Nyro and Tim Hardin, were also bringing jazz elements into their far-reaching songs. Hardin was even responsible for another early jazz fusion band forming, enlisting the flute player Jeremy Steig to form the Satyrs to back him up in 1966.

Wanting to know what it felt like to be in this whirlwind, I tracked down the trumpeter Randy Brecker, who played in Blood, Sweat & Tears with Kooper, and asked him about what life was like in the Village then. "I remember Richie Havens, Warren [Bernhardt] was playing with him," he said, mentioning the folk-blues pioneer who helped inspire Joni to try open tunings and the jazz pianist who'd go on to form the fusion group Steps Ahead. "Tim Hardin was on the scene. The Café Au Go Go had a lot of singers and also instrumental groups like the Electric Flag and Blood, Sweat & Tears and Jimi Hendrix's drummer, Buddy Miles. Across the street were the folkie clubs. It was all on the same block." The scene Becker describes was multigenre and multiracial, but jazz fusion gets a bad rap in part because the bands who had its biggest pop hits, like Blood, Sweat & Tears with "Spinning Wheel," were overwhelmingly white. The jazz band Joni enlisted for her *For the Roses* follow-up and first full fusion effort, *Court and Spark*, was mostly white, too, though Felder and the keyboardist Joe Sample played on the album. Yet fusion did create a space for interracial bands like Dreams (Brecker was a member) and welcomed an international array of players, especially from Brazil and other points south. The album that many consider fusion's big bang represents the full integrative potential of the style. It's a Joni favorite, a high point in the career of one of her heroes, Miles Davis—*Bitches Brew*.

Most historical accounts of jazz fusion call this riveting, electric, studio-manipulated masterpiece its center, if not its origin point. It sold five hundred thousand copies in 1970, its first year of release, bringing jazz back into the mainstream in a different way than Wes Montgomery had with his strings-laden, easy-flowing fusion experiments. The *Bitches Brew* band—well, sort of a band, since Miles conducted the album sessions as a highly stressful game of round robin, keeping tape rolling as he'd usher players in and out of the studio—featured many of the style's then and future stars, including three—the saxophonist Wayne Shorter and the percussionists Don Alias and Airto Moreira—who'd later become key in growing Mitchell's sound. The leaders of major fusion bands Weather Report and Return to Forever, keyboardists Joe Zawinul and Chick Corea, also appear on *Bitches Brew*, as do the guitarist John McLaughlin and the drummer Billy Cobham, whose Mahavishnu Orchestra influenced multiple generations of jam-band weirdos. Davis designed the project this way, a maximalist outing that would yield maximum results. He further ensured the album's revolutionary impact through innovative editing techniques and sound effects that turned the studio into an instrument: something rock bands like the Beatles and the Beach Boys had done, but Davis fully claimed these innovations for jazz, producing a double disc that sounded like it had been recorded live—maybe on Mars.

Especially in the latter half of the 1970s, the *Bitches Brew* effect shows up clearly on Mitchell's albums—on extended tracks like "Paprika Plains," through the pioneering sampling on "The Jungle Line," in the dreamlike interweaving of elements on *Mingus*. As a Miles stan, she'd always happily acknowledge his influence. But just as her story has overshadowed many smaller, worthy ones within the singer-songwriter lineage, the titanic *Bitches Brew* has come to define fusion to the exclusion of others. I wish I could stay in fusion's wide open field forever, sharing stories of the supreme showman Charles Lloyd, a saxophonist who brought flower-child aesthetics to the genre; of Howard University professor and trumpeter Donald Byrd, who traced rhythm's journey from West Africa to Motown on the albums that transformed him from respected bebopper to renegade; of drum prodigy Tony Williams, whose work in his own band, Lifetime, and on Miles Davis's *Nefertiti*, grounded jazz fusion in rock and roll flash and insane rhythmic complexity. But the Joni road leads this history back to Los Angeles before jumping to New York, and to the studios where fusion happened fairly naturally, in the name of a paying gig.

SESSION MEN

Mitchell was a studio rat from the first time David Crosby brought her to Sunset Sound in 1968 and had her sing into the guts of a grand piano to create an ethereal vibe (that experiment unfortunately

failed, and the album's a little wan because of it). She became her
own producer after that, in partnership with the engineer Henry
Lewy. They played around together, starting to multitrack her
voice and bring in guest jazz soloists as early as *Ladies of the Canyon*. After the almost artificially spare sound of *Blue*, she wanted
to try more of that: she wanted new effects, experiments, fresh
brains to pick.

The best-known story about her and jazz fusion has her in
conversation with Russ Kunkel, one of the few session guys she let
into the *Blue* sessions. With remarkable honesty, he told her that
her newer songs were too thorny for him, and that she needed to
build a band of improvisers who could follow her weird tunings
and time signatures. Soon after, she went to see Tom Scott's L.A.
Express at the Baked Potato on Cahuenga Boulevard, where all
the hottest session players hung out. She liked what she heard, and
a collaboration ensued.

As usual with Joni legends, this one is in reality a little bit
more complicated. In fact, Scott had appeared solo, playing
reeds, on *For the Roses*, as part of an expanded lineup of collaborators including Muscle Shoals, Alabama guitarist Wayne
Perkins; violinist and Electric Flag cofounder Bobby Notkoff;
and Motown percussionist Hall. Before that, she'd enlisted the
proto–New Age flute player Paul Horn and veteran percussionist
Milt Holland for *Ladies of the Canyon*. So Joni's jazz period actually began years before she made it official with the L.A. Express.
And she was hardly alone in her tentative genre-jumping. Holland recorded with the Rolling Stones, the Monkees and Captain
Beefheart; Perkins appears on Bob Marley and the Wailers' 1973
reggae classic *Catch a Fire*. Horn toured as a duo with folk faerie
Donovan; Hall was ubiquitous, a tween prodigy in Detroit who'd
become everyone's favorite, appearing on classics by Janis Joplin,

Stevie Wonder, Carole King, Bill Withers, Marvin Gaye, the list goes on. In both Hollywood and New York at the turn of the 1970s, this is how the session scene worked. Everybody went jazz because the finest players were pragmatically open-minded, many of them jazz expats looking to expand their horizons and make some extra cash.

The turn Mitchell made didn't reorient her toward jazz as a sound or lineage, exactly, but toward jazz*men* (almost entirely men, with Hall, who wouldn't have called herself a jazz musician anyway, a rare exception). She needed to change the dynamics within her creative process and become a true collaborator, not dictating her fellow players' moves but trusting their skills and instincts as she led more instinctively. She could do that with her boys, but they were trying to do the same thing on their own albums and brought too much baggage into the room. New matches made through the arranged-marriage system of the studio could allow her to start anew.

The L.A. Express connection was unique in one important way—this was a regular band whose members, though all session stars themselves, had a vibe together and could take it on the road. Scott, their leader, also brought in incredible arranging skills. A prodigy whose dad had written scores for film and television, Scott made an early fusion LP at nineteen, experimenting with electric sitar and covering the Beatles. He was twenty-two when he recorded his take on "Woodstock," and that's how Joni found him. He didn't even know her music then; Quincy Jones, the legendary producer, another important fusion originator, was the first to play the song for him. "I was floored," Scott said in a 1974 interview. "Especially with her voice. So I did the tune using a recorder, kind of imitating Joni's voice. She heard the track and asked me if I'd like to play on her new album, which at the time was *For the Roses*. A few nights later we went to the studio and struck up a very rewarding relationship."

"It was easy and a fun way to make a living," said Randy Brecker, describing his early-1970s New York life supplementing twenty-dollar jazz gigs with big paychecks from Blood, Sweat & Tears and session work. "That's how the jazz scene could thrive, because guys weren't depending on it, you know? They were all studio cats. You'd go to record a jingle, and Thad Jones would be sitting next to Mel Lewis on drums or Snooky Young or Ron Carter or Herbie Hancock," he continued, rattling off a list of jazz greats. "They were all doing sessions."

Session work also allowed a curious player like Brecker to leapfrog from genre to genre. "There was a true potpourri of musicians mixing together, so you couldn't help but be influenced by all this stuff," he recalled. "One day you'd be playing for Johnny Cash, and the next day, you'd be playing for Eddie Palmieri." Fusion's man of all trades, Brecker laid down tracks with James Taylor, Todd Rundgren, Carly Simon, Lou Reed, Bette Midler, Ringo Starr, Laura Nyro, Average White Band, Elton John and many other stars while maintaining his own jazz career. He played the indelible solo on Bruce Springsteen's "Meeting Across the River" and was there when Parliament recorded *Mothership Connection* and Steely Dan made *Gaucho*. He toured with the bass god Jaco Pastorius and was in Larry Coryell's band Eleventh House. He never played with Joni, but his sibling and Brecker Brothers bandmate Michael did, and they were all pals who hung out after midnight.

Opening their ears, singer-songwriters and bandleaders challenged themselves conceptually, too. In 1973, for example, Carole King released the now-overlooked song suite *Fantasy*, in which she imagined an identity-fluid utopia. *In fantasy*, she sang, *I can be*

Black or white, woman or man. The album is dotted with dramatic monologues through which King inhabits Puerto Rican, Black, and Mexican characters fighting for a more harmonious America. It was a flop, sadly. "An unintentional travesty," Stephen Holden wrote in *Rolling Stone.* More successful were the diverse artists who didn't try to shift race or gender, but still challenged older ideas of what a folk troubadour or a rock provocateur could be. Was Phoebe Snow a cabaret singer, a jazz chanteuse or a folk queen? Hits like her "Poetry Man" cast her in all of those roles at once. Same with Roberta Flack, whose early albums eased their classically trained maker from gospel stomps to jazz standards to freedom songs like "Angelitos Negros," sung in Spanish. These are just two examples of the fruitful restlessness of the time.

Flack perfected the calm, powerful sound that made her a superstar, in part, by working with the jazz bassist Ron Carter, who appears on three of her key albums. Such strong ongoing relationships stand out amidst all the creative spit-swapping of the recording-session scene. Joni, who entered this period already knowing herself to be a serial monogamist in art as well as in life, excelled at forging meaningful connections. Mixing work and pleasure again, she hooked up with the L.A. Express drummer John Guerin, a love match that meant a lot artistically as he became her guide to the scene and its key players. A few years later, the percussionist Don Alias would occupy that dual role in her life. As important were her musical soul mates, especially Wayne Shorter, the brilliantly idiosyncratic saxophonist who'd played on one of her favorite Miles discs, *Nefertiti*, and who would end up on ten of her albums, and the bass innovator Jaco Pastorius, whose tone and daring thrillingly synced with hers. These were not just session men. They were friends and catalysts. Touring with Pastorius and a band that also included the guitar maverick

Pat Metheny in 1979, Joni solidified the new style and preserved it on *Shadows and Light,* one of the finest live albums of the era. Those dates and an earlier round with the L.A. Express helped her find new ways to perform as well as record.

As Guerin and Shorter did later, Scott introduced Mitchell to people who'd bring her experiments into focus. One was Larry Carlton, whose reverb-heavy guitar parts on "Help Me" from *Court and Spark* helped make the song a big, sexy hit. Carlton was a top-shelf studio rover, playing on some of the 1970s' most enduring favorites—most famously, Steely Dan's "Kid Charlemagne," singled out on poll after poll as one of the greatest guitar solos of all time—while maintaining a vital solo recording career. Seeking someone who could describe a West Coast session man's daily life, I sought him out and got him on the phone.

Like Scott, Carlton began his career as a teenager, playing in clubs near his home of Torrance, California, and eventually securing a gig touring with the Black vocal group The 5th Dimension. Once he entered the realm of sessions, the money started rolling in. "I bought a home right off of Cahuenga Boulevard," he said. "Out of my kitchen I could see Universal City. I moved there because I got so busy in the studios that I wanted to be close. I could be down to Capitol Records or other studios in like 10 or 12 minutes. I got married when I was 22. So as far as hanging out, I wasn't. I was a homebody between sessions, I'd go home for dinner, as opposed to going out to a restaurant with the guys."

As a teenager he'd been recruited to join the Crusaders, an all-Black band that had relocated from Houston and dropped the word "Jazz" from its name to be able to cross into R & B and pop. That group's keyboardist, Joe Sample, also played in the L.A. Express. That's how Carlton met Mitchell. By that time he'd begun to develop his own sound, and that's what he brought to the *Court and Spark* sessions.

"In the beginning, I didn't have an identifiable sound," he said. "Every session I went to, I was just the guitar player. But after the Crusaders' first record was so successful, my volume-heavy pedal style and the way I bent the notes became something that nobody else was doing. After that, when I would go to a session, they wanted me to play like me." That's what Mitchell wanted. Carlton recalls those early Joni sessions as experiments, for her and for him; he was honing the sound that would become his trademark as she figured out how to sing in the broken middle of jazz.

Mitchell loved the effect Carlton produced by controlling the volume of his guitar lines using a Sho-Bud volume pedal. For her, it resembled the arc of a dolphin leaping within the ocean's waves. In fact, Carlton said, she was more attached to it than he was by the end of their time working together. "I don't remember which Joni album it was. After *Hejira*," he said. [He played on all of her studio albums from this period except *Mingus*.] She brought me in to do some overdubs. By then the volume pedal thing had kind of run its course for me. And Joni asked me, 'Can you give me some of those swells and stuff?' I remember going, 'Well, I haven't done that in a long time. But sure, I will.' I'd moved on stylistically in my head to something new or something different. But that's what she wanted to bring out of me, you know?"

It's easy to understand why Joni wanted him to repeat himself. Carlton's arcing guitar lines grace one of most sublime tracks from 1976's *Hejira*, the heaven-bound "Amelia." The lyrics of that song are about getting lost in the air, and that's exactly what Carlton's guitar sounds like, jumping and curving. It's a perfect example of a tuned-in, adept jazzman tuning in to exactly what a singer-songwriter needs to make her lyrics go beyond the confines of storytelling into poetry, the realm of metaphor. Carlton recognizes that synergy. It's all a session man could ask for.

At the end of our conversation, I asked him if he played Mitchell's songs in his solo shows; I knew he frequently performed a Steely Dan set. He said he didn't, expressing just a touch of the elitism I'd expect from a jazz snob, not one of fusion's greatest session men. But in this version of the story, it's Joni, not jazz, that stands apart. "Joni's lyrics are so important," he said. "I'm just afraid at this point to have a flute or something play the melody so I can play my background parts, you know? She's a great artist, you know. I don't want her songs to sound like a lounge band."

A BLACK THING

You know who else didn't want to step anywhere near the territory of "lounge band," that ultimate insult to jazz players, the blandification of the sacred practice? Joni Mitchell. She had a different goal in mind, and stated it to the boys and the session men, to her right hand and confidante Henry Lewy, to the rock press and the suits at her record label. They smiled, nodded, didn't really listen. What Joni wanted was to have some of what Stevie Wonder was having. Or Marvin Gaye. She longed to become a soul man. Or maybe a soul woman, though she never mentioned Roberta Flack or Minnie Riperton, whom she could have considered peers as they moved in their own lanes through the broken middle, making fusion music without earning that name from the jazzbos.

The jazz establishment has only rarely acknowledged Black pop as a wellspring of fusion. "Fusion meant . . . oh, this band has some white people in it," late-1970s Joni collaborator Herbie Hancock's white manager David Robinson once told the jazz

critic Steven F. Pond. Definitions have a way of obscuring possibilities, and so fusion became a white/Black thing, a rock/jazz
thing, yet another byproduct of America's essential racial inequities. This critique mattered, but it also excluded Black pop (aka
soul, or R & B) artists working in the realms the industry had
designated as their own. Meanwhile, Wonder—to cite just one
outstanding example—deployed Greg Tate's jazz definition, "the
exploration of sound, timbre, technology and expressive musical
effects," with astounding success.

Let Joni herself correct the record. When asked about her influences in a 1974 CBC interview, she did not make her usual move
and cite Bob Dylan first. That prize went to Stevie. "I think that
he's like a musical genius, I really do," she gushed. At that very
moment "Help Me" was becoming the biggest hit she would ever
enjoy—a song that strongly echoes Wonder's 1973 charmer, "You
Are the Sunshine of My Life," from its first chords onward. At
the end of the year, *Rolling Stone* named Mitchell and Wonder co-
artists of the year, and in 1975 both were nominated for the Album of the Year Grammy award. Wonder took the statue and three
others.

Mitchell and Wonder are rarely aligned within current tax-
onomies of 1970s music, even though they shared so much in
common. Both were polyglots exploring new rhythms and extended melodic lines within arrangements that pushed the lines
of their home genres. Both had astounding album runs in the
early-to-mid-1970s. Both could write a devastating love song and
then, on the next track, spin social commentary with ease. Both
led big bands on major arena tours. And both took unexpected,
critically questioned turns into esoteric projects near the decade's
end—Mitchell releasing *Mingus*, her spiritually driven collaboration with the legendary jazz bassist Charles Mingus, and Wonder

delving deep into synth-driven moods on *Stevie Wonder's Journey Through the Secret Life of Plants*.

A photograph from 1998, when Mitchell finally connected with Wonder on a Herbie Hancock–led tribute to George Gershwin, shows the stylistic divide that may have obscured their affinities in their prime. On one side of Hancock, Mitchell wears an Annie Hall–style relaxed men's blazer and chews happily on a pen. Wonder, on the other side, is resplendent in a dashiki decorated with a huge appliquéd ankh. White liberal feminist cool and Afrocentric pride did not mix much in public in the 1970s. The structure of the culture industries reinforced this lack of dialogue. Wonder and Mitchell met at awards ceremonies and on the Top 40 charts, but their music was packaged by different labels, marketed to mostly separate audiences and rarely written about in tandem. Wonder was a superstar and a widely acknowledged genius, but while an artist like Mitchell earned descriptors like "experimental" and "deep" from white gatekeepers, he remained "funky" or "soulful." Wonder himself rejected genre categories, saying in 1972, "It doesn't matter what color you are or whatever. People say, if he is black, he is a soul artist . . . I don't feel I should be bound to any one particular thing." The respect he rightly earned couldn't defeat the categorizations he resisted.

Mitchell wanted to follow Wonder's lead, but the men in her life discouraged her. Henry Lewy, usually so in tune with Mitchell's choices, dissuaded her from trying a Wonder-style Moog synthesizer on *Court and Spark*. "I know that Stevie Wonder was using Moog and stuff," she told Malka Marom in 1979. "Henry would not let me do it, but he couldn't tell me why. So I took him to a Stevie Wonder session. And I said, 'You see? Listen to this. The bass, the bottom end is getting fatter. Why can't we do it?' Still, no reason." The arranger Dale Oehler similarly discouraged her from invoking the string arrangements on Marvin Gaye's song "Trouble Man"—which she loved so much she wrote her own version, *Court and Spark*'s "Trouble Child"—on *The Hissing of Summer Lawns*. Her jazz moves made sense to these trusted advisors, but apparently Joni didn't strike them as the right kind of lady to dip her toe into Black pop.

The question is not whether Joni could really hang with the likes of Stevie or Marvin, but why those artists and many other Black innovators of the 1970s have been largely excluded from fusion histories. They employed jazz session men and women and often took those players on tour. Their classic releases stretched the possibilities of album-oriented music as much as did anything by Weather Report or even Miles Davis. They were inspired by those kin from across the genre gap, too—Randy Brecker, who toured with Wonder, remembered him as a major fan of jazz pianist Chick Corea. In the strictest terms dictated by measures of improvisation and time signatures, they may not have been jazz artists. But they certainly were jazzy, as Joni also called herself. As I tried to grasp what fusion was, is, or could be, poring over old issues of *Down-Beat*, *Ebony* and *Rolling Stone*, I soon realized that while the story was unfolding, the intermingling of soul and funk with rock and jazz was just as crucial as the summit between jazz and rock.

Let me take a paragraph and honor the Black pop elites who belong in the history of jazz fusion if we put Joni there, too. One list, incomplete:

Bill Withers, who like Mitchell was often classified as folk, but whom one reviewer in 1972 declared "unbaggable. What he writes and sings isn't exactly blues or jazz or pop or rock or folk." Valerie Simpson, like Mitchell a writer for others first (with her husband, Nick Ashford; for decades they were king and queen of New York Black glitterati), whose 1971 solo debut took the top spot in

Rolling Stone's reviews section with a rave from future Bruce Springsteen herald and manager Jon Landau. Gil Scott-Heron. Earth Wind & Fire. Isaac Hayes. Charles Wright & the Watts 103rd Street Rhythm Band. Post-Supremes Diana Ross. Post–Muscle Shoals Aretha Franklin. Curtis Mayfield. Joni's friend and occasional background singer Chaka Khan and her band, Rufus. Leon Ware. Terry Callier, who had a duo with David Crosby early in his career and helped him understand jazz. Labi Siffre. Patrice Rushen. The Persuaders. The Sylvers. The Spinners. The Main Ingredient. Tower of Power. War. Roberta Flack.

This list could form the basis for a whole other book. I want to write that book. But I pulled myself back to Joni, and it wasn't so difficult, because as much as she loved Miles or Mingus, Joni lived in the orbit of these Black pop auteurs, too. Sometimes the overlap was literal. Minnie Riperton's 1970s albums, for example, not only shared sonic elements with Mitchell's, the two women sometimes enlisted the same collaborators, including Lewy, who produced 1979's *Minnie*, and Larry Carlton, whose arrangements add fusion flair to 1975's *Adventures in Paradise*. In recent years Riperton, who died young in 1979, has been the subject of a posthumous revival. She is celebrated not only for the birdlike high notes that graced her signature hit single, 1974's Wonder-produced "Lovin' You," but for the cinematic imagination at the core of albums like *Come to My Garden*, her 1970 debut. That lush work was produced by jazz vibes player and symphonist Charles Stepney; its delicate, fanciful sound and mystically introspective lyrics recall *Ladies of the Canyon*. Riperton and Mitchell also shared fashion sense; in not one but two *Los Angeles Times* features on L.A.'s haute-post-hippie couture, they're spotted shopping at the same designer boutique. I like to imagine them meeting over a rack of Holly Harp's "cream puff" dresses at the Right Bank Clothing Company on Rodeo Drive, perhaps exchanging notes on Carlton's guitar work as each plotted further musical expansions.

Mitchell did meet and befriend Chaka Khan, the young singer for the funk band Rufus, enlisting her to sing on *Don Juan's Reckless Daughter* with a phone call in the middle of the night. Their life-long friendship attests to the relative diversity of the musical circle Mitchell was building. Like Riperton, Khan was an early favorite of Stevie Wonder—he wrote Rufus's best-known song, "Tell Me Something Good," on the clavinet in the studio where the group was making its second album after Chaka rejected another song he'd offered her. Her boldness at twenty-one must have been part of her appeal to Joni, who like her didn't have many women friends then. Also, her taste. Interviewed by the *Chicago Defender* in 1974, she listed her three favorite artists: Wonder, spiritual jazz pioneer Alice Coltrane and Led Zeppelin.

Black artists traveling across the pop spectrum in the 1970s embraced the spirit of fusion even when that term would never be applied to them. Racism is one obvious reason why the connection was rarely acknowledged at the time, despite the general understanding that these were leading innovators. Excellence didn't guarantee entry into the musical categories white record men and media types had determined would both sell and enshrine popular music. "Being a black pop singer isn't easy," wrote Vince Aletti, one of the era's least prejudiced critics, in a Dionne Warwick album review for *Rolling Stone*. "There are too many definitions, expectations and demands that have to be sidestepped, too many people wondering where you at."

If fusion represented a de facto integrationist impulse within popular music, it was still defined by hierarchies that put Black communal pleasure at the bottom, even among those who revered acknowledged geniuses like Wonder. Jazz fusion's unfolding history excluded certain kinds of sounds and scenes, and especially Black sounds and scenes that didn't fit white-defined ideas of what forms of self-expression are truly meaningful. This is why, even as white and Black musicians were playing together on the same sessions, helping make the same classic albums and mount the same legendary tours, only certain Black artists' groundbreaking efforts are remembered as helping recast sonic borders in a lasting way. As fusion became codified as a trend, then a disputed but identifiable subgenre, these divisions persisted even as everyone involved declared themselves to be fighting against them.

A SPANISH FEEL

One thing that brought Wonder and Mitchell together, at least aesthetically, was a love of Latin rhythms. Her time in Florida exposed her to the varied sounds of the Caribbean diaspora, an influence maintained in Laurel Canyon by friends like Stephen Stills, who grew up a military brat in places like Costa Rica and Panama. Even if folk friends like Stills hadn't turned her on to mambo, son cubano and salsa, the jazzmen in Mitchell's life during the 1970s would have soaked her in it. She started incorporating more percussion into her sessions, nabbed the flamenco-style virtuoso José Feliciano in the A&M Studios hallway when he was playing on John Lennon's *Rock 'n' Roll*—the encounter led to his springy guitar parts on her "Free Man in Paris"—and dove in deep on 1977's *Don Juan's Reckless Daughter*, which features four percussionists and is centered on their improvised piece "The Tenth World," with vocals in Spanish by the Peruvian Alex Acuña.

That piece leads into "Dreamland," which features Airto Moreira, the rhythm man from a family of healers who'd brought

the Amazon to Miles Davis's *Bitches Brew* sessions and become a
star on the scene in his own right, often performing with his wife,
the extraordinary singer Flora Purim. "Dreamland" was inspired
by a trip to Brazil that Joni took with Guerin, the first of several
rhythm players in her life. Just as Joni's closest companions in her
folk-rock years held up mirrors that helped her perfect confessional songwriting, time spent with bassists and drummers ori-
ented her toward ever more complex rhythmic palettes.

The bottom of the mix was where it was at in jazz fusion, with
people like Airto Moreira mapping it. His mark is everywhere on
fusion's line through time and space. Following Purim from Rio
to L.A. in 1967, he ended up in New York, playing on not only
Bitches Brew but as part of Davis's Cellar Door set from 1970,
which Davis combined with studio tracks, including three compositions by Moreira's fellow Brazilian and close friend Hermeto
Pascoal, for the classic album *Live-Evil*. He and Purim then joined
Chick Corea to form Return to Forever, the fusion band that ensured Brazil's place at fusion's center. He also played on Paul Simon's solo debut, helping secure that singer-songwriter's status as
a major pop interpreter of global sounds. These are just a few of
his moves. Carrying his suitcases full of "little things and gadgets,
rattles and shakers and things" that he'd collected as a self-taught
student of Brazilian folk traditions, Moreira traveled from session
to session, seeding the bottom on every kind of track imaginable.

Inhabiting a third space where Blackness traveled along
the colonized routes of the global diaspora, Airto and his cohort
were uniquely suited to the fusion moment. They inhabited a social margin, as did Black artists, but also represented movement
and hybridity. "I'm from Brazil of course, so I was not totally
white, so I could mingle with them," Airto once recalled about
his camaraderie with Miles Davis and other Black jazz stars. This

comment, of course, hints at the complexities of race and colorism within Brazil itself, where colonialism is as strong and destructive a force as hybridity is a healing one. Airto's ability to "pass" in both directions (the musicologist Kaleb Goldschmitt describes it as "ethnic illegibility") allowed him to travel across racial boundaries in ways that were prohibited for Black musicians—and for Mitchell, who would have loved to have been accepted as the Black man she felt she was in her soul.

Latin and particularly Brazilian elements within many fusion-era projects imparted a sense of mobility, even lightness, that appealed to musicians, fans and listeners of all kinds. After the saxophonist Stan Getz's massively popular 1964 collaboration with João and Astrud Gilberto, "The Girl from Ipanema," Americans tapped into Brazilian sounds via "easy listening" albums by the likes of Rio's unofficial ambassador Sérgio Mendes, whose Brasil '66 band claimed the first global Portuguese-language hit with a version of Jorge Ben's "Mas Que Nada." Listeners seeking a relaxing form of the exotic may have gravitated toward such recordings, but within the smooth grooves, that complex hybridity still shone forth.

From Miles Davis's New York to Moreira's Rio to the tossed salad that was L.A., fusion's songlines held musical connections that engendered seemingly endless possibilities. For Mitchell, always longing for movement and change, its promise was irresistible. It was in fusion that she found her most adventurous voice, not only as a writer but as a bandleader and collaborator. She took from every source it offered, Black, white or brown, sometimes maybe too much. This was how she grew her own way out of the box that confessional songwriting had become. All this context sets the stage: now let's consider what Joni made of it. For one thing, at least at first, she made some money.

THE SOUND OF MONEY

In 1974, David Geffen had a birthday party. Joni's music biz mentor was flying high the week he turned thirty-one, with three albums on his label moving up the charts: Bob Dylan's *Planet Waves*, Carly Simon's *Hotcakes*, and *Court and Spark*, the breakthrough he'd been wanting Joni to give him since he first helped her become a folk oracle. The soiree in the Beverly Wilshire Hotel's Le Grand Trianon ballroom was fit for such a ringleader, organized around a carnival theme by Geffen's close personal friends Dylan and Robbie Robertson, and his then-girlfriend and "almost constant companion," Cher. Robert Hilburn, chronicling the shenanigans, described them as "lavish," detailing the seventy-five to one hundred guests and "carnival atmosphere—fortune tellers, knife throwers, strolling troubadours." Hilburn doesn't note Joni's presence among the night's glitterati, which is a little weird, because she and Geffen were still tight then, though a few years later they'd have some temporarily alienating arguments over (what else?) money.

Maybe Joni felt she could blow off the carnival because she'd already paid tribute to Geffen in the most indelible way possible: on that moneymaker *Court and Spark* she included a song written not just for him, but effusively sung from his point of view. Even better, it made the Top 40. "Free Man in Paris" was the album's second-highest-charting single, becoming a staple on what were then known as "easy listening" stations, where it would remain an album-oriented-radio favorite throughout the 1970s. The tune is in fact a pretty easy listen, its musical signature a sparkly flute fanfare played by Scott and echoed on Joni's guitar, its lyric a fond reminiscence of a European idyll from the vantage point of a charming, if harried, businessman. But a few things make this song more complex.

The little bump of ascending notes that begins it, followed by Mitchell's and José Feliciano's percussive acoustic strumming and a lick from Larry Carlton that hits like cocaine rubbed on your gums, sets the stage for the monologue that follows. *The way I see it, he said, you just can't win it,* the lyric begins; unusually, Mitchell is relaying someone else's confession. According to the critic Sean Nelson, who wrote a short book about *Court and Spark*, this is what makes "Free Man" the pinnacle of her songwriting career: "It's the ultimate extension of her effort to be personal without being autobiographical." Letting Geffen's voice inhabit her—she has said that the song contains actual phrases from their conversations after a French holiday they took with Robbie Robertson and his wife—Mitchell fully embodied that leisure-suited, deal-making, self-actualizing 1970s male ideal.

Joni heads to her lower register to voice the cynicism that dooms the Free Man despite his awareness that he'd be happier away from the machinations of the music biz. Carlton's guitar lines circle behind, slick and forceful, as the Free Man continues his argument—like many of her songs, an expression of internal conflict that's fully evident but never resolved. The complaints continue, carried along by the music, until the chorus, a plunge into memory: in Paris, the Free Man declares, he felt *unfettered and alive, there was nobody calling me up for favors and no one's future to decide.* He should just go back. He will! But by the end of the first chorus he's talked himself out of it. So many people need him, and he has to keep this engine humming, the star maker machinery he designed and only he knows how to properly run. And so the song unfolds exactly like a one-sided conversation during a coke binge, a steady stream of contradictory arguments and impulses. Its key phrase—*a good friend of mine*—changes meaning each time Mitchell intones it. False friends, secret friends, intimate friends, imagined friends. All the people who make the Free Man feel important, because they love him, need him, make him money, take his time.

"Free Man in Paris" resonated in the hedonistic, stagflationary 1970s, when the culture industries kept pushing new luxe ways to consume fashion, food, travel, entertainment and even sex, requiring middle-class Americans to work harder and harder to purchase those fondue sets and Chevy Corvettes and tickets to the Triple-X art film showing downtown. And, as the lyric says, to buy the popular song, a commodity funding massive concert tours even when the OPEC-driven oil shortage threatened the production of those little wheels, LPs. Jazz is the right soundtrack for this quintessential struggle of the ascendant American male: a music born of marginalization and oppression, but quickly adopted as a signifier of refinement among the elite, who then confined it within spaces—exclusive clubs, high-end stereo systems, cruise ships—where its disruptive qualities were less appreciated.

This is a song about what money can buy, and how, once money has trapped you, no purchase is ever enough. It can also be heard as the story of Joni in the land of fusion, wandering blissfully into new doorways, able to afford the best sidemen and studios, acting on her unquenchable impulse to set down stakes in the unfamiliar. Though the closeted Geffen worried about "Free Man in Paris" because of its coy but potentially gossip-inducing line about a same-sex foreign idyll (one *very good friend of mine* is definitely a date), what gives that line its true meaning is the way Mitchell flips the phrase *good friend* from the first verse, where it represents social climbing, to the second, where it entices with a vision of soothing social oblivion the Free Man knows he will never actually pursue. "Free Man in Paris" enacts the paradox of consumer capitalism: when status is determined by purchasing

power and intimacy occurs in spaces available only to the rich
(Paris, for example, a jet-set destination), there can be no pleasure
without a tab. Geffen's idyll, allowing him to engage in same-sex
adventures and ignore his Rolodex, parallels Mitchell's fusion trip,
where she bathed in Caribbean rhythms and relished the gleam
of a great horn line. In both cases, the rightful inhabitants of
these exotic milieus are sweetly acknowledged, yet remain in the
background.

Throughout *Court and Spark*, Mitchell asks the question, how
does the transactional become personal? In 1974 she was tempera-
mentally suited to explore this question, having fully reestablished
herself in Beverly Hills after her ruralizing time in Canada, hanging out in clubs where models and actors shared lines with the
band in the bathroom during breaks in the show. She retreated in
and out of the social scene, sometimes spotted stepping out of a
limo and sometimes holing up with Guerin within diving distance
of her pool. She also started spending time in Manhattan. When
she did venture out into clubs where the L.A. Express played, she
found herself in heady company. "The crowd was the prime fascination," gossip columnist Joyce Haber wrote about one of the
band's New York gigs in 1975. "It included Mick Jagger without
Bianca; Faye Dunaway in trench coat and black cloche, right out
of 'Chinatown'; [and] 22-year-old Dino De Laurentiis Jr." There
to sing backup, Joni had to mingle with the actors and other Tinseltown types rubbing up against the rock stars.

Money made all this possible, and gave it a cynical perfume.
That's how some jazz musicians felt in the fusion era, too, as
chronicled in accounts by morally outraged journalists. "How
would you define the stomping, infectious essence of their general
direction? Is it jazz/rock? Disco music? Funk 'n' roll? A better
name would be money music," Leonard Feather wrote about

fusion's stars in 1975, a couple of years after he'd first condemned
them in a scathing *DownBeat* article entitled "A Year of Selling
Out." "So many expert artists are playing money music today that
a great deal of creativity is thwarted along the way. But along the
way also lie huge record sales, big auditoriums, cheering crowds."

Feather was white; a leading Black voice railing against fusion
was Amiri Baraka, the poet, playwright and music writer formerly
called LeRoi Jones. Declaring that "fusion, in the main, had no
soul, because it smelled of corporate dilution and money tricks,"
Baraka saw this period of pop experimentation as a threat against
the primacy of Black musicians within jazz. He connected bands
like the post–Joe Sample L.A. Express to other white ensembles
benefiting from Black culture from 1920s Dixieland bands to
1950s rock and roll stars. The endgame? "Maximum profits, racial
segregation, and discrimination, black national oppression maintained." Though Baraka's denouncement is harsh, it hit home
with jazz ideologues, who weren't interested in the fact that half
of the stars within fusion were Black.

It's undeniable that for all of the boundary-crossing happening in recording studios and clubs, white fusion artists often occupied the biggest stages and found the warmest reception among
the larger rock and pop audience. The inequities that elevated
Bob Dylan and, yes, Mitchell above Black folk musicians like Len
Chandler or Odetta surfaced again. In her jazz period, Mitchell
was clearly aware of these tensions around race and tried to respond empathetically by declaring herself essentially Black—the
most controversial move of her career. Unlike her, most white
jazz snobs weren't all that interested in the racial disparities within
fusion; they cared about some ineffable quality in the music, the
same one Mitchell had heard misting out from the horn of the
anonymous clarinet player in her *Ladies of the Canyon* ballad "For

Free," which juxtaposes her growing wealth against his impoverished anonymity.

Mitchell sometimes used jazz settings to color satirical portraits of the 1970s high life, including its colonialist tendencies;
in this, she was not alone. Walter Becker and Donald Fagen, the
acerbic social critics behind the mostly studio project Steely Dan,
were leaders in this endeavor, with hits like "My Old School" and
"Show Biz Kids" satirizing the neuroses of both East Coast sci-
ons (Becker and Fagen met at the tony liberal arts college Bard)
and West Coast arrivistes, and "The Royal Scam" painting a cruel
portrait of Puerto Rican immigrants flimflammed by the American dream. Janis Ian, coming back to herself after teenage fame as
a protest singer had derailed her life, recorded thoughtful ballads
about the cost of success like the modern torch song "Stars." Carly
Simon, struggling through a drug-affected marriage to Joni's old
heartbreaker James Taylor, wrote affectionately and sometimes
wryly of her life as part of a monied New York family. But Mitchell was the best at tapping into the fusion sound with the right
balance of musical acuity, emotional nuance and self-awareness.

Peter Asher managed and produced James Taylor and Linda
Ronstadt in their 1970s prime; he also briefly managed Joni and
is her longtime friend. In a conversation we had over lunch in
the kind of haute hotel restaurant 1970s rock stars frequented, he
remembered the era as a time when labels were kinder and gentler
than ever before, or since. "Letting people make the record they
wanted to make and changing things around the next time if they
wanted to, that all made sense," he said. "Because the payoff was
big enough. Now, the payoff is smaller, the timeframe is faster,
you need results now. We made whole albums and people from
the label wouldn't have heard any of it. It's not like anybody told
us what to do."

That's how Mitchell could make a record like *Court and Spark*'s follow-up, *The Hissing of Summer Lawns*, which further developed her social critiques in musical settings that augmented the L.A. Express lineup with half a dozen more instrumentalists, Moog synthesizers and, on the stream-of-consciousness account of the jazz diaspora "The Jungle Line," an innovative sample of the African Royal Drummers of Burundi. On *Hissing*, Mitchell's questions about the leisure class only intensified, taking on a feminist tone, though she rejected that then-incendiary identifier. Two of its songs—the title track and "Harry's House"—examine stifling marriages between beautiful women fiercely protecting their own worth as breadwinner men ignore them and dally with others. "Shades of Scarlett Conquering" examines fractured femininity in a dissection of the Southern belle. "The Boho Dance" is a more capacious satire borrowing a phrase coined by the journalist and social critic Tom Wolfe to describe how ambitious artists use the signifiers of bohemian impoverishment to sell themselves to titillated wealthy patrons. Expanding on the scene she'd built in *Court and Spark*'s "Raised on Robbery," a monologue by a charming but manic sex worker, "Edith and the Kingpin" depicts a gangster enticing a new lover with the promise of comfort, drugs and not much else; here, Mitchell describes the transactional relationship with less humor and more angst. The music throughout *Hissing* is humid, thick, seductive and only rarely danceable.

If *Court and Spark* intrigues by acknowledging luxury's allure, *Hissing* challenges by relentlessly chronicling its costs. The evolution made sense culturally. By autumn 1975, when it was released, the malaise of the 1970s had fully set in. Americans still aspired toward ever-fancier suburban homes and jet-set lifestyles, but the energy crisis limited their movements, President Nixon's fall in the Watergate scandal tested their idealism, and rising divorce rates threatened their hopes at home. America was a pretty place whose ugly underbelly was increasingly exposed.

Mitchell was trying to find herself, the former hippie–turned–rich Bel-Air babe, within this milieu. Her songs became more scopious and harder for some to parse. For the first time since the release of her first album, she faced serious negative reviews alongside the glowing ones. The liner notes she penned for *Hissing* announced that the album should be received as a "total work"; in the *New York Times*, John Rockwell responded, "This really is the 'total work' she tells us it is, and if that means she shows her warts, her warts are slicker, more glamorous and more interesting than anybody else's." That was a positive take. Others called the album's songs "smug" or containing "almost impenetrable mystery."

Despite Mitchell's full embrace of the artistic freedom Geffen allowed, she was affected by the declining support for her approach. "It was a premature experiment; people thought I'd lost my marbles," she said years later. To some she seemed like just another rich Californian, playing with disruption even as she stood in her swimming pool wearing her custom-made Boyd Elder boots, molded to perfectly fit her legs. That image, from a 1978 *Vogue* piece on the latest Hollywood excess—haute Western wear—shows the Joni that fit in with the rock scene, but it missed the heart still beating beneath the finery. The heart of an outsider, now a jazzwoman, always a thorn in the star makers' sides.

A WOMAN'S SENSE OF TIME

For me, a story from Joni's early years illuminates the deepest purpose of her jazz fusion experiments. She was dating Leonard Cohen and trying to become a better artist in every way. Frustrated with her attempts at sketching—"It's too naive and too ornate," she said—she sought the advice of Cohen's best friend, the sculptor Morton Rosengarten. "Let's go to Washington Square Park," the sculptor said. Once there, he sat on a bench and said, "Joni, draw me and don't look at the paper."

She did, and subtly, suddenly, everything changed for her. No longer focusing on her own quivering hand, she felt free of her ego. Later she told Malka Marom that this was the moment that made her work "more realistic and more immediate and more modern"—not only her drawings and paintings, but her music. She started experimenting with song structures even then, "more rhythmic, less classical, more rocky jazz." Her kind of fusion. In music, drawing without looking at the paper meant creating something that would get her out of her head and make her want to dance.

Rock and roll rhythms, extending into funk, fed many fusion experiments. Purists hated that aspect of the music, saying rock's simplicity squashed everything else fusion players wove into their mix. It's true that an insistent beat could overshadow the other elements in the music. The newly minted jazz fans laying out cash for a Weather Report show might not have recognized the cumbia or son rhythms invoked, but their asses moved when they felt the influence of Jimi Hendrix or James Brown.

For Mitchell and her singer-songwriter crowd, though— mostly white kids who loved Chuck Berry before they'd ever heard of Woody Guthrie—turning back toward the rock and roll of their teen years necessarily loosened things up. Many did smell the money that nostalgia always generates, and kept things simple with cover versions or rewrites of the jukebox songs of their childhood. James Taylor and Carly Simon redid Inez and Charlie Foxx's hopped-up soul stirrer "Mockingbird"; Linda Ronstadt covered

the Motown-ish Dee Dee Warwick jumper "You're No Good."
Others mimicked 1950s jukebox hits to craft their own: Elton John
and Bernie Taupin's "Crocodile Rock" openly borrowed from the
Australian band Daddy Cool's 1971 raver "Eagle Rock," which it-
self owed everything to Chuck Berry's "Brown Eyed Handsome
Man." The money rolled in for these artists, whose fans were
ready to return to times before the 1970s wrecked their roll, as
Joni saw it, and have some fun again.

Why do the songs from Mitchell's fusion period so rarely feel
like throwbacks, then, unlike the *American Graffiti* reduxes other
white singer-songwriters created? Partly it's because, as with her
open tunings, when it came to rhythmic composition she gave herself permission to consistently veer from the norm. She'd start
writing something in 4/4 time but then throw in a section in 5/8
or 4/8—aiming, as she said, for something "sideways." Guerin
invented a system of transcription to guide the band, a way of mapping her hip shakes, so the jazz guys confronted with her eccen-
tricities could get into her groove. She didn't read charts herself.
She was just trying to "sophisticate my music to my own taste."

The pianist and composer Brad Mehldau, who has interpreted
Mitchell songs throughout his career, attributed her inimitable
boogie to her conviction that music is a form of conversation.
"Joni Mitchell's unique rhythmic approach to melodies has to do,
for me, with a total conversational ease. A wonderful feeling of
casualness that makes the music all the more arresting because
there is so much pathos implied in the way she variously clips,
staggers, and extends each phrase; in the controlled huskiness
of her voice, and in the lyrics themselves," he wrote in the liner
notes to a 2007 Mitchell tribute album. This makes sense to me:
she was always a talker, bubbling over in interviews with journalists delighted to keep their tape recorders rolling past the allot-

ted time, sharing long giggly anecdotes from the stage when she performed, even finding talk erotic, or as she put it in "Help Me," *sitting there talkin'* before *lyin' there not talkin', didn't it feel good?*

Mitchell made intimate talk one of her main vehicles and subjects, and found, in her fusion years, that such talk is a lot like dancing. It has its own rhythms, choreography, moments of sublime synchronicity and painful, even fatal stumbles. Mitchell tapped into the bottom end of her music to expand how she could talk about talk, and particularly about how inner talk and the art of persuasion might collide in one woman's mind and mouth. She used slant time signatures and metric interruption to mimic conversation's verbal twists and arcs. Talk, in these songs, is a woman's job, her tool, her hope, her burden. And it's what distinguishes her from a man.

Again I talk too open and free, she sings in 1977's "Talk to Me," supposedly written for Bob Dylan, who refused to spend much time *sittin' there talkin'* while she was with him on his Rolling Thunder Revue tour. *I pay a high price for my open talking, like you do for your silent mystery.* She then squawks like a chicken. The rhythms of animal language, of rain and fire and muggy heat, of moving vehicles, of anger and lust and frustration, of memory: Mitchell reoriented her music around these essential, often hidden pulses.

Mitchell's musicalization of talk connects to an even more heady preoccupation that unites her fusion-era albums: a challenge to common perceptions of time. Other Joni scholars have identified this mission. In her insightful monograph *The Songs of Joni Mitchell*, Anne Karppinen connects her music to the work of feminist philosophers like Luce Irigaray and Alison Stone to illuminate how Mitchell communicates the "fluid pluralism," as she writes, of women's experience and self-expression. I startled when I read a quote from Stone that Karppinen shares in her book's introduction, demanding a way to describe "human bodies as made of rhythms, forms and fluid materials, remaining close to our lived experience of our bodies"—this is precisely what I think Mitchell's broken-middle music does. It runs time through a body that can dance.

Writing about *Mingus*, Mitchell's 1979 collaboration with the great jazz bassist of its title, Kevin Fellezs focuses on the two artists' shared desire to expose time as an invention that only partially keeps the unstructured essence of human experience in check. Both Mingus and Mitchell stretched out the song form to disrupt the orderly listening experiences that conventional approaches encouraged while staying grounded in familiar styles: Mingus in blues and gospel, Joni in folk, jazz standards and rock. In Fellezs's view, they integrated the straight-ahead and the avant-garde in ways that stressed the intuitive and nonlinear aspects of human expression. In "The Wolf That Lives in Lindsey," one of *Mingus*'s most arresting songs, Fellezs hears Mitchell echoing the bassist's classic compositions like "Fables of Faubus," which frame improvised passages with composed ones to musically demonstrate, in his words, "how human will deludes itself into thinking it has structured order from the seeming chaos in which it finds itself, in contrast to the greater order of 'chaos' that swirls just beyond human comprehension." Music arises within time, but in a song like this one it also strains against it.

Maybe I can simplify all this theorizing by going back to Mitchell's own words about her process in these years, modeled on Miles Davis: "very alert and very sensual and very unwritten." I fixate on the word "unwritten." It strikes me as the opposite of confessional. To try to make unwritten songs is to avoid the crafted narratives of autobiography, to reach for what can't be said, though it can still be shared. Perhaps "unwritten" music goes beyond the boundaries of human communication itself to incorporate other howlings—of the wolf, the wind, the orgasmic lover, the subconscious—that language can't really ever grasp.

Rhythm was Mitchell's way into the unwritten. Some of her songs, like *Court and Spark*'s "Trouble Child," explore the way psychological or spiritual unrest can both uncage a person and make them dangerous. Others make the riskier move of projecting the listener into dreamlike spaces where time is disrupted via African-diaspora virtuosity. One of her most experimental efforts, "The Jungle Line," exemplifies this. Its rhythmic bed is a sample taken from a 1967 field recording that Mitchell had first heard incorporated into a French novelty song called "Burundi Black." She paired the drums' looped, jagged rhythms with her own blippy, fuzzy Moog-generated bass to form the sound bite for a surrealistic lyric that follows a time-traveling Rousseau, that white painter of fantasized jungle scenes, on a journey through the Black neighborhoods of the postcolonial world. Mitchell's words expose the way the white mind exoticizes Blackness even as she participates in that process, pairing "charging elephants" with "chanting slaving boats." The song implies that what Blackness offers is an alternate chronology: "the jungle line, screaming in a ritual of sound and time." Part of what that line marks is the history of jazz, the ultimate musical disruptor.

"The Jungle Line" is one of Mitchell's strangest songs, arguably a failed experiment in her ongoing quest to fully comprehend the Black American culture with which she increasingly identified. But its rhythmic disjunctures shed more light than even Mitchell may have realized on the way that the stories we tell are also undone by time's flux—history distorts the realities of those who lived it but didn't write it, and even the most empathetic artist will fail in capturing another's perspective, because she is still caught within her own view.

The key collaborations Mitchell cultivated in her fusion years fed her fascination with irresolution and unraveling narratives. I hear challenges to straight time in all of them. Chief among them is the one that began with *Hejira*, the album that followed *Hissing*: her dialogue with Jaco Pastorius, a mercurial, rhythm and blues–trained, rock-star attitudinal musician whose brief life (he died at thirty-five in 1987, addicted and homeless) established him as the most influential bassist in jazz or rock. Joni was introduced to his debut album by the guitarist Robben Ford, another fusion trailblazer who played a key role in her 1970s live bands, and she instantly felt she needed to work with him. Pastorius's legend is tied up with his recordings and short touring life with Mitchell, and his personal life was, too—though he was married, they were lovers, at least briefly. On record they developed a highly intuitive dialogue in which Mitchell's singing and his high-on-the-fretboard melodic lines intertwined and supplemented each other. He answered her call from *Court and Spark*: *you could complete me, I'd complete you.* That lyric could also apply to her deep friendship with Wayne Shorter, whose approach to both composition and improvisation was as "metaphorical" as Joni's, in her own words, and who remained her guide and foil until his death in 2023.

And she learned rhythm from the drummers in her life. First Guerin, then Don Alias. He was a Harlem-raised percussionist, the son of immigrants from St. Martin with an encyclopedic understanding of the many different beats of the Caribbean diaspora. Their affair was volatile—later, Mitchell said that he was occasionally abusive. (Guerin, on the other hand, was gentle and attuned but chronically unfaithful.) That must be said. Yet she did learn from him. Randy Brecker, whose club with his brother Michael was only a few blocks from Joni's New York loft, told me about hanging out with the couple in the late 1970s.

"Joni was on the scene with Don," he said. "And he's one of the greatest purveyors of Latin music. He just knew more about Latin rhythms than anyone I ever met. You could talk to him for hours about rhythm. And he knew every little beat, from every country. It was just encyclopedic. He was Joni's man for quite a long time, so I'm sure a lot of his stuff rubbed off on her. It sure rubbed off on us."

Ever searching for a partner who would feed both her insatiable creativity and her heart, Mitchell has nearly always formed intimate bonds with other musicians. She wanted to live inside the compositional process, even when her lovers didn't get what she was doing fully, even when Jaco would tell interviewers, "I really dig Joni but she's not a jazz musician. My personal opinion: she's not a jazz musician. But she's exceptionally talented and a very good person and she can paint her butt off." Some of her jazz compadres still didn't totally consider her an equal, it seemed. But in the studio, she was in charge and their prejudices dissolved like the smoke from her cigarettes.

She asserted her bona fides twice by covering vocal jazz workouts originally recorded by her childhood heroes Lambert, Hendricks & Ross. "Twisted," on *Court and Spark*, is a send-up of psychoanalysis that had served as a showcase for the droll and dagger-sharp Annie Ross. Joni's version mirrors Ross's original nearly note for note, but it's notable for the way she pairs it with "Trouble Child," her far more personal, emblematically contemporary study of mental illness. The two songs simultaneously enhance and erase each other, one a joke with a bitter punch line, the other a lament with an exasperated edge. Together they dwell in the irresolution that surrounds mental illness and its remedies. What helps? Humor? Mourning? Time? Honing in on a mood, or spacing out? The slipstream groove of "Trouble Child" echoes silently through Mitchell's "Twisted" and makes its joke a ruse.

Mitchell again pairs a Lambert, Hendricks and Ross number with one of her own compositions when their "Centerpiece" is preceded by "Harry's House," a tale of marriage unraveling in a well-appointed home. On that song, Mitchell's vocal line moves calmly forward as nearly every player on the track—from guitarist Robben Ford to keyboardist Joe Sample to trumpeter Chuck Findley—lays down fluttering, entangling lines that keep making a mess in its living room. Harry, a businessman cutting through traffic and distractions to make a very important meeting, is facing a crisis—his wife has just left, telling him *just what he could do with Harry's house and Harry's take home pay*. Unable to imagine a future without her, he dwells on a mental snapshot of her as a girl shining with suntan oil at the local swimming pool. He has everything, yet he has only that memory.

When the band shifts and organizes that snarl of music and moves on to "Centerpiece," the thick air of "Harry's House" hovers in the background, weighing on the comical clarity of the jazz song's paean to partnered bliss. Joe Sample's barrelhouse piano speeds the song toward resolution, but Joni's vocal drops some syrup on the keys. This is fusion of the highest order, music that refuses to be one thing any more than an individual is ever really only one person. Collapsing two musical styles—and two jazz eras, swing and fusion—into each other across the span of seven minutes, Mitchell shows how the present is both formed by the past and haunts it, through the pain of disrupted memories.

6

hejira means pilgrimage

Throughout the 1970s Mitchell made music in defiance
of pop's familiar forms of containment and stretched
her lyrical approach to match. Fusion's game of
upending expectations inspired her to not only continue
shifting her sound, but to fully erase the patina of
preciousness that clung to her during her folkish years.
Continuing to expand her songs beyond confession
and close observation, she tried social critique, allegory
and even free association. She explored storytelling
as a tool for mining the subconscious, inspired by
psychoanalysis, meditation and possibly peyote.

Three journeys in the mid-1970s put her firmly back in voy-
ager mode—a tour cut short by her imploding relationship with
John Guerin, an exhilarating, frustrating stint on Bob Dylan's
circus-like Rolling Thunder Revue tour, and a spontaneous road
trip, at first with a couple of boys in tow and then solo, from L.A.
to Maine and all the way down the East Coast and across the
Southern states back to California. As she drove, she continued
to document her inner journeys, which sometimes got positively
wild. From this flight, this work, would come a trio of studio albums offering her freest music yet, crowned by one of her greatest,
Hejira.

She'd found the word "hejira" in the dictionary, trawling for
something that evoked her desire to traverse the borders she felt
were hemming her in. Arabic for "pilgrimage." Wanderlust again
put Mitchell squarely in the center of American popular consciousness, taking over just as mobility resurfaced as a central topic in
public conversation. Social mores were loosening even as political
and economic realities grew more challenging for the very people
supposedly freed by the previous era's cultural shifts. Road movies and travelogues became popular again, and a feminist version
emerged, with women as the protagonists seeking to escape men's
stifling presence and find themselves. These stories reflected the
hopes and struggles of women trying to seize opportunities in the
workplace or their postdivorce personal lives, running into road-
blocks and devising new routes.

As women (and, in aligned movements, people of color and
queer people) worked to erase the bounds imposed on them, the
paladins of the old American dream often seemed utterly upended. On the screen, antiheroes were in. The decade's heart-
throbs ranged from scruffy street renegades like Robert De Niro
and Al Pacino to nutjob Jack Nicholson and everybody's favorite

unreliable date Warren Beatty. These men had the dislocated air of sons unable to manage their inheritances, echoing the pathos of the current social climate: everyone wanted to get somewhere or away from somewhere. Just don't stand still.

The history of this period is, to steal a line from Joni, written in the white lines of the freeway. But that freeway is a place of stasis as much as a conduit to change. *Play It as It Lays*, that novel of female sadness that had so well complemented the nascent women's liberation movement, was relevant again, this time for its portrait of unrest as visible on L.A.'s gleaming overpasses. In a 1973 *New York Times* article, Joan Didion reflected on the neurotic driving habits of her antiheroine Maria Wyeth. "She didn't have anything to do, she was kind of in limbo," Joan explained. "When you're in that state, marking time and trying to stay together, you've got to have something to do to organize your day. The freeways give you a spurious sense of organization. You do have to be organized and in control." Maria drove in circles, as Joni did sometimes, to reassemble herself. Didion's words make me think of the way the songwriter Dan Wilson describes the music of *Hejira*: "endless loops." Loops within loops within loops. Always moving, never landing.

LADY DRIFTERS

The story in *Play It as It Lays* can be reduced to a short sentence: Maria Wyeth takes a drive. Her aimlessness on the days when she just sets out to go nowhere, escaping the failed family relations and self-destructive friends who populate the novel's plot, motivates her to stay alive. It is a meaningless kind of freedom, the only kind she thinks she deserves after failing (that's her feeling) as a model, an actress, a wife, a mother, a friend. Unhappy with what she is, unable to imagine herself otherwise, she makes a life of endless transitions.

I believe Joni Mitchell would have barely tolerated Maria Wyeth if she'd been a real person and they'd ever met. She disliked weak women. As much as her own road songs similarly alight in liminal spaces, our Joan has too much vigor, too much actualized desire, to give in the way Didion's heroine does. If anything, Didion's lady driver recalls the characters in Mitchell songs who doom themselves by sitting still. The unnamed socialite in "The Hissing of Summer Lawns," who responds in despair to a busted television in her mansion, *Tube's gone, darkness, darkness, darkness, no color, no contrast.* Or the former poolside beauty Harry weds in "Harry's House," who reeled him in only to tell him to shove his wealth and status up his ass, but who probably doesn't leave him in the end. Or the dissatisfied aging ingenue in "Shades of Scarlett Conquering," tied up by her conviction that *a woman must have everything* but only men can fulfill that demand. Even the title character in "Song for Sharon," a real friend whom Mitchell loved, gains only faint praise for remaining on her farm making meals and singing to a crowd only the size of her nuclear family while Joni remains on the road, heading out of the Los Angeles chaparral toward something green.

There was so much more on offer in the 1970s for women who might be thinking a trip could be nice. Take your pick from the top of the bestseller list or the bottom shelves of the feminist bookstore, from Saturday matinee offerings and jukebox hits— women on the move were everywhere. Some authors behind the era's travelogue boom were on Mitchell's radar—her fellow L.A. babe Eve Babitz; the Canadian Margaret Atwood. Others she likely didn't know, like the Black science fiction trailblazer Octavia

Butler. They all shared a spirit, an insistence that the guys who'd claimed those freeway lines stop hogging the road.

Bob Dylan released his own road record, *Desire*, in 1976, brimming with swashbuckling ballads about romance and quests for treasure in exotic locales. Compared to Dylan's heroics, Mitchell often wrote of her journeys in an almost pedestrian way. He bragged about mystical outlaw princesses that drew him into catacombs and gunfights; she focused on hotel room trysts and the bitter coffee sheepish lovers drank in diners the next morning. She did see visions, heavenly hexagrams formed by jet planes, but she also noticed the antique dolls in the bed-and-breakfasts where she spent the night. This was a gift that women's travel stories offered, not a shortcoming. Within the heterosexual cliché, a traveling man can leap into the realm of fantasy, while a woman often ends up cleaning up the mess that adventurer made, especially if she made it with him. Think of Rayette, the wishful, pregnant waitress played by Karen Black, whom Jack Nicholson's Bobby abandons at a rural gas station at the end of *Five Easy Pieces*. Director Bob Rafelson's film leaves her stranded, pathetic. The songs and stories many women wrote in the 1970s take up right after this moment, showing the dirty diapers and the temporary jobs that fill a woman's life as she tries to locate her own power outside the typical hero's tale. The singer-songwriter Maggie Roche, who like Joni became a single mother at twenty and entrusted her son in adoption, succinctly expressed how responsibility landed on such women adventurers when their men wandered off: *The world is handout on the corners and the burden of proof is on you.*

Some women singer-songwriters focused on such messes, and the costs and comforts of sticking around to manage it. A profile of Carly Simon stressed her homebody side. "She confesses she doesn't like to travel," the piece reads. "Among other things, 'I am paranoid about eating out of town tuna fish sandwiches.'" Simon made a neat 1970s career of critiquing the domestic life she and James Taylor imperfectly modeled (he continued to struggle with heroin as they became parents to two, eventually divorcing in 1983); hits like "We Have No Secrets" and "Haven't Got Time for the Pain" exposed the imperfections of the swinging-while-married upper middle class. Her image as a mommy sexpot tended to overshadow Simon's incisive side. In the late 1970s her ode to women's slow-building orgasm, "Anticipation," was repurposed in an iconic Heinz ketchup commercial that deflected the song's sensuality into the hungry hands of children. Family fare at its latchkey-kid best.

Mitchell, meanwhile, sought a broken middle again, this time between the masculine and feminine. Her songs convey the conflict she and many women felt between the desire to escape old roles and the awareness that there were no real new models for maintaining safety and security within a self-determined life. *Again and again, the same situation* . . . She allegedly wrote that line from *Court and Spark* about Warren Beatty, an unusual flirtation for her, an actor and notorious Lothario. The situation was this: she wanted to be in love, which for her also meant making a home, but only if she could also leave that nest when inspiration and, as she called it, *my struggle for higher achievements* demanded. Doing both sometimes seemed to require that she bend time and collapse space.

Many women's travelogues in the 1970s teetered on this lunch plate's edge between the quest for liberation and the realities many women couldn't leave behind: kids, partners, homes, communities. Faith, the middle-aged heroine of Grace Paley's 1974 short story "The Long-Distance Runner," takes up the sport to allay domestic emptiness as her children age out of their teens; in a surreal twist, she temporarily holes up with the Black family who has moved into her Bronx childhood home. But she soon returns to her sons and unreliable boyfriend. Joan Foster, the romance novel–writing heroine of Margaret Atwood's 1976 novel *Lady Oracle*, lives a lifetime of escapes—from adolescent obesity into svelte adulthood, into marriage and then out of it, in affairs, and through the Gothic romances she authors—until her various alternate realities become so jumbled that she fakes her own death to elude them. She, too, seems destined to return to home and husband after her ruse is uncovered, although she may have a new lover in tow. Even Isadora Wing, the emblematic libertine in Erica Jong's *Fear of Flying*, tries many positions with a few different men but ends up back with husband Bennett after a sexual assault convinces her that the "zipless fuck" she's seeking is meaningless without emotional connection. Jong's phrase became a catchword for liberation, but women's road stories rarely if ever idealized the anonymous encounters it signifies. In them, freedom came through better connections with men or sometimes women, and through greater self-awareness—not full abandonment of traditional coupling's intimate bonds.

This pattern of breakaways and returns was one that many people, especially women, understood. New horizons could be reached creatively and spiritually, but love (and marriage in particular) often put the vehicle back in park. Some writers turned to science fiction as a way out of this plot limitation—for Atwood, Marge Piercy and Octavia Butler, time and space travel allowed women freedom that seemed unimaginable otherwise. Some of its spirit enters into Mitchell's mid-1970s songwriting, as her metaphors soar: *The eagle and the serpent are at war in me*, she sings in the title track from 1977's *Don Juan's Reckless Daughter*. *Scales to feathers . . . crawl and fly*. Compare this to the scene she painted in

"The Same Situation," of herself contained within Beatty's mirrored bathroom, primping and questioning her urge to do so. The
timid pretty girl has become an airborne Gorgon, her internal
struggles mythologized.

DOG LOVERS, DARK ROADS

Bob Dylan designed his Rolling Thunder Revue tour to be a
generative mess, inviting dozens of friends and collaborators
on board in 1975 for fifty-seven dates in convention centers, on
college campuses and even in a gym or two. Meant to evoke the
vaudeville tent revivals and carnivals that Dylan felt represented
the real, raw America, Rolling Thunder Revue fought back against
the encroaching dullness of standard arena rock. The band wore
slapdash gypsy costumes, Beat daddy Allen Ginsberg improvised
poetry and David Bowie's right-hand man Mick Ronson inter-
jected glam-rock guitar solos into folk song choruses. The reunion
of the star with his long-estranged singing partner and paramour
Baez added sexy buzz to the goings-on. Gossip, magic, hokum and
greasepaint were what held this mad moving convocation together,
and Joni had to let her satin shirts get dirty when she joined up at
the end of what had, for her, been a fairly sedentary year.

She'd been scheduled for only one night in New Haven, Con-
necticut, but Joni had so much fun—and was so glad to get away
from the troublesome intensity of her life with Guerin, the nearly
perfect guy who couldn't keep his "pachyderm" in his pants—that
she stayed on for a whole month. Unlike on her own recent tours,
where some fans voiced their disapproval of her swing toward
jazz, on Rolling Thunder Revue she brought down the house.
They listened, rapt, to her musical contributions, and then . . . the
songs she started to write testified to what came next.

The most famous is "Coyote," about the playwright and tour scribe Sam Shepard, with whom she dallied when she wasn't flirting with the Band's Rick Danko or trying to get Dylan to sit down with her for more than five minutes. (He was busy negotiating an emotional triangle between himself, estranged wife Sara and Baez.) In her jittery lyrics Joni portrayed the notoriously randy Sam as an animal tamer who kept his own manhood wild, a romance novel type who had horses on his ranch and a lady down every hotel hallway. The song's most famous line is her dirtiest anywhere: *He picks up my scent on his fingers while he's watching the waitresses' legs*. In "Coyote," she's not only responsive to this dog's sniffing, but suddenly desirous in a new, uncontrollable way. She's a hitcher with her thumb extended, brought into the album's encounters by fate, with her will playing along.

Joni finished writing *Hejira* by staying on the road, this time only to chase herself. After Rolling Thunder she embarked on a tour supporting *The Hissing of Summer Lawns*, but tensions with Guerin cut that short and soon after she headed out on her own. Part of the time she had traveling companions—a lover from her earlier roving days and a new flame, a trouble child she'd met at Neil Young's house one night, whom she took to bed and memorialized in the album's most furtive rocker, "A Strange Boy." She then drove alone deep into the South, where she took on assumed names and even sometimes wore a wig, supposedly so she wouldn't be recognized, but the noir-movie fugitive fun of it all must have kept her going. She wrote back to Guerin via a vampy cocktail jazz parody she titled "Blue Motel Room," playing off the keyboard chords she was hearing in the lounges where she made transitory friends. The most memorable songs on *Hejira* have a snapshot quality of scenes captured and developed quickly, with a shake of the Polaroid picture. She was cruising on a dry desert road when a nearby air show put six fighter jets above her in formation, and she thought of Amelia Earhart, writing a song for her and for those trick boys overhead: *the drone of flying engines is a song so wild and blue*. She met a friend in Memphis and they did the roots music tour, finding the old landmarks decrepit; from that came "Furry Sings the Blues," *pawn shops glitter like gold tooth caps in the grey decay*. On a New York stop she took the ferry to Staten Island and passed a window full of a wedding dress: it's in "Song for Sharon," *some girl's gonna see that dress and crave that day like crazy*. These passing thoughts ravel around each other and undo the maps directing Joni forward. They challenge her to accept the detours that lead her away from her presumptions. The stories do not resolve; the journey won't end. That's the point.

Hejira sounds like Rolling Thunder Revue, even though it also sounds like the fusion Joni was deep into mastering. Its songs spin out and drift, their wheels muddy, with no choruses anchoring them. Though she was preoccupied with the lupine Shepard and all the other men who kept her away from another failed stab at domesticity, Dylan's vagabond aesthetic is the most audible inspiration for these songs. Rolling Thunder Revue was shaggy and grand, and so is *Hejira*. The difference is one of periodization. Dylan wanted to keep his America historic, made shabby chic by patina shades of hokum and lore. Joni saw the contemporary heartland, taking snapshots of the liminal spaces where women linger with bad-choice boys or dream of different matches, or of ways to be alone: diner booths, hotel rooms, store windows, dance floors. An America for the uncaged housewives and the freaks feeling themselves, the new vanguard, all hitchers, imagining themselves at the wheel.

THE INNER JOURNEYS PLAYLIST

In the 1970s, Joni was connected, reaching out, taking it all in. The shy girl and the party girl did a little boho dance inside her, trading places depending on what day it was. *I'm always talkin', chicken squawkin', bigawwk, bigAWWWK!* she yakked in "Talk To Me," musicalizing the women's art of conversation as it goes off the rails. That song from *Don Juan's Reckless Daughter* is an extrovert's embarrassing indulgence, the final shove from a pushy broad: *Romeo, Romeo, talk to me.* She sure did like to run her mouth off. But then she'd do an about-face, retreating into solitude. Reflecting on this period later, she'd describe the 1970s as a time when she moved away from the introversion that had reached its nearly claustrophobic peak on *Blue* and toward a new role as an observer, telling others' stories as she encountered them on the road. Yet in another, fundamental way, she remained inwardly focused. She just had a different framework for doing so, one emblematic of the time. A silent listener sits across from her in *Hejira*'s songs as she recounts her excursions. Herself, in the role of analyst.

I tried to run away myself, Mitchell sings in "Coyote," *to run away and wrestle with my ego. Hejira*'s opening salvo identifies her travels as both geographical and psychological. She ranges through her own mind as much as anywhere else, but her lyrics show signs of a new mindset. The scholar David Shumway identified the Freudian couch as the source. "Ambivalence is a characteristic of neurotic states, but it is also a product of the work of analysis," he wrote in his book *Rock Star*. "Mitchell's work depends heavily on the discourse of, if not psychoanalysis proper, then the therapy of the talking cure in a general sense."

Damn, you're right, I thought when I read these lines, a little envious that he'd made the connection before me. Bringing psychoanalysis into the conversation explains so much, not only about Mitchell's 1970s preoccupations, but about the nonlinear, strangely looping, overflowing structure of her songs as the decade progressed. I wasn't surprised to discover that Mitchell's own experiences with therapy were at best mixed. In 1973, bereft after a brief fractured romance with Jackson Browne, she started seeing Dr. Martin Grotjahn on Warren Beatty's recommendation; David Geffen was the German shrink's patient, too. Mitchell dove in, but to no one's surprise then or now, she soon decided she could do the job better herself. Pretty soon, references to analysis started slipping into her work: *Court and Spark* includes both the haunting portrait of an unstable patient, "Trouble Child," and the analysand's retort, "Twisted." From then on, therapy's terminology turned up in her lyrics again and again.

This was not unusual in the "Me" Decade, as some dubbed the 1970s—everybody had a shrink and a stack of self-help paperbacks in the den and talked that jargon with the ease and enthusiasm of the newly enlightened. Mitchell managed something unique, though. She remade the song form to reveal her inner journeys.

As she sped along the highways of an America increasingly turned on to its own navel, Mitchell's compositions became as evocative of that historical moment's ideas about self-actualization as they were of the changing landscapes outside her vehicle windows. Her conversational vocal style became a means for embodying rumination, that mental state in which thoughts unspool and recombine, dragging a person down until she can identify which of them might be a lifeline. To accommodate her intuitive writing style, she abandoned hooks and clear refrains in favor of soliloquies and sonic meltdowns, all serving insights that paid off without resolving. More than any other music of the time, this was the sound of a brain inquiring about itself.

"An artist needs a certain amount of turmoil and confusion and I've created out of that, even severe depression," she told a reporter from the *Toronto Star* in 1974, explaining why she started therapy. "But I had a lot of questions about myself, the way I was conducting my lives—life, what were my values in this time." I imagine her keeping two notebooks, marked up in different inks for every town through which she passed—one recording details about landmarks, people, incidents; the other devoted to moods, memories, the ghosts she carried around with her. Loops within loops within loops: that's rumination, the mental *talk-talk-bigaawwwk* that simulates motion while keeping a person stuck in the past. A meditation teacher would call it the monkey mind, always slapping away the serenity of concentration and insight. A gestalt therapist might say, *Joni, you're talking to an empty chair*; that technique employed such metaphors to help people process life's half-completed conversations. A shaman might hear her free-associating and decide she's on a vision quest.

I've done some chicken squawking in my time. Definitely the variety Joni outlined in "Talk To Me"—the begging for attention from a man too cool or repressed to care. But also the kind on the couch, to medical professionals trained to keep their distance. I returned to therapy while writing this book, in a little room five miles away from my house. I sat upright on the cool gray love seat in my analyst's office, putting a pillow behind my back and leaning forward to better hear his gentle, often nearly inaudible responses to my yammering. Later we switched to the phone because of the pandemic, and I trod around the neighborhood with my dog and my headphones, happy that I could discourse into space. I'm not a great analysand. Even when I start a session ready to talk about ugly things, my need to be liked takes over and I'm performing. In "Talk To Me," Joni lists all the things that might

interest her hero: religion and gossip, Charlie Chaplin and Ing-
mar Bergman. The topics of the day. During my appointments I
think about what might interest my shrink: a funny story from my
childhood, a memory that will elicit sympathy but still cast me in a
good light. I've already put these anecdotes through the mechani-
cal wringer of contemporary therapy and self-help so many times.
It's something I share with Joni, this appetite for new methods of
laundering the old noggin. I got it from my mom, who loved a
good self-help book.

Here's a list of what those bestsellers offered when I was a
kid, beyond the warm fuzzies of my family's preferred method,
transactional analysis, which I've already discussed: reality therapy,
behavioral therapy, cognitive behavioral therapy, nude marathon
therapy, and of course encounter groups. In her book, *Encountering America*, historian Jessica Grogan calls the "Me" Decade a
time when "Americans were confronted with an 'imponderable
dilemma of choice.'" I'd add to the list all those esoteric practices
that intersected the field of psychology, from Transcendental Meditation (TM) to peyote dosing, from Nova Yoga ("the yoga of the
imagination") to EST.

Joni stuck to the middle but sometimes flirted with the edge.
Her psychic trips took many forms, as they did for her closest
friends. Here's how her pal David Geffen described his own path
in 1993: "I'm a person who's been in therapy, analysis, Lifespring,
EST, the Course in Miracles, for the last twenty-five years." Joni
sampled from the same buffet. I'm pretty sure she tried psychedelics, given her interest in spiritual seekers who embraced the
practice; she was a devoted fan of the anthropologist Carlos Castaneda, whose shamanic training manuals touted the wonders of
peyote. She definitely got into TM—her name appears in several
different 1970s gossip columns among the countless celebs who

paid the Maharishi for their mantras. She did yoga, though she never went macrobiotic, enjoying hot dogs too much.

With the language of psychotherapy permeating everything from novels (again, Jong's *Fear of Flying*) to films (*Annie Hall*) to prime-time sitcoms (*The Bob Newhart Show*, with the comedian as a charming shrink), music followed suit. Male rockers incorporated tales of madness into their lexicon of questing heroes, from Elton John's "Madman Across the Water" to Pink Floyd's "Brain Damage." Women rarely explored the subject in the same way, and the exceptions were marketed as pop novelties. I loved these songs. Their main avatar was the preternaturally calm Australian singer Helen Reddy, who counted several portraits of madwomen among her many hits. In the converted basement den that was my bedroom, I made up elaborate dances to these Gothic tales. My favorite was "Angie Baby," an account of teen breakdown in which music itself drove its poor heroine over the edge. I valued this song because its mad girl turned out to not be crazy after all. Her radio really did have magic powers. It allowed her to imprison a neighbor boy who'd broken into her house "with evil on his mind," upending his plan to assault her and turning him into the "secret lover who keeps her satisfied." I always sang the song's punch line at the top of my lungs: "It's so nice to be insane. No one asks you to explain!" Upstairs but within earshot, my mom scheduled another transactional analysis appointment.

I didn't discover the one woman who openly explored her own breakdown and recovery in song until I was well on Joni's path, looking around for others who took risks the way she did. Dory Previn didn't sell a lot of records, though her story certainly made the tabloids. She'd found her place among the Laurel Canyon–adjacent elite, partnering with her husband, André, on film soundtracks and theme songs like the wistful theme from

Valley of the Dolls, a movie about, what else, women having break-downs. Their partnership imploded when André took up with Dory's friend Mia Farrow, twenty years her junior, who, in the lyricist's own cutting words, had "admired my unmade bed." Dory's subsequent collapse on a cross-country flight landed her in a psychiatric hospital—not that uncommon a fate for well-off women who weren't coping well with calamitous life changes. But Dory didn't keep mum about the experience afterward; in fact, she did the opposite, recording her brutal, brilliant album *On My Way to Where*.

That song cycle relates the story of her husband's betrayal and her derangement with a clarity rarely matched by other song-writers. Martin Kasindorf profiled Dory for the *Los Angeles Times* when *On My Way to Where* came out, declaring her the sole prac-titioner of "her sui generis musical genre, the poetry of therapy." The writer compared her to Mitchell and Judy Collins, identifying her songs as "starker" but "more singable, besides—a predictable result of the fusion of Freud with the work of the woman who set words to the *Valley of the Dolls* theme." Dory talked openly of writing these songs as "self-prescribed hospital therapy." She told Kasindorf, "I had said it, lived it, screamed it, but still I was afraid of dealing with my background. There was nothing to do but set it down on paper. I had to get my demons in the open and say, 'OK, I have to live with you, so let's hassle it out.'"

The sound of Dory Previn hassling it out is unlike anything else recorded in those years. She went even further than Joni in creating sometimes monstrous, all-too-human characters in her songs. But her combination of musical-comedy razzmatazz and psychoanalysis-inspired inquiries only resonated with a small cult of listeners. Letting it all hang out had its limits when it came to being a pop star.

Mitchell figured out how to balance self-exposure and a sense of mystery more effectively. Her songs invoking psychotherapy and other vision quests are sometimes humorous, often skeptical, never conclusive. Mystery remained attractive to her, as did the safety net of occasional discretion. *I am returning to myself, these things that you and I suppressed*, she sings on *Hejira*'s title track. But this homecoming wouldn't be simple or direct.

In her essay on Mitchell, Anne Hilker calls "Amelia" the best example of Mitchell's grounding in melancholy—a Freudian term not simply synonymous with sadness but denoting the unresolved losses that afflict and divide a person's psyche. Musically and lyrically, Hilker writes, the song "gestures toward perpetual movement." It wavers between two keys, F major and G major; its suspended chords, with their built-in dissonance, reinforce its sense of exile, as does the circular structure, never offering the climax of a bridge or a chorus. Plus, the song is a riddle: its refrain, *Amelia, it was just a false alarm*, is never explained. Is the false alarm a reference to the famous aviator Amelia Earhart, her body never recovered from a crash no one saw? Might Mitchell be speculating on the moment the plane went down, a fault in the wiring that ended Earhart's legendary restless life? Or could the false alarm be plaguing Joni herself, as she sets out for places unknown within her own subconscious, surveying patterns built from memories and impulses that she only partly understands?

"Amelia" is one of two songs on *Hejira* that doesn't have a bass line, another reason it feels ethereal, ungrounded. This album foregrounds Joni's sonic twinship with Jaco Pastorius; his bass playing, overdubbed after her parts on the album were completed, answer her voice and guitar so intuitively that they seem like extensions of her own thoughts. I think about Jaco as another voice inside Joni's own head. The bass is an aspect of her monkey mind, an instrument of rumination, but also of insight. In certain moods I can't listen too much to *Hejira* because of its intensity; it weighs on me, reminds me of how my own mind can fill with chatter. Why turn Jaco's bass up so high? I've sometimes wondered. But I think this is it—he provided the final element of unrest that realized Mitchell's goal of replicating an inner life in a way that conventional songcraft, with its neater harmonies and resolutions, could not. And sometimes those bass parts push her questioning to a whole new level.

By her next album, 1977's *Don Juan's Reckless Daughter*, Joni was leaning out of the psyche's language and into mysticism. Jaco was with her. The record's great psychedelic moment is the song suite "Paprika Plains," but plenty of other examples of vision questing surface on this complicated, truly over-the-top recording. The album's very title, though seeming to poke sweet fun at Mitchell's status as a female Casanova, also expresses her appreciation for Castaneda's Don Juan books, fictionalized accounts of his hallucinatory journeys with a Yaqui shaman. The "split-tongued" spirit Mitchell conjures in the title track, whose dual nature— world-bound serpent and transcendent eagle—presides over these songs, is exactly the kind of guide Castaneda continually evoked in his bestselling books.

It makes sense that Joni's inner journeys would get more psychedelic as the 1970s wore on. By 1977 Mitchell had moved past psychoanalysis through various forms of meditation, trading in a cocaine habit acquired on the road for more organic routes toward enlightenment. Urged by Robben Ford's wife to seek out the guidance of the Tibetan sage Chögyam Trungpa Rinpoche—a guru as popular among Hollywood habitués as the psychoanalyst Grotjahn had once been—Mitchell had a confrontational encounter with the monk that, according to her, put her into a three-day state of what Buddhists call satori, or no-mind. "I left his office and for three days I was in an awakened state," she said in a 2005 interview. "The technique completely silenced that thing, the loud, little noisy radio station that stands between you and the great mind."

That major reset tipped Mitchell's writing more toward the mystical. With this turn, she was again in step with American culture. Overshadowed by the medicalization of mental health and the mainstreaming of New Age self-help movements, psychotherapy remained an important tool and Freud's talking cure a historical touchstone, but no longer was it a definitive force within Americans' understanding of their inner lives. But Mitchell would continue to look within and sometimes use Freud's language to do so. "I can't quit analyzing; I'm an artist," she'd told Rinpoche before he zapped her with his breathing technique.

THE TENTH WORLD

After the cross-country sojourn of *Hejira*, Mitchell later told a reporter, she saw herself turning her back on America, musically at least, and departing for the "Third World." She was a hippie sophisticate exploring her notion of the foreign to clear her head. Musically, she ranged from Miami to the Caribbean and deep into Latin America's jungles, where she believed the magic she'd read about in Carlos Castaneda's books was afoot. She'd grown disillusioned with America's violence and corruption, and in the rhythms of the African diaspora she sought some kind of return to harmony, if not innocence. "My intention was in a way to go around the world and embrace a lot of different cultures, and distill it all down," she told one interviewer.

These were sonic journeys that took place in various rehearsal rooms and studios, culminating in songs like "The Jungle Line,"

"Dreamland" and "Paprika Plains." Forging paths with new fellow travelers, Mitchell sought a kind of mutual recognition—a genuine rapprochement with the brown and Black voices who originally laid down these songlines. In her lyrics she acknowledged the power dynamics involved when white wayfarers claim space in others' homelands, even as she made her own appropriations. Mitchell's visions of these encounters are complex; she knew that in the history of conquest, the best intentions are often wrapped in poison blankets. In the vacation fantasy "Dreamland," she calls herself out for her colonizing gestures, identifying herself as a "suntan slave" in a starlet's "Dorothy Lamour sarong." But this indictment of tourism ends on a sympathetic note for the visitors rejuvenated by their escape from their snowy Northern lawns. "Dreamland" calls back to "The Jungle Line," replacing the sampled Drummers of Burundi with African diaspora percussionists right there in the studio. The earlier song about the thrill and risk of colonizing sets up the later one about conquest's aftermath at the beachside snack bar. The tone of these songs is buoyant; they are critiques of "going native" that acknowledge the pleasures of doing so.

What I hear throughout *Don Juan's Reckless Daughter* is the dislocation and irresolution of *Hejira* extending beyond the limitations of one mind and one eye. Its love songs slip into mythology; its painted scenes span deserts, jungles and teeming inner-cityscapes. Instead of bringing her inner visions to the analyst's couch, Joni rolls with them. This is dream music, hallucinatory, not easily interpretable. No longer do the songs move in loops within loops. They are more unhinged now, more discursive, sometimes finding relief in old-fashioned jazz forms but more often growing thick and hard to navigate.

In the title track, Joni expresses her uncertainty: *What strange*

*prizes these battles bring, these hectic joys, these weary blues; puffed up
and strutting when I think I win, down and shaken when I think I lose.*
The grittiness in her voice feels foreign, revealing a part of herself
she hasn't wanted to confront. She is trying to claim its power and
its unfamiliar nature. The music evokes her reach toward what
theorists call "the other" through Pastorius's bass lines, now not
duetting with Joni but sparring, going deep in the hole and sneak-
ily surfacing, and through Don Alias's percussion lines, the root
web of everything.

Where was she going with this music? Nowhere and wherever. Mitchell sacrificed a European tour to write these songs,
claiming exhaustion but still traveling for self-edification. She
traveled to New Mexico with Alias, now her beau, in search of her
hero Georgia O'Keeffe. And she was often out in the clubs in both
New York and L.A., mingling with her new jazz fusion friends. As
a musical collaborator, Alias helped Mitchell claim the world. A
polymath who could explain every percussion pattern from Brazil
to Haiti to the Bronx, Alias added topographical layers to Joni's
maps that she could have only imagined on her own.

Percussion dominates *Don Juan's Reckless Daughter*, so much
so that two tracks privilege it above all else. For "Dreamland,"
Airto Moreira, Alex Acuña and Manolo Badrena were enlisted to
expand the arrangement; Pastorius took up a cowbell and Chaka
Khan added vocal flourishes to Mitchell's lead. It was all very
spontaneous—Khan recalls Mitchell calling her at three a.m. to
join the session the next day. Pastorius brought in Acuña after Joni
decided the album's title track needed some ankle bells. A report
in *Circus* magazine indicates just how unfamiliar most American
writers were with such cross-cultural exchanges. A hot tip from
an unnamed studio assistant led writer Wesley Strick to paint an
almost cartoonish scene:

Mitchell decided, mid-session, that she really needed "ankle bells" for "tempo and atmosphere." Long-time engineer Henry Lewy put out a frantic call, with no luck. "Finally," the assistant laughs, "somebody came up with a dancer named Alejandro Acuña. They dimmed the lights, stuck her on a little stage, and ran the tapes. I think they got her from the Screen Actors Guild, actually. But she is a real Indian."

Alex Acuña, who's not a "real Indian" woman but a Peruvian man, remembered in a later interview that he was the one who owned the ankle bells and performed a dance native to his home region upon Joni's request. She recalls it differently—the bells were hers, and she persuaded him to strap them on and move across the baffled floor to create a "pow-wow sound." In her description, Acuña was temporarily crippled by the exertion: "It was a bent-knee dance and when the song was done, he limped off the baffle. He couldn't straighten up for an hour, but he agreed it sounded great." Shaman or somewhat put-upon studio musician going that extra mile? In these interactions, apparently, power dynamics continued to blur the roles.

An even thornier entanglement of Joni's fantasies and the lived histories of colonized people produced one of her greatest and most challenging songs, the sixteen-minute-long "Paprika Plains." Mitchell recorded the base of this hallucinatory return to childhood as a series of piano improvisations over the course of several months. Jaco Pastorius had shown her some harmonic approaches that she found freeing; she explored their outer limits. Henry Lewy and she then edited them together. She wrote the song's vocal part and recorded that, and then she got together first with her band in London and then with an arranger and a chamber orchestra in New York to map out the piece in 3-D. Later, she enlisted Mike Gibbs, a jazz-trained composer and arranger who'd also worked with prog-rock groups like Manfred Mann and Uriah Heep, to create a film score–style framework for the song. And she wrote its 650 words, many of them not sung but included on the album packaging. They describe her experience of recovering the girl Roberta Joan within a mental flash flood, a flashback, a vision that overwhelms, and then, with deep breaths, a return to the now-enhanced present moment.

Everything about "Paprika Plains" eradicates the comfort zone of pop. Dynamically it ranges from crickets-quiet in the beginning to booming full orchestration at its peak. Joni's piano is washed in Technicolor, augmented by Gibbs's string arrangements evoking the trippy pastoralism of early Disney movies. The wild creatures Joni calls forth are not bluebirds and bunnies, though; they are snakes and lizards. In the poetic lines printed on the album's gate-fold but uttered only in her head as she recorded, she conjures a crow, then a phoenix. This is her dream, the one she had while Dylan slept in a nearby room during Rolling Thunder Revue. The grandiose and the banal mix surrealistically, as they do in the surfacing subconscious.

"Paprika Plains" is a song made for getting lost, in the jazz way and the psychoanalytic way, and the psychedelic way, too. Yet as unique and compelling as it is, it bears evidence of rich white hippie self-delusion. As much as I admire its dazzling depiction of how the traces of the past surface in the mind's eye and ear, sitting with it nearly half a century after she recorded it makes me squirm even as I swoon. The archetypes Mitchell conjures aren't that far from stereotypes. Debates raged over who has a right to Indigenous imagery in the 1970s as they do now. Anyone can find herself on the sunburnt Great Plains the Mandans call the Okaraxta, or on the prairies that are part of what the Lakota claim as the Beautiful

Country, Makxoche Washte. Mitchell did, as a child and again in later adventures. Whether everyone has the right to speak from those places, even in alliance with their first residents, is a question that remains unresolved.

In Mitchell's lyric, ochre-shadowed figures gather in front of a small-town general store. "Saskatchewan" is Cree for "fast-flowing river," but little of the rest of the region's First Nations culture—representing not only Cree people, but Lakota, Dene and others—was preserved by the white settlers of the pioneer territory where young Roberta Joan was raised. On the back cover of *Don Juan's Reckless Daughter* is a photograph of her in an "Indian" costume; mirroring the lyrics of "Paprika Plains," this image, though confronted far less frequently than the notorious blackface costume she wears on the front cover, shows how Mitchell both imagined herself as akin to First Nations people and misunderstood their lived experience from childhood on.

Her activism on behalf of Indigenous causes has been a mainstay of Mitchell's adult life, so much so that she was even granted the name Sparkling White Bear Woman by the Saulteaux people in a civic ceremony in 2018. Mitchell also believed for many years that her own genetic makeup included the blood of the Sámi, the first people of northern Scandinavia, home of her great-grandparents. (This has been disproven.) She clearly feels a deep emotional bond with the distant neighbors who, to her, seemed like fellow outsiders in her lonesome prairie youth. But she is not a member of a First Nations community; she was and can only be, at best, an ally, and at worst a romanticizer. Indigenous imagery runs through Mitchell's lyrics, especially from the 1970s onward, and often works as the seed of protest. At the same time, when she pictures the non-white people in her memory or dreams as corrupted by the white man's influence, she doesn't always consider their resistance or accurately portray their survival in the industrialized Canada of her adulthood.

"Paprika Plains" isn't a historical account of anything; its distortions are the point. Yet I wonder if Mitchell ever heard, as a child, about the actual fight waged by First Nations folk like the ones she saw and mimicked in her preschool years? The Cree, Saulteaux, Sioux and other Indigenous people of Saskatchewan were among the most poverty-stricken in Canada at midcentury; after World War II, some who had enlisted in the army organized to protest the treaties that had removed them from their land and put many of their children in brutal residential schools. The Indian Act was revised in 1951, around the time young Roberta Joan went through her own hellish battle with polio. Mitchell would likely have known this history well before writing "Paprika Plains": her friend and mentor Buffy Sainte-Marie is a lifelong activist, as was her onetime Toronto neighbor, the poet and musician Duke Redbird, who was a friend to her during her pregnancy. Was Mitchell thinking of them when she placed at the center of the unsung portion of "Paprika Plains" a *blanket figure* who *springs with a fist raised up to turquoise skies like liberty*? Is it her right to share this image, even if it came from her own memory, her own dream?

THE UNDERDOG

My twenty-first-century qualms about "Paprika Plains" took me back to the question at the heart of every argument over appropriation: Who owns the stories we tell? It became central for Mitchell in April 1978, when she was contacted out of the blue by Charles Mingus, the bassist and composer legendary for his huge personality and his gift for revivifying traditional jazz forms through an experimental lens. Having claimed his place in the canon with new standards like "Goodbye Pork Pie Hat" and major works like the primal fusion suite *The Black Saint and the Sinner Lady*, Mingus was facing down a diagnosis of the neurodegenerative disease ALS and hoping for one last creative outburst. He'd been introduced to Mitchell's music by the Italian film producer Daniele Senatore; "Paprika Plains" jumped out at him, as did that cover image of Joni in blackface. (Mingus had interrogated his own Blackness in outlandish ways at times, depicting himself as a pimp in his some-times pornographic memoir, *Beneath the Underdog*, and perhaps smelled a fellow provocateur.) His wife, Sue, a well-connected arts journalist who'd devoted herself to managing his career, was starting to think about how his music might live on for new audi-ences after he'd gone. An alliance with a pop star would benefit everyone involved, and this one clearly had the kind of peripatetic spirit such an effort would require.

The first task the dying Mingus set for Mitchell was to help him set T. S. Eliot's "Four Quartets" poems to music, but she found she could not adapt the late English poet's otherworldly masterwork to the vernacular language Mingus desired. A few months after they'd called it quits, Mingus reached out again. By this time ALS had put him in a wheelchair and was starting to take his speech, but his mind remained intact. He'd written several themes for Mitch-ell, offering them as a prompt for lyrics that would be a kind of epitaph: a recounting of key moments in his life and a document to carry across the river into legacy's realm.

Mitchell recognized her work with Mingus as her full entry-way into the jazz realm—thirty years later, she'd tell Robert Hil-burn that this was the only album she'd made that existed within the genre's laws—and both her compositional style and her voice changed as she negotiated its parameters. Still forcefully her own woman, she rejected half of the tunes Mingus offered her, writing one track—"The Wolf That Lives in Lindsey"—wholly by herself and adding her own lyrics to his signature "Goodbye Pork Pie Hat." She let him steer while he still could and when she had to take over, she sought guidance from his echoing spirit. Mitchell was working hard to hear and preserve Mingus's voice, his subconscious, within her own process. She assembled a series of interstitial "raps," snippets of his conversation recorded by Sue in those later years, to hold the songs together. She tried out dozens of musicians, the coolest jazz names she could find, before settling on a band mostly consisting of Weather Report friends and family—Shorter and Pastorius at the center, with another crucial player in the fusion world, Herbie Hancock, on the keys—in her familiar stomping grounds at A&M Studios.

In her mixed review of the album, Ariel Swartley wrote in *Rolling Stone* that the Joni who embraced Mingus was not so much an outsider as a "habitual non-expert"; a tourist, a hitcher. Swartley saw that as a weakness, but years later, *Mingus* echoes forward precisely because of Mitchell's confidence in getting lost.

She does strut a bit as she travels. Over the course of thirty years, Mingus composed for some great jazz singers, and *Mingus* takes on this challenge as a chance to flex. "The Dry Cleaner from Des Moines" is a rapid-fire scat session, more ambitious than the Annie Ross tributes she'd tried before; "Goodbye Pork Pie Hat" has her playing with Billie Holiday–style blues timing, elasticizing the beat as Pastorius tickles her phrasings. Mostly, though, Mitchell lets the currents created by her remarkable band—and the spirit of Mingus, waning, waxing—carry her as she explores an approach that's both meditative and deconstructive, elongating phrases until each word drips with different meanings, evoking different kinds of inner journeys than the ruminative rambles of her other jazz explorations. "He was preparing to die and was

in a very reflective state," she told the pianist and writer Ben Sidran of Mingus. He told her that his mind was mostly focused on
the things he was losing by leaving the earth. Listening to him, she
said, "I simply became him in my imagination and wrote what he
would miss."

In the slow ballads "A Chair in the Sky," "Sweet Sucker Dance"
and "Goodbye Pork Pie Hat," Mitchell shifted her own perspective
in a way she rarely had, and escaped her own tendency to chicken-
squawk and showboat for attention. Her remarkable instrument
became the boat floating on otherworldly waters, conveying a consciousness in flux, a spirit cleansing itself for the afterlife. "It's a
different kind of breathing," she told Sidran of these vocals. "And
ironically, it's a more natural form of music for me as a singer than
my own music, because you have such creative liberty within the
bar." Mingus's melodies gave her a chance to go, again, to a place
she'd explored on *Blue*, at a moderate volume, with nuance and
subtle dynamics. "Like Miles Davis," she said to Sidran. Again.

Mingus himself was known for his volatility and showman-
ship, but also for the sheer beauty of his melodies and a lush ex-
pansiveness that did often connect to the spiritual, always with a
strong erotic pull. This was a quality Mitchell could embrace. The
bassist's outspokenness about racism and other forces oppressive
to creative people gave him a reputation as "the angry man of
jazz," but as his biographer Nichole Rustin-Paschal writes, "Mingus is all about love: musical, familial, sexual, and spiritual."
Dedicating herself to exploring all of what she told Sidran was
Mingus's "wide emotional spectrum," Mitchell on *Mingus* ends up
in a numinous space, where the torrents of words that she'd been
raising to explain her dissatisfaction with quotidian love and life
give way and instead the air is calm, the night sky star-marked and
cloud-streaked, the heat of restlessness diminishing.

Mingus gave Mitchell a whole new underworld to explore, and she was thankful. But the world did not respond the way she had hoped. The album received mixed reviews—one notable exception was Tom Reed, a critic for the Black newspaper the *Los Angeles Sentinel*, who concluded, "Synopsis: White woman does justice to Black man on record." I agree with Reed. With this one man, Mingus, depending on her to relay his final visions in words and voice instead of a field of strange figures culled from memory and fantasy, Mitchell took her time listening. Her preconceptions still surface in her lyrics to his tunes; a line in "Goodbye Pork Pie Hat" opines that a lynching would be unlikely in the 1970s, neglecting the various forms of racist violence common then— the ghost of Fred Hampton, the Black Panther leader shot in his bed by police in 1969, might want a word on that. And she does dare to adapt Mingus's mode to suit her own voice, especially in "A Chair in the Sky," one of the rare Joni songs that could be called a prayer, offering his dream of being reincarnated in style. In the end, though, *Mingus* still belongs to Mingus. Joni remains his envoy. The sound of this album reminds me of what a wise person once told me is the essence of being an ally: listen first, and let the other person speak as much as they want to, as much as they can.

7

for art's sake

One of the fundamental principles of Joni Mitchell's life is that an artist must be free, must value above anything else the right to move and change. There can be no limits when it comes to pursuing something new, even a different face and name. For one leg of her *Hejira* road trip in the late 1970s she turned South in her white Mercedes and disguised herself in order to explore its regions unrecognized.

One pseudonym she used venturing all the way to the Alabama Gulf Coast was "Joan Black." Later, she returned to Los Angeles, and made another crossing.

Still playing with her new jazz cat persona, Mitchell darkened her visage and put on a wig and a fake moustache and became, in her mind, a Black man whom she'd alternately name Claude and Art Nouveau. She did it as a lark, but then she did it again as a way to be a muse to herself, and again as an artistic statement she made sure was visible to all. Her choice to inhabit this character, which she's never denounced, is inconceivable today. It's shocking to realize that she felt no hesitancy when she buttoned up her vest and topped her polyester Afro with a brightly banded fedora. But few around her questioned her costume then, and most friends, fans and chroniclers have tread lightly around the worrisome subject since. It's tough, they say, to even talk about it, especially because this is Joni, the unimpeachable, the treasure so many feel compelled to protect.

Shocking—but is it, really? I think again about where we're at as a nation—a world—stained by the ongoing effect of racism. Sorry, Joni, we can't get ourselves back to the garden on this one. Blackface, the hideous act of assuming another's features in order to steal their energy, is one of the foundational American arts, traceable within any musical form grounded in Black culture but dominated by white stars. Big band jazz, rock and roll, country; Al Jolson, Elvis, Eminem. It's always there. I say this shamefully, as a white person aware of my own transgressions—never something so obscene as applying brown greasepaint to my cheeks, but my use of slang, my dance moves while drunk at a party, my mindless rapping along with a song on the radio that contains the N-word—I can't deny such everyday breaches, despite my desire to transcend them. And I've loved and identified with countless white musicians who've applied their own Black markings through a shimmy of the shoulders, an exaggerated drawl, an overdone diva wail. Joni is just another of these pretenders. Still, she was so bold. She didn't just cross a line—she refused to acknowledge its existence. It matters, saying this out loud, not wishing away what she's done.

It was 1976 when she first openly claimed Art Nouveau as her own. She had been invited to a Halloween party at bassist Leland Sklar's house and was popping into shops on Hollywood Boulevard in search of an outfit. At some point she got catcalled by a Black man who, in her words, "walked with a New York diddy-bop kind of step," as a jazz fan might say. She'd later tell interviewers that at that moment she felt possessed, overtaken as she had been by the Indigenous ghosts in "Paprika Plains." A few steps beyond this point of encounter she found a costume shop and began to assemble her look, which she later described using a word that signifies the declassé and the disrespected. "Sleazy." "I went into a sleazy menswear [shop] and bought a sleazy hat and a sleazy suit and that night I went to a Halloween party and nobody knew it was me, nobody." She took her purchases to Peter Asher's house and augmented them with some of his clothes, because they were about the same size. Then, off to the party. That night she called herself Claude. Sklar and party guests like the photographer Henry Diltz and Joni's occasional lover J. D. Souther have all confirmed Mitchell's claim that she was so thoroughly transformed as to be unrecognizable. This is preposterous. The general agreement among her friends that her transformation was believable is one of the strangest aspects of the whole saga, and in fact the many stories about that night contradict one another. But whether people didn't know at first that this "Claude" was actually Joni didn't matter much, because pretty soon he was a regular on her circuit.

She doubled down on developing this character, whom, it turned out, she'd been keeping close to her heart for a long time. Her evident reference points were the blaxploitation movies directed by auteurs like Gordon Parks and Melvin Van Peebles, and the album and book covers in a similar vein—including Corky McCoy's for Miles Davis's *On the Corner*—through which Black artists reclaimed the images, descended from minstrelsy, that made them objects of ridicule. She might have also come across another source, Adrian Piper's Mythic Being series, for which that Black feminist conceptual artist assumed a similar fly identity. (Thanks to Daphne A. Brooks for pointing this out to me.) Mitchell could have seen Piper's work in New York, where parts of it were published in the *Village Voice*. Did she think, *If they could do it . . . ?*

The following year, Mitchell took the performance public, including Claude—renamed Art Nouveau by now—in photographs by Norman Seeff within the montage of archetypes (a child, herself dancing) presented on the cover of *Don Juan's Reckless Daughter*. In 1980, invited by producer Barry Levinson to contribute a segment to *Love,* an all-woman-made omnibus film "on the subject of love, preferably from a sexual point of view," Mitchell brought Art out of the closet again. That fourteen-minute avant-garde oddity written by Mitchell and directed by Swedish actress and arthouse filmmaker Mai Zetterling, entitled *The Black Cat in the Black Mouse Socks*, begins with Mitchell completing her outfit (though she's already blacked up) and entering a costume ball full of fantastically clad beautiful people where she encounters an ex-lover on a date with a new flame. "You really do look like a black cat!" the man, who's wearing a toga, declares. After showing him her socks adorned with knockoff Mickey Mouse illustrations, she responds by saying, "I really am this cat, you see. It's the truth." Her whiteness is the fakeout. "It's the pallor, that's the good makeup." Both laugh, a fond feeling of recognition passing between them. It's weird as fuck.

Confronting these episodes forces any Mitchell chronicler to seek insight but resist making excuses. It's a crucial question for a writer—can you go to ugly places with your subject? How do you commune with the ugliness in them? Her previous biographers have dutifully reported the blackface story but not focused on it, citing the messed-up racial politics of the 1970s as the background, if not the motivation, for Joni's missteps. More recently, scholars including Eric Lott and Kevin Fellezs have faced down Art Nouveau and tried to explain Mitchell's bizarre racial logic within the larger context of segregation and sexism.

From Lott's essay on Mitchell I learned about the urban policies that had made the L.A. enclaves where she lived part of a "white or white-dominated city" cut off from the megalopolis's Black and brown neighborhoods by a series of freeways constructed in the early 1960s, just as the pop scene that produced the singer-songwriter phenomenon was coalescing. Isolated from the inequities that caused Watts to erupt in riots in 1965, "Laurel Canyon scarcely batted an eye." Such obliviousness is a form of complacency that Mitchell resisted, at least, even if her songs exploring racial dynamics were fantastical. Lott calls Art Nouveau her "black mirror," granting her both power and distance among her white male peers. Fellezs, a musicologist in contrast to Lott's cultural historian, helped me think about Mitchell's intentions, both musical and personal, in donning this taboo guise and insisting it was actually her deepest self. (A famous Mitchell remark, often repeated: the first line of her unfinished autobiography would be "I was the only black man at the party.") He makes the connection between this alter ego and Mitchell's desire to inhabit "alterity"—a mutable position of strangeness, otherness— throughout her musical career. "It not only spoke to Mitchell's increasing distance from mainstream pop songwriting practices and concerns," he writes, "but also demonstrated her efforts to develop as an artist whose aesthetic concerns were not necessarily circumscribed by gender or race but [by] attempts to articulate the universal from the subjective."

These views resonated with me. As I'd grown closer to identifying with Mitchell, I could feel the passion and even desperation in her refusal to be categorized, especially as a woman. Fellezs's reading of the Art Nouveau guise as one way Mitchell demonstrated the artifice of any identity tracked with the Joni I was getting to know—a woman who would not be pinned down by essentials. I also appreciated that both Lott and Fellezs empathized with her struggle to be wholly understood within her male-dominated milieu. As Lott put it, "It's as though the best you could do in this crazy new exploding industry as a female artistic sole proprietor was aspire to hustle yourself, be your own pimp— that was Mitchell's implicit, and then explicit, claim." Without fully pleading Mitchell's case, these theorists of her transgressions made it more understandable.

Yet, I thought, is understanding enough? I arrived at this juncture not long after America's mass witnessing of the murder of George Floyd, a Black man killed in Minneapolis by a policeman's knee on his neck, ignited a wave of protest and ongoing deep discussion about anti-Blackness in America and beyond. The images of his death, recorded by teenage bystander Darnella Frazier on her cell phone, took their place in my haunted consciousness alongside other widely circulated images of other brutalized Black people: Trayvon Martin, Eric Garner, Philando Castile. The killers in these cases aren't always extremists; they are just as likely to be indistinguishable from the white fans of Black culture who feel it's their right to use racist words in casual conversation or to laugh at the caricatures that also come at them through their screens. As I faced down the legacy of Art Nouveau in the wake of such horror, I no longer felt the impulse to spend time comprehending how a white person, even one as supposedly in tune with Black artistry as Joni Mitchell, could do violence to someone who doesn't look like them. And I knew that whatever else it was—homage, satire, possession—her creation of Art Nouveau did involve a kind of violence. The theft part of appropriation always does.

BLACK IN THE BACKGROUND

When did Art become Black? That's something I could never fully determine. Mitchell has insisted that she and Art Nouveau were inseparable since the night she snuck him into Sklar's party nearly fifty years ago. In fact, Art's existence predated his embodiment as a Black man. She first mentioned him publicly in a 1974 *Time* magazine cover feature declaring her "Rock 'n' Roll's Leading Lady." Reporter David DeVoss wrote that "she deeply believes in a male muse named Art, who lends her his key to what she airily calls 'the shrine of creativity.' Her relationship with him is easily the most serious and enduring thing in her life. 'I feel like I'm married to this guy named Art,' she whispers. 'I'm responsible to my Art above all else.'"

At that point, Art didn't have a body, as far as anyone could see. In 1976, Mitchell debuted "Furry Sings the Blues," which she would record for *Hejira*. That song makes evident that Mitchell herself is *not* Black, but a white upper-middle-class intruder on the inner-city Memphis existence of the song's subject, bluesman Furry Lewis, whom she describes as a hostile presence interested only in the liquor and money she might bring him. The year before, on Rolling Thunder Revue, she witnessed Dylan and Baez

donning whiteface during some performances in support of the
Black boxer Rubin "Hurricane" Carter, whom they believed had
been wrongly convicted of assault. The critic Janet Maslin would
note in her review of the film that resulted from the tour, *Renaldo
and Clara*, that the smeared and dripping white greasepaint appeared highly unnatural on Dylan's face, offering "the sense of a
person at war with a mask." Complicated by Dylan's Jewishness
and Baez's half-Mexican heritage, the performance was nonetheless jarring. Mitchell's Rolling Thunder Revue stint left her skeptical about Dylan's discernment regarding race; she questioned
his and Baez's public support for Carter, whom she felt was a "bad
person" and not the victim of injustice her friends believed he was.
Meanwhile, she was expanding her circle to include more Black
friends and collaborators, growing close to Chaka Khan, who'd
joined the Black Panthers as a teen before finding fame in the interracial band Rufus, and Wayne Shorter, whose leaping mind led
him to not only defy jazz rules but to think of racism as an existential crisis that could be challenged, if not defeated, through creative acts. In 1977 she became lovers with Don Alias, eventually
sharing a loft with him in New York. Though no one can know
the exact formation of a concept within another person's mind, it
feels logical to speculate that as she grew more confident about
her real-life connections to Black musicians, Mitchell imagined a
new skin for her muse.

The seeds of her presumptuousness may stretch all the way
back to childhood. Mitchell's professed favorite childhood book,
Rudyard Kipling's *Kim*, centers on an Irish boy abandoned and
footloose in colonial India; to avoid being sent to a white orphanage, he hires a prostitute to apply brown dye to his already tan face
and passes as a native. "Sahibs are always tied to their baggage,"
he tells the woman after she calls him "shameless." Using a familiar

term to describe ruling-class men who can't escape their responsibilities, Kim is articulating the mobility he believes he will gain by abandoning that class and posing as a brown boy.

Only a white person would have imagined that a brown or Black body would render them freer. The truth is, many have done so. The myth of Blackness as an escape route from an uptight white life runs through Western culture from Kipling's adventure tales to the stories of jazz-baby slummers and teenage rock and rollers to *Easy Rider* to Joni's own songs. She tapped into all of those sources. In "Dreamland," the track that features a percussion ensemble led by Alias as well as Khan's Latinized background vocals, Mitchell both skewers touristic American fantasies and expresses her enjoyment of them. The Black man Mitchell imagined burned within her is both a trickster and a sage, but most of all, he's a chimera constructed of her own long-tended fantasies.

But wait. I'm contextualizing, which when it comes to Art Nouveau can feel a lot like making excuses. She was called out by a few folks in the 1970s. When *Don Juan's Reckless Daughter* was released, its cover raised more eyebrows than visions of a racially hybrid future. "Joni the Drag King wearing blackface. I'd suggest she stay out of Watts," wrote Michael Snyder in the *Berkeley Barb*, while Tom Reed, one of the few Black critics to review the album (and a fan of her later project *Mingus*), wrote in the *Los Angeles Sentinel* that its cover image showed her as "a pimply-looking negro" and declared, "the music content is unlistenable." Alias later told Sheila Weller, as far as I know the only Joni biographer who interviewed him, that he found Norman Seeff's shot of Joni as Claude/Art Nouveau troubling; he worried some might assume the pimpish figure was based on him.

Alias was one of Mitchell's crucial collaborators, introducing her to the complexities of the African diaspora rhythms that became as fascinating to her as open tunings had in the past. But his role in Joni's history has become a challenge to discuss. In David Yaffe's biography, Mitchell went on the record with the claim that the possessive Alias had abused her during their relationship. The percussionist was no longer alive to refute or confirm this claim, nor to offer his view of another encounter she shared with Yaffe. The biography's chapter on *Don Juan's Reckless Daughter* concludes with an account of Alias taking Mitchell to the home of Miles Davis, her idol, who turns out to be a cartoonishly aggressive creep high on drugs and testosterone: "He lunged towards me on the couch and I jumped up," she told Yaffe of the scene, "and he flew off the couch with his hands around my ankle—and passed out." This story stands out among the others Mitchell has told of her encounters with Davis, most of which happened later and were civil, if a bit distant.

It is wholly possible that Miles Davis did make a lurid pass at Joni Mitchell in the Upper West Side apartment where he'd retreated into paranoia and crack cocaine, and that Alias was "insanely jealous" and assaulted her more than once. Both men are dead, so other evidence stands in for their responses. In his 1989 autobiography *Miles*, Joni's hero openly admitted that he hit his three wives, and the women themselves spoke of the abuse in their own interviews and memoirs. As for Alias, Yaffe has said that several of Mitchell's jazz collaborators had told him that the percussionist had "smacked her up," and that's what prompted him to inquire about it. He did his due diligence and reported what he'd heard.

The aura of silence around the aggression of these men strangely winds around the reticence about Mitchell's Art Nouveau impersonations. Two root problems, sexual violence and racism; two relatively unexplored areas of a much-explored life. I believe Mitchell's account of her relationship with Alias. Why would she lie? At the same time, I believe Alias's assertion that he experienced insensitivity bordering on racism at times when in Joni's company. How else could he have felt when his partner flaunted that Afro wig? For example, Alias told Weller that he never felt accepted by her high-powered white L.A. friends, feeling that some viewed him as an interloper out for Mitchell's money. He also said that at one point, Joni painted him partially nude, with an erect penis, and displayed the canvas in the loft they shared in New York. Only after his protests did she modify the painting, deflating his dick, but she fought him on the change "all the way."

Mitchell identified with Black men and sought intimacy with one, who remained her companion for three and a half years. Sometimes, Black men also threatened and hurt her. (She has said that Alias is the only boyfriend who physically abused her, though others broke her heart.) Is the complexity of her experience evident in her depictions of them? Art Nouveau is a caricature, fabulous, the product of her imagination. In many ways he does resemble the nonwhite characters in her songs from these years, who are almost always observed from a distance. The shiny dancers on Cotton Avenue and the "black babies" busting moves in front of the Pork Pie Hat Bar. The Muslims sticking up Washington in "Otis and Marlena." Furry Lewis sticking out his bony finger in "Furry Sings the Blues," saying to her, *I don't like you*. These florid figures play key roles in her portraits of the adventurous life and its consequences. They often come across as timeless, pulled beyond historical context. I wonder, as I consider the entitlement she and every white artist inevitably bring to their appropriations of Black music and culture, if she created these semi-fictions in part as a way of having the final say about the contradictory realities of her own experiences.

I'd found plenty of instances among Mitchell's peers that raise questions about their perspectives on race, especially in the

2020s, when the conversation around these matters has changed
so much. Buffy Sainte-Marie spent her life fighting for Indigenous
people's rights; as a young woman she was also adopted into a
Cree family. Yet late in life she faced credible accusations that she
had faked her bloodline; she has called them disingenuous, but
the questions remain unresolved. Other singer-songwriters made
connections far more casually. A comment from Jackson Browne
from 1974 leapt out at me when I first read it. At that point Browne
was tired of always being lumped in with his fellow sensitivos,
Sweet Baby James and the like. "Don't ask me about those people, man," Browne said hotly to *Crawdaddy* writer David Rensin.
"Ask me about Merchant, this 40-year-old spade cat who used to
work in the kitchen at the Troubadour when I was doing Hoots
there." I doubt the guy who made his hamburgers back then appreciated the epithet Browne used to describe him. Browne would
later devote much of his life to activism and forge real relationships across many intersecting lines. But he clearly wasn't there
yet when he called upon the spirit of Merchant.

The media and the music industry aided white artists in their
attempts to break the racial boundary. A *Rolling Stone* review of
Carole King's 1971 album *Music* called her "naturally, unaffectedly, black." When John Lennon and Yoko Ono released their song
"Woman Is the N——— of the World" the next year, talk-show
host Dick Cavett gave them ten minutes to rationalize the use of
that word in the song's title, with John dismissing its critics by noting that "most of them were white and male." In 1978, Patti Smith
released "Rock 'n' Roll N———," a song she continued to perform
for decades, and interviewers accepted her explanation that her intention was to recast that most destructive word as more universal.

No excuses, but these other examples do explain, at the very
least, why Joni didn't feel self-conscious when talking about her

"Blackness" to writers and friends. Many bought its existence, and supported her right to show it off. The scene in Norman Seeff's studio when Mitchell donned the Art Nouveau costume to be immortalized on *Don Juan*'s album sleeve would have been read as charming by many white music lovers even in 1985, when writer Angela LaGreca recalled it in a feature for *Rock Photo* magazine. What Mitchell told her starts with typical self-justification but ends with a clever insight:

"'In the song, Don Juan is really the art of the tongue, it's rapping—coffee house poet talk,' says Joni who dressed up as a black guy for the LP's cover and sleeve. That's her, too, underneath the Indian garb. The shooting sessions were upbeat, with Joni trying on different dresses and dancing around while Norman Seeff clicked away. When he asked for another change of clothes, he hardly recognized the black character that strutted from the dressing room five minutes later. 'At that point, I realized I really enjoy character acting,' she says."

She is a woman who loves a great costume: bird feathers, fairy gown, yuppie pantsuit, she's worn many. Imagination is one of her greatest gifts, after all, and in those years she was busy crafting her own picaresque volumes, a Chaucerian bard taking it all in. The encounters she wrote about were real and concocted at the same time, which is true of every artist on some level. Mitchell made up her visions of the "Third World," as she'd called it, from a wide swath of experiences: real-life road stops at the homes of Black Americans; musical collaborations with percussionists, especially those hailing from points along the African diaspora; remembered scenes of youth, like the one in "Paprika Plains"; and communion with the parts of herself that she thought of as Black. Describing her encounters with Blackness fit in with her wider storytelling, and she's really never stopped doing so. As late as

2015, she told Carl Swanson of *New York* magazine that years be-
fore a dentist had told her, "You have teeth like a Negro male."
That comment, she said, partly inspired the construction of Art
Nouveau, the costume that became her muse.

Mitchell's inability to grasp the casual racism of her invoca-
tions of Art Nouveau does distress even her loyal fans. No one's
standing up for bigotry in this story. Joni supporters and friends
have politely played them down, in part, because of a seeming
contradiction: Mitchell genuinely can claim some of the era's
most progressive Black musical legends as close collaborators.
Fusion-era friends like Shorter and Alex Acuña continued to
work with her in the 1980s; in the 1990s she formed a rich musical partnership with the drummer Brian Blade. Members of the
Black intelligentsia noticed her dedication to these players. She's
always welcomed praise from the elite group of Black artists, including Nona Hendryx, Janet Jackson and Prince, who have cited
her as an influence and covered her songs. (Prince even offered
her a song once, but she kindly demurred, declaring it too racy.)
In turn, they have enjoyed her interest and approval. Greg Tate
spoke up for Mitchell's right to identify at least partly as Black in
a 2004 essay playing on variations of the phrase, "Joni Mitchell is
so black that . . ." Tate, who died in 2021, was one of the greatest
music writers ever to be born, and he loved nothing more than
to challenge others' easy assumptions with a cool look and a shy
smile. I was at the conference where he presented that tribute; Joni
was in the front row, beaming, when he said that he saw the *Don
Juan* cover as "more *brujo* than minstrel show." *Brujo*: the Spanish word for "sorcerer." Tate was saying that Joni had accessed
some deep magic to transform that way. I wonder now if he'd
still believe that such a metamorphosis is possible, or desirable. I
should have asked him. Tate also immortalized the phrase "every-

thing but the burden" to encapsulate what white people take from Black culture, using it as the title of an anthology he published the year before he extolled Mitchell in Montreal. I just can't believe he wouldn't question the worth of her attempts to shape-shift now. Or is my thinking that he must have changed his view of Mitchell simply my own Art Nouveau move, the expression of my desire to be of like mind with this man so different from me, so much cooler, with his New York diddy-bop walk?

SWEET SUCKER DANCE
(A Conversation with Miles Grier)

Confronting Mitchell's racist moves—not dancing around them with phrases like "her tricky relationship to race"—required me to check my own. For all of my certainty about her transgressions, I'm a white woman, raised to be unaware of my own privilege. I'm not better than others who've tried to confront this aspect of Mitchell's work and life. The most effective way to fight against the easy look away, I decided, would be to enlist someone who would hold me accountable. I immediately thought of the one scholar I knew who'd had the guts to not excuse the existence of Art Nouveau.

Miles Grier is a Joni fan and has his own measure of sympathy for her. Grier, who teaches at New York's Queens College, was the first person I heard make the connection between Mitchell as a maligned woman artist and her desire to claim Black masculinity as a possible way out of that trap. I first saw him present his findings, later published in an essay, at a conference in 2011. "Mitchell's 'best Negro' riposte illustrates that her Black pimp persona provided an authoritative position from which to criticize sexism *as if it were racism against Black men*," Grier argues (italics are mine). Mitchell's transformation into "an overlooked and undervalued Black male musical genius" was a canny way of entering into the rock canon, he writes, since its gatekeepers fetishize such geniuses—that's an aspect of racism, too. But he concludes that "her beating the white rockers at their own game should not be confused with having changed the game."

Grier's analysis of Joni's run as Art/Claude is the one that most plainly refuses to let her off the hook. Yes, he agrees, her motivations included genuine admiration for Black music and musicians, not to mention Black swagger and style. And she was in a fix herself as a white woman in a white male–ruled scene. Yet Grier insists that as Joni fans we acknowledge her full humanity, warts and all, by really seeing that Black man at the party, not rolling our eyes at her antics and quickly looking away. The unique self-possession and resilience that Black Americans have cultivated over centuries of oppression cannot live within her, no matter how much it inspires her. Relating to someone across the lines of race and gender doesn't land you in their body or their life.

That's what thinkers like Grier are insisting music fans acknowledge as they set the frame right regarding popular music history. He is hardly alone in his work. Right now, a revolutionary retelling of that history is underway, led by Black scholars and writers. As I was on Joni's path, I read their books—Daphne A. Brooks on Black women and the sonic archive, Maureen Mahon on Black women as rock stars, Danyel Smith on Black women pop stars, Kim Mack on the blues, and Francesca T. Royster on Black artists in country and Americana, to name a few of my recent favorites—and my brain changed. These geniuses are the ones toward whom I look these days when I contemplate the subject of Art.

As I pondered this weird figure, stuck not on the question of how he came to be but on why he has been able to survive mostly unchallenged for so long, I kept Grier's essay foremost in my mind. I had questions. Had his thoughts about Mitchell changed in the era of Black Lives Matter? Could he listen to her music today, knowing she still clung to this inappropriate muse? So I reached out, arranged a time to talk. Our conversation clarified my thoughts and loosened the knot inside my stomach. Simply put, Grier helped me see that it's possible to love Joni and still hold her accountable—in fact, that such love is meaningless without accountability. Here's what we had to say to each other.

A: Hey Miles, thanks for talking with me today. I really need help here. I'm so grateful for your work on Joni and race—as I've been flailing around, I keep asking myself, what would Miles think? That's why I wanted to get your voice on the page instead of just doing the quote-and-footnote thing.

M: I appreciate that. It's a strange group to be in, we skeptical Joni scholars. Where should we start?

A: Well, I'm trying to figure out why Joni gets a pass so often. Certainly some critics called her out for the Art Nouveau character, and after your essay, a handful of others have been published about her adoption of blackface. But aside from you, most end up essentially defending her. That's been true of fans and the musicians around her, too, whether Black or white or Latiné, whatever. The line is, well, she's really great anyway, so we're not going to worry about this. I'm trying to figure out why that is.

M: I was trying to do exactly what you said—to try to explain how she got there but also call her on it. The Claude/Art Nouveau mask was absolutely a reaction against sexism, and part of the reason people don't want to jump on her is that the dilemma that she faced is so real, and is so abiding. People don't want to be seen aligning themselves with sexism. Also, she was brilliant in figuring out that the white dudes around her—all sexists in one way or another—wanted to be Black men themselves. And she thought, well, all right. I'll trump them. She was very canny about how to play the game.

A: I want to say something that, I think, reflects my own white entitlement. When I was younger, I looked at that cover [of *Don Juan's Reckless Daughter*] for years and didn't recognize that she was supposed to be a Black pimp. I was like, who is that weird looking person? Just some weird . . . I don't even know what. Do you think the image is instantly legible to people?

M: No, I don't. And that's one of the really tricky things around terminology. Like, do you call it blackface? Because she was trying to *pass* as a Black man. That's not minstrelsy, not blackface, right? And I think it's interesting that she was successful in this passing. At this party [at Sklar's house] she passes . . . but would she actually have been able to go to Watts and pass?

A: For sure not! But even though J. D. Souther says he didn't recognize her, I don't know if I believe him. These are really famous rock stars. Would they have just let some random person into the house?

M: I always wondered whether it was a case of nominally liberal white people not wanting to be racist. So they're like, that must be somebody's black friend, and I don't want to question it.

A: Oh, that's interesting. Like maybe a weird cloak of invisibility descended. People thinking, *That person makes me uncomfortable. This guy is at my friend's party and I don't want to look at him because it's just too weird that he's even here.*

M: Right. And also, *I'm not going to call the cops on this person.*

A: Do you locate what she did in relationship to other white musicians doing similar things in the 1970s, or was she an unusual case?

M: I haven't really thought about her too much in relation to the men—like Jackson Browne or even David Bowie, who was taking so much from Black culture in his *Young Americans* phase. I think of her more in comparison to Laura Nyro and Bonnie Raitt. I found a photograph of Nyro playing with Miles Davis. They were rehearsing together! I thought, that must have burned Mitchell's bacon. She makes all these claims that Miles wanted to record with her but couldn't because she was white. Which is just crazy because he played with white musicians almost his entire career! It is true that he wouldn't record with certain singers. Come on, though, y'all just didn't work together. I'm not sure why she had to make it into this larger thing about Miles's racial politics. [Note: In 1997 Mitchell admitted that Davis's son Eugene corrected her misperception that race was the reason his father wouldn't work with her. "It was because you are a singer," he said.]

A: It's the basic predicament of biography that everyone tells stories about themselves that are partially untrue. We all do. But when it comes to creating Claude/Art Nouveau, where does the "art" come in? How do we read the character as an artwork? Is it even worth reading?

M: I'll just echo what I wrote in my essay: I think it's a remarkable parody and critique of white men's pimplike relationship to white women, and of white men's homoerotic desire for and rivalry with Black men. As that, it's amazing.

But I also think Joni got lucky. Because Black male musicians who became her closest collaborators were of a certain generation and political bent. They did not like being pigeonholed as Black. This is not to say they weren't proudly Black, but they definitely felt—for some good reasons—that being categorized as Black musicians put them in a lesser category, restricting their opportunities and giving them less stature as artists. And that is the level on which they bonded with her. Because that's how she talks about being called a female singer-songwriter.

A: Oh, that make sense.

M: Mitchell is either a year older or a year younger than my father. He's a photojournalist and hates being called a Black photojournalist. And my whole childhood I was like, you are Black and a photojournalist. Why do you hate this? I mean, I do understand historically why they did it and what they were fighting against.

A: Herbie Hancock talks about that directly in his autobiography. He writes that he wanted to play funk music, but didn't want to get trapped there. Everybody around Joni was crossing boundaries.

M: I've always said that the fear of reverse discrimination—that Black people are going to discriminate against and exclude white people—is really overblown.

A: Thank you for checking me on that! Deserved.

M: But one other thing, too. In your research you may have noticed that Black artists did begin to cite Mitchell as an influence in the late 1970s. You asked earlier where Joni fits in the history of Black music. As jazz sort of wanes and people like Stevie Wonder are stretching the boundaries of [R&B] or soul, citing Joni as an influence becomes, for some Black artists, a way of saying, "Don't pigeonhole me." Prince did it when he came out, for example.

A: Well, Joni herself doesn't want to be compared to anyone, except Bob Dylan. What do you think about the whole Dylan thing with the benefits for Rubin "Hurricane" Carter? Joni was the one who questioned Dylan's motivations, saying that Carter was a violent predator and that white liberal support of him might be misguided.

M: For me, [that] was the one potentially salvageable moment in her adventures in blackface. When she sort of goes, all these white liberal patsies are running around here and they can't see that this man is jive. And after he was released, he was [accused of assaulting] a woman. A Black woman, by the way. The way Joni has framed that whole episode is that they were running around in whiteface apologizing for being white, and she was the only one saying, this is a bad dude.

I haven't dug into her relationship with Dylan. As I said, I went toward Bonnie Raitt and Laura Nyro, because I like them and I like their music. And they supported Black musicians. Laura Nyro made an album with Labelle. Bonnie Raitt provided decades-long financial support to the rhythm and blues artists whom she considered mentors. That's the conversation we need to be having instead of just thumbs up or thumbs down on Joni. Instead of the question, is this photograph or song racist or not, which we could debate forever, why don't we ask, does this help Black people or not? I care about whether our conditions change.

A: Well, her closest Black collaborators have certainly always felt that Joni treated them as equals in the studio . . .

M: And that's great! But honestly, Ann, I think this whole debate is in many ways about white writers and their own guilt. Sort of like, *Well, I can't do anything to stop racism.* And so, you know, better to have not done a racist thing. Or to call out an artist for something in their work or self-presentation. That's when the nitpicking starts: well, is it blackface, or something else. This is not a matter we shouldn't talk about, but the conversation can't stop there.

A: Ugh, that's so true. You're hitting on why people like me get so worked up about the issue. I keep thinking about it as the gray elephant in the room. Should I cancel her? What would be the point, though? So much of cancel culture is about exactly this: I feel paralyzed for some reason, I can't go out and solve the problems right around me, so I look to popular culture for offenders whom I can refute without actually having to do anything.

M: If we focus on representation only, then the question becomes about Joni's intentions and her feelings about Black people. As long as her feelings were the right feelings, then people can wipe their brows: it's okay. In the end, scholars and biographers aren't that different from fans. There's a lot of good feeling toward Joni. And it's hard. It was painful for me to write that essay. I literally couldn't listen to some of my favorite Joni albums for a little while. It went away, but for a while, I couldn't, because of her racial essentialism, her racial arrogance, that line in "The Boho Dance": *Just another hard-time band with Negro affectations.* Negro affectations? I cringe every time I hear it.

I did have to really confront something and lose my affection for her music for a while, and maybe that's what people don't want. Because to really accept how fucked up her racial politics are does cost you something. But I think it's important that people don't just take her word for it about these things. You really have to look.

A: Joni has given herself permission to do a lot of things.

M: Which is why her art is great! But it's also partly why these problems arise.

Saying goodbye to Grier, I felt elated. He'd poured more insight into my brain in one hour than I'd generated myself in months of pondering. Yet after a while I realized that even though I felt more enlightened about my own motivations as well as those of everyone involved in the dance of desire and repression that created space for Joni to manifest Art Nouveau, I wasn't really any closer to knowing how to live with the fact of his existence. I had recognized her in her wig and fake sideburns, fake gold tooth gleaming, and refused to look away. And I'd also heard her trading shimmering vocal lines with Wayne Shorter on saxophone; I'd come to believe in the kindness and respect she'd extended to Charles Mingus, and to love the music that came from it. I believed that, when she walked away from the mic and let Alex Acuña vocalize on "The Tenth World," or gave Chaka Khan that shining part on "Dreamland," grace, if not humility, led her. Like

Grier, I don't think Joni Mitchell is nothing but a racist, or that her racism strictly defines her. What I know about her and about myself is that as white women, we can enact racism even at times when we think we are being generous and full of affection. This is the condition of our lives in a society based on such dehumanizing divisions. And our choices can reinforce those hierarchies even when we think we're eradicating them. *It's a long, long, way from Canada*, Joni sang once, imagining her Third World, a utopia that, on some level, is always falling apart. It's a long, long way from that place she called Dreamland, too.

8

the marriage

By the time the 1980s rolled around, Mitchell was ready for another change. So was I, here in the twenty-first century, as I continued on my quest to reconstruct her steps. I'd lost myself completely in the weeds of jazz fusion and bushwhacked myself out. Faced with the saga of Art Nouveau, I'd confronted the most difficult aspects of her legend. As I went through these phases of following her, I found myself feeling closer to her as an artist and as a person. This familiarity, I realized, was a projection—as my original hostility toward Joni the Ice Queen had been.

The patina of perfection I'd mistaken for her essence started falling away, a little more each time I learned about another difficulty she'd faced down or another wave of self-doubt she'd wrestled back and turned into free verse. I could now recognize that she was always knocking herself off pedestals, even as she maintained the belief that greatness was hers by right. She'd been less complicit in her own glamorization than I'd suspected. Or . . . it was complicated. Like anyone—like me, on a much smaller scale, when I was feeling my oats about this very book—she wanted people to recognize her insights, her labor, her charisma, her artistry. And she did have massive, sometimes unwieldy, dreams. But her music itself cast suspicion on hyperbole. As she grew older and faced the challenges encountered by any woman who survives past her unwrinkled youth, her craving for honesty only increased.

Approaching forty, Mitchell realized that the pop-star privilege she'd enjoyed and sometimes mocked was now slipping out of her hands. Record sales were down; critics had started to question her acumen. Meanwhile, at the mirror, she eyed the nearly imperceptible sag in her jawline. The untouchable beauty with the grabbing heart now realized that while men certainly still glanced her way, the urge—and maybe the ability—to conquer them was fading. She needed a palate cleanser, something that would redirect her energies and carry her into a new period.

It was time for a new relationship, not only with a man, but with herself.

So she decided to try something she never had before: officially sanctioned domesticity. She settled down with one last prize, and what a guy—not only very cute and still in the bloom of young adulthood, but a musician who actually admitted he had things to learn from her. Larry Klein, her one and only genuine husband, put that starter marriage and all those cases of serial monogamy into a wholly new context. From 1982, when they met in the recording studio (of course), until their divorce in 1994, Klein was her partner in morning yoga, cat care and Malibu house refurbishing. But mostly, in music. Here was another reason '80s Joni became the one I began to like the best—she was no longer an overweening solitary "I" but the peaceful, happy half of a productive "we."

When I wrote the paragraph above, I was idealizing. I knew it. The marriage, surviving after divorce as friendship and ever more fruitful collaboration, had its ups and downs like any other. Larry had to deal with being shadowed by the celebrated "Joni Mitchell" while he was still figuring out how to love the woman behind that name, and to be his own whole self in the meantime. Joni suffered in these years, too, from the emblematic survivable disasters of midlife—body aches, money pains—compounded by post-polio syndrome and the creeping feeling that her cultural authority was slipping. Middling reviews and the fading support of her music-biz champions hit her hard. Not that she needed the money, but no longer was she the queen who could always tell the record label guys exactly what to do. She was now a rich woman who, like many her age, felt precarity creeping up everywhere.

Still, there was the sunshine of that marriage. The soul connection. The warmth and heat of it. And the creative spark that sent her leaping into new musical terrain, learning a different way to work in the studio and taking on subjects she'd only dabbled in before.

The music Joni Mitchell made within her marriage is the most overlooked in her body of work. I turned to it with a contrarian's enthusiasm, eager to argue for its value. The best of what she and Klein made together—their adventures in sampling and synthesized sounds, framing big ideas about the state of not just one woman's heart, but the world—is more relevant than ever before. Synth pop is again in fashion, and the political turmoil of the Trump era made protest music relevant—and popular—again. And there's been a change of the tides regarding Mitchell's work, as well; think pieces recently began to appear calling the Joni of the 1980s a "fearless, futurist auteur."

Yet there's no groundswell around this Joni era, no echoing mythos. Her 1980s albums are her problem children, loved but disappointing. "I seem to be out of sync with the times in this decade," she told Kristine McKenna of the *L.A. Times* in 1988. "I've come to accept that I must write what I feel when I feel it and only do what is given me."

The Joni who looked askance at her 1980s work is a very relatable figure—a woman who got something different than what she'd hoped for out of a partnership and, after it's faded, sets herself right by fiercely reclaiming the narrative. However, her occasional assertions that she and Klein let musical trends get the best of them, and that at times she hadn't wanted to try those things he pushed on her, don't really bear out. Though a blockbuster breakthrough eluded them, Mitchell and Klein spent more than a decade on a real sonic adventure, taking chances that her most daring earlier songs clearly show she'd always wanted to take. The albums extending from *Wild Things Run Fast*—they fell in love during its making—to *Turbulent Indigo*, which they coproduced as they separated, show a pattern of growth through experimentation that recalls her folk arc from her debut to *For the Roses*, or her jazz immersion from *Court and Spark* to *Mingus*. Together, Klein and Mitchell really got somewhere.

I wanted people to realize this.

As I made my case, I also knew I'd have to fight my own tendency to sentimentalize artistically fruitful intimate relationships.

This is my romance-novel ideal come to life: not the celebrated pairings with the hippie princes and sexy, shady sidemen immortalized in Joni's best-loved songs, but that day-to-day connection that develops over years, despite all the little rifts and misunderstandings. Looking at adorable photos of Joni and Larry in complementary New Wave T-shirts or playing together onstage, grins as huge as the moon, I convinced myself that Larry Klein was her match made in heaven, her lucky guy.

They did have bad times, sometimes. A weird glitch in California's tax laws put a lien on her publishing for a while, and a litigious housekeeper kept her in court for a few years. A serious car accident on the Pacific Coast Highway bonked her head and did worse to Larry, and she suffered repeated insults under the drill of an untrustworthy dentist. Worst, an unexpected pregnancy at forty-two ended in miscarriage, a tragedy that her young husband didn't take as seriously as he should have (he later admitted), causing a crack in their bond that never really healed.

But I'm still intrigued by the wide turns she took with Larry beside her. She was painting a lot more during these years, and the impulse to compose visually compelled her. She experimented with pastiche, electronic manipulation and a vocal style grounded in something very different from the acrobatic virtuosity of her youth. In the 1980s Mitchell was arguably the most daring of her old singer-songwriter friends, making music that took its cues from younger pop innovators. She was immersed in new processes alongside her partner, a mutual promise to create, create, create.

MEET CUTE

Joni and Larry, Larry and Joni. To tell their love story, I'll have to figure out what to call the husband, this most significant object of our subject's affection. Examining the way names can shape a narrative might be a good place to start. Mitchell has always given a lot of thought to the syntax of romance, the way calling a loved one *king child father mean old daddy honey coyote my vain darling* declares a certain ownership, the right to define a person, to control a dynamic even as you're negotiating its limits. She always called Larry "Klein," as if they were starring in one of those golden-age romances featuring fast-talking lovers who spar with as much fervor as they embrace. Rosalind Russell and Cary Grant trading quips at lightning speed in *His Girl Friday*. William Powell and Myrna Loy sipping martinis and solving crimes as married detectives Nick and Nora Charles. Such Hollywood couples modeled what sociologists called companionate marriage, in which erotically electric friendship and mutual respect mattered as much as the status this legal connection could confer. Joni and Klein were big movie buffs, spending many an evening holed up with popcorn on the couch. I imagine them laughing at these films together, each internally perfecting the banter they'd employ the next day in the recording studio.

For me, Klein is a familiar character, the kind of nerdy-charismatic scholar-practitioner I've met over and over in my own career. He was one of the first people I reached out to about Joni, and I have had some contact with him over the years of walking on her roads. Early on in my research, I drove from my home base in Northeast Los Angeles all the way to Santa Monica, where Klein charmed me over brunch, told me he would not talk on the record and gave me a wry smile as he let me pick up the bill. I left him in peace. Then, as I was working on this chapter, I found myself in need of some clarification about gear. Larry and Joni really dove into the new technologies on offer in the 1980s, and I couldn't always tell which synth was on what album track, or how he got a certain bass sound, or how she used tape loops and other effects. So I sent him an email, and eventually he replied with some very helpful, detailed answers. I felt a sneaking sense of accomplishment that my muso questions had drawn him in.

Joni met Klein through her ex John Guerin, the one whose rambling had damaged the similar connection they'd had. "I loved playing with John," Klein told me. "He had a looseness and a shuffle to the way that he approached things that was all his own." Guerin frequently tapped Klein for gigs; the younger player was both flexible and inventive. His early ambition had been to play with every jazz great he admired. He cut his teeth at twenty-one with Freddie Hubbard's hard bop band, standing out in that group and others as a kinetic player on both upright and electric bass. By his midtwenties he wanted something different: less emphasis on chops, more exploration.

Maybe he also wanted to make more money. He'd spent a year with Guerin playing in the band for television talk-show host Merv Griffin and, though most of his recording experience remained jazz-oriented, had started to venture elsewhere—his early discography includes easy listening auteur Neil Norman's space opera *Not of This Earth* and an album by hard-rocking singer Anne Bertucci, once of the power pop band the Babys. "I wanted to learn to use the studio as an instrument," he told an interviewer in 2020. "John really helped me make that transition by telling people about me and calling me for certain things." In the versatile and eager Klein, Guerin recognized a promising way for Mitchell to get over Jaco Pastorius, the man at the heart of her jazz dialogues from *Hejira* to *Shadows and Light*. Jaco was lost to her by the end of the tour that produced that live album, overtaken by his struggles with mental illness and drugs. "He was a giant of an innovator, and to try to sound like him would be a losing game," Klein said of Jaco. "I tried to find different ways to use the instrument without emulating him; using higher melodic material either in a more orchestral manner or a combination of harmonics and swells to get at different textural effects. I tried to get at sounds with it that sat in cracks in between identifiable sounds and effects."

It's unclear whether Guerin, who died in 2004, suspected Klein also might help Mitchell get over Don Alias, with whom she'd finally split. By 1982 Guerin must have been used to pheromones flying in every direction around his ex. She still kept her former lovers creatively close—even Alias, who is credited with "rhythmic arrangements" on one *Wild Things Run Fast* track, "Be Cool." The album also contains evidence of her return to speaking terms with James Taylor, following a truce brokered by Peter Asher, who stepped in as Mitchell's manager after what she perceived as benign neglect caused her to sever her longtime ties with Elliot Roberts. (She and Roberts also stayed friends; he hosted her wedding to Klein at his Malibu home.)

A couple of tense but recuperative phone calls with Taylor set the stage for an encounter straight out of 1971. One day during the *Wild Things Run Fast* sessions at A&M Studios, Taylor, working on his background singer David Lasley's solo album, ran into Joni in the hall. She pulled him in for vocal support—on a song, "Man to Man," about her own lifetime of serial monogamy. Some slurping notes from Klein's bass kick that track off. Everybody must have had a good chuckle over it.

With Joni and Klein, it was all talk at first, and game-playing— but not the duplicitous and jealous kind that repeatedly brought down her relationship with Guerin and inflamed her time with Alias. *Talk to me, bgawwk bgaaaawwk!!* Klein did. He and Joni would confer for hours while playing the studio's pinball ma-

chine, and he taught her video games, his generation's version of
that bar sport. Their conversation wound around itself and grew
taller, a beanstalk of chatter about movies, music, gear, Buddhist
philosophy, books. Eventually, their late nights turned into early
mornings. As this happened, Joni also started thinking that this
guy's ideas might be useful not just as fodder for new lyrics, but
in the studio, too.

Does this meet-cute sound too corny? Klein was corny, according to Mitchell, who made the band do a remake of the Leiber
and Stoller tease "(You're So Square) Baby I Don't Care"—one
of the few Elvis Presley hits the King actually played on, and bass,
no less—as part of her Larry-wooing process. It does seem amazing that as their bond rapidly evolved no one around Mitchell
raised an eyebrow. But then, many of her sidemen had been in
these weird friend-lover configurations with her before—and her
lovers were also used to Mitchell kicking them out of the studio
after they'd played their parts. This time, at her request, Klein
hung around. He hesitated at first. Did she really need him in the
editing and mixing process? But she insisted. Headed into a new
phase, she recognized in him a soul who was also on the move,
trying to go beyond his jazz upbringing and grasp the new tools—
synthesizers primary among them—that would change music in
the 1980s. Klein was a newcomer with an open heart and a lot of
confidence, enough to surprise and charm the woman in charge.
Yet he didn't expect to fall in love with her. "It was wild and surprising to us both," Klein said, decades later. "And yet very organic
and kind of innocent in the way it happened."

Truth be told, Klein reminds me of my own husband, Eric,
a music journalist–turned-academic with whom I've worked off
and on while making a home and a family over thirty years. Also a
younger Jewish guy with soft, lovable features and a penchant for

flashy T-shirts. (In one of my favorite pictures of Joni and Larry, she's all in black and he's wearing a Picasso self-portrait tee and tennis shorts.) I was twenty-five when we met in 1989; he was a cherubic-looking twenty-three. A little less than two years' difference, not fourteen. Yet I see some parallels between the relationships. At the time I held a modest power position that represented an opportunity for him. I was an editor at a local alternative newsweekly. He'd just graduated from Princeton and relocated to the West Coast. He wanted to become a music writer. I could give him assignments. He didn't hustle me, though—like Klein with Joni, he led with enthusiasm. That was more than thirty years ago. The commitment to living within music held us together even when the differences that surface in youth threatened to pull us apart. And yet, like Joni and Klein, sometimes each of us felt overshadowed by the other. As we pursued our careers together and separately, tensions often bubbled up about who really owned the life story we were co-authoring. Who would decide where we'd live, what kind of work would dominate our lives together? We learned that an intimate partnership striving for equality is a real roller-coaster ride. You're strapped into the car together, but it has a split down the middle, and it can break apart as one engine pushes upward and the other stalls. All you can do is reach out beyond your own side of the car and grab that hand.

UNDERNEATH THE STREETLIGHT

Before Guerin brought Klein in, Mitchell had been working on the *Wild Things Run Fast* songs for a while without finding the groove she wanted. The previous year she'd spent six weeks in the Caribbean, writing and listening to both reggae music and the new rock bands tuned in to that Jamaican frequency—the Police, Talking Heads, punk, ska. With Jaco gone, Wayne Shorter busy with Weather Report, and her potential as a charting radio artist dimmed after *Mingus*, she wanted to rock, but in that rolling island way.

Klein got this. Stepping away from jazz himself, he too had *Outlandos d'Amour* in his Walkman headphones. John Guerin wasn't the only drummer in his social circle, either. When Guerin's style turned out only half appropriate for the *Wild Things Run Fast* sessions, Klein enlisted Vinnie Colaiuta, also jazz-trained but best-known by then for his breakneck playing with the uncategorizable Frank Zappa (Colaiuta would later become the drummer in Police frontman Sting's band). In one of the most effusive and thorough interviews she gave after it was released, Mitchell told Vic Garbarini of *Musician* magazine how Klein's influence helped *Wild Things Run Fast* become the grooveful rock album she wanted it to be. "He's twenty-five and he's come up in an era that's more sound-conscious than the previous wave. He stretched my ear in certain areas, like drum sounds, which we'd never fussed much with before."

As she and Klein grew closer, he became her main creative confidant. Along with engineer Larry Hirsch, he spent months with Mitchell at Paramount studios perfecting the album's sound, taking cues from English New Wave bands and the gleaming, radio-ready rock of American chart-toppers like Journey. "We were a perfectly balanced team in that I handled the treble aspects and placement of the vocal and horn sounds," she told Garbarini. "They handled the rhythm section sounds and certain things I couldn't hear. But I heard that the snare had a certain quality, and its placement was related to what we'd liked on the Police albums.

And I could hear that supersonic sheen on the Journey album. There's a place on our record where it sparkles so much that if you listen to it too long it'll make you nervous."

A lot of *Wild Things Run Fast* shines; the rest of it glows. On the album's ballads, Mitchell reflects on her past decisions and their consequences. Desire and anxiety are still the catalysts in these stories, but instead of trying to turn them into wheels that would never carry her far enough away, she rests in these unsettled emotions. In the haunting opening track, "Chinese Cafe/ Unchained Melody," she returns to the memory field she visited in "Song for Sharon," but instead of pushing herself back toward the future, she lets the past permeate the atmosphere. The song's watercolor arrangement floats synthesizer lines around her spare piano parts as Steve Lukather's guitar echoes in counterpoint with Klein's bass. The music's gentle complexity complements a lyric that again puts Mitchell in dialogue with a childhood friend (this one is named Carol) who is raising a family instead of following the lonely path of the artist. Mitchell mentions her daughter, too, a rare nod. Kelly is a lingering trace: *I bore her but I could not raise her.* Mitchell's recollections give way at times to the lyrics of songs she and Carol once played on hometown jukeboxes, like "Unchained Melody" and "Will You Love Me Tomorrow." Her multitracked voice becomes a choir of angels who haunt even as they bestow grace. *Nothing lasts for long*, Mitchell murmurs, yet the song itself is evidence that the losses of youth do linger, translucent and ever present. Lost and lasts are not opposites. "Chinese Cafe" is a throwback to the sad philosophical Joni her fans adored, but its contemplative calm tempers its sorrow.

Throughout the rest of the album, she lives and moves. There are philosophical meditations like "Love," based on a passage from Paul's epistles. There are breakup songs—the scathing "You

Dream Flat Tires," whose lament, *struck by precious love*, may refer to the violence Alias wreaked in her life; and "Ladies' Man," in which cocaine is the other woman her companion (maybe Guerin?) can't kick. The romantic songs, the ones obviously for Klein, are the most fun. *Yes I do, I love ya!* Mitchell declares in "Underneath the Streetlight," a bop radiating hot sex with its lines about *gay boys with their pants so tight out in the neon light* and *the truck at the stoplight with his airbrakes moaning*. The album's most Police-ish cut, "Solid Love," percolates on a slightly hyper off-beat rhythm, with Colaiuta doing some mobile snare work that's clearly in dialogue with that band's Stewart Copeland. *We got a chance, hot dog darlin'!* Mitchell cries in what has become the album's most quoted lyric—embraced, by most reviewers, for its unpretentious joy. "Dreaming on a dime, she listens to the past with hope for the future," wrote John Milward in his *Rolling Stone* album review, extolling Mitchell's fresh perspective.

There's a video for "Underneath the Streetlight" floating around on the Internet, mislabeled "Street Light." In it, Joni and Klein unabashedly flirt with each other as they perform—she makes kissy faces at him, they rub noses, he smiles like he just ate a canary. It's shameless and delightful. Fuck your power dynamics! Their interplay challenges anyone who'd cast a gimlet eye on what they've found. This is Joni insisting, after a period of questioning, that love can be real and, in becoming real, that it enlivens everything. *Shoving back the shadows!* she exclaims.

THE END OF SEX

True to her zeitgeist-savvy ways, Joni shacked up with Klein just as marriage was making a comeback, in popular culture at least. A few months after they moved in together, Joni picked up an issue of *Esquire* magazine with a heart made of thorny roses on the cover and, in white block letters, the words "THE END OF SEX." The words inside hit her hard. Their writer, George Leonard, was a founding father of the human potential movement, an aikido master and early architect of Esalen whose first book, published two decades earlier, was called *The Decline of the American Male*. Now he was mourning a different social construct—heterosexuality of the mostly white middle-class kind, which his instincts, backed up by some dubiously interpreted research, told him was exhausted and on the ropes.

"The ultimate erotic challenge, in fact, lives not in racing from bed to bed, shirttails aflame, but in the quest of what I call High Monogamy: a long-term relationship in which both partners are voluntarily committed to erotic exclusivity, not because of moral or religious scruples, not because of timidity or inertia, but because it is what they want. Because they seek excitement and adventure through the love of another person," Leonard wrote. Unsurprisingly, given her newlywed status, Mitchell found this directive inspiring. Six years later, she was still talking about Leonard's essay. "The thing the writer said that sticks in my mind," she told reporter Ben Fong-Torres, "is if you want repetition in a relationship, see other people. If you want infinite variety, stay with one person."

"The End of Sex," which Leonard soon expanded into a book, did seem to mark a turning point in attitudes among the white middle class. The divorce rate dropped throughout the 1980s after an all-time high at the start of the decade, and the celebrity trend analyst Faith Popcorn coined the term "cocooning" to describe monied couples' revived interest in tastefully cozy interior decoration and "Mom foods" like chicken potpie. Mitchell had again zeroed in on her generation's mood. Solid second marriages, entered into by self-aware adults like Joni herself, particularly resonated in popular culture. In step with the political and social conservatism ushered in by Ronald Reagan, the right's most beloved divorced dad, the hopeful aura Joni cast around a well-made match in the lyrics of "Solid Love"—*tested and blessed, darlin', I'm gonna give you my very best*—reflected the bloodied-but-unbowed attitude that her fans, mostly now in their midthirties, brought to domestic lives augmented by deep-seated sofas and Cuisinarts.

Yet marriage did not return to the center of America's imagination unscarred. As Susan Faludi would write in *Backlash*, her 1991 exposé of the media-driven "war against women" that raged during the Reagan era, Hollywood and the publishing industry fed and even created the drive to conventionally couple by stoking fears of infertility, social marginalization and loneliness. With the Wall Street–mandated need to hustle for more and more money replacing the countercultural possibility of thriving differently, the nuclear family again came into view as the bulwark of success. But the white-lace dreams Mitchell fondly recalled in "Song for Sharon" were no longer so easy to fulfill. Faludi quotes a typically contradictory message from a 1986 *Advertising Age* article: "The media are having a swell time telling us, on the one hand, that marriage is 'in' and, on the other hand, that women's chances of marrying are slim. So maybe marriage is 'in' because it's so hard to do, like coal-walking was 'in' a year ago."

In *Backlash*, Faludi argues that 1980s romantic comedies like *Working Girl* and *When Harry Met Sally* adjusted the classic marriage plot to accommodate working women with dreams beyond the altar—while dragging them back there. The same applies to some of the era's biggest radio hits. Stevie Wonder put aside the fiery social commentary and cosmic visions of his 1970s masterworks to streamline the love song, beautifully but soporifically, in "I Just Called to Say I Love You." Steve Winwood, who'd sung some of the most searching ballads of the previous era (Blind Faith's "Can't Find My Way Home" and Traffic's "The Low Spark of High-Heeled Boys"), set monogamy as a life goal with the bouncy "Higher Love." Stevie Nicks stepped away from the tangled web of Fleetwood Mac with relationship-advice classics and the pop-metal wedding ballad "Leather and Lace." Mitchell's friend Lionel Richie, whose songs with funk band the Commodores had made a case for sexual freedom with titles like "Easy" and "Sail On," settled into superstardom with ballads like "Stuck on You." Incidentally, he sang background vocals on *Wild Things Run Fast*.

The best songs about mature, monogamous bonding complicated the narrative. None fits the bill better than "The Boys of Summer" by Mitchell's occasional 1980s collaborator Don Henley, built around a floating bass line played by none other than Larry Klein. A lost-love lament swathed in sweetness, "The Boys of Summer" can be interpreted a few different ways. On the one hand it's an update on "Lyin' Eyes" by Henley's band the Eagles from the point of view of the bad boy the cheating wife in that 1975 weeper can't quit. In "Lyin' Eyes," Henley sang cruelly, condemning a good girl turned bad; here he's all forgiveness. The song's sound—a luxury-car engine built of synthesizers, starting with a LinnDrum beat that never relents and growing smoother and more efficient with every additional layer of synths—marks this as a 1980s story of propulsion away from youthful experimentation into adulthood. Its immortal line *I saw a Deadhead sticker on a Cadillac* was inspired by Henley glimpsing the ultimate hippie band's logo on a Cadillac Seville, which he called "a symbol of the bourgeoisie and the right wing generally." That sighting could have inspired rage, but Henley cultivated an air of resignation that

makes the song irresistibly sad. *A little voice inside my head said,*
"Don't look back, you can never look back," he sighs. That phrase,
coming immediately after Klein's hooky bass playing moves to
the fore, makes this the ultimate anthem of the brokenhearted
baby boomers eschewing freedom for the soporific comforts of
the good life.

Much of the most admired writing, visual art and cinema
of the 1980s—the kind Joni and Klein were most likely to consume in their homebody-ish life of watching movies, reading and
checking out the art scene—explored the same themes Henley's
hit made musical. Art films, which Klein told me they preferred,
played against Hollywood's standards and stereotypes, and when
it came to the marriage plot, the counterpoints it offered ranged
from softly lit and meticulously scripted "small stories" to wild
surrealism. Films as different in tone as David Lynch's *Blue Velvet*
and Steven Soderbergh's *sex, lies, and videotape* portrayed coupled
domesticity as a minefield, not a citadel. Mainstream rom-coms
presented the complexities and even the perversions of private life
as predicaments that could be fixed with love, but still suggested
that the process of breakdown was built in. Fiction followed suit.
Bestsellers like Tom Wolfe's *The Bonfire of the Vanities* and Don
DeLillo's *White Noise* depicted 1980s society as a teeming mess,
with marriage both a casualty of the chaos and a cause.

As these sprawling social novels took home major prizes, short
story writers dissected marriage more delicately—especially the
"dirty realists" who took over the literary scene. Mitchell loved
these writers, citing Raymond Carver as a favorite in a conversation with Sean O'Hagan in the *New Musical Express* in 1988.
"There's no one really cutting it so you gotta turn to the short
story tellers," she said, slagging off her old pals Bob Dylan and
Neil Young as passé compared to them. She went on to say, as she

often would during this period, that the degraded state of the pop scene was making her wonder if short story writing was her true métier.

Writers like Carver and Ann Beattie, who first became famous in the 1970s and was sometimes compared to Mitchell, might have agreed. Their best-loved stories read very much like variations on her observational classics, like *Blue*'s "The Last Time I Saw Richard." Marriage is often the enclosing element in these stories, inescapable even when characters stray or leave. It represents the ultimate goal—connection—and its seemingly inevitable failure. Domesticity builds lives through little details and, in its repetitiveness, simultaneously erases their value.

If this focus on marriage's static scenes seems like the opposite of what Mitchell does in her story songs, which so often capture the moment in which she realizes she's imprisoned by a feeling and breaks free, note the shift that occurs in the small group of songs she wrote about marriage during her years with Klein. After the love explosion of *Wild Things Run Fast*, only a handful of her songs dwell in this personal space, a shift engendered by her apparent conviction that a mostly happy relationship should be kept private. Yet those few show Mitchell riding the changes others were exploring in film and fiction.

"Moon at the Window," from *Wild Things Run Fast*, is a perfect melding of her jazz sensibility with more direct pop melodic lines and rhythms; it beguiles, but its lyric is sorrowful. This may be the closest Mitchell ever came to achieving a dream she'd had since childhood, of singing in spiritual kinship with Billie Holiday. It's one of her first deep musical collaborations with Klein, whose layered bass parts—four in all—build a harmonic context for her guitar playing and underscore the song's sense of stasis and isolation. It's a counterpoint to the brighter songs on *Wild Things Run Fast*, Mitchell's blue study of the institution she would soon enter.

"The song is quite a dark poem about agoraphobia and the fleeting nature of happiness in romantic relationships and marriage," Klein told me. "After we had gotten a basic track that felt definitive to everyone involved I proposed the idea of building an orchestral group of bass tracks to function as an ensemble that ran through the song to Joni. The dark nature of the poem somehow suggested this to me as an interesting possibility, and Joni was up for me experimenting with the idea. I had never heard this done before in this context, and it felt fresh to me. Joni gave me the room to experiment with it, and in the end we felt that it worked well."

Mitchell plays delicately syncopated guitar on "Moon at the Window"; Klein's bass parts range into their zone and Wayne Shorter's saxophone takes the high end as Guerin keeps a characteristically light beat. An Oberheim synthesizer played by Russell Ferrante subtly recombines these elements so that the song sounds both spare—lonely—and expansive. It's the ideal setting for the story of an abandoned wife haunted by the presence of a husband who still confines her, though now as a ghostly memory. Mitchell has said that the titular phrase, *At least the moon at the window, the thieves left that behind*, refers to a note written by Brad MacMath, her daughter's father, when he left her, three months pregnant. (He'd lifted the phrase from a poem by the Zen master Ryōkan.) Her own experience of confinement and uncertainty helped her craft a subtle portrait of a marriage broken yet still oppressively unfinished.

On *Chalk Mark in a Rain Storm*, the 1988 album in which her fiction-writing aspirations fully surface, two marriage portraits suggest her lingering doubts about the institution despite her own happiness. "The Tea Leaf Prophecy" employs the pastiche techniques her growing command of synthesizers afforded her to build a complex view of her parents' marriage, which she pictures as both a product of routine and a never-ending cold war. "Snakes and Ladders," with Henley providing guest vocals intentionally manipulated to sound inseparable from her own, portrays a very 1980s match between a corporate climber and the "Barbie doll" he envisions as perfection, though he never really sees her. The song chugs along like radio fodder, but instead of hearts and flowers it offers a story of betrayal and recycled desire: in the end, the doll on the shelf, never really a human presence anyway, betrays him. He, in turn, throws her to the dogs of gossip and finds another Barbie girl. As in a Beattie story, marriage here is portrayed as the union of two solipsists, unable to truly reach each other even within their avowed intimacy.

By her 1991 album *Night Ride Home*, perhaps because her marriage was then starting to show the fissures that would end it a few years later, Mitchell risked singing openly about herself and Klein—their anxious moments as well as their contentment. She also started critiquing marriage and the family in terms that could be called feminist despite her lifelong hostility to that word. "Cherokee Louise" exposes a father's sexual abuse of his foster daughter. "Not to Blame," on 1994's *Turbulent Indigo*, calls out an abusive spouse who *beat the girl you love the most*. That latter song generated much gossip upon its release; domestic violence was claiming headlines nationwide as football hero O. J. Simpson faced murder charges in the death of his wife, Nicole Brown Simpson, and her friend Ron Goldman. He was acquitted of murder, but was later found responsible for the deaths in a civil trial. Two years earlier, a much-discussed incident had brought the matter of violence between intimates to the fore when something happened between Jackson Browne and his then-partner Daryl Hannah that drew police to their Santa Monica home. Browne denied rumors that he was responsible for a black eye Hannah later sported in public, and was legally cleared of all responsibility. Hannah never directly accused him. Nonetheless, many listeners have speculated that in "Not to Blame" Mitchell points a finger at her former lover. In an album release interview with Robert Hilburn, Mitchell shied away from that suggestion, saying that she "should have put a disclaimer . . . 'any resemblance to people living or dead is coincidental.'" As for Browne, he later told the *Dallas Morning News* that the song was "all about carrying a torch for twenty years . . . she just thinks that I'm, like, you know, the antichrist."

What is sure is that unlike many of her earlier songs about problematic men, the central crisis of "Not to Blame" is not just interpersonal but openly political. Mitchell casts scorn on the *six hundred thousand doctors* who blame women whom they *see bleeding through their lives* instead of apprehending the men who hurt them. Like the tragic, bruised heroine Isabella Rossellini plays in Lynch's *Blue Velvet*, the unnamed women in "Not to Blame" are complicated people destroyed by confinement within marriages to dangerous men. Mitchell takes care to put not just one man on notice, but the institution of marriage itself.

By the time she recorded "Not to Blame," she was questioning marriage's value in her own life. There's more rapture directed toward Klein on *Night Ride Home*, but by *Turbulent Indigo* they had separated, and Mitchell's attitude toward love's possibilities grew dark. She mostly continued to look beyond herself, as in "Sex Kills," a fierce diatribe against sexualized greed and violence and, implicitly, the hypocrisy of the government during the AIDS crisis; or "The Magdalene Laundries," a keen for the unwed mothers driven to their deaths on an Irish work farm. But one song on her marriage playlist stands apart. I think it's the most personal she ever wrote about Klein. A coda, it breaks the heart.

The arrangement on "Last Chance Lost" is spare. Only the two of them play on the track: her guitar and voice, his bass and keyboards. She climbs and falls along a melody that ascends in stairsteps and continually collapses on itself. The lyrics are spare, too; this is a pained description of what happens when words fail. Real people to each other all those years, the married couple revert into stereotypes: *the hero cannot make the change, the shrew will not be tamed*. Klein's usually buoyant bass, for the first time ever and clearly on purpose, actually sounds a bit stolid. The song's last image is of the two soon-to-be exes bickering on a rifle range. The multitracked harmonies that end the song, just little short phrases, careen like bullets and lean sharply, like bodies dodging something. Marriage is exposed here as the bond that binds and wounds. The song seems to end abruptly and, at the same time, feels incomplete.

ENGLISH BEATS

Joni and Larry, Larry and Joni. Mitchell and Klein. This marriage wasn't like the cracked edifices her favorite writers deconstructed and articles like "The End of Sex" sought to reinstate. It came closer to another ideal coming back into vogue in the 1980s—the swashbuckling duo, bonded by complementary strengths and driven by a passion for risk-taking. In this vision of the marriage, Klein is Harrison Ford, the ultimate 1980s action hero–slash–romantic lead. Or maybe that's Joni; she always liked a good fedora. Flipping roles as it suited them, Mitchell and Klein mastered technology like Han Solo and Princess Leia in their *Millennium Falcon*; in search of new sounds, they risked it all, like Marion Ravenwood and Indiana Jones seeking the Lost Ark. Creative breakthroughs sparked this romance, grounded in teamwork, a commitment to mutual learning and a little healthy rivalry.

Reading the interviews Joni and Larry did together, I reveled in the gearhead connection that hummed beneath their conversations when both were learning about synthesizers and drum machines and other new studio wizard tools. In one "rock master class" in front of a small audience, the interviewer introduced Klein by ribbing him about being "ridiculously good-looking" and winning the hand of a woman he and millions of other male admirers had long fantasized about. I cringed for Klein as I read this exchange, but he simply deflected, going right into a lengthy explanation of how he and Joni made their *Dog Eat Dog* demos at home and why they decided to bring in engineer Mike Shipley and rising synth-pop star Thomas Dolby to help them speed up on the learning curve. Explaining how they created a particular effect on the song "Good Friends," Klein dove into the details:

"There's two chords where it see-saws back and forth from one to another and she'd sing those stacks and then we sampled those with an AMS digital delay and then triggered them with, like, a rim shot or something like that. And so what you're actually hearing is these two different samples being triggered: da-da da-da / da-da da-da."

Mediated glimpses of Joni and Klein's life together, always marked by the claws of journalists' digging for details of a "private life" beyond their musical collaborations (they never offered much beyond expressing affection for their cats), reinforced my idea of them as a working unit above all else. I found this thrillingly romantic. After all, that's one way I think about my marriage. The way Joni and Klein speak to each other in these interviews shows how a creative couple devises its own means of mutual translation—she speaks in metaphors, he's more technical, but they listen to each other and invent a new dialect through which both can be heard.

The hard parts, when teamwork slips into competition, resonate with me, too. When Eric and I met, I immediately knew that his Princeton education and bookworm superpowers had granted him more relevant frameworks for writing criticism than I'd built from my ramshackle library of poetry books and tarot card manuals. Though Joni had so much more recording under her belt than he did, Klein was the one who could talk sequencers with the guys at the soundboard—the one who'd bothered to learn that lingo. The tensions between them that sometimes erupted into "semi-war," a phrase Klein used in conversation with Bill Flanagan in 1988, seem mostly related to these clashes regarding expertise.

"I've learned a lot about how to be a good producer," he told Flanagan. "Joan's got very good musical intuition. On some of the previous things I would voice my disapproval of an idea before the idea had time to reach fruition, before it paid off. That really bothered her. She's not used to having someone present any kind of negativity at the birth of an idea. I've learned through the course of these records how to time my input."

Flanagan, a great interviewer who could meet musicians on the geek ground where they lived, nonetheless turned Klein's talk of "trust" toward discussions of sexual infidelity, quoting another point in the conversation where Joni says she doesn't mind if Larry takes a female pal out to lunch. Of course she didn't— she knew what her husband truly valued, and she had it. He was a studio rat, and so was she. Even if she didn't know the lingo, what other woman in the early 1980s could take charge behind a mixing board, much less command a room full of session players, guiding them to go beyond their clichés in service of her vision? (There were a few, in fact, like Roberta Flack and Patrice Rushen, but mostly women were still shut out of that boys' club.) As a creative team, Mitchell and Klein had the kind of potential that Joni and Larry both cared about—the kind that Joni had cultivated less successfully with Guerin, Alias, even James Taylor. They could make great music together as equals, shoring up each other's weak spots and bringing out hidden strengths, their intimacy heightening their ability to absorb each other's most provocative ideas.

If one way to dream about this marriage is to see it as Joni's reward for years of broken hearts and valiant efforts, another is to see it as an even more old-fashioned kind of union that, in the 1980s, also felt up to the minute: arranged. It was a love match, but also, in a strange way, a practical one. Klein was already well on his way toward behind-the-scenes stardom when he met Joni; the widening connections to various studio gangs she made possible helped him further escape the jazz box he found confining. She had access to nearly any player she wanted, and to those expensive synthesizers already starting to dominate the young decade's sounds. As for Mitchell, her jazz immersion had left her alienated from a wider audience that, despite her insistence on putting art first, she still wanted to reach. And she was curious about the potential of those synths and other electronic tools—she'd been playing around with them since *The Hissing of Summer Lawns*, when she sampled the Drummers of Burundi and manipulated her voice using an ARP string machine. Teacher, meet student. They could switch those roles at will.

One thing Klein gave Mitchell was currency with a younger generation of pop experimenters. She wasn't the only 1960s refugee trying on these new methods. Henley's "The Boys of Summer," cowritten and coproduced by Tom Petty's guitarist Mike Campbell, was a home run; many others tried such routes with varying degrees of success, some before she did. Linda Ronstadt (who was managed, like Joni in the '80s, by expert trend watcher

Peter Asher) looked to New Wave songsmith Elvis Costello for the 1980 album *Mad Love*. Carly Simon hooked up with Tim Curry, a hero to New Wave kids for his polymorphous turn as Dr. Frank-N-Furter in *The Rocky Horror Picture Show*, for her syndrum-punctured semi-hit "Vengeance." Neil Young went full sci-fi for *Trans*, a droning noise fest with highly processed vocals that saw him trying to invent a new musical language, in part to communicate with his cerebral palsy–afflicted son Ben. That was a heartfelt exploration of technology's possibilities; other efforts, like Grace Slick's 1984 album *Software*, were blatant bids for commercial success that didn't pan out.

Jazz fusion, always a space where new technologies thrived, had incorporated synthesizers throughout its evolution, and many in that field followed the trend toward poppier synth sounds in the 1980s, too. Wayne Shorter made his most composed and pre-programmed album, *Atlantis*, in 1985—enlisting, who else, Larry Klein on bass. Soul fusion pioneer George Duke used a boppy Michael Jackson–style Moog bass on Deniece Williams's 1984 number one hit "Let's Hear It for the Boy." Most impressive was Herbie Hancock's massive success with the 1983 single "Rockit," which utilized not only synthesizers but a brand-new "scratching" turntable technique borrowed from hip-hop, and won him his first Grammy in 1984. His performance that night featured breakdancing robots and Herbie on a keytar.

Joni didn't really incorporate new jazz directions into her work with Klein, though. Maybe she was tired of engaging with the tradition after *Mingus*, or maybe leaving her thirties made her feel the need for a perk-up. She turned to the kids connected to the new British movement known as New Wave. The most famous origin story about the pivot on her first full Klein collaboration, 1985's *Dog Eat Dog*, had her dancing in that Caribbean bar to the Police and becoming obsessed, *da doo doo doo da da da da* sticking in her head for months. What she liked best about that trio with the platinum dye jobs was Stewart Copeland's drum style, heavy on the light-as-air snare and dropped reggae beats. She even tried to get the Police to join her for some recording sessions, but schedules didn't permit.

Mitchell was interested in using electronic elements to help make songs sound oppositional, or at the least, a little bit alien. A paradox loomed: How could the most commercial sound on the pop market also serve challenging musical storylines? Trying to figure that out, Joni's and Klein's ears got caught up in signals mostly emanating from England. There, New Wave music had morphed out of punk as a means for retaining the disruptive spirit of that movement's loud, raw style while diversifying its sonic possibilities—and making it more marketable.

As Prince and other American R&B artists were using the novel sounds of synthesizers to lead listeners into new ways of thinking about pleasure and fun, British stars like Gary Numan, Tears for Fears and Thomas Dolby explored those same effects as prompts for pondering dystopian futures or inner unrest. At the same time Mitchell got interested in writing about the political power games she'd partially explored in songs stretching as far back as her second album's "The Fiddle and the Drum." British synth-pop gave new shape to the outsider spirit that, in her bougie adulthood, had become hard for her to grasp. Behind a Roland keyboard, she could be a new Joni Mitchell: an oracle, in a way.

Klein was drawn to electronic music's possibilities for different reasons. Having already taken up the fretless bass to loosen the hold of standard fingerings (as Jaco Pastorius had before him), he was thrilled by the seemingly unlimited sounds the newest machines made possible. Here he is in an email to me, describing his first encounters with the Fairlight, the first synthesizer to

incorporate a sampler and a very rare and expensive rig when he
first got his hands on one. I'll let him tell the story:

> The Fairlight was the first and most expansive computer musical
> instrument that was developed during this time. I was fascinated
> by what was being done with sampling. It really seemed to be an
> entirely new palette to work with. I decided to figure out a way
> of learning about how the instrument worked, and how to work
> with it.
>
> The local office for Fairlight in Los Angeles was located
> very close to where Joni and I were living, and I approached a
> guy who worked there about the idea of coming into the office
> for 90 minutes on weekday mornings to show me how the
> instrument worked, and to give me some lessons in operating it.
> The more that I worked with it, the more excited I got about the
> possibilities of what could be done with it. The people who were
> doing the most interesting work with the Fairlight were Trevor
> Horn, Tears for Fears, and Thomas Dolby. Of course, as I was
> listening to the music that was being made incorporating this
> technology, I was sharing it with Joni.
>
> Joni is an artist who is, and has always been, in search of
> fresh territory to work in, so the best of what was coming out of
> the sampling technology was exciting and interesting to her as
> well. During that time Joni and I moved to Malibu Beach, and
> I had a little studio in one of the bedrooms of the house. I had a
> Fairlight and a Sequential Circuits Prophet synth set up in this
> studio, and was gradually developing some facility on them. I
> was writing music upstairs while she was painting downstairs.
>
> Here and there something that I was working on would
> catch her ear, and she would say "Oh! . . . I like that one . . . let
> me work with that one!" As time went on Joan started writing

lyrics to some of the pieces that I was working on as well as songs that she started developing on guitar and piano, and what felt like the beginnings of a new album began to emerge.

Klein and Mitchell enlisted Thomas Dolby and engineer Mike Shipley to help on *Dog Eat Dog* because Klein, still taking classes to master the thing, wasn't quite confident enough on the Fairlight. Received wisdom about that album, reinforced by Mitchell in the bitter interviews she gave after it failed commercially and received mixed-to-bad reviews, is that she and Dolby didn't get along and their conflicts botched the whole project. His working methods interfered with the intuitive Klein-Mitchell team effort. Dolby preferred to build tracks and present them for Mitchell's input, while she wanted to be in on everything from the ground up. She captured the struggle best in a 1986 interview with Los Angeles journalist Iain Blair, saying, "I don't want to be interior-decorated out of my own music." She got on better with Shipley, who worked with her throughout this period.

The scorn and dismissiveness she sometimes communicated in the aftermath of her marriage sour the narrative and make it difficult to hear the music she made with Klein in a fully positive light. Speaking about *Dog Eat Dog* to David Yaffe years later, she called Klein and Dolby "puffed-up dwarfs" and accused her husband of isolating her from everyone who supported her approach to music-making. Yet beyond that account, Mitchell's recollections of making *Dog Eat Dog* were more exasperated than accusatory. "People think Klein took me over, but he didn't," she told Malka Marom. "We just changed the palate, and I played nearly everything on there, everything was under my guidance."

What to believe? I'm choosing to listen to the music, and trace its evolution from the experiments Mitchell had been tentatively making for a decade before she met Klein to the subtle, integrated sound they achieved on *Night Ride Home* and *Turbulent Indigo*. I believe that every marriage, and every close working relationship, involves a lot of agita intermixed with love. I also know that for most of the history of popular music, men have been wired—by homosocial creative cultures that have long viewed women as helpmates at best and objects at worst—to expect to dominate the few women who share their workplaces. From a distance, it seems to me that the long Mitchell-Klein partnership nearly always ran on strong support, yet it did sometimes fall prey to complicated power struggles stemming from his sense of entitlement as a man and her equally strong determination to remain independent, singular, apart. The fundamental problem during the making of *Dog Eat Dog*, as Mitchell herself usually described it, was that she and Dolby had incompatible work methods, and that nothing about him made her trust him enough to let go and let him twiddle the knobs the way he wanted to. Yet even on that album, one of the last lyrics includes the word "trust," fondly directed at Klein. I know in my own marriage the sore spots are never entirely resolved. Eric and I will carry certain contested stories to our graves. That seems to be true about *Dog Eat Dog*, too.

What gets lost when *Dog Eat Dog* is dismissed as a failed experiment is its crucial role in the evolution of Mitchell's songwriting. It is the album that takes her beyond a common idea of the personal, not only via the subject matter its songs address— most of the album's tracks are protest songs that apply poetic logic to issues ranging from yuppie consumerism to mass-media overload—but through its sound. While more than a dozen musical collaborators contribute to the mix, including mainstays Shorter, Colaiuta and Alex Acuña, synthesizers dominate. They meld with Mitchell's singing, which echoes and pings, sometimes sounding more like another synthesizer than the conversational, vulnerable woman listeners have long known. Firmly committed to her middle and lower register, she explores the many ways her voice can sound like the instruments with which it's interacting— like a drum, or a fretless bass, or a sample. Samples themselves surface on songs like "Tax Free" (in which the actor Rod Steiger voices the character of a televangelist, the target of Mitchell's ire, his voice mingled with others Mitchell plucked from her television) and "Shiny Toys" (clips of a blasé Dolby uttering *I'm excited* and Klein proclaiming *I love my Porsche* anchor this song about rampant spending). It's the beginning of a new phase in Mitchell's explorations of pastiche, a technique borrowed from the visual arts that she had long wanted to apply sonically. The synths made doing so really possible.

A mostly forgotten track on the album shows how *Dog Eat Dog* opened new doors for her and Klein. "Smokin' (Empty, Try Another)" begins with the sound of a vending machine—the actual machine in the recording studio where it was made, recorded by Mitchell herself. Its janky rhythm pushes against Klein's bass line, which is a bit of a throwback, funky and spare. Mitchell repeats the phrase *empty, try another*, multitracked and spliced into infinite enjambment. This little soundtrack to a bad habit implicates the voice at its center in a fascinating way. For a moment Mitchell and Klein have figured out how to pinpoint the spot where one person's addiction intersects with the greed and compulsion that the rest of the album so forcefully calls out. It is personal, but in a new way.

The now-"dated" sounds of *Dog Eat Dog* come alive when considered as part of a larger pop moment in which virtually every major artist was trying to adapt the creative process to fit within a digitized world. If most of Mitchell's work in the 1980s was grounded in character studies that showed a kinship with the short story writers she treasured, this album is her Big Novel— her *White Noise*, recasting interpersonal stories within a large and loud milieu of blaring headlines and televisions constantly turned on. *Empty, try another* is as much a definitive statement about the 1980s as *we've got to get ourselves back to the garden* was about the 1960s. It's just been difficult for people to hear over the voice of their beloved, confessional Joni, still ruling in their heads.

THE LADY PROTESTS

In 1985, with Ronald Reagan set for a second term in the White House, Klein and Joni's shared worldview was a common one in their social circle. Pessimistic. "This country is going very conservative, very right wing, and a lot of the progress made in the ['60s] through liberal law-making is being undone," she told Mick Brown of the *London Times*. "I think there is a sense of powerlessness developing among people. A lot of people I talk to say they feel angry. I feel it myself."

This wasn't really a political awakening, though interviewers then and Joni historians now often characterize it that way. Mitchell had long incorporated gentle strains of protest into her music. Her occasional antiwar statements fit alongside environmentalist and women's liberationist impulses within a balanced portfolio of high-hippie concerns. Her desirous, compassionate, sometimes patronizing attempts to connect with marginalized people added more to the ledger. And she'd turned a cynical eye on her own community, too, in the critiques that filled *The Hissing of Summer Lawns* and her other portraits of private lives made ever more arid by quenchless consumerism. Apprehending the topics of *Dog Eat Dog*—corporate greed, government and corporate malfeasance, the deadly dissatisfactions of the rat race—she was really making a return.

Her political analyses were not always sophisticated and sometimes self-motivated. "Tax Free," for example, was a personally compelled protest. Mitchell found herself facing a huge bill due to a quirk in the California sales tax laws. Newly signed to Geffen, the new label her old mentor David had named after himself, she found that the company had put a lien on her songwriting royalties to pay off the debt. The case was overturned in 1988, but for a few years, Mitchell found herself in a financially precarious situation, compounded by other struggles, including that lawsuit involving her housekeeper, which dragged on for several years. These messes interfered with her and Klein's peaceful life and sometimes put Mitchell in what Klein once called a "Caine Mutiny" mood. She was looking for conspiracies in her own life, and, reading the newspaper, found them in the bigger world.

One of her most powerful songs from *Dog Eat Dog*, one she later claimed Nina Simone herself praised when they met by chance one day, is "Ethiopia." Mitchell wrote the dirgelike lament about life and death in that famine-stricken country because she'd grown disenchanted with charity movements like Band Aid and USA for Africa, which assembled wealthy pop stars to croon anodyne anthems raising money for impoverished developing nations. Mitchell sometimes joined in these top-down efforts, singing on the Canadian version, Northern Lights's "Tears Are Not Enough," and showing up for the heartland-oriented Farm Aid and more pointed political events like the 1986 Get Tough on Toxics concert to raise awareness about tainted drinking water in Los Angeles. But she questioned the value of charity in such politically troubled times. As she had in her *Hissing* days, Joni looked at her rock-royalty peers and saw hypocrisy. "Ethiopia" was her rejoinder.

Her view in the song is cinematic, in line with her previous imaginative forays into foreign environments. But this time the journey offers none of the psychedelic release of "Dreamland" or "Paprika Plains." Mitchell's visions in "Ethiopia" are nightmarish, connecting Western wealth with African privation and calling out the white middle class for empathizing only when the famine is sentimentalized on television. *A T.V. star with a P.R. smile calls your baby "it" while strolling through your tragic trials*, Mitchell intones in its most devastating line. Compare this to the hook from Band Aid's treacly charity single, especially offensive considering that many Africans are Muslim: *Do they know it's Christmastime?*

What makes "Ethiopia" so haunting isn't the lyrics, as unflinching as they may be. It's the song's resonance, a stunning hybrid of the warm, enveloping sweep of Mitchell's earlier fantasias and the strangely disembodied mood that synthesizers could create. Sparer than most of *Dog Eat Dog*'s tracks, it gains its eeriness via the obscured, manipulated tones running beneath the main instrumentation, evoking the whir of an airplane making an airdrop, children's cries, even the sub-Saharan heat itself. Conventional instruments, including Kazu Matsui's Japanese bamboo flute, are combined and recombined, becoming the voices of the landscape and the people tied to it. Providing the close-ups in this hazy milieu, Mitchell's vocals are pitched low, with a heavy edge.

"Ethiopia" is a prime example of how Joni and Klein's musical approach suits her dark scenarios during this period—and of how their bigger frameworks made such protests possible. Always a complicated thinker as both a guitarist and a songwriter, Mitchell now had ways of fleshing out her narratives that were not possible, exactly, even in the busy jazz arrangements that had suited her late-1970s stories of love and wandering. The confessional school's assumption that a song needs to be grounded in the personal shifts once the limitless voices of the Fairlight and other synthesizers enter the room. Before the 1980s, Mitchell's songwriting had always privileged the view from within her own head, even when she was observing others. Now she could adopt the wide lens of the filmmaker. The songs seem to move through Mitchell instead of from within her. She lives in these landscapes, pays witness to them, but mostly, she is not at their center.

The change had to be intensely liberating for Mitchell despite whatever struggles she faced learning how synths worked and collaborating with men like Dolby and her sometimes overconfident husband. Since her young adulthood she had been a portraitist, mostly a self-portraitist. Now she pursued much larger visions. It's not coincidental, I believe, that during the 1980s Mitchell also grew exponentially prolific as a visual artist, producing semi-abstract work for the first time, and exploring photography. In the painting originally designated for *Dog Eat Dog*'s cover, she filled a massive canvas with a blue-and-brown cubist whorl showing the partial figures of dogs in seething motion—"God dog, Jesus dog, you know, and racial dogs in conflict and so on," she called them—emerging and sinking back into the churn. It is a great distillation of the album's overarching view of the impending crises that oblivious, overfed North Americans were hardly noticing. The marketing department at Geffen rejected the cover. They wanted her face. So she made a collage in which she became one of the dogs, who were now jumping all around her. There would be no clear-eyed self-portrait with Joni gazing at her fans as she holds a flower, inviting them in. No shot of her in a swimming pool. She refused the center. She showed herself as part of a pack, strengthened by the bond.

DUETS

She would go even further outside herself on her next album with Klein, *Chalk Mark in a Rain Storm*. Almost twenty years had passed since she'd first appeared on the cover of *Rolling Stone*, representing songwriting's turn toward the personal and poetic. She'd constructed so many selves since then. Now she was preoccupied with life beyond the edges of the self. Partnered intimacy, political consciousness, the fictive art of living in others' skins. On her thirteenth studio album, she would go fully cinematic, letting stories expand beyond her instead of staying grounded in her rowdy mind and sensitive gut.

Chalk Mark began forming during a pause in her musical productivity. She'd miscarried an unexpected pregnancy, and that experience unsettled her blissful communion with Klein. His choice to keep working after this calamity further strained the marriage. Have you ever noticed the similarity between "marriage" and "miscarriage"? Families of two can be difficult to maintain in a world that fetishizes childbearing. Joni had lost a daughter who was still out there. She may have been ambivalent about this accidental pregnancy, scared, secretly thrilled, I don't know. But it had to have hit hard.

Thinking she was managing on her own, or perhaps unable to deal with her grief, Klein had decamped to England to produce an album for singer Ben Orr from the Cars. "I was a big fan of the Cars from the first time that I heard them," Klein told me. "I felt like they were doing something new and interesting in every way. It was an abbreviated and direct mode of expression, both musically and lyrically. I was actually brought in on the Ben Orr project by the great engineer and my good friend Mike Shipley, who had worked with Mutt Lange on their *Heartbeat City*. Working on Ben's album was what actually brought me over to England. At a certain point where the period that I was supposed to be there had long elapsed, Joni and I decided that it would be good for her to come over to England and stay with me."

Mitchell was intrigued by the artists Klein was getting to know. "I remember her saying something to the effect that the writing of that period, and this would include the songwriting of groups like the Cars, was emphasizing the description of *what* things were, not how one felt about them . . . that it wasn't an era of writing about how one felt about things." Klein is identifying a certain constructedness, a distance between author and subject, that lends much 1980s pop a chilly glamour. On *Chalk Mark* Mitchell explored this approach both lyrically and through a blend of traditional instrumentation and electronics. The album grew out of the time she and Klein spent in a rented cottage in the village of Frome, and at Ashcombe House, the home studio of another rock star finding power in new storytelling techniques, Peter Gabriel.

Gabriel had first found fame as the singer for the progressive rock band Genesis, crafting surrealist mini-operas about late-capitalist alienation and spiritual rapture. He'd found his pop voice after leaving that band and tightening up his grandiose tendencies. Hits like the fractured wail of jealousy "Shock the Monkey" and the vaguely environmentalist lament "Red Rain" made him an elder statesman of the synth-driven British scene. His fascination with both high tech and global beats made Ashcombe House a percolating center for new musical ideas.

Chalk Mark was recorded in several different studios and completed back in Los Angeles, but its open-ended spirit, fortified by the wealth of synthesizers and other goodies that Gabriel had amassed, is rooted in the work Joni and Klein did in England. There, they were in the orbit of a community of musicians they admired, and who adored Joni. (Kate Bush, the young mistress of the Fairlight, also lived nearby, and I just had to ask Klein if they'd met, but they never crossed paths with her.) They would visit several other studios back home after their time in the Cotswolds, but *Chalk Mark* remains, in some essential way, an English album.

It's also a highly collaborative work, in a different way than the big-band outings of Joni's jazz years. Half the album's tracks are duets. A rumor bubbled up then, and has stuck since, that pairing with other big voices like Gabriel's was an attempt to shore up Joni's waning commercial value. But listen to the way Joni's voice tumbles against Don Henley's on "Snakes and Ladders," and how it streaks across the sonic Texas sky of "Cool Water" alongside Willie Nelson's. On these tracks, the counterparts she's enlisted cut apart the perspective, the way the collage-like blocks and shards of images in the paintings she was making disrupted the figurative style she'd long maintained. As the director of these songs, Mitchell chose each collaborator to best represent the often male characters speaking through her. "I cast voices just like I would cast faces for a film," she told one reporter.

It was hardly new for a singer-songwriter to adopt others' viewpoints—other's lives—to make points and pull heartstrings. Men were granted this privilege more than women. Dylan had written others' stories for nearly his entire career, as did John Prine, Randy Newman, Springsteen. Women were still expected to write from their own experience and emotions, the culturally designated sources of their authority. Still, in the 1980s, new stars—Suzanne Vega, Rickie Lee Jones, Tracy Chapman—were showing that they could pull off complex character studies, too. Klein was working with some of these women as a producer. Joni hated being compared to them, but she couldn't help but have heard how much they owed her, and noticed variations on the aspect of her own work that had too long been overlooked: the observational tactics of the flaneuse who even on her first, folkie albums had experimented with sketches of a cabdriver, a pirate, the ladies in her canyon.

Mitchell's development of other characters' voices on *Chalk Mark* goes beyond those brief encounters toward a greater letting go—what Raymond Carver named as the "detachment" necessary to write characters that seem to exist apart from the author's hand. Even when singing in the first person, she softened the impact of her own personality throughout the album. On its lead single, "My Secret Place," she cast herself as a woman on the threshold of intimacy with a potential lover, with Gabriel playing the mysterious man leading her away from the lonely crowd. The pair trade off lines seamlessly, peeling away layers of mistrust as they begin to finish each other's phrases. Late in the song, the lyrics bend toward her old introversion: *Why did you pick me?* she sings. But as the swirl of keyboards continues to cocoon her and Gabriel's voices, that question falls away, defeated. The woman Joni is in this song may be tempted to live in her head, but as she is seduced and seduces, her own ego boundaries melt.

Mitchell traveled widely in her imaginings for *Chalk Mark*. "The Beat of Black Wings" goes inside the mind of an army veteran with PTSD, its samples invoking the helicopters whose noise still echoes in his brain, dissolving his damaged consciousness until it smears like *chalk marks in a rainstorm*. The lyrics interpolate early rock and roll songs to evoke memory's fluctuations. For "Cool Water," her duet with country kingpin Nelson, she became a dusty trail rider hallucinating her way toward a dry death; again she interpolated older songs to widen her scope, combining a chorus best known from Hollywood Westerns with contemporary images of drought that recall the international crises charity singles were meant to help solve.

She did fall into her old bad habit of racial appropriation on the sonically stunning but lyrically questionable "Lakota," an anthem written in the spirit of Indigenous ghost-dance laments and intended to support the land claim the Sioux are still staging against the U.S. government in the southwestern Black Hills. This song epitomizes 1980s Joni at her most impassioned, creative and occasionally clueless. Melding sharp keyboard lines with a looped Native chant and traditional percussion elements, "Lakota" delivers one blessing: it powerfully removes Indigenous music from the "anthropological folk" category where it had been frozen. Mitchell's spare lyrics call on the earth itself as a savior—*grass, pity me; rocks, pity me*. The effect is powerful. But she does not manage to fully decenter herself, repeatedly crying, *I am Lakota!*, which she most definitely is not. The fact that the vocalist she'd enlisted as a background singer was Iron Eyes Cody, a famous Hollywood "Indian" (he's the man with one tear rolling down his face in the ubiquitous anti-litter ad campaign staged by the Keep America Beautiful nonprofit in the 1970s) who was not actually Lakota, but Italian-American—his real name was Espera de Corti—further deflates the power of this musically rich but politically problematic song.

"Lakota" is the shimmering artistic centerpiece of *Chalk Mark*, with irresistible rhythms and a soul-enveloping combination of Indigenous and synth-pop elements. Yet as its failings show, even as she dared erasing herself in the name of empathy, Mitchell was still that privileged dreamer who swathed herself in Navajo blankets and designer turquoise, that utopian, sometimes myopic hippie romanticist she'd always been. Peter Gabriel had made a similar potentially awkward leap across racial divides in his anthem "Biko," an elegy for the South African freedom fighter

Steve Biko, who was murdered while detained by police in 1977. Somehow his foot landed on more solid ground. That song's chorus included the Xhosa phrase "yihla moja," in English "spirit come down"; Gabriel sings it without changing tone or rhythm in a lyric that is otherwise in English and from his perspective. "Biko" works while "Lakota" raises questions because its white protagonist doesn't try to imaginatively occupy the body of the marginalized person he's invoking. Momentarily, he adopts the language of the man he laments, yet he remains himself. "Lakota" could be reclaimed by Native voices—Mitchell's empathy goes that far—but in her version she does not cede enough territory. Such are the limits of her collage technique.

This misunderstanding of the limits of empathy was common among liberal musicians in the 1980s. When she and Klein made *Chalk Mark*, they were spending time with white English artists caught up in causes very similar to those Mitchell had long embraced, including support for Indigenous people on colonized land. Gabriel eventually put his money where his ideals were, creating Real World Studios as a place where artists from all over the world could work together, but even he could not transcend his whiteness, presenting a highly idealized, reductive view of the former English colonies whose musical lineages ran through some of his biggest hits. ("Biko" was his best; the overheated "Rhythm of the Heat," about revered psychoanalyst Carl Jung's first visit to Africa, might be the worst.)

Mitchell never could completely dissolve into her music; few of her fans would have wanted her to do so. But the character studies of *Chalk Mark* actually sharpened her self-reflective skills as she returned to the old Joni on her next album with Klein, the last of their happily married days.

HOME AND AWAY

I've been telling the story of Joni and Klein, Larry and Joni, Klein
and Mitchell, as it unfolds in recording studios, not at home. Of
course I'm curious about the personal stuff, too. Something made
that romance last for more than a decade, even as Joni spent more
time in her art studio and Klein became a sought-after producer
for other artists. Then something put salt in their small, accumulat-
ing wounds, leading the pair to separate while they were making
Turbulent Indigo. Maybe another woman. Or another man. The
miscarriage, always haunting. The failure of their music to chart.
Health problems, money problems, the stuff everybody faces.
Their partnership was exceptional, but their parting, it seems, was
ordinary.

Before the split, Joni and Klein made *Night Ride Home* together, at home this time, away from the stimulating distraction of
other people's influence. It's a favorite among fans and, for many
younger ones, has been an entryway. Upon its release in 1991,
Night Ride Home was heralded as a return to form. Compared
to *Chalk Mark*, the production is restrained; instead of the electronically enhanced big-sky arrangements of that previous album,
these tend toward quietude, with Mitchell's acoustic guitar again
in the foreground and her voice, recorded "dry" (without extra
effects), landing right in the listener's ear. The closeness was back.
Things felt personal again. "*Night Ride Home* is her umpteenth
comeback," wrote the ever-acerbic critic Dave Marsh. "This one
works."

That's how *Night Ride Home* sounds on first listen—like a
sigh of relief and a settling into old ways. More attention reveals
that this album wasn't a return as much as an integration of past
lessons within a fresh approach. Another step in the evolution.
Linda Sanders of *Entertainment Weekly* heard this, writing, "It

simply sounds like the distilled essence of everything that's come before."

Klein remembers the time making *Night Ride Home* as a happy one, grounded in the creative bond at the center of his and Joni's relationship. They'd finished their home studio and christened it the Kiva, in reference to the underground structures the Indigenous Pueblo people use for their religious rites. Always ready to get working, Joni and Klein invited in old friends like Alex Acuña and Vinnie Colaiuta and new ones like guitarist Bill Dillon and a couple of the young artists Klein was producing, David Baerwald and the Innocence Mission singer Karen Peris. They workshopped new songs in the give-and-take way to which they'd become accustomed, with Klein often coming up with music and Mitchell responding with her own tunes and rhythms and writing lyrics.

Within mostly analog arrangements, they still experimented with some synthesizers, like the Omnichord, which is shaped like Joni's longtime favorite the dulcimer, and the Birotron, which makes loops using 8-track tape. Joni played those synths herself. Such elements contributed to a sound that almost leans toward the ambient instrumental music then becoming popular via artists like the guitarist Michael Hedges and Mark Isham, an electronics-loving flugelhorn player who'd later play with Joni—lots of room, a kind of circular feeling to many of the songs, but peaceful. (When I brought this up with Klein, he rejected the New Age comparison, except when it came to the master of that benighted genre, Brian Eno, whose music both he and Joni love.) Within this sonic framework Mitchell let her mind roam freely, back to her childhood, into others' stories, or pausing within her own experience and seeing what it's like to sit with hard things.

"Our studio was in a leg of the house, and we were living the music night and day," Klein said in a 2021 interview. "It was an incredibly catalytic time. Not being able to get away from what we were working on was intense, and it put some strain on our relationship, but on the musical side of things, it was a great period. . . . Production-wise, we were braiding together technology with an organic kind of feeling, sequencing certain elements and then playing naturally against those things, combining programmed elements with played parts."

The ellipses in the above quote are there because I removed Klein's assertion that their personal life was a little boring at that point. "One starts to wonder where the poetry can come from," he joked. If her lyrics on this album are any indication, Joni wasn't wondering—she benefited from the calm, the space to return to herself. Having left confession behind on *Chalk Mark*, here she brought it back gracefully, without fanfare, having learned from her time in the heads of other characters that her "I" didn't have to be so pushy. She could gather herself gently within a song, letting the atmospherics speak.

That's what happens in the title track, a memory song about a drive she and Klein took during a quick Hawaiian getaway. The melody turns on "grand, sweeping curves," Lloyd Whitesell notes in his analysis. "Its beauty does not depend on ornament or rhythmic complexity but on the elegant counterpoise of bold movements through space." The tune is like a wheel turning, and Mitchell's words invoke the experience of looking out a window as the world goes by. Fragmented images caught in the moment blend with stray thoughts and recollections as she sings, *like some surrealist invented this*. Joni's "I" is part of the landscape as she sits next to her man. Instead of the incessant back talk and rumination of earlier songs, she rests easy. *We love the open road*. The generosity of her repose makes the song feel like a hymn.

Not all of *Night Ride Home* is this peaceful or contained. The old brio resurfaces on Mitchell's adaptations of great works—the New Testament's crucifixion story in "Passion Play (When All the Slaves Are Free)" and W. B. Yeats's famous poem "Slouching Toward Bethlehem." She also seems to have stooped to take another swipe at the housekeeper with whom she remained legally embroiled on "The Windfall (Everything for Nothing)." (This was around the time they settled out of court.) The tracks that won the hearts of both critics and the new listeners who discovered her in this period, however, are ones that neither rail nor pronounce.

One, "Cherokee Louise," is another encounter with the Indigenous people with whom Joni so deeply and often problematically identifies. This time, though, it's not an anthem laced with the poison of overidentification. It's a real memory from Mitchell's childhood, about a friend (actually a Cree girl, she has said) who, like so many First Nations children of Mitchell's generation, had been taken from her birth family and placed in a foster home. Mitchell's lyrics describe the sexual abuse Louise suffered at the hands of her stepfather and her decision to run away in order to escape it; she imagines her friend dashing through the tunnels where they'd play in the dust *like bubblebath*. The vocal on "Cherokee Louise" comes closer than most to Mitchell's old rapid-fire talk-talkin' style, but she holds back enough to keep its main character at the center, letting Wayne Shorter's skittering sax part become the running figure the song follows and eventually loses. Unresolved, grieving, hopeful against hope, "Cherokee Louise" captures the painfulness of a memory that cannot be resolved through analysis or political anthemizing.

This is the beautiful thing about *Night Ride Home*: the directive it gives to sit with unanswered questions, not try to outrun them or think them away. Reviewers called this an effect of "middle age," and Joni didn't disagree. That's as good a metaphor as any to encapsulate what is actually the span of a lifetime lived one moment at a time, with an eye on the horizon. *I am not old, I'm told, but I am not young*, Joni intones in her smokiest alto on "Nothing Can Be Done," a broken love song with music by Klein that trades the antsy anticipation of her earlier "Car on a Hill" for the twilight calm of knowing that intimate connections wax and wane, and cultivating patience within that reality.

The crowning moment of *Night Ride Home* is "Come in from the Cold," a seven-and-a-half-minute-long meditation on the search for love, with ambition a thread running through it. It's a little autobiography that also manages to become an epic—an apt description of many of Joni's most beloved songs, this time with a different energy. The music takes that gently arcing form that makes *Night Ride Home* a unified work. This time, though, the circle never closes, instead becoming more like the endless motion of waves at the shore. A subdued reggae rhythm sets the pensive mood. The lyrics move from "we" to "I" without explanation or apology; no overweening ego here, just a wise person's ability to see that her experiences—of teenage sexual frustration, of adult sexual disappointment, and of grander letdowns, too, rooted in the implosion of the baby-boomer dream to change the world— are shared by many, in some ways by all. Mitchell's multitracked vocals on the core refrain, *come in from the cold*, call to herself and to the listener simultaneously.

Mitchell would edit this song to make it more palatable to radio, but I always need to hear the full version: Joni's mind drifting from adolescence to her prime and on toward an uncertain future, the internalized shifts in mood exemplifying adulthood in all its tedium and obstinate lingering promise. The song never really ends; it only fades and begs the listener to add her own verses, her own accounts of romantic striving and humiliation and reconciliation with a self who will never not want to go beyond its own skin. Such peace in this song, and such unrest.

For me, "Come in from the Cold" marks *Night Ride Home* as a masterpiece. When Joni and Klein won a Grammy five years later for *Turbulent Indigo*, the final album of their marriage, the pop establishment recognized them for an integration of elements they'd managed with this older release. *Turbulent Indigo* is, to my ears, less adventurous musically, but it is the perfect afterword to this marriage story. Klein sees that set of songs, connected within the theme of romantic disillusionment, as another step forward, though for them it marked an end. "It was a difficult album to make, but mostly because it was a programmatic album about the disintegration of our marriage," he said. "It was a sad time, and there was a lot of sadness to illustrate in the way that the music fit together with the poetry. I don't think of it as a return to any previous era of Joni's work. She has always been searching for fresh territory to explore, and I think that with *Turbulent Indigo* we were trying to do that in new and different ways. Different instrumentation, different musicians, different methods of building tracks."

Onstage at the Shrine Auditorium the night *Turbulent Indigo* won a Grammy, after their names had been announced and they walked to the stage arm in arm, Joni began her acceptance speech with some qualifying words. "Considering we made this album in a state of divorce . . ." He grabbed her hand. "Well, we had two cats for help." Some giggling, more embraces. Klein leaned into the mic. "First of all, I'd like to thank Joan, who is I think the best songwriter around these days, for ten years of instruction in the arts." She kept his hand in hers until they returned to their seats and their new companions.

9

weaving garlands

Throughout my time winding along Joni Mitchell's path, her songs infiltrated my brain. They directed my emotions, faded and changed to others. "Nothing Can Be Done" is the one that stuck as I turned toward the later phases of her life. I consider it a blues, maybe not musically—the music, written by Klein, is a minor key variation of the soft-rock "Boys of Summer"—but in the way that genre designed to carry ancient pain encompasses both complaint and a certain hard acceptance. In the song, Joni confronts her lover, who's just grabbed his keys to head out toward something or someone she can't be.

But she also faces her aging self as she questions her impossible longing to keep things as they were. The song captures the feeling of being on the threshold, wavering, unbalanced, knowing there's no choice but to accept gravity's pull. Those words: *I am not old, I'm told, but I am not young*. Mitchell delivers them in clipped syllables. She's not yet sure how to settle this argument with herself. Middle age equals ambiguity, and for women it can hit at any point after fertile young adulthood wanes, graying the days before the onset of whatever illness or other calamity finally fells you. Joni Mitchell must have thought about this as she stared down solitude again at fifty.

Nothing can be done but grow older, more damaged and wiser, more accepting of life's cruelties, Joni sings. Then she asks: *must I surrender with grace the things I loved when I was younger?* She's talking about sex, at least the ridiculous fire of it, the way it dominates and opens doors and burns down houses. She also might mean her own ego—that fiery "I" that has so much power over people, making them think they can thrive dependent only on themselves. Nothing can be done, Joni murmurs, besides opening up a little to the idea of compromise, to the possibility that others might know something that you don't immediately understand about the way the world operates, or even about how you operate, how your life and work fit into a picture bigger than yourself. To surrender with grace is to open your arms. Share access to the life you've made with people who care about you, and trust that what you've done will live beyond the border of your fierce protectiveness. Let others reinterpret what you once insisted only you could say.

This is the work of making a legacy, and Mitchell turned toward it after *Turbulent Indigo* won its unexpected Grammy for Best Pop Album in a category that included younger and hotter stars like Madonna and Mariah Carey. That album had already signaled a new phase, away from the ebullient experimentation of her prime Klein years and toward a more contained reckoning with imperfection in the world and her own life. She still staged protests, in songs like "Sex Kills," about AIDS and objectification, and "Borderline," which bemoans the racial and gender divisions afflicting America. If, as Klein and Mitchell have both said, *Turbulent Indigo* is about the dissolution of their marriage, she processed her pain in lyrics that reached out toward others: the abandoned mothers in "The Magdalene Laundries"; the battered women of "Not to Blame." As for her own predicament, this was still Joni: she identified with the most fabled sufferers, the biblical Job and Vincent van Gogh, in whose image she crafted a self-portrait for the album cover. *All my little landscapes and all my yellow afternoons stack up around this vacancy*, she sang in the title track, dedicated to him, identifying loneliness as a source of madness, or at least its main companion.

How to move on? She still had herself, the Joni Mitchell she had created within music over more than a quarter century. The future felt uncertain, but the past was right there. And the market was hungry for it. Before turning fifty, Mitchell had stayed away from retrospectives, though Reprise issued a limited-edition one in 1971; she didn't want to look back. But now she started to think about how to witness her life in full.

As the 1990s turned toward the new century, Mitchell continued to create, though at nowhere near her previous pace. She did start releasing compilations, her way. The autumnal decades of her life would require patience and perspective. One thing about reaching maturity is that you realize that even as the future becomes ever more unclear, you cannot really be alone as you head there: there are the people who've forged this road, the ones who still walk with you even if you tried to walk away from them, and the ones who follow, to whom you owe your light, that legacy. Joni recognized this as she became the matriarch she'd never exactly planned to be.

GATHER THE FLOWERS

Building a legacy can be a beautiful act of gathering, like weaving a fragrant, flowery chain—anthologies were called "garlands" in the old days. But it can also feel like setting up shop in a bomb shelter, shutting out the present and securing essential goods so that the whims of time don't destroy them. Flowers rescued from the trash. From the rock and roll generation committed to living in the present tense, this kind of estate planning wasn't a natural move.

As tough as it was for the children of the incomplete 1960s revolution to attend to activities as banal as estate planning, many realized by the time they hit their fifties that they didn't want their music to fade away; plus, the money legacy work promised was awfully attractive. Joni was a garland weaver who also knew the value of a secure vault. She had always invested a chunk of her thought processes in the past, her lyrics knotting memories together within yarn-ball assemblages and challenging her fans to unravel them. Her life as a painter gave her a framework for the act of anthologizing: visual art runs on documentation, retrospectives and catalogs, curatorial activities that help determine how reputations form. So maybe she was more inclined than some of her generation to take on legacy-building as a creative act.

Still, when she turned toward her life's work, it had to feel a bit like a door shutting, one of those heavy wooden library doors that seals the room against outside air. She'd just won two Grammys, for God's sake; her name held currency on the pop scene again. Yet here was the latest record executive in her life (not her increasingly detached friend David Geffen, nor her onetime benefactor Mo Ostin, but a new kid from the punk world who'd taken over at Reprise, Howie Klein—no relation to Larry, by the way) telling her she needed to up her sales. Do a greatest-hits package, he said. She relented. With Larry gone, easels calling to her from her painting studio and her post-polio syndrome continuing to flare, she didn't feel too excited about making new music. Give the people what they want! The old stuff. But of course she couldn't just do that.

Recognizing that Howie Klein would be intimidated by her legend (and he was, telling Neil Strauss in the *New York Times* that "I have so much respect for her that I'm willing to subsume my own way of thinking to hers"), she came up with a plan to get something for herself out of the tedious process of packaging her most popular songs. When *Hits* came out in 1996, it had a twin, *Misses*. The first did what the title said, including "Both Sides Now" and "Big Yellow Taxi." The second went for the deep cuts, from "The Arrangement" to "Sex Kills." Mitchell wasn't the first to wordplay her way into gaining exposure for songs she thought had been overlooked; the New Wave band Devo released its *Greatest Misses* compilation in 1990, and rap pioneers Public Enemy did the same in 1992. For Mitchell, though, this wasn't just a way of making sure the songs she called her children all had a fair shake. The *Hits* and *Misses* projects launched an archive-making practice that has consistently stressed the generative possibilities of mining the past.

After *Turbulent Indigo*, legacy-building became one of the three main outlets for Mitchell's expression, alongside her dwindling number of new compositions and her steady work in visual art. In a rare case of synergy with the music business she so loved to oppose, her innovations as an archivist suited the needs of those wanting to make money from her music. Compilation albums were nothing new in the 1990s, and a few significant packages—the Beach Boys' *Endless Summer*, Neil Young's *Decade*, the Beatles' "blue" and "red" double albums—showed artists making a case for immortality as early as the 1970s. As these stars and the musical culture they'd created hit midlife, anthologizing became more elaborate, even high-concept. The best examples established an artist's historical relevance while having fun with the stuffy process of canonizing itself.

As often happened, Mitchell's favorite rival, Bob Dylan, defined the approach. His *Biograph* came out in 1985 and created a new category, only hinted at by earlier multidisc packages: this was the dawn of the boxed set. Its five albums' worth of material included many of the bard's most notable songs, but alongside them stood outtakes, alternate versions and unreleased songs that, up until that point, had been available only on the gray market, where bootleggers ruled. Beautifully contained within a package adorned with an Andy Warhol–esque Dylan portrait, *Biograph* also offered a thirty-six-page booklet containing notes from the artist himself and an interview with Joni's favorite journalist, Cameron Crowe, who'd become a famous Hollywood director. The monumental project was greeted with skepticism by some—*Philadelphia Inquirer* critic Ken Tucker called it "a chancey commercial prospect" whose organization was at times "confusing and annoying"—and, in an interview with longtime friend Mikal Gilmore, Bob himself said, "I've never really known what this thing is supposed to be." But *Biograph* opened a door. The following year, Bruce Springsteen copped Bob's move with the release of a five-album live set, and after that, dozens of classic rockers and others followed suit. The box set soon became a standard item under every holiday menorah or tree. Dylan continued to lead the way, with the *Boot-*

leg series he originated in 1991 eventually expanding to seventeen volumes (and counting).

Mitchell wasn't ready to catalog her stuff that elaborately yet; thus, she offered the limited capitulation of *Hits* and *Misses*. She also released one album of new material during this decade—*Taming the Tiger*, her 1998 collaboration with the young drummer Brian Blade. But nostalgia was coming for her whether she wanted to confront it or not. A full generation had passed since the glory years of the 1960s, and the market for trophies—and institutions to display them—was booming. The Rock & Roll Hall of Fame, which had mainly existed as a tony annual awards dinner since its inception in 1983, opened its museum doors in 1995, in a glass pyramid designed by world-class architect I. M. Pei, on the shores of Cleveland's Great Lake Erie. Mitchell was inducted in 1997 and won many other prizes in a few years' fell swoop: the Billboard Century Award in 1995; the Canadian Governor General's Performing Arts Award and Sweden's Polar Music Prize in 1996. She entered the Songwriters Hall of Fame in 1997.

During this onslaught of recognition, Mitchell expressed her doubts, repeatedly questioning whether the prize-givers had honorable motivations or understood her music. When the Rock Hall inducted her, she stayed away from the festivities. A year later, during a private concert staged for a television special, she accepted her trophy from her old paramour Graham Nash, who brought it to her in a garbage bag. (They had a laugh about that, establishing a new piece of Joni lore, though later she quietly revealed that the cheap container was necessary because one of her background vocalists had broken the statue's base backstage earlier that day.)

Anthologies and tributes complemented each other as ways of keeping older artists in the spotlight. Reissues added another layer. Then as now, effective marketing campaigns for any popular musician over forty seemed beyond the ken of the major record labels, but resurrecting their old material—and younger images—worked. As English journalist Dave Simpson wrote in the *Guardian* in 2002, after Mitchell announced for the second time in a few years' span that she would no longer be releasing new music, "Execs have realized that if they have the back catalog, they don't need the aging artist." Instead, they dug into their bank of assets, with little recompense for the music's originators. In 1996, for example, as Murray Lerner's documentary about the 1970 Isle of Wight Festival hit theaters, Sony Music was ready. They released a companion recording as part of their Vaults series that featured Mitchell's somewhat shaky appearance there.

What could an artist like Mitchell do to maintain control in the garland game? She did some fairly typical things, releasing a book of songs and poems in 1998 and embarking on a nostalgia tour with Bob Dylan and Van Morrison that same year. Certainly recognizing that the crowds at her feet displayed a sea of graying hair, she continued to beef to interviewers about the pop world's fickleness; within those screeds were some solid ideas about respecting the wisdom of elders. "Rather than thinking of me as a bitter old fogey, like the young press would like to do, if they thought about it as mature artists, if it was the old guild system, it would be respected that I knew something," she told Dave DiMartino of *Mojo* in a characteristically vitriolic interview.

After all, Mitchell knew a world where elders were respected—the jazz realm, where artists continued to record and headline festivals long past retirement age. Maybe that's why, when she did make a fully engaged turn toward her own past, she did so in satin and heels. Two jazzmen she trusted set her on this new path—Herbie Hancock, who invited her to lay down some vocals on a Gershwin tribute released in 1998, and Klein, who served as musical director for a benefit concert Don Henley organized to help preserve the forest around Henry David Thoreau's beloved Walden Pond that year. These projects connected Mitchell with her lifelong love of the American standards songbook. The Walden Woods event also showed her the pleasures of singing with a full orchestra. Henley had wanted something "elegant" for this nature-preservation fundraiser, and Klein, employing his Rolodex of up-and-coming women artists, suggested an all-female intergenerational lineup. Joni claimed her space in front of the sixty-six-piece orchestra alongside Stevie Nicks, Natalie Cole, Sheryl Crow, Björk and others, and discovered that the torch song style of pre-rock jazz and pop chanteuses suited the alto voice her years of smoking had gifted her. As usual, she and Klein got to talking. Pretty soon, two new albums were in the works. Both told Mitchell's life story in ways that new songs could not.

The first, *Both Sides Now*, is a standards set augmented by two vintage Mitchell originals—"A Case of You" and the title track. Klein enlisted the young composer Vince Mendoza to create string arrangements; he ended up winning a Grammy for his efforts in 2001, and the album claimed the prize in the Traditional Pop category. Listening to this lush record, I picture Joni and Klein relaxing over a nice glass of Château Lafite Bordeaux and winding their way through her record collection: the Harry James Orchestra, Judy Garland, Billie Holiday, Sinatra at the Sands. Songs by these longtime Joni favorites became the spine of a concept album reenacting a love affair from first thrill to final smoking embers. "Being a writer herself, we were very careful to select songs that Joni could really feel were her own, that she sang with the same intensity as if she had written them," Klein said in a 2020 interview in *Uncut* magazine. Klein and Joni's neatest trick on *Both Sides*

Now is their inclusion of those two originals, recast as torch songs
and fitting right in. The title cut, in fact, became many fans' favorite rendition of that chestnut, with Joni's weathered voice lending
gravitas to lyrics that had always seemed a bit flighty before.

Mitchell had plenty of company as she followed the sound of
violins into dignified elderhood. Linda Ronstadt had restarted her
career in the 1980s by joining forces with the legendary arranger
Nelson Riddle and his orchestra; she also recorded several albums
of Spanish folk songs she'd learned from her Mexican father, accompanied by a mariachi band. Carly Simon made two orchestral albums of her own. Willie Nelson had set a precedent for this
trend in 1978, when his Grammy-winning standards set *Stardust*
helped him find a pop audience. And two years after *Both Sides
Now*, the rocker Rod Stewart turned this approach into a one-man
industry, climbing up the charts with the first of five volumes of
American songbook selections.

Jazz-tinged orchestral pop wasn't the only means of career
revitalization in the 1990s. Another method emerged that's relevant to what Joni and Klein did after *Both Sides Now*. In 1993, the
young producer Rick Rubin went into the studio with the country
music titan Johnny Cash. Cash was struggling, still dealing with a
longtime drug problem and banished by pop's fickle tastemakers
to the tacky realm of Christian cable television. Rubin talked Cash
into abandoning that market and making a spare, highly intimate
album featuring unexpected song choices from throughout rock
and folk history—including current heavy-metal and alternative-
rock songs and a version of the murder ballad "Delia's Gone" that
became an MTV hit.

American Recordings became a template for many older artists,
some turning to Rubin and others to legacy-minded musician-
producers like Joe Henry, Daniel Lanois, and Wilco's Jeff Tweedy.

These projects revived artists' legacies through strategic song selection that matched surprising covers with remakes of emblematic originals. Sparely produced and organic-sounding, they showed that an older voice did not have to respond to fleeting musical trends to make an album that people of all ages could embrace.

Whether Klein and Joni had *American Recordings* in mind when they made their second retrospective album, *Travelogue*, doesn't matter as much as the context that Rubin and Cash's success created. A space had opened up for innovation in the garland game. Joni and Klein, still inspired by the orchestral approach, decided to apply it to her embarrassingly rich songbook. *Travelogue* is an autobiography in twenty-two tracks, a retelling of stories once swarmed by immediacy in the voice of one now able to apply a little distance. The miraculous moments on the album occur when, reaching for the meanings of now-decades-old songs from "For the Roses" to "Be Cool," Mitchell holds them delicately, slowly disassembling her own words and reshaping them. "At a certain point it's all in the phrasing," she told James Reginato in *W Magazine*. "I'm a better storyteller now."

After *Travelogue*, Mitchell announced that she would no longer be releasing new original music. She soon proved herself wrong, but anthologizing her work and enjoying the tributes that kept coming her way did become the core of her musical activity. Interpreters from the jazz and pop worlds kept her classics circulating—friends like Diana Krall, Cassandra Wilson, Norah Jones and Hancock, whose Klein-coproduced 2007 tribute album *River: The Joni Letters* won the Grammy for Album of the Year. Joni got the documentary she deserved in 2003, when Susan Lacy's *Woman of Heart and Mind* debuted as part of the PBS American Masters series. A shelf of books on her career began to grow with the publications of Sheila Weller's biographical *Girls Like Us:*

Carole King, Joni Mitchell, Carly Simon—and the Journey of a Generation and Lloyd Whitesell's musicological *The Music of Joni Mitchell* in 2008. She even had another hit, in proxy, when the rock band Counting Crows and the singer-songwriter Vanessa Carlton teamed up for a bouncy version of "Big Yellow Taxi" in 2002.

Still, Joni wasn't done. Five years after *Travelogue*, she released a new set of songs recorded with Blade and Klein, connected to a dance staged by the Alberta Ballet and released by the coffee company Starbucks as part of a deal that allowed her the creative control she required. *Shine* is minimalist in tone and wide-ranging in subject matter, pairing songs inspired by Mitchell's experience as an older woman with others based on movies and books. One of its grandest moments is the reimagining of the Rudyard Kipling poem "If" that closes the album—another in a series of interpolations of classic literary works that comprise the third way that Mitchell has built her legacy. On *Night Ride Home*, she'd transformed the Irish poet W. B. Yeats's masterpiece "Slouching Toward Bethlehem" into a song; on *Turbulent Indigo*, the Old Testament got the Joni treatment in her version of the book of Job, "The Sire of Sorrow." As she wove her past and present views together, Mitchell was able to do what she'd long insisted was her right—to place herself in conversation with the men whose works stood enshrined at the center of the culture. She had spent so much of the past four decades insisting she could and should leave her mark there. Kipling had been the one whose words transported her out of herself as a child. Now she wrote him into the life story that would survive her. His poem offers advice to his son about how to be a man; Joni's revision extends a hand to all, but ultimately circles back to herself, transforming the Victorian poet's exhortation to be vigorous and productive into a testament to the value of creativity in and of itself. *If you can fill the journey of a minute with sixty seconds of wonder and delight, then the earth is yours*, her version goes. She's describing songwriting, the generative heart of all she's given.

JONI AS MOTHER

For many years Mitchell publicly discussed only one form of her progeny: those songs that came from her like living things and followed their own trajectories. She referred to them as her children and acknowledged their different personalities. "I like the life that it has," she told writer David Wild in 1992, describing "Big Yellow Taxi" as one of her most gregarious offspring. Letting go of her songs was easy; finding her human daughter, even wanting to do that, proved much more difficult.

Did Joni Mitchell ever really want to be a mother? I ask this question rhetorically, and even then it feels invasive. The clear answer is yes, she had her baby and knew what it meant to go through with the pregnancy, even if she couldn't figure out a way to raise Kelly Dale while becoming the Joni she and the world required. But it's also possible to conclude that she had no real desire for that role. Not only did she walk away from raising her kid, but throughout her career she deflected the nurturing role that even childless women often take on in friend circles, workplaces and even their creative work. Call her a lonely painter or a black crow, a wild thing or a radio. Both her biographer Sheila Weller and the critic Claire Dederer have made the convincing case that Mitchell's great ambition was in part triggered by the huge sacrifice she made of her chance to raise her child. "She separated the self from the art, as many women have had to do—privileging one over the other," Dederer wrote in her 2023 book about problematic creators, *Monsters: A Fan's Dilemma*. So don't put an apron on her

or assume she'll sit so you can climb into her lap. The scorn with
which she sang, *You think I'm like your mother* in 1972's "Woman
of Heart and Mind" lingers in the air.

Yet to ask whether Joni Mitchell ever wanted to be a mother
is to assume that she, like any woman, could hold only one desire
within her body at any given time, much less over time. Whether
Mitchell playacted motherhood with dolls and other girls during her
Saskatoon childhood has little to do with how she reacted when,
at twenty-one, she found herself pregnant and broke and overwhelmed, or what she felt a few years later, noticing that she was the
only woman who could really hang with the Laurel Canyon boys
while the other women around chased toddlers or sat in their condo
kitchens elsewhere, too hemmed in by domesticity to enter the fold.
Nor can anyone but her know what went through her head when
she told a journalist that she might have a baby with Don Alias, who
loved but also scared her, or how she dealt privately when she lost
that pregnancy with Larry Klein, who always made her feel safe.

Public motherhood came for her long after the point when another biological child would have been possible. By that time, she
would later say, she had begun trying to find the girl she'd never
abandoned in her heart, having trusted that others could care for
such a vulnerable creature when she could not. In 1997, Mitchell
received a fortuitous, shocking call from Kilauren Gibb, then
thirty-two years old and a lifetime away from her birth name. The
reunion began very happily, but Mitchell's embrace of motherhood
and grandmotherhood has had its ups and downs. In the end she
mostly shut up about it, as did Kilauren, figuring out some kind
of balance but no longer showing it off. Her grandson Marlin and
granddaughter Daisy have accompanied her to certain Hollywood
parties of late, but her daughter tends to keep to herself, and Joni
seems okay with that.

This is the point where I have to share one of my very few personal encounters with Mitchell. So late in these pages, I'm admitting it: I did meet her in 2004, awkwardly and distantly, when she received that honorary doctorate at McGill University in Montreal. I have told this anecdote many times to friends and occasionally in public, not to shore up my bona fides as a Joni expert but to demonstrate my discomfort with the weird structures connecting artists with those who chronicle their lives and critique their work. I've always emphasized how humiliated our interaction made me feel, how distanced from the blonde glow of her glory. Twenty years later, I can see that Joni and I were, in that moment, in one version of the same boat. We were both newly visible mothers negotiating uncommon definitions of that term.

The conference took place nine months after I became a mother through open adoption, standing just outside the door in an Oregon hospital when her birth mother bore the daughter we would name together. We were in the early months of developing family bonds that would make room for all of us, a deeply emotional, difficult, lifelong process that has brought plenty of joy and pain to everyone involved. (The story of our family isn't mine to tell alone, and I won't say more; to do so would require another book with a shared byline.) I'd been invited to fly from my then-hometown of Seattle to Quebec and share some thoughts on *Blue*, and warned that because she was receiving an honorary doctorate, Mitchell might be in the room when I did so. Greg Tate and the performance artist John Kelly, both great thinkers whom Joni admired, would be my copanelists. At the time I was adrift in the dream state of sleep-deprived early parenthood, complicated infinitely by my uncertainty about the role I'd wanted so desperately to inhabit—about whether I had a right to motherhood at all. The trip to Toronto was to be my first extended time away

from my daughter. I arrived nervous and, jet-lagged, slept only
three hours the night before the conference. Zombie-walking my
way through the day, without a cell phone to check in on my family, I hid my agitation and drank plenty of strong Canadian tea.

When my panel began, Mitchell was indeed in the front row,
sitting next to Kilauren. The looming presence of one of the
world's most famous birth mothers reunited with her beaming
adult daughter pushed me from exhausted nervousness into full-
blown anxiety, as did Kelly's highly personal talk about his close
artistic bond with Joni and Tate's bravura performance celebrating her connections to Blackness. As I presented my meditation
on *Blue*, built in ten sections to mirror the sequence of its songs, I
stumbled when I reached "Little Green," the brokenhearted love
letter that Mitchell had written for Kilauren—her Kelly—only a
few years after their separation. Mentioning my own daughter,
I began to cry. From that front row I heard a voice: *You can do
it!* It was Mitchell. How powerless I felt, reduced to the status
of a grade school sprinter encouraged by this real mom—not a
fake like me—and desperate to cross the finish line and get out
of there. At the small reception after the conference, where Joni
stood looking for conversation partners while nibbling on carrots
and dip, I avoided her. I surrendered my chance to make her acquaintance because I felt barren in that moment, worthless. The
only thing I could see was the gap between her authenticity and
my pretending.

Now my daughter is grown, but I can still hear Joni's nurturing
voice in my head: *You can do it.* But you know what? It turns out
that I made it up. A video of my talk can be found on her website,
in the extraordinary fan-sourced archive that is a boon to me and
all other Joni scholars. When I discovered this I avoided it, afraid of
reliving that painful embarrassment. Many others have watched it,

however, and one such person told me that I'd misheard or mis-remembered her encouraging words. She didn't give me that ma-ternal cheer I would later shout at my kid when she was playing soccer, drumming in her punk band, applying to colleges. She sim-ply said, "Go on, go on." A neutral injunction, as likely springing from irritation as from concern. Or so I suspect; even after being reassured of the moment's sweetness, I won't click the link.

So did Mitchell want to be a mother? Can I hear a long legato note moving through her music, saying *you can do it* to the child she couldn't keep in her sights? Or do I hear *go on, go on*, directed at herself in her most driven moments and her weakest ones? Should I call that sound regret? In her songs, the clues reaching toward the child she signed away in the family name don't tell a linear story, either. For much of her career, *Blue*'s "Little Green" stood alone as a clear signal, but countless listeners who loved that album didn't grasp the story the song told. With no baby in sight, her fans, including the journalists who only asked her about motherhood in the future tense, left the matter behind. As her am-bitions expanded and the way she told stories changed, Mitchell did often mention mothers, but usually in kindly or sometimes acerbic contrast with herself. Sharon, with her husband and her family and a farm, but no one who cares when she starts singing. Carol, whose kids are coming up straight—is that a good thing? In Carol's song, "Chinese Cafe," Kelly Dale appears again, one clear glimpse, almost named: *My child's a stranger/I bore her, but I could not raise her*. I could not. Don't ask.

Mitchell released that song fifteen years before Kelly would reveal herself as Kilauren in what a long article about the reunion in *Maclean's* magazine would describe as "a blaze of media atten-tion." The heat soon overwhelmed the young woman, who even then shied away from the spotlight, enlisting her then-boyfriend to strike deals over her availability to reporters. Later, Mitchell told James Reginato of *W Magazine* that the pair had worked through the strange tangle of kinship and alienation that haunted their first years as a recognized family. "Our relationship is beautiful," she said. "Since I didn't raise her, we don't have the scar tissue that's frequently built up between mother and daughter." She also spoke of how becoming a tangible mother instead of a ghostly one had filled a hole within herself, claiming that her voice had changed because of it. "I was recording some music with Wayne Shorter and Herbie Hancock recently and they were going on and on about my [vocal] tone, which was odd because I've known and worked with those guys for years, so why should it be different now?" she told Greg Kot of the *Chicago Tribune*. "And the only thing I can think of is that the coming of my family has done something to my central core. It's like there was a hole in there that is fleshed-out now."

The song most associated with Joni and Kilauren's reunion is called "Stay in Touch." It's an attempt to clarify the feelings that surface when a complicated love affair begins. She wrote it, Mitchell has said, for Donald Freed, a Canadian folk singer who was her generally behind-the-scenes companion for most of the 1990s; Kilauren contacted her after it was written but before it was recorded. When she played it for her and her boyfriend, he immediately turned to Kilauren: "This is about you." Mitchell shared that moment with radio host Jody Denberg in a 1998 interview, accepting the reading: "It applies to any new, terrific attraction. It's basically how to steer yourself through that smitten period."

"Stay in Touch" inches toward the indescribable rather than trying to fully capture it. In her borrowing-from-the-greats mode, Mitchell rooted her melody in Rachmaninoff's "Variations on a Theme by Paganini"; she told *Musician* magazine's Robert

L. Doerschuk that she felt the song's words of encouragement and warning required "the highest melody I've ever heard." Yet this twist on the famed violinist's extravagant melodies never ascends toward an emotional climax; instead, it ebbs and flows in a tidal pull of mixed emotions. *This is really something*, Mitchell sings in wonderment at the song's start, and the lyrics unfold in counterpoint—enthusiasm (*I'm grinning like a fool*) pulled back by caution (*we must be loyal and wary*), poetic wisdom interrupted by little outbursts of doubt. Synthesizers wrap around Mitchell's vocal, pushing at the edges of subdued delivery, forming an antigravitational field that both supports and washes over her sometimes breathless phrasing. Mark Isham's Harmon-muted trumpet makes a warm intervention; instead of intensifying Mitchell's lines, his gently augment and echo hers, making this rumination one that continually checks itself. Mitchell lands on an aphorism culled from the *I Ching*—*in the middle of our time on Earth we perceive one another*—but the song goes out on its title phrase, which could be casual or the most heartfelt lover's plea. *Stay in touch*. The song does feel a lot like motherhood: the never-ending dance of holding close and letting go.

THE OTHER DAUGHTERS

Mitchell sometimes talked of Kilauren in those years using the language of cosmic synchronicity. She was reading books on astrology and noticing how their stars aligned, with Joni as a "discoverer" and her child as an "explorer"—a pairing that promised tension and accordance in equal measure. Their reunion did seem blessed by the stars in one way: it occurred just as popular music took a turn that made room for Mitchell as a mother figure writ large, with a whole raft of daughters reaching toward her as they claimed their own space within the singer-songwriter tradition, taking on the same questions about freedom and identity that she had.

The 1990s saw a renewed interest in women singer-songwriters as the climate shifted away from the shiny, synthesizer-driven sounds of the 1980s toward something that, to many, felt more authentic and oppositional. Feminism also entered another period of adjustment. The daughters of those 1970s women's liberationists whose paradigm-shifting challenges had paralleled Mitchell's own were coming of age and asserting their right to define the fight for equality.

A new shelf of bestsellers reflecting and furthering feminism's ongoing debates, like Susan Faludi's *Backlash* and Naomi Wolf's *The Beauty Myth*, reworked earlier polemics in fresh language. Other third-wave feminists, as this new generation was sometimes called, challenged the received wisdom of a movement that, in their eyes, had never been diverse or flexible enough, or had grown dangerously set in its ways, even puritanical. Writers like Katie Roiphe and Rebecca Walker (both daughters of notable feminists) challenged women's movement truisms from very different perspectives—some verging on neo-traditional, others demanding an even more radical, expansive view of pleasure and fulfillment. Among gender theorists, the category of "woman" itself came under intense scrutiny, defusing the essentialist view of woman-as-goddess that some earlier feminists had taken to extremes.

These conflicts, it turned out, only helped secure Mitchell's new unsought stature as a pop matriarch. What better role model existed for younger artists who felt it was their right to speak frankly about issues like harassment and sexual self-determination, but who also rejected anything with a doctrinaire aroma? Joni made for a perfect wandering North Star. Interest in her music rose throughout the decade. In 1987, only six musicians recorded versions of Mitchell songs; in 1997, there were sixty-four. By the turn of the twenty-first century, more than one hundred artists per year were delving into Mitchell's songbook. The shift had been enacted by the young women who emulated Mitchell across the radio dial.

Those hewing most closely to her example included Tori Amos, Natalie Merchant, and Alanis Morissette, all of whom openly professed their debt to her. Sarah McLachlan, who founded the all-woman-headlined touring festival Lilith Fair, even had a business connection to Joni—Mitchell's manager during these years, the Canadian impresario Sam Feldman, was McLachlan's booking agent. McLachlan approached Mitchell to play the first Lilith, but she passed due to health reasons and perhaps a certain skepticism about this fresh round of inheritors trying to claim her. Still, the cries for her blessings echoed forth, often prompted by journalists and other music-biz types who couldn't resist lumping women together as they always had. The 1995 compilation album *Spirit of '73*, which benefited pro-choice efforts to change consent laws affecting abortion rights, included two Mitchell covers—country music innovator Rosanne Cash's version of "River" and McLachlan's languid version of "Blue." Asked about taking on her fellow Canadian's classic, McLachlan quickly told an interviewer, "God knows I can't play like Joni," and acknowledged that respect would only let her go so far in reworking that treasured primary text. Tori Amos, asked about Mitchell's hold over her and her peers, also pointed toward the sacred nature of her work. "She took the clay and molded it in a way we hadn't seen before," Amos told a radio interviewer, extending the mother metaphor until Mitchell became the Creator herself.

The 1990s also marked the moment when Mitchell's influence surfaced in R&B, via another young woman rethinking her own musical parentage—Janet Jackson. Jackson's "Got 'Til It's Gone," featuring avid Mitchell fan Q-Tip of the rap group A Tribe Called Quest, interpolated the chorus of "Big Yellow Taxi" and became one of Jackson's biggest hits. In *Jet* magazine, Jackson talked about listening to Joni as a child in rotation with her Stevie Wonder and Marvin Gaye records. "Joni's songs spoke to me in an intimate, personal way," she said.

In the wake of this renewal, Mitchell remained imperious. Unsurprisingly given her unflagging desire to reach a Black audience, she embraced Jackson's praise; she also expressed admiration for the Icelandic singer Björk, naming her as an original even as she called most 1990s singer-songwriters derivative (rockers, too; she was dismissive of noisy new superstars like Nirvana). When she did connect publicly with younger women artists—most notably at the Walden Woods benefit concert that featured her on a bill with ten women singers and a full orchestra, and included her and Björk playfully duetting on Cole Porter's "What Is This Thing Called Love?"—it was at the behest of old friends like Don Henley and Larry Klein. Klein, in fact, had become renowned for bringing the best out of women with a string of successes by emerging artists including the Innocence Mission, Shawn Colvin, Julia Fordham and the all-female band the Murmurs. Mitchell occasionally found her way into collaborations with these artists. The Innocence Mission's Karen Peris sang background on *Night Ride Home*, and she provided some handclaps on Colvin's *Fat City*, recorded at the Kiva, steps from her kitchen. Colvin, in turn, wrote in the album's liner notes, "and to Joni Mitchell—me wimp, you master."

Still, Mitchell never settled comfortably into her role as spiritual/musical mother, even as she embraced her own birth family.

At the time I found her resistance confusing, but looking back, I get it. In the 1990s, I was forging my own career as a music journalist who often wrote about women, and I perpetually felt weird about doing so. I've come to think of that period as the Decade of the Year of Women in Rock. Real work done by women fighting the threats to women's autonomy then posed by anti-abortion legislation and the specter of sexual assault could be reduced to an opportunity for corporate branding by record labels and magazines eager to cash in on a "girl power" trend. The notion that feminism could sell led record labels and media outlets to package women together even when they had little in common. Being thrown into a box marked "female" could feel suffocating even when it offered career opportunities. At one point in the middle of the decade, I grew so weary of my designated role on the girl-power beat that I told my editors I would write only about men for the foreseeable future. That phase didn't last long, because women's stories kept drawing me in. I was lucky that I'd gained enough respect from the men who dominated my field that I could flex my ability to do what they'd always done: excel in any context, not just the one marked "ladies first."

I also can't forget the intergenerational battles that divided women in those days. It became popular in the 1990s to say, "I'm not a feminist," even when the work you were doing clearly reached back toward earlier women's efforts. The daughter's urge to leave Mom behind, to clear space and differentiate, was that strong. I remember the buzz in my Brooklyn neighborhood about the aging radical feminist Andrea Dworkin, often spotted in the back of a popular cafe called Cousin John's, eating coffee cake alone. We made fun of her. As much as I never have and never will agree with Dworkin's polemics declaring all women victims and all heterosexual encounters a form of violence, I now wish, so much, that I'd pulled up a chair and talked with her. I would have learned something. I rejected her because I thought her ideas were dangerous, but also because, as she sat there in her overalls with her unkempt head of curls, she seemed out-of-date—old.

No younger artist accused Joni Mitchell of being old in the 1990s, but most only went so far in embracing her as a spiritual mother. She made sure of that, with her endless comments about the hollow nature of contemporary music and her silence when she was asked about what younger artists she admired. Mitchell was equally unkind in the title track from her 1998 return to the studio, *Taming the Tiger*. Its lyrics bemoaned the radio dominance of "formula music, girly guile, genuine junk food for juveniles." The vitriol she directed toward the younger generation, to be fair, transcended gender. Rap, she said, "came out of a pimp's tradition," and though she'd once admired that stereotype of the Black man enough to make it her own as Art Nouveau, she felt its effects on music in the '90s had become problematic. And '90s rock was pathetic. Later, in 2002—after pop music's postfeminist surge had given way to the teen-oriented spectacles staged by Britney Spears and a young Beyoncé—Mitchell couldn't find herself in pop at all. Telling James Reginato that all the music business wanted from women was "a look and the willingness to cooperate," she laughed at her chances, asking the room, "What would I do? Show my tits? Grab my crotch?" What Mitchell wanted was what she'd always demanded: to remain, in her own words, "raceless and genderless."

Then, as always, all she wanted was to define herself. No labels. This made her a paradoxical emblem of third-wave feminism's bloody struggle to adjust at a time when the very idea of gendered personhood was thrown into question. If I'd been able to look past what she often said in interviews—her diatribes that seemed so dismissive of other women, though she also stood up for some—I might have grasped the potential of Mitchell as a metaphorical mother of a movement that was fragmenting to make room for different voices, different ideas of what freedom and full personhood means. But I also believe that if I'd had a chance to ask Mitchell about her spiritual daughters back then, she would have rebuffed me. I think she would have said this: *Mother yourself.* A legacy is worth preserving only if it remains unfettered by others' definitions. The paradox of motherhood, after all, is that people define the role as both necessarily limiting and the ultimate realization of a woman's potential. Joni walked away from it, carried it with her, turned it into a metaphor for her creative process, embraced its reality when it came back to her and finally accepted it, I think, as a cultural designation that people were going to grant her whether she fought against it or not. But as with any role, she never did fully rest within it. Her example continues to raise that key question—what does it mean to never stop pursuing the person you could possibly be?

BAD DREAMS ARE GOOD IN THE GREAT PLAN

One way we honor our elders is by taking care of them. Joni welcomed such care when it came to her music; the tributes and the archival work accomplished by compilations and other artists' versions of her songs kept her catalog thriving when she herself was busy with her newfound family and her painting, which continued to spark her creatively. But when it came to her own body, care became more complicated. In 2006, an affliction seized her that caused others to question her sanity. Morgellons is a skin condition that causes unrelenting itching, the feeling that tiny parasites are constantly crawling under your skin. Named in 2002 by a former lab technician who used a RadioShack toy microscope to home-diagnose her itchy toddler, Morgellons spread—as an idea—via the newly ubiquitous Internet, where sufferers dismissed by their doctors compared notes and photographs of colorful, near-microscopic fibers they saw growing from their skin. The CDC looked into the disease and, in 2012, concluded it was psychosomatic; the fibers, their scientists said, were normal residue from fabric, pets and their own hair. But Joni, like the others filling online forums with their complaints, believed in her own diagnosis. In rare interviews, she said that her torment was the reason she then rarely left her house. The itching was relentless; she sometimes couldn't even wear clothes. Her spasms reminded her of her polio years. "My body is like Afghanistan," Mitchell told an interviewer in 2010, referring to the South Central Asian country then being torn apart by endless war. Even in her torment, she could make that leap from her own experience into an expansive metaphor.

What she couldn't do was be in the world, much of the time. "Yes, you can call me a recluse," she told another reporter. She preferred living alone in her L.A. and British Columbia retreats. Self-portraits filled her Bel-Air house, which began to resemble a gallery. She did open her doors to Alberta Ballet artistic director Jean Grand-Maître, who persuaded her to help him use some of her more political songs as the basis for an antiwar ballet, *The Fiddle and the Drum*. That collaboration demanded a few new compositions, and soon Mitchell had enough songs for *Shine*. She called up her guys, including engineer Dan Marnien, with whom she'd worked since the late 1980s. The album's foundation emerged with Joni at the piano and Marnien there to document her process, letting her try out whatever ideas she had. Eventually, she enlisted Klein, Brian Blade, pedal steel guitarist Greg Leisz and saxophonist Bob Sheppard to enact her delicate compositions, with percussionist Paulinho Da Costa and James Taylor showing up in the guest chair. Some songs on *Shine* feel peaceful, a reflection of this contemplative phase in Mitchell's life, and the album's sound overall is delicate. The title track is a civil rights anthem burning with a candle's luminous flux. Elsewhere, Mitchell's lyrics communicate a wretched weariness, prophetic as they were in the 1980s but now more like blind Tiresias lamenting at the end of *Oedipus* than the wild witches of *Macbeth*. "Bad dreams are good in the great plan," she sings in "Bad Dreams," quoting something Kilauren's boy Marlin had said to her, the inscrutable wisdom of a child. In that song and others, Mitchell cries out the woes of a beleaguered planet, calling less for change than for simple awareness of how much humans have wrought upon it, like the tiny eaters she felt on her own skin.

Shine was moderately well received, and for a while Joni stayed as active as most crone matriarchs, accepting interview requests, showing her now mixed-media art, battling her illness in private but making it out enough to occasionally rejuvenate herself. Fallow years alternated with ones where she continued to shore up her legacy. Then in 2015, alone in her California kitchen, she experienced a brain aneurysm. Joni the self-described recluse was not found for a span of time that worsened the aneurysm's effects. Hospitalized for more than a month, she found herself unable to speak clearly at first, and as when polio struck her, could no longer walk.

Music fans often mark the calamitous moments in their favorite artists' lives by recalling the exact spot where they stood when they heard the news. In 2015 I hadn't begun my Joni journey yet, but I can put myself in my little sunlit office in Tuscaloosa, Alabama, where Eric had taken a university job, watching the world freak out via the computer perched on my desk. I sat there astounded. People were falling apart. This was before the deaths of David Bowie and Prince, when mourning in cyberspace revealed itself as a global ritual of both community-building and legacy-guarding, with thousands of fans sharing their most personal memories alongside the YouTube clips or streaming-service playlists that formed the arguments for their overwhelming grief. I hadn't before witnessed so many people desperate for the recovery of a rock star.

In the early years post-aneurysm, Mitchell remained hidden from view, though still up front in her fans' hearts and online conversations. When she reemerged in 2018 to attend yet more tributes, wielding a gold-tipped cane and a beatific smile as she leaned on the arm of her physical therapist, she was greeted with an outpouring of admiration and relief. So many people could not tolerate the idea of a world without Joni. Here she was, surviving for them. And then the stories trickled out: she was walking better, welcoming friends to jam sessions in her home, gaining strength and showing her good humor, even, finally, sometimes singing. Her healing process became a source of light, each step she took a testimony that others, too, could overcome life's merciless onslaughts.

I've thought about why Joni's Morgellons years resonated so differently, even among her admirers, than her recovery from her brain injury. As usual with this woman, this lightning rod, her story resonates outward. Morgellons is a controversial condition that fits within the category of women's laments, especially in the early twenty-first century, when autoimmune and other hard-to-diagnose illnesses have become a more-discussed aspect of public health. The nonlinear nature of chronic illness makes people deeply uncomfortable; it reminds healthy onlookers of the egg-shell nature of good health, something that can be shattered with the slightest unexpected move. Mitchell's aneurysm engaged a different kind of response partly because she was in mortal danger, but also, as she began to heal, because her recovery was relatively linear, a hard-earned gradual triumph. In what feels like a perilously unstable new century, with the climate itself both the victim of carbon emissions and an assailant on an endangered planet, Mitchell's return to public life and, eventually, to the stage has offered a strange kind of stability. Step by step, she learned to walk again, to sing again, to be Joni Mitchell again. Her personal recovery was mirrored by another kind: the reclamation of her place at the center of a musical conversation that never really banished her to the sidelines, but which now explicitly focused on the unique importance of her work. She made it back to the matriarch's chair, where she so deserves to be.

In the process, she gained more daughters and sons. Her aneurysm and the (coincidentally) subsequent publication of David Yaffe's major 2017 biography occasioned a new round of career-spanning appreciations. And her return to performance, mightily supported by a new ally, the ascendant singer-songwriter Brandi Carlile—the first woman to become her regular musical companion—has been greeted by an unceasing wave of adoration from fans ranging from her fellow rock stars to the people whose hearts she won when she was young, now bringing their children and grandchildren and even great-grandchildren along. Emerging artists from Lana Del Rey to Harry Styles cited her as a primary influence. Former president Barack Obama put her on his annual summer playlist. More prizes came; she won a Grammy for her latest archival work. When she spoke now, from those stages, it was not in bitterness but in gratitude: interviewed by her old friend Cameron Crowe, she said that Thumper, the sweet rabbit from the movie *Bambi*, was her new guru, quoting his famous line: "If you can't say anything nice, say nothing at all." This new kind of vulnerability made Joni feel a different kind of love— for her inheritors and for her friends. Embraced, she finally fully hugged back.

10

emissaries

As she made her way into genuine elder territory, Mitchell looked for new friends to support and inspire her. It took a particular kind of person to get her right, whether they were collaborating with her, interpreting her music or supporting her through difficult times. As I made my way to the end of my road with Joni, I wanted to talk to these people. They offered me a way into the mysteries of this iconic figure who always insisted on being just a woman, but not just any woman—into the flux she represents, between ordinary life and extraordinary insight, human imperfection and artistic transcendence.

I focused on three who became Joni's allies as she girded her legacy and continued to expand it. Their stories illustrate how different ways of encountering a legend—partnering, inhabiting, apprenticing—can clear away the weeds of renown and make room for new growth. They were the final stop on my own expedition. I wanted to hand over my maps to them and learn what they'd learned as they stood next to Joni, making footprints on her road.

PART ONE: PARTNERING

Brian Blade became Joni Mitchell's main musical partner in 1995, after the producer and noted legend rehabilitator Daniel Lanois brought some of the drummer's recordings over to Mitchell's Bel-Air place on a sunny afternoon. Lanois had worked with Bob Dylan in the late 1980s and enlisted Blade to play on *Wrecking Ball*, the late-career breakthrough album by Emmylou Harris, who'd achieved a status not unlike Joni's on the country side of the singer-songwriter world. It makes sense that Mitchell met with Lanois, but also that she ultimately felt no need for his production help. Besides, despite the success of *Turbulent Indigo*, with Klein out of the house she'd felt increasingly more drawn to the easel than the studio soundboard. There was something about the touch of that twenty-five-year-old drummer from Shreveport, though, that fit with a few musical ideas floating around her head. So she called Blade. He picked up.

I smiled thinking about how those first conversations went, because I'd had my own charming exchanges with the openhearted Mr. Blade. He is a man who goes deep quickly, eager to comprehend the intricacies of creative exchange, but he does so with the kind of light and playful touch that instantly dissolves anxiety. I met Blade in a parking garage in 2018; I walked up to him and handed him a Post-it. We were both in the bowels of the building where the Los Angeles Philharmonic rehearses, adjacent to the Los Angeles Music Center's Dorothy Chandler Pavilion; in a few days he would lead the band at Joni 75, a star-studded celebration of Mitchell's seventy-fifth birthday. He didn't know me from Eve when I announced I was working on a Joni book and wanted to interview him at his convenience, maybe if he passed through Tennessee one day. But he greeted me with the enthusiasm of an optimist. A few months later, we sat together in a Nashville recording studio and he told me the story of how he'd partnered with the woman he calls Joan to become one of the key players in her later creative life.

Blade has a way of speaking that reaches out and embraces the listener; that comes from his preacher dad and his own Christian faith, grounded in delight in creation. As we talked, his philosophy of collaboration became clear. Not long after he'd made *Taming the Tiger* with Mitchell, he succinctly described it to another music critic, Tom Moon, comparing his intuitive approach on their work together to the attunement he'd cultivated with his Fellowship Band and in jazz sessions with greats like the saxophonist Kenny Garrett. Moon succinctly described it as "the noble art of accommodation." Not deference: rather, Blade overcomes obstacles like ego or anxiety by making space, in his own playing and through his interplay with others. "It's like, we'll be playing and suddenly this intangible thing comes to the foreground," he told Moon. "Everybody feels it and respects it. And it's that thing, not what any of us was doing, that makes it interesting."

When he first met Mitchell, a few things stood in his way. First, his own nerves. He definitely had some flutters when she called him on the phone. Since his teen years, he'd been a major fan.

Devotion is the rule among Joni collaborators, but Blade, born the year before Mitchell released *Blue*, grew up with her in his ears in a way her earlier musical partners hadn't. A road opened when a family friend slipped him some tapes of her music at sixteen, not long after he first learned to drive.

"That gift!" he said to me, breaking into the sunshine grin for which he's rightly known. "You never know, when you give someone something, what it means. I mean, is it a coffee mug? Or is it two cassettes that are essentially scrolls?" The tapes came from Roger Barnes, a pianist and singer he'd met around Shreveport as he added jazz to the gospel repertoire in which he'd been raised. They held *Hejira* and *Mingus*.

"I had a 1973 black Volkswagen Beetle that my father bought me. Restored for me, actually," he continued. He jumped into the present tense, where the memory still lives for him. "And I have a cassette player. And you know, I'm going to school every day and I put this in the player, and it's unlike anything I've ever heard up to that point in my life. And I instantly feel this—I don't know how to describe it, this, something, something revealed that that is going to continue to feed me, nurture my life, enrich my life and give me a greater outlook. Perspective."

He broke into song, one of Joan's of course. "*Your life becomes a travelogue, picture postcard charms* . . . you know, heart, humor and humility, all these thoughts that she's sharing from her refuge on the roads, written as she drove along. I was also driving. It doesn't matter if it was 1975 for her or 1986 for me. This scroll, it continually opens another door and another door and you start to believe more deeply in that gift that she gave and [feel]—long before I met her—that I know her somehow. It's just immeasurable."

Bringing all this love from afar into their initial encounters, Blade could have easily overenthused. Instead, he focused on listening as Mitchell filled him in on her perspective on music, the business, midlife creativity and possible next steps. "I was living in New Orleans. She was at a point where she was going to stop playing music. She had an invitation to play [at the annual New Orleands Jazz & Heritage Festival]." Unable to play guitar in her old way because of recurrent polio pain, Mitchell found a solution via Los Angeles guitar store owner Fred Walecki, who custom-made her a Stratocaster-style instrument equipped with a Roland VG-8 synthesizer that contained programs triggering her myriad alternate tunings. "[They] can happen digitally, these tunings she has," Blade explained. "It allowed her that freedom. She no longer had to have eight acoustic guitars stand by."

She did want Blade to stand by, but he was committed to another tour on the date she was supposed to be playing her New Orleans "swan song." (She was really getting attached to that designation; it was the first title she suggested for *Taming the Tiger*.) "'Come wing it with me,' is what she said. I was like, wow! What kind of trust is that?" he said. "I hadn't even met her face-to-face yet!"

Alas, Blade is a man of his word, and wasn't willing to disrupt the cosmos by reneging on his other commitment. Anguished, he resigned himself to a broken connection with Joan. But that's not what she wanted. She wanted to continue exploring her new guitar with him on rhythm. "We got another chance," he said.

The new relationship grew closer when Mitchell, in New York to play a few songs at a benefit for the progressive advocacy group People for the American Way, spontaneously organized a duo gig with Blade at the au courant downtown nightclub Fez. She mostly played songs from *Turbulent Indigo* with a few chestnuts thrown in. I was there that night, drawn in by the buzz around a rare and unexpected appearance, though at that point Mitchell's music didn't hold the personal significance to me that it now does. What I remember from the night was a rowdy Chrissie Hynde—one of my greatest punk rock heroes—shouting encouraging words at the bemused heroine onstage and getting in trouble when she playfully put Carly Simon, who was trying to shush her, in a choke hold. That and Brian Blade. I was struck by his elastic presence on the drums, a touch so light and sensitive; it obviously relaxed the somewhat nervous Mitchell as she offered her first New York concert in more than a decade. They laughed together. The floridly decorated Fez, home of the yuppie Cosmopolitan cocktail, felt like a living room that night as we all witnessed two people becoming not just collaborators, but friends.

Then came the bigger version of Blade's second chance. He flew to L.A. to join the sessions for *Taming the Tiger* as part of a crew that included the stalwarts—Klein, *Turbulent Indigo* guitarist Michael Landau and Shorter—and some newer friends, including pedal steel player Greg Leisz and trumpeter Mark Isham. Having played with musicians all along the jazz-rock continuum, Blade was used to adapting to different bands, but with Joan he had to change up his whole lifestyle game. Upon arrival he found himself drawn into a session for the album's showcase piece, "Harlem in Havana," that stretched on toward dawn. "I'm an early-to-bed, early-to-rise person," he recalled. "But we're in the studio and it's two in the morning and we're just getting started. I think I was falling asleep at the drums as she was coaching me. I'm playing, and she's telling stories, and we're dancing it out. I woke up out of my bleariness, and she was saying, 'That was great!' I was like, what?"

It makes so much sense that Joni would be drawn to this curious and convivial man, not only due to the youth that, to her, always promised new forms of engagement, but because of his grounding in the Zion Baptist Church back home, where he'd learned to subsume his own impulses within gospel music's highly responsive ebb and flow. "In that flow," he told me, "what becomes most important isn't that we go to the four chord after four bars. You have to be watching and listening and feeling. What's needed in this moment? Experiencing that early on, I was being prepared for Joni, or for Wayne Shorter. It gave me this knowledge about how to serve the song. Don't come with a bunch of preconceptions, trying to put your thing on."

Taming the Tiger doesn't sound anything like Black church music or the gospelized jazz that Blade has created with his Fellowship Band. Aside from the '80s-Joni throwback "Lead Balloon" (about her old foe, *Rolling Stone* publisher Jann Wenner) and "Harlem in Havana," another entry in Mitchell's catalog of cathartic songs about interracial encounters (this one inspired by a traveling burlesque show she saw as a child at a provincial fair in Saskatchewan), the songs are spare, tending toward introversion, like pastel sketches more than landscapes in oil. Mitchell's synthesized guitar dominates as she explores the hybrid sounds of the instrument. The band's interplay with her is crucial, gently giving shape to songs that might have otherwise sounded a bit like demos, incomplete. Decades as a bandleader had taught Mitchell that self-sufficiency is overrated within musical production, and that her most inward-turning songs still benefit from the presence of other voices: Shorter's dialogic horn, Klein's harmonic bass lines. And always the drummer. Blade's work shifted her sensibilities, his embodiment of listening allowing her to follow her own dreaming mind without ever having to play the exhibitionist.

In those witching-hour recording sessions, Blade watched and listened to Joan and took in new lessons. "I learned a little more about how to be nimble and quick," he remembered. "There's a foundational aspect of the rhythm section—what's the ground?

What are we building? But there's also that lyrical color and sensibility required to execute grooves, that makes that waist-down feeling feel so good, but then also makes the heart light. She helped me with that, so much. I knew if her body got straight, something wasn't in a groove, you know? But then when that sway came back, and her shoulders would go left and right, then I thought, okay, here we go. Now we can tell the story."

After they completed *Taming the Tiger*, Blade joined Mitchell, Klein and Leisz for a brief West Coast tour, not knowing it would be Joni's last time in the clubs of North America. After that she settled into her life of attending tribute shows, giving extensive interviews and occasionally joining musical events as a featured or (more often) unannounced guest. It would be nine years until she released new music, and on that album, *Shine*, only half the tracks would feature his drums. But even in those seemingly fallow years, Blade remained central to Mitchell's creative process.

He joined in her project of building a legacy. He played drums on *Travelogue*, finding his pocket amidst that album's rich, string-dominated arrangements, as well as on the intimate *Shine*. And he was involved in many of the tributes that kept Mitchell's candle burning in the 2000s. The producer Danny Kapilian staged one of the first major Joni tribute concerts, Joni's Jazz, at Central Park's Summerstage in 1999. Living Colour guitarist Vernon Reid led the band that night, but Kapilian made Blade his musical director when he extended the concept at several venues in the 2010s. One was Toronto's Luminato Festival, where Mitchell herself made a rare appearance, performing three songs as Blade sat behind her on his kit. (She also persuaded him to join her for an onstage interview with *New York Times* pop music critic Jon Pareles.) Joni 75, where I met Blade, saw him sharing musical director duties with Fellowship Band keyboardist Jon Cowherd. Blade brings his practice of deep listening to this work, bringing in notable players from throughout Joni's history when he can (doing so, he says, establishes an atmosphere of trust for Mitchell) and always striving to put her vision before his own predilections.

"I know her scrutiny," he said. "I've seen what it takes for her to release and birth the songs into the world. And to not regard that and treat it as precious would be a misstep. So that's my priority. Whoever might have to render those songs as a singer, that's their business, you know, they have to deal with that man in the mirror. I am responsible to her. I try to put as much of myself in it as I can, almost without touching the original structure."

Reaching for a metaphor to describe the art of tending to another's body of work, Blade transported himself back to one of his early collaborations with his friend Joan. As usual for this spiritually advanced man, he was thinking about what it means to be blessed, and to tend to something blessed. "When we made the *Travelogue* recording at Air Studios in London, it's a beautiful cathedral, declared a historic landmark," he explained. "So you can't touch the inner wall. That's what I want to do—I want to build right within those walls without messing up [the] beautiful cathedral that she's built."

PART TWO: INHABITING

In the same underground room where Joni played her last twentieth-century New York show with Blade, she met another friend of her later years, this time one who would literally make her see herself differently. John Kelly started singing Joni Mitchell songs in public in 1985, when he was twenty-six; that same year, he also started being Joni Mitchell. Kelly is a performance artist who began exploring drag in the early 1980s as part of a raucous downtown New York punk scene whose trademark was challenging every preconception available, including those that upheld the culture of old-fashioned gay New York. Old-school drag queens worked to carefully tuck and pluck, staying gaudily femme; punk drag artists like Kelly, who gathered at Manhattan's annual Wigstock festival, ripped their stockings and pushed gender roles off-kilter. He debuted his tribute to Mitchell at the first Wigstock. It aimed for a new kind of verisimilitude, gender-fluid and eerie in its subtlety. The act was peppered with monologues Kelly took from Mitchell's interviews, delivered in a perfect California-Canadian cadence as he delicately pushed the tresses of his hippie wig from his face. The subtlety was the point. Instead of performing an archetype, as most drag queens did, Kelly used acute attention to detail to reach a remarkable level of immediacy, finding universals in Mitchell's specifics that spoke of the complexity and partialness of gender as a form of self-definition.

Kelly's Joni Mitchell performance is only one element in a multifaceted career that began in dance and expanded to include visual art, songwriting, essays and scripted shows, though Kelly always puts gesture first, calling himself a "mute storyteller." All of his many works address one question, as he wrote in his autobiography: "What does it mean to be a man? And: how dare anyone tell me?" When I met him in his somehow elegantly cluttered Hell's Kitchen apartment in 2019, Kelly recounted his wide-ranging history, remarking that his Joni performance has defined him, to many, as "merely" a drag artist. "It's so funny, you do drag once and you're a drag performer," he said with a laugh. "Just like, you can fuck 800 thousand women and suck one cock and you're a cocksucker." His words made clear the need to acknowledge that bigotry still limits drag's definitions. Yet I understand why his Joni show was the one that had brought him the

biggest audience. It touches her essence in a way that other interpretations of her music have not.

I saw Kelly perform a midcareer version of the show, then
called "Paved Paradise," in 1996 at Fez—the same club where,
the year before, I'd witnessed her playing with Brian Blade.
Kelly's sinuous personification fascinated me; he was not hiding
within the act of becoming Mitchell, but letting her draw out hidden aspects of himself grounded in his own histories of listening, of learning how to move through dance and finding his own
reedy, resonant voice. That night was particularly charged, because Mitchell herself was in the room, seated at Kelly's request
at a back table, obscured from his nervous vision. He needn't
have worried—Mitchell had signaled approval of Kelly's self/
portrait before she'd even seen it, after hearing about it from
friends on the West Coast, where he'd brought it earlier in the
decade. I'm sure no one there that evening was surprised to later
hear that Joni ended up backstage after the set, enveloping Kelly
in a bear hug and, in a touching anointment, giving him one of
her dulcimers.

She must have appreciated the musicianship he brought to her
work. He had mastered her tunings on both acoustic and electric
guitar and even later bought a Roland VG-8 like the custom instrument she'd played on *Taming the Tiger*. He also enlisted an ac-
companist to play keyboard so he could evoke the grandeur of one
of her favorites from her own catalog, "Shadows and Light." This
high level of dedication to craft is characteristic of Kelly's work;
in the name of "presence," his highest goal, he dedicates himself
to a kind of possession by his subjects that can be achieved only
through meticulous care. For Mitchell, always quick to question
whether those praising her really understood her, to be honored
so empathetically must have felt deeply restorative.

Kelly recognizes that his way of undoing and remaking drag can be a little bit hard to comprehend. "The drag characters I've done, it's weird shit," Kelly said. "Those are not the bright queeny things—they're homages, but they're deliberately obtuse. I was trying to turn drag upside down in a way. Or—not so much that. I was just lovingly needing to embody these characters." His connection to Mitchell began when he was twelve years old in early 1970s New Jersey, sneaking time with the Victrola in the family basement and his older sisters' copies of *Ladies of the Canyon* and *Blue*. What he heard in Mitchell's songs was the kind of romantic sensibility that he'd later flesh out in theatrical works with poets, painters and saints at the center. "It was my first exposure to soliloquy, to wanderlust, to a certain lyricism," he said. "And her piano has a kind of classical music cast, which, I'd been exposed to none of that." He also loved Mitchell's range. "Joni's songs, they were each so different. Sometimes there's a similar musicality, possibly—like 'Rainy Night House' and 'For Free,' there's that plaintive piano, but they're completely different ideas, and they go to different places."

Making the pilgrimage to New York as soon as he could, Kelly embarked on his lifelong practice of troubling the binaries confining both gender and art. He studied ballet and enrolled in art school by day and found a chosen family among the East Village's club kids at night. Fellow travelers, like Joey Arias, John Sex, Lady Bunny and Michael Norman (aka Tanya Ransom), were infusing drag with a punk sensibility that challenged the art's self-imposed rules. What did Joni Mitchell have to do with this? It makes sense that a young Kelly would have lip-synched to songs by outrageous punk women like Nina Hagen on top of the Pyramid Club's bar, or, when he got up the courage to sing in his own haunting countertenor, created the character of Dagmar Onassis, the great diva Maria Callas's secret daughter. Both punk and opera favor the flamboyance of drag. Mitchell's persona, on the other hand, is nothing if not naturalistic; her charisma is grounded in highly intimate acts of self-exploration and disclosure. So Kelly kept Mitchell's influence to himself—until an occasion demanded that he let her out.

That event was the first official Wigstock, an annual festival that took over various downtown parks from 1984 until 2005. (It's been revived a few times since then as drag has become a staple of cable television, though not since right-wing legislators have taken up its abolition as a cause.) The fest's main catalyst, Lady Bunny, invited Kelly to participate, and recognizing that every great countercultural happening needs an anthem, he decided to work up Mitchell's "Woodstock" with new lyrics that celebrated their community. In that song and the brilliant yet melancholy voice of Mitchell, Kelly, who'd lost a lover to the new AIDS epidemic in 1982, located the tone Wigstock needed: visionary, cathartic, mystically political. "All of those things I was doing very quickly became prayerful missions on my part, to move people to make sounds and show up in a way that was beautiful," Kelly said. "At Wigstock, 'Woodstock' became a prayerful moment where people would literally hold up their lighters as I sang."

Kelly played with Mitchell's lyrics to suit the times. "Since it was a dirgey, mournful, bright and pale—or dark and shiny—song, it was completely appropriate for what was really going on, which was that people were fucking dying left and right," he explained. "The first year I sang *and I dreamed I saw the drag queens spraying hairspray in the sky. And they made all the yuppies die across our nation* . . . Soon after that, though, it became *and I dreamed I saw the drag queens, and they were all dressed up like maids. And they had found a cure for AIDS across our nation.*" He's continued to adjust the lyrics to confront the endless stream of threats queer people have survived.

"Wigstock/Woodstock" became a Kelly trademark, and he began thinking about how he could go further in exploring a form of Joni emanating from himself. He started performing an early version of his show at the Pyramid Club, joined by two friends representing different points in Mitchell's career. Soon Kelly had learned enough of Mitchell's repertoire to stage a full club act centered on her music. In his dancer's way, he focused on how her physicality might reflect her sonic narratives.

"What is the image of her?" he said, remembering the process through which he brought Joni to life within. "Well, it's long blonde hair, bangs. Kind of willowy. No eye makeup; it's all about the mouth." He worked from memory and instinct. "I'd maybe seen some films of her on TV years ago, but there was no access to the Internet then, and I didn't get to the library to find them. But I remembered her, that kind of slightly hunched kind of swaggering lope of hers, which I concocted based on somebody who plays the guitar a lot and thinks a lot. She's leading with the head, kind of ponderous but in a good way. Very thoughtful and kind of almost spaced out, like a cat."

Evolving over thirty years, Kelly's Mitchell show honors the whole of her career, going beyond the familiar parameters of *Blue* and *Hejira*. It incorporates the absurdist humor that also runs through his other work—sometimes his gestures can be heavily stylized. These actions further destabilize his Joni embodiment; audiences laugh, but soon recognize that for Kelly, this is serious stuff. "I don't make a joke out of it," he said. "You lure them in with the beauty, and then you clobber them." He added, "My favorite place, which I've said before, is right on the line between irony and pathos."

There is a picture in Kelly's book of him with Mitchell at the Fez. They are both grinning, a mile wide, but with their mouths closed. It's remarkable how the curve of their lips—remember, the mouth is central to Kelly's depictions of Mitchell—is exactly the same. "I don't think I look like her," Kelly told me, "but I made myself feel like I sensed how she felt or showed up. That's an acting thing. A button that gets flicked. And out of that came along the long-limbed, flaxen-haired ingenue."

After the Fez show, Kelly continued on his nonlinear path and kept in touch with Mitchell. He continued to revamp the Joni show with new set lists on many different stages as he mounted many other works, collaborated with musicians and composers like David Del Tredici and Laurie Anderson and taught as an artist in residence at Bard College.

Sadly, his friendship with Mitchell hit a bump around 2010, and they've talked only occasionally since then. Kelly mourns his close connection with this woman who'd become a part of his own soul—or, perhaps more accurately, whose way of being had opened up new avenues he could recognize. But he continues to sing her songs—now, often, as himself, not in drag.

Kelly's performances as Joni transmute her legacy into something still forming, open to reinterpretation. In this act, he shows his audiences that identity itself is indeterminate. "Each song is essentially a character itself, and also about some aspect of a character," he said. "And probably about some aspect of her character. That makes those songs possible to embody. There's a journey that's unfolding in the moment, but also an awareness and a critique of the journey." Like the lives we all live, and perform. "You're witnessing it as you're living it."

PART THREE: APPRENTICING

Brandi Carlile hummed into a plastic straw as she paced across the gray-carpeted floor of a rehearsal room at S.I.R. Rehearsal Studios in Hollywood, doing her vocal exercises and burning off nervous energy at 10 a.m. on a sweater-weather Friday in 2019. She sat down for a minute on a leather couch next to her wife, Catherine, and turned her attention to the band running through "This Flight Tonight," with Jon Cowherd leading from behind the baby grand. "You play just like Joni!" she exclaimed to him. He smiled with a rueful little shake of his head—*come on, no.* The song ended and Carlile's longtime bandmates, the brothers Phil and Tim Hanseroth, deposited their guitars on stands and headed to the mood-lit hallway to call a wife or grab a snack. Russ Kunkel uncurled himself from behind the drum kit. He was the coolest guy in the room—after all, he'd been inside this music before, playing on original sessions with Joni Mitchell across the neighborhood at A&M.

The mood among the players, whose ranks also included the guitarist Marvin Sewell and the violinist Scarlet Rivera, who'd been on Dylan's Rolling Thunder Revue tour, was effervescent but a little tense. In a week's time, Carlile and her collaborators would bring this show to Disney Hall in downtown Los Angeles, resurrecting *Blue* in its entirety, track by track. Joni would be in the audience, along with friends from throughout her life, like David Geffen and Brandi's other guiding musical light, Elton John.

Like so many singers roped in as flower bearers at past Joni tributes, Carlile was nervous about simply hitting the notes. But her fear went beyond even what Elton had expressed when, before singing "Free Man in Paris" as part of a Mitchell tribute in 2000, he'd declared it an occasion more intimidating than playing for England's queen. Carlile was not entering the kind of athletic competition that a multiartist bill honoring Mitchell always becomes; she would stand alone at the lead vocal microphone, in communion with the album most people considered the master's greatest work. This would be Olympic medal territory, a gymnast's double twist and a blind landing on the mat, and at the same time not a competition at all but a gift given and received, a bond cemented.

Carlile, possessor of one of twenty-first-century rock's most magisterial voices, would need to enter a paradoxical state to perform *Blue* as she desired: so thoroughly attuned to Mitchell's music that she would vanish, in a way, and become a channel for the wisdom she'd learned from all of her listening, and at the same time still be herself, relaying the lessons only she could have learned from that listening. She turned to Cowherd as the band, back from break, prepared to give the album's title track a try. "I'm glad we lowered the key," she told him. "I like to do it like me, not Joni. Just this one."

Carlile had been Mitchell's greatest champion since meeting the elder artist after the Joni 75 event, where she supported an ailing Kris Kristofferson in a tender rendition of "A Case of You." That night the two women spoke briefly, and Joni gave Brandi a jazz-cool compliment. "I met her and I told her in very brief terms how much she meant to me. She said, 'Right on, man! You did a great job,'" she later told a *Rolling Stone* reporter. "I'll never forget that Joni Mitchell called me 'man.'"

By the time of her *Blue* concert, Carlile's acquaintance with Mitchell had grown into a friendship reflecting unspoken mutual hopes and needs. Carlile had decided after Joni 75 that she'd love to perform *Blue* as a whole and started laying the groundwork to make that happen. At the same time, Joni was growing more interested in this woman nearly forty years younger than herself. Unlike other potential protégées in decades past, Carlile, who was raised in rural Washington State, was well established as a country-leaning troubadour before she met Mitchell; she'd never borne the burden of being declared a "new Joni," instead forging relationships with mentors Amy Ray and Emily Saliers of Indigo Girls and Pacific Northwest friends like Pearl Jam. She'd had several breakthrough hits, and one of them, 2018's "The Joke," won two Grammy Awards, carrying her from cult status to mainstream superstardom. (As of publication, she has nine Grammys.) Mitchell, conversely, had receded after suffering the 2015 aneurysm that forced her into seclusion as she worked to relearn basic motor skills. Now Brandi had come to Joni as a kind of student, ready to sit and listen and learn instead of either downplaying her influence or engaging in blatant imitation.

Their meeting was serendipity: a legend in the shadows starting to contemplate a return encounters an aspirant able to help in that process. It helped, too, that Carlile values humility, a surviving precept of her post-hippie Christian upbringing, and that in the aftermath of her brain injury Mitchell had by all accounts lost the bitter edge she'd acquired after the music industry set her on the legacy shelf. These two women were ready for each other. The question in the air at S.I.R. Studios was, could Carlile demonstrate the worth of their new connection to the world?

Knowing of my own circling around Mitchell's myth and many realities, Carlile had invited me to be a fly on the wall as she prepared for this test. We had met several years before and quickly established a pattern of occasional exchange, remaining journalist and subject, but trusting each other enough to express respect and enthusiasm for each other's work. I'd been there as Carlile's audience grew, witnessing her charisma work magic on increasingly larger and more impassioned audiences. A notoriously generous soul, she has a knack for making her "I" feel like a "we" for many listeners—very much like the Mitchell of the album she was about to perform.

Carlile later reflected on Mitchell's impact in a *Seattle Times* interview. "Joni shook me . . . because she's unlocked, and there are very few people who are unlocked. She's in touch with the source of where music comes from, the muse, you know. . . . I realized that more and more as an artist, I was wanting to become the kind of songwriter that would write a song that would impress Joni Mitchell one day." What that meant for Carlile was tapping her own experience—as a queer woman, a mother, an idealist whose hope had been shattered by the world many times, despite her evangelical urge to lift others out of their own heartbreak. "I wanted to write for me, but I wanted to write in a way that was at least nodding to the unlocked."

Carlile hadn't recognized this as a goal until she started to explore Mitchell's music, and she did so alarmingly late in life. Like me—but even more so, because she's eighteen years younger than me, and that much more steeped in the indie-punk ideals of our shared home region, the Pacific Northwest—she initially found Mitchell's music "wimpy"; she wanted to rock. It was Catherine who insisted she listen to *Blue* and really grasp its blood and guts. On an early date, she sat Carlile down and told her the lost-daughter story behind "Little Green," made her sink into the regret and loneliness of "River." And it was Catherine who connected Brandi to Joni in the real world, expressing interest in purchasing one of Mitchell's paintings. That contact led to dinners and phone conversations and, eventually, to this night. Another thing connecting Carlile and Mitchell, Brandi and Joni, is their comfort with blurring creative and intimate connections.

So here was Brandi now, a self-enrolled star student in Joni's musical university, but also an emissary for her greatness, which

had not faded in anyone's eyes, but like any legacy, required pe-
riodic renewals. She had a vocal coach on hand at S.I.R. to help
her achieve a tone and range as close to Joni's original as possible;
that's why she was doing what's called "straw phonation," a technique that calms and strengthens the breath. At the rehearsal she
pulled me aside and elaborated on her approach. Gesturing at the
Hanseroths, her rock and roll phalanx since she started as a teenage busker in Seattle's Pike Place Market, she said, "I'm trying
to strike the right balance between being our band and trying to
serve the people in the audience who are never going to be able
to hear the album live, because Joni can't do it anymore." This
was a point she would return to many times as she took her *Blue*
beyond this one performance, to Carnegie Hall in 2021, and in
other shows that eventually included a still-fragile but remark-
ably rejuvenated Mitchell herself. Carlile's unwavering belief that
the world needs to hear Joni's voice—literally or through others'
interpretations—became the strongest motor carrying the former
recluse back into the center of things.

Carlile sings Mitchell as a kind of amanuensis, striving to
maintain the original brushstroke even as she inevitably adds her
own subtle flourishes. About "All I Want," *Blue*'s opener, she told
me, "On this song I had to learn not the lyrics but the breaths. Joni
takes the weirdest breaths and if you don't take them where she
did you won't make it through the song!" Not for the first time, a
celestial metaphor leapt to my mind: she is a Jedi knight learning
from her personal Obi-Wan, following each gesture to its core,
trying to surrender to the Force.

THE AIR WAS PRETTY CLOSE IN THAT REHEARSAL ROOM. I NEEDED SOME PERSPECTIVE, SO
I grabbed Jon Cowherd for a coffee once the day's longer lunch

break ensued. I'd met him before through Brian Blade, with whom he'd played in the Fellowship Band for nearly thirty years, and through whom he had become one of the most notable arrangers of Joni's songs. Like Carlile, he considers Mitchell a towering figure, but he'd been working with her on and off for years and knew her affable and occasionally irascible sides. He had a handle on the practical requirements for this momentous occasion.

Cowherd told me about his own evolution as a Mitchell ally and interpreter, from one of his first meetings with her at a private Fellowship Band show at Daniel Lanois's Teatro studio to claiming the musical director spot for Brandi's *Blue*. Affable and casual, with a jazz player's ease around mythic figures and classic repertoire, Cowherd kept me laughing as we talked about his Joni history. Their first brush was a doozy: after the Fellowship Band had finished the recording sessions for its 1998 debut album, Lanois decided to host a small listening party to see how the tracks would land for civilians. Except these civilians, Cowherd said, were "Joni Mitchell and a bunch of movie stars. Billy Bob Thornton, Laurence Fishburne, Dwight Yoakam, John Sayles—all these people. And Joni sat just a few feet away from me. One of the songs I wrote on that album, as we played it, I thought, oh no, I've lifted this from her song 'Jericho.' I looked at her after we were done. She had this big smile on her face. I thought, yes!"

This is the jazz way, not the pop or rock and roll way—to uphold legacy through reinterpretation, respecting authorship, but aware that in some ineffable way, the music that unfolds over time is one great song with infinite players. Cowherd brings that openness into his work while recognizing that Mitchell's songs are more tightly woven than the jazz standards that have often inspired her. After serving as co–musical director (with Blade) on numerous Joni tributes, he's figured out a way to be faithful to her work, top to bottom, while letting it breathe.

"Especially in Joni's case, so much of the instrumental side is a pairing with the vocals and the lyrics," he explained. "For this show, I transcribed pretty much every note of the piano parts. Because there's certain things that she plays, accents and dynamics, that go with the meanings of the melodies or the words. There's a line in 'My Old Man' about a warm chord, *he's the warmest chord I ever heard*—and it's a warm chord that she wrote! So I try to put that vibe on it when we get there. It doesn't mean that I have to play note for note, but I want to retain the vibe and the feeling." This diligence has earned Mitchell's trust. "In Toronto [at Luminato], she took me aside and said, 'Thank you for paying such attention to the details of the arrangement,'" he said.

Often, however, Cowherd has found himself having to navigate the distance between Mitchell's originals and what the artists who love her want to execute. "Sometimes they've wanted to do something radically different," he said. "So there is that balance. I have to be myself as an artist but still honor all the work that went into her production and arrangements, the way she delivers things. I think you can do that. I think there's a way to study even the way she delivered certain lyrics and still use your own voice."

He was watching this process unfold with Carlile. "I really hear her singing a lot of the subtleties, and she's a great singer," he said. "Joni comes from a wide stylistic background, and you hear that in *Blue*. It's not just folk singing. I feel like Brandi can do that, too. Even in her version of 'Shine'"—the one non-*Blue* number in the show, performed as an encore—"she did a little bit more of a gospel thing. She has a wide palette and a wide ability to do all this different stuff."

I mentioned the way that Carlile, a tightly wound ball of energy between takes, could relax into a song the moment the first chords were played. "She does make a lot of it sound easy," Cowherd agreed. "And it's hard! I think this record is hard, not only technically. There's a lot of emotion involved, and at times there are moments that tend to be the opposite of what you think they should be. Some of the lyrics in 'California' are about being frustrated, but the song is so infectious. You have to deliver that with a little bit of tongue in cheek. Brandi does that kind of thing so well."

The band as a whole was happy to follow his and Brandi's lead through the fairly orthodox arrangements, he said, partly because they had guidance from the source. Tim Hanseroth, who'd never played a dulcimer before, went to Mitchell's house for a personal lesson. What he got was vintage Joni—more cosmic wisdom than technical advice. "Just tune it up and hit it like a conga or a bongo or something," she'd told him. This little story led us into a discussion of the rhythmic roots of Mitchell's compositions, even on the relatively spare *Blue*.

"*Blue* doesn't feel as connected to jazz as some of her later work, but I feel that, rhythmically, it is. Especially on songs like 'Carey' and 'California.'" He snapped his fingers, evoking the song's swing. "That's the Charleston rhythm, which is in so much jazz," he said. "And with 'Carey' there's a Caribbean influence. After all, she's singing about Africa. That feeling's in the song even without the percussion we've added."

Absorbed in these musical details, Cowherd kept Carlile's call for emotional accuracy foremost in his mind as he created the evening's arrangements. He recognized that the mood at this show would be different from the party atmosphere that drove the multiartist Joni shows he'd organized. This was a milestone for

Carlile, and, by extension, for Mitchell—an act of both transmission and renewal.

"*Blue* has gotten a lot of attention, and a lot of people love it," he concluded. "But a lot of times I feel like Joni as a whole doesn't get enough. There are so many levels of artistic achievement on her records. There's the lyrical and the musical and vocal. It's like going to the opera, where there are so many things to check out at one time, you know. You have to zero in on a few things at once. I don't know if people really recognize that."

AT DISNEY HALL, AS PREPARED AS SHE WOULD EVER BE—SHE'D EVEN TRIED A SESSION with a hypnotist to calm her nerves—Carlile leaned into that recognition. The band moved through Cowherd's arrangement with a playful spirit, shining light on the music's understated complexity while adding those rhythmic elements and color strokes evoking the larger arc of Mitchell's career. Following the lines etched out by Mitchell's breath, Carlile awakened the original spirit of Mitchell's most beloved songs. As she did so, she talked the audience through her process, making sure this experience would be protean: a virtuosic triumph for her, the student living up to her sensei's example; an emotional journey for the listeners who treasure *Blue* as a Bible of the personal; and a polemical argument for considering this and Mitchell's other music as central to the popular music canon. "We didn't live in the time of Shakespeare, Rembrandt or Beethoven," she said before she began her performance. "But we live in the time of Joni Mitchell."

She told the story of Catherine converting her to Mitchell, and of her getting to know the woman she had quickly grown to idolize over wine-filled dinners and jams at the Bel-Air house. She hyperbolized about Mitchell's musicality, noting that "it takes about

13 people onstage to do Joni's one job," and praised her emotional intelligence, saying that *Blue* had shown her "how much toughness there is in femininity." Her running monologue chronicled one person's romance with the album—one rock and roll–loving lesbian convinced to slow down and listen and open up her heart—in ways that anyone in that boat-shaped symphony hall could recognize. This narration, interwoven with the arrangements that were both uncanny and unrepressed, made an argument for Mitchell as the central figure in modern songwriting history, and for Carlile as her worthy, steadfastly humble heir.

The *Blue* performance secured Carlile's spot alongside Blade, Cowherd, Herbie Hancock and Klein as one of the key stewards of Mitchell's legacy. As it turned out, she was also becoming a caretaker of the legend's voice. In the year since they'd met Mitchell, Brandi and Catherine had become regular visitors to her home, and witnesses to the slow improvement her diligent work with physical therapists was making in her body. As Joni learned to walk for the third time, she tapped into the grit she'd developed as a polio-afflicted child. Her body remained weak, however, and her speech was affected; she feared she would never sing again. But Carlile's magical optimism helped return Mitchell's voice.

Brandi and I stayed in touch, as we long had, after that night with *Blue*. I'd been the first journalist to write about "The Joke" in 2017, and sometimes when she came to Nashville we'd touch base. By the early 2020s she was building an empire, but one unlike most seen in the music biz: this one was based on what the writers Aminatou Sow and Ann Friedman have dubbed "shine theory," the idea that when a person succeeds, she redirects that glow toward worthy members of her community, and the chain reaction lifts each person higher as the others achieve their goals. Carlile's shine chain connected older artists like the country rebels

Tanya Tucker and Wynonna Judd to emerging ones like the multi-instrumentalist and songwriter Allison Russell and the two-woman string section SistaStrings. She created a festival, Girls Just Wanna Weekend, to highlight her growing community, produced albums for friends and made sure to give them space in the many media appearances now dominating her pop-sensation life. Carlile's relationship with Mitchell is her spiritual anchor as she builds her volunteer navy of peers, mentors and protégées; their time together has been transformative, enacting the miracle of healing as well as the hard-won pleasure of public recognition.

Her visits to Mitchell's house eventually became more than gabfests, turning into informal jam sessions that a person versed in the healing arts might also recognize as music therapy. Friends would gather around Mitchell's piano and sing standards, hippie hits from the Laurel Canyon days and, often, Mitchell's own repertoire. At first Mitchell just absorbed the joy—"Oh, that's gone," she said of her singing voice in a 2021 conversation with Cameron Crowe—but, true to her self-challenging spirit, she couldn't stay silent forever.

One afternoon not long after the *Blue* show, as I shopped with my daughter at the local craft store, my phone dinged and I saw it was Brandi calling. "Ann," she said breathlessly, "I have to tell you what happened at Joni's last night." Our conversation was between friends and not for publication, but soon enough what she'd told me turned up in a conversation she and Bonnie Raitt had for *Rolling Stone* in 2019. "She swore off music," Carlile said. "But we've been doing these get-togethers at her house. We drink wine, she tells stories, then we play music. I played my song 'Cannonball,' and I was shaking. I brought Hozier and he played a song—and Chaka Khan walks in. She's cracking everybody up, stealing people's wine. Joni got real loose when that happened.

"Then Herbie Hancock walks in. I think it was Joni's cruel surprise, to make these kids squirm. He sits at the piano, and he's hovering on this chord; nobody knew what it was. But Joni did. And from the middle of the room, you hear *Summertime and the living is easy*, and it's Joni fucking Mitchell, singing for the first time since her aneurysm."

It reads almost like a fairy tale, this rejuvenation of the queen's throat. Soon, she was singing along with her own songs, and then it began to seem that she might be inching toward performance. That would be a miracle, her fans began to whisper. In reality Mitchell's gradual, ongoing recovery comes down to hard work on her part and resources, including great therapists, that allow her the best in care. But I have no doubt that Carlile, whose good cheer can be overwhelmingly persuasive, has played a significant role in bringing Mitchell back into the public eye, not only as an icon but as a living presence.

Meanwhile, accolades began to collect around Mitchell the way that they had in the 1990s, but instead of questioning the sincerity behind them, the old dame now graciously accepted each new decoration, beaming beatifically from the audience and rising with the help of her cane to give a blessing as each unfolded. In 2020, she became the first woman to receive the guitar-oriented Les Paul Innovation Award. 2021 brought her a Kennedy Center Honor for a lifetime of contributions to the performing arts. Her seventy-eighth birthday that year was commemorated with a special gift as Carlile brought the *Blue* concert to Carnegie Hall to rave reviews. Then came more. Mitchell was honored as the MusiCares Person of the Year as part of 2022's Grammy festivities and the first volume in her new Archives series earned a statue for Best Historical Album. In 2023 she received the Gershwin Prize for Popular Song from the Library of Congress.

Carlile was usually on hand to add excitement to these celebrations and make them feel intimately connected to their honoree. After all, she was now Joni's confidante. It never felt like she was taking advantage of that role, but instead that she was making necessary introductions between Mitchell and a younger generation of artists who revered her but only from a distance, as well as music industry higher-ups whose admiration may have calcified.

Partly because of the story she offered, of grasping Mitchell's central significance long after she should have, Carlile has demonstrated a unique ability to refresh the aura around the legend. She's intensified the glow of greatness while making this canonizing process feel personal. No longer would Joni Mitchell's insistence that hers is a voice forgotten at others' peril seem like vanity. She had been fully restored to the center where she always lived, if in a slippery, idiosyncratic fashion. And that slipperiness, the Joni swerve and sway, is what made this return all the more satisfying. Even weighed down by laurels and the inevitable downturns of a life fully lived, she is finding a way to kick off her shoes at the party in her honor, and dance.

NEWPORT

The rumors started circulating a couple of months before that cloudy afternoon in July that Brandi Carlile would be bringing her most special friend with her to play at the Newport Folk Festival. I heard tell of it a couple of months earlier, from Allison Russell, who swore me to secrecy while bubbling over with her own excitement at the prospect. Russell would be there at the historic fort in Rhode Island, onstage during Brandi's closing set, always a semi-informal gathering designed to capture the fest's temporary-autonomous-zone spirit and send attendees back into the world in the grace of fellowship. Russell had brought Mitchell's lifelong pal Chaka Khan to the Sunday night performance she'd organized the year before, the older singer's multi-octave voice echoing across the fields of Fort Adams State Park. Now Carlile would be leading the love-in, and it seemed like a safe bet that Mitchell would return to claim her crown.

Fifty-five years earlier, another woman had championed her in this space: Judy Collins, who'd organized that fabled afternoon singer-songwriter session where Mitchell met Leonard Cohen and made a new leap in her ascent on the American folk scene. Jay Sweet, Newport's current organizer, loves nothing more than a ringing symbolic gesture—except perhaps an unparalleled news event guaranteed to take his festival viral. Joni showing up would certainly do that. I'd seen Sweet schmoozing around backstage after Carlile's first *Blue* show, so I wasn't in the least surprised he was milking his connections to make history happen.

Yet I didn't scramble to rearrange my life, secure a plane ticket and a hotel room and finagle my way into the cramped area at the side of Newport's main stage. I'd witnessed Joni receiving her flowers so many times by that summer that I felt I could take a pass. Little did I know this would be the breakthrough moment of her septuagenarian redemption arc, the reemergence Carlile had been dropping hints about when she kept mentioning the "Joni Jams" and said at one of her concerts that she and Joni had been "kind of jamming." Or maybe I did know, deep inside, and just didn't want to deal with the glad-handing and access issues and insider bullshit that always submerges staged pop music "special events" in the viscous poison of power and influence. I made a note of Allison's intel and cleared my schedule for that Sunday, in case I needed to tune in.

I made the right decision. The bragging rights would have been sweet, but my experience of Joni Mitchell's first full concert

since 2000, which is what this public version of the Joni Jam became, unfolded in a way that I could fully embrace as the fan I'd
become while writing this book. Two years into the COVID-19
pandemic, I'd evolved into a semivirtual version of myself, taking
in music via webcasts instead of cramming into the clubs and connecting with both artists and fellow music lovers via the flat magic
of Zoom meetings and FaceTime. Though I longed for the mystical communion with strangers I felt when electrified rhythms
moved through a crowd and into me, I'd used these isolated years
to explore other pleasures. Even as I tiptoed back toward live
performances, I knew that experiencing music via my computer
I could sometimes hit a level of deep listening that came when all
of the extra stuff—the anxiety about where I fit at any gathering,
what my hair looks like, how my hearing is being affected by that
amp turned up to ten—falls away. Experiencing Joni's return re-
motely also helped me think about how greatness in the digital age
translates in streams and memes, how the highly crafted intimacy
of her art might work within the new century's shifting definition
of authenticity.

That Sunday, I started paying attention to Newport online in
Tennessee around the time Carlile first took the stage, right before
sunset. It wasn't too long before the tweets started buzzing. *Word
is Joni Mitchell herself is here and is going to sing!* Phones raised
aloft at Fort Adams captured Carlile's opening words about the
power of folk music to create and sustain community, and of the
festival as a living testament to that endeavor. The Bramily, her
ever-expanding inner circle, began to fill the stage. The Hanseroths, of course, and Allison, and her regular background singers Jess Wolfe and Holly Laessig of the band Lucius, whose most
recent album Carlile had produced. Also newer friends like the
English folk star Marcus Mumford and the producer Blake Mills,

and a couple of Newport's favorite sons, like Taylor Goldsmith of the band Dawes. Wynonna Judd was there too—a younger and newer addition to Brandi's pantheon of elders, emotional that night not only because she was standing so close to her lifelong musical hero but because she'd only recently suffered the loss of her own mother and singing partner, Naomi.

A well-cushioned rococo chair in the center remained empty. Then, escorted by her longtime physical therapist, Sultoon, Mitchell emerged resplendent in a beret, beads and satin. Jumping around on my social media feeds, I could watch the whole set unfold. Joni first only tentatively joined in on the most familiar lines from her songs as the all-star chorus sheltered her. But even in her beatific state, she proved to still be the woman who wouldn't be banished to the chorus. She claimed the lead on "Big Yellow Taxi" and "Amelia," and even took up an electric guitar. Between songs, she shared some of the stories she's told for years, ones I'd memorized after reading scores of her interviews. They felt fresh again, renewed within a voice that had, in public at least, long been limited to a few halting words.

Is Mitchell restored now? The Newport set would be followed nearly a year later by a concert at Washington State's majestic Gorge Amphitheatre, whose tickets rapidly sold out at thousands of dollars a pop. There, Mitchell would sing more than ever, surrounded by the friends now holding her in their love: not only Brandi, but women representing every singer-songwriter era since she'd emerged, including Annie Lennox, Sarah McLachlan, and her old friends through Prince, his former bandmates Wendy and Lisa. Her Newport companions were mostly there, too, as were a new batch of boys: Hozier and Marcus Mumford and Brandi's bandmates, the Hanseroths. The evening was a triumph, starrily reviewed, a historic occasion that felt like a rebirth.

From Newport on there have been whispers about more public Joni Jams, a new album, a real autobiography, whatever variation of "comeback" makes sense for an eighty-year-old woman long afflicted with health problems but surrounded by love and an unrelenting hunger for her presence. Across my phone screen as sunset wound down into night and in the days beyond, the testimonies and the tears flowed. *Weeping profusely at the brilliance of Joni at Newport* and *watching Joni Mitchell at Newport folk clips at a coffee shop daring myself not to cry in public* and *the videos of Joni at Newport make me feel like there's a knitted blanket around my brain* and *Joni Mitchell showing up at Newport proves that God (or whatever sustaining grace you believe in) has not yet left the building.* All that feeling zinging around the underground cables of our connections. And new souls opening themselves to her energy, too. *Joni Mitchell at Newport Folk Fest I think just changed my life*, wrote one, who couldn't have been more than a college sophomore, judging by his picture on the app.

I felt a pang of recognition. I had traveled so far to get to the point where this spectacle meant as much to me as it did to her most ardent fans. I still stood apart in some ways. After all, I hadn't bought that ticket, made that plane, stood on the grass and felt the Rhode Island salt air on my face along with inevitable tears. And yet, miracle of miracles, I was there. And I thought: *I am with you, Joni fan. I feel you, rushing toward her voice; pausing to try to get her into focus; turning toward the me you become, the traveler, when listening to her. On her road, which is our road, too. Forever circling, round and round and round.*

Viva

a moving conclusion

As Brandi grew closer to Joni, and Joni began stepping back into the world, I found myself moving in a different direction. Not opposite, exactly; witnessing the doyenne get her flowers was, as always, pleasurable, and the fan in me—yes, that fan who'd shyly begun showing herself to me as my immersion quickened— loved that Joni was getting well through music, *in* music, held in recovery by those who loved her as both an artist and a person.

But my inner fan's sister, the skeptic, still staged her arguments. I knew what I valued most about Joni's music and her life story—its thorniness, the way it always took unexpected turns, its perfectly contained audaciousness. The Joni who tentatively began to find and use her voice again faced limitations that would have sunk a meeker soul, and the very effort moved me. But there was no way that the woman who'd once flown so close to the clouds that she could see them from all angles would return. The aneurysm, escalating the inevitable decline of aging, had changed her. Delighted as she seemed—glowing, radiant, every breathless media report used those words—she remained subdued during her triumphant appearances. She was grounded, a term that can describe someone at peace, but also, a creature unable to soar.

It's never easy to watch the heroes of our youth grow old. Not only does their aging put the ultimate loss that is mortality clearly in sight; the process itself is a series of little murders. The ideals embodied by the young and those in the prime of life—quickness and nerve, the magnificent aplomb that grows with each accomplishment—grow shaky as the body gives in. I hadn't been besotted with Joni in my own callow years, but I'd come to treasure the twenty-five-year-old who had lugged her guitar through Laurel Canyon, and the thirty-two-year-old who commandeered the open road, and the forty-eight-year-old who raised her arms in love and wisdom even after many struggles and said, *come in from the cold*. Every one of those Jonis was her own person above all else. She welcomed acclaim at every stage, but mostly she wanted to keep heading somewhere else, never to rest at the front of a receiving line. And to never let others define her, even in adoration. Even though I knew from those spending time with her that she still ran her own show as best she could, the new, soft face she was showing the world disconcerted me.

I realize that most people will find my reluctance to unabashedly cheer the Joni renaissance unreasonable. Here was a septuagenarian woman lifting herself from her sickbed and insisting that as long as she lived, she would do so as fully as possible. Undeniably inspirational! And here was her songbook, lifted off the shelf, for longtime fans to celebrate and new ones to claim and renew. Yet all the glorious fuss took me back to the very beginning of my time following her, raising the same questions I had then. The Joni being celebrated often struck me as more monumental than the one I'd come to value but also far more contained. All legend, less bite. The beautiful boxed sets that began arriving in earnest, solidifying her archive, documented every aspect of her vast catalog, yet the swell of adoration around her obscured their complexity. And through it all, Joni smiled. She beamed! She appeared to be happy in a way she hadn't been for decades. That thing she'd said to Cameron Crowe about emulating Thumper started to really bother me. "If you can't say anything nice . . ." *Joni*, I thought, *what you gave us was the chance to say everything that isn't nice. To be neurotic, mean, confused, rude. While also being wise, sensual, empathetic, honest. Honest above all.*

I was wrestling pointlessly with my feelings over Mitchell's comeback. Pointlessly! Because why squash joy? Who would want me to do that? I could see that her rejuvenation was following the same inspirational arc that had given music some of its most powerful milestones. Elvis Presley wallowed in ignominy until donning black leather and returning to his early material in his 1968 comeback television special. (Aging too fast, he was only thirty-three.) Tina Turner became the rock star she always should have been after surviving her husband Ike's abuse and spending years in the wilderness searching for the right champions. David Bowie pushed back cancer long enough to produce some of his greatest work at the end of his life. Such stories matter because they show that even after great pain and shattered strength, recovery is possible. People give in so easily to their own suffering. It confines them. When Joni told Crowe that after her aneurysm she had learned to walk again for a third time, and described doing so with no bitterness, it didn't matter that she would likely never return to making vapor trails on her guitar or hitting notes that made the spine tingle. She was living fully, as best she could, a fundamental human accomplishment.

Yet I wasn't alone in my complicated feelings. Michelle Mercer, whose book on Joni's blue period I so admire, posted her own conflicting thoughts about Joni's resurrection in her newsletter, *Call & Response*. Acknowledging the draw of the story's human-interest side, Mercer wrote that she missed "the dissecting, skewering gaze, that difficult genius" that once made Joni as moody as she could be hilarious, and which was nowhere evident as she sat resplendent on stages receiving the kind of love she might have once called sycophantic. A jazz critic, Mercer also missed the players from that world who rode Joni's vibe wherever she would go, and led her to take risks she might have otherwise not dared. She wanted "both the analytical and the carefree parts" of Mitchell, and "Joni's observing artist self who could recognize and express this dualism in lyric and song." Mercer concluded that Joni's happiness may have been born of that dualism's death. "The great tragedy," she wrote, "is that it seems Joni had to lose so much of herself in the aneurysm to become the accepting, happy person she is now."

In her book on Sylvia Plath, the great biographer and interrogator of the form Janet Malcolm famously wrote that "the freedom to be cruel is one of journalism's uncontested privileges," and the same is true for critics. I know Mercer feels the same hesitation I do to express her doubts about old Joni's flowers and sing-alongs;

fans will call us cold-blooded. But what is criticism, if not a balancing act between the mind and the heart? Love can be defined in many ways. It generates acceptance and, at the same time, the kind of sustained attention that can turn into questioning, dissatisfaction and doubt. To be a critic, like being an artist, is to love in a way that is as careful as it is passionate. I have tried in this book to trace my own oscillations within this range and to understand why Joni Mitchell's music and her presence can raise so many different emotions in me. Mercer did the same when she voiced her doubts, even as she concluded that Mitchell's late fluorescence was in itself an amazing gift to the world. In return, Mercer later wrote, she received more death threats from Joni fans than compliments. If Janet Malcolm were still alive, she might have said, *Well, what do you expect?* The journalistic knife is often turned back on the one who wields it.

If the Joni Mitchell who sits on a dais and greets her weeping fans with the declaration "Viva la old age!" as she did at the Gorge, is not the Joni who most interests or pleases me, the best I can do as a critic and chronicler is to try to comprehend my feelings and communicate them. I can reflect on my own unwavering attachment to underdogs and rebels, to eccentrics and outcasts, and recall how at different points in her life, this now fully acknowledged queen occupied and illuminated all of those roles. I think about the solitude that formed in her as a child, which she later made her signature and her burden; I key into the longing that she knew came from loss, but which she transmuted into hunger for men, for acknowledgment, and for escape. All of these qualities remain even in the most simplistic renderings of her music. They are embedded there, in acerbic lyrics and odd tunings, sometimes in the way she utters a single phrase, like *They say I've changed*. Other people will always make Joni Mitchell into what they need her to be, and she's survived all of those handlings, the callow dismissals and the smothering hugs alike. If the throne is Joni's final stop, it exists on her nonlinear map alongside all the other places she's rested and departed, rejected and reclaimed.

Not long ago someone asked me an impossible question: Why does Joni Mitchell matter? I blathered on about the usual stuff, like her supreme skill and groundbreaking innovations, and her embodiment of womanhood—personhood—in a time and place when those always mutable terms were in violent flux. I was bored with my own answer. But then it hit me, what mattered to me about Joni after all this time. It is simply that she has sustained her conviction that it's always worth giving something a try. What does it mean to be an artist? She has pontificated about greatness, and I have questioned her definitions; she's noted the cost of creativity in tears and weariness and I've thought, yes, but it has given you so much. In the end nothing that she or I could say about her music or the life she has given it means more than the fact that she kept picking up her tools. A song comes into being only after fingers hit a fretboard or a keyboard. A performance begins in rehearsal, even before that on the stage in a woman's mind. Joni Mitchell went through so much to grant us all that she has, and in turn she has enjoyed adulation. But where I leave her, when I leave her, is in that place, alone or with others, where she says, *Okay, let's start.*

ACKNOWLEDGMENTS

The metaphor that grants this book its title represents a process that took the better part of a decade. In that time I struggled, triumphed, went under, returned, ran away and returned again. It was not easy, and I wouldn't have made it without the support and encouragement of many people, from close collaborators to loved ones and acquaintances who offered kind words, insights and material aid. I am sure I have forgotten to include some here. Forgive me.

Traveling would not exist if not for Denise Oswald, that New York editor who called me to say I should try to do the impossible. I thank her so much, though in all honesty I've also cursed her over the years. Sarah Lazin, my agent, has always been my champion and wise advisor, and never more than in the time I was struggling with this project. Carrie Thornton took up the torch when Denise left Dey Street Books, and has been a stalwart supporter. Anna Montague—what can I say to the editor who pushed me to try again and do more when I handed in messy pages and half-finished thoughts? Anna, you are as gentle and kind as you are persuasive, and I deeply appreciate you. Corinne Cummings is the greatest fact checker in the world, and saved me so many times it's both humbling and astonishing. For a thorough and thoughtful legal read, I thank Trina Hunn. Thanks to Janet Rosenberg for catching my errors in the copyedit, and to Sarah Grant for help on the endnotes.

I talked to many people in the course of *Traveling* and their stories tie the book to the earth. Some interviews did not make it into the book, but every one mattered. Some of these subjects have left us, and I treasure their words all the more. In no particular order, thank you to David Crosby, James Taylor, Graham Nash, Tom Rush, Judy Collins, Michelle Phillips, Len Chandler, Olga Adderley Chandler, Leah Kunkel, Bobby Ingram, Ed Pearl, Alice Echols, Russ Kunkel, Peter Asher, Randy Brecker, Larry Carlton, Taj Mahal (more talk than interview but I loved every minute, Taj), Wayne Shorter, Flora Purim, Roberta Flack, Larry Klein (Larry, I'll wait for your answers anytime), Brian Blade, John Kelly, and Miles Grier. Miles, thank you for being an open and brilliant interlocutor; I can't wait for your Joni book! To Brandi Carlile and the entire Bramily I send love and admiration that goes beyond the boundaries of this work. Robben Ford, I'm sorry we never connected, but I appreciate your warmth as we tried.

So many people helped me arrange these encounters, research the book and gather my thoughts. Thanks to Lisa Ducore and the staff of the L.A. Philharmonic, Asha Goodman, Tom Huizenga, Kerry Thompson, Josh Brown, Bryn Ingram, Sheila Weller, Michelle Mercer, Carolina Shorter, Michelle Conceison, Michael Kramer, Alissa Kingsley, Angela DeDominick, Katherine DePaul, Keith Putney, Elaine Schock, Suzanne Koga, Roberta Cutolo, Marc Satlof, Paul Ingles, Clem Hitchcock, Stacey Anderson, Rob Sevier and David Shumway. I spent happy hours in the archives at the Rock & Roll Hall of Fame and the Country Music Hall of Fame; thanks to Andy Leach, Jennie Thomas and the whole RRHOF staff, and to Michael Gray, Ali Tonn, Katherine Campbell and the CMHOF staff.

This book is a work of scholarship as well as storytelling, and I'm happy that it will sit on a shelf with other great Joni tomes. I must praise those whose efforts laid the groundwork for my own, particularly Malka Marom, Sheila Weller, David Yaffe, Michelle Mercer, Lloyd Whitesell, Susan Whitall, Barney Hoskyns, Anne Karppinen, and Ruth Charnock. Kevin Fellezs's work on jazz fusion helped me begin to understand that much-misunderstood phenomenon. Patrick Milligan and the staff at Rhino Records are doing incredible things with Mitchell's archival releases; thanks to Jason Elzy for the hook-ups. Most of all, the late Wally Breese and Jim Johanson and the incredible fan-archivists who have made jonimitchell.com the best music site on the internet deserve an ovation. They embody the true meaning of the heart-word "amateur."

As I followed and approached Joni, I was always working on other things, and I appreciate the patience of my colleagues. Alison Fensterstock took on the enormous task of leading another book project that I could not helm because of this one, and has done miraculous things with it. Casey Kittrell, Jessica Hopper and Sasha Geffen at UT Press have been accommodating beyond the call as I pushed off our collaborative work to stay with Joni. Lauren Onkey, Keith Jenkins, Anya Grundmann, Otis Hart, Suraya Mohamed, Marissa Lorussso, Hazel Cills and everyone else at NPR helped so much. Jacob Ganz, you above all.

To my friends, interlocutors, confessors, comforters: without you I'm nothing. Tim Higgins is my number one conversationalist when it comes to all things Joni. Thank you for every observation, story and YouTube clip. Aaron Sanders Head, you were in on many of those exchanges and I treasure your insights. Jordan Hamlin is not only an extraordinary musician and engineer herself, but one of the best when it comes to articulating love for '80s Joni and beyond. To my group text, Jody Rosen and Carl Wilson:

thanks for staving off insanity and for emergency edits. The intellectual power trio of Gayle Wald, Daphne A. Brooks and Sonnet Retman provided essential insights shaping the "For Art's Sake" chapter, the ideas therein are theirs as much as mine. (Thank you, Gayle, for getting me to think about others' complicity in relationship to that character.) Pauline Mauro offered a bed to sleep in and fellowship in Los Angeles. Jill Sternheimer, my soul sister, I am so glad that you joined me on several of my key Joni adventures, and I treasure your unflagging support and empathy. Jewly Hight, you win the medal for best encouraging words. Nick Popovich, Whitney Pastorek and Mary Ho, when I need a laugh or an ear, you come through. To Amy Weisbard, my sister-in-law: your care for our family and our long talks provided immeasurable help. Jen Le Coguic is a brilliant physical therapist who kept my body in shape when my brain was totally fried.

To Eric and Bebe Weisbard: you endured my absences and my crises, the late nights with my study door shut, and my tears when I felt I could not complete this journey. Eric, as another book weighs down the shelf that we share, I feel so much admiration for you and gratitude for our love and our partnership. Bebe, during the time I wrote this, you grew from a young teen to a woman. I am so proud of all you are, and it is my joy to continue getting to know the wise adult you are becoming. Thank you for every hug and *How are you doing, Mom?* They got me through.

Frank-N-Furter Nietzsche Weisbard, you share a name with Joni Mitchell's cat, but you are a Maltipoo without peer. I am very glad you joined our family. I am also aware that as a dog, you can't read, but I love you.

And finally: Joni Mitchell, I thank you for your endless complexity. It gave me so much to explore, and I'll never regret my time following you.

NOTES

Introduction: Drawing the Maps

3 *"I feel sometimes like I'm a multiphrenic person"*: Malka Marom, *Joni Mitchell: In Her Own Words* (Toronto: ECW Press, 2014), p.158.

3 *"many selves and self-representations that conflict"*: Kenneth Gergen, *The Saturated Self* (New York: Basic Books, 1991) p. 16.

3 *"Will the real me stand up, you know"*: Marci McDonald, "Joni Mitchell Emerges from Her Retreat," *Toronto Star*, February 9, 1974.

11 *"I knew she would turn on me"*: Elon Green, "Q&A: David Yaffe on Reporting a Biography of Joni Mitchell," *Columbia Journalism Review*, September 13, 2017.

13 *"This is the effect that listening"*: Zadie Smith, "Some Notes on Attunement," *The New Yorker*, December 9, 2012.

13 *"After everything"*: Meghan Daum, "The Joni Mitchell Problem," *The Unspeakable: And Other Subjects of Discussion* (New York: Farrar, Straus and Giroux, 2014), p.167.

13 *"periods when I get tangled up"*: Ron Rosenbaum, "The Best Joni Mitchell Song Ever," *Slate*, Dec. 14, 2007.

14 *"I guess I'm going through something of a phase"*: Merek Cooper, "Mitchellin Man: Destroyer's Favourite Albums," *The Quietus*, August 12, 2015.

14 *"All girls go through a Joni Mitchell phase"*: Tift Merritt, "Tift Merritt—Triple Threat," *No Depression*, January 1, 2000.

14 *"You don't meet too many"*: Lisa Cholodenko, director, *The Kids Are All Right* (Focus Features, 2010).

15 *"there was pure genius sitting in front of me"*: Graham Nash, *Wild Tales: A Rock & Roll Life* (New York: Three Rivers Press, 2013), p. 116.

16 *"It's like a ghost is writing a song"*: Robert Hilburn, "'I Always Admired True Artists, So I Learned from Them': When the Enigmatic Bob Dylan Opened Up in 2004," *Los Angeles Times*, August 4, 2004.

17 *"like peeping in a window"*: Karl Dallas, "Joni, the Seagull from Saskatoon," *Melody Maker*, September 28, 1968.

18 *"I always smile when I'm nervous"*: Caroline Boucher, "Joni: 'My Personal Life Is a Shambles,'" *Disc and Music Echo*, January 10, 1970.

18 *"She is fulfilling something of a 'goddess' need in American rock"*: Jacoba Atlas, "Joni: Let's Make Life More Romantic," *Melody Maker*, June 20, 1970.

19 *"a stainless steel bullshit detector"*: Lindsay Zoladz, "Joni Mitchell: Fear of a Female Genius," *The Ringer*, October 16, 2017.

19 *"When I record, I'm not a human"*: Michele Kort, *Soul Picnic: The Music and Passion of Laura Nyro* (New York: St. Martin's Griffin, 2003), p. 74.

20 *"I'm a painter. Painters paint women"*: Margaret Atwood, *Cat's Eye* (Toronto: McClelland and Stewart, 1988), p. 101.

22 *"If you see me in my songs"*: Jian Ghomeshi, "The Joni Mitchell Interview," CBC Music, June 11, 2013.

22 *"That's as close as someone"*: Michelle Mercer, *Will You Take Me As I Am: Joni Mitchell's Blue Period* (New York: Free Press, 2009), p. 49.

23 *"penitent"*: Stephen Holden, "The Ambivalent Hall of Famer," *New York Times*, December 1, 1996.

23 *"It's better than a poem!"*: Kelsey Osgood, "A Band of Her Own," *Harper's Magazine*, October 2014.

23 *"an emotional immediacy"*: David Shumway, *Rock Star: The Making of Musical Icons from Elvis to Springsteen* (Baltimore: Johns Hopkins University Press, 2014), p. 164.

23 *"I have a compulsion to be honest with my audience"*: Cameron Crowe, "Joni Mitchell Defends Herself," *Rolling Stone*, July 26, 1979.

23 *"Music pours over"*: Anne Sexton, "Music Swims Back to Me," *The Complete Poems of Anne Sexton* (Boston: Houghton Mifflin Harcourt, 1981), p. 6.

24 *"Thus the frightened"*: Maxine Kumin, "How It Was," in Anne Sexton's *The Complete Poems* (Boston: Houghton Mifflin Harcourt, 1981), p. 30.

24 *"like my guts were on the outside"*: David Yaffe, *Reckless Daughter* (New York: Sarah Crichton Books/FSG, 2017), p. 174.

24 *"the new uterus of popular music"*: Jon Landau, "Rock 1970," *Rolling Stone*, December 2, 1970.

25 *"I was in the womb all along"*: Anne Sexton, "Menstruation at Forty," *The Compete Poems*, p. 137.

25 *"would be punished by circumstance"*: Malka Marom, *Joni Mitchell: In Her Own Words* (Toronto: ECW Press, 2014), p. 38.

25 *"Oh, Joni, save something for yourself"*: Lindsay Zoladz, "Joni Mitchell: Fear of a Female Genius," *The Ringer*, October 16, 2017.

26 *"They were glad to be sheep"*: Ben Fong-Torres, "Introducing Joni Mitchell," *Rolling Stone*, May 17, 1969.

27 *"She was like a storm"*: Yaffe, *Reckless Daughter*, p. 86.

27 *"those wonderful, vulnerable cheekbones"*: Michael Gross, "Joni Mitchell: Nassau Coliseum," *Swank*, March 1976.

27 *"That's the way the world worked"*: Katherine Monk, *Joni: The Creative Odyssey of Joni Mitchell* (Vancouver, Toronto, and Berkeley: Greystone Books, 2012) p. 52.

28 *"Women? I guess they out to exercise Pussy Power?"*: Eldridge Cleaver quoted in Robin Morgan, ed, *Sisterhood is Powerful: An Anthology of Writings from the Women's Liberation Movement* (New York: Vintage Books, 1970), p. 38.

28–29 *"Black men still didn't like short hair"*: Michele Wallace, "A Black Feminist's Search for Sisterhood," *But Some of Us Are Brave: Black Women's Studies* (New York: The Feminist Press at CUNY, 1982), p. 5.

29 *"the groupies were generally better-looking"*: David Crosby and Carl Gottlieb, *Long Time Gone: The Autobiography of David Crosby* (New York: Dell, 1990), p. 167.

30 *"Even the most beautiful"*: Simone de Beauvoir, *The Second Sex* (New York: Vintage Books, 1952), p. 614.

31 *"Ah Joni"*: Greg Granquist, letter to *Rolling Stone*, March 29, 1973.

31 *"a process of making up, or making over"*: Hermione Lee, "Virginia Woolf's Nose," *Essays on Biography* (Princeton, N.J.: Princeton University Press, 2015), p. 37.

31 *"They do exist"*: Hermione Lee, *Body Parts: Essays on Life-Writing* (London: Pimlico, 2008), p. 28.

31–32 *"Masturbation, dental work, body odor"*: Hermione Lee, *Body Parts*, p. 4.

Chapter 1: Childish Things

Chapter 1 includes an original interview with James Taylor conducted in 2018.

38 *"Perhaps the act of skating"*: Marco Adria, *Music of Our Times: Eight Canadian Singer-Songwriters* (Toronto: James Lorimer Limited Publishers, 1990), p. 65.

39 *"When I was a kid"*: Susan Gordon Lydon, "In Her House, Love," *New York Times*, April 20, 1969.

40 *"judgment was so sucky all the time"*: David Yaffe, *Reckless Daughter* (New York: Sarah Crichton Books/FSG, 2017), p. 17.

40 *"My parents are both color-blind"*: Yaffe, *Reckless Daughter*, p. 19.

41 *"I wasn't lonely, but I was a lone person,"*: Brent Lannan, "On Being a Flatlander," *Saskatoon Report*, October 1990.

42 *"A lonely adult recalls earlier moments of loneliness"*: Hayden Herrera, "Childhood in Coyoacan," *Frida: A Biography of Frida Kahlo* (New York: HarperCollins, 1983), p. 31.

42 *"The hallucinatory lyrics"*: Lloyd Whitesell, "Harmonic Palette in Early Joni Mitchell," *Popular Music*, May 2002.

44 *"A man translates himself"*: Leonard Cohen. *Beautiful Losers* (New York: Knopf Doubleday Publishing Group, 1993), p. 19.

46 *"nothing is real"*: John Lennon and Paul McCartney, "Strawberry Fields Forever," Capitol Records, 1967, 45 rpm single.

46 *"My father always promised us"*: Judy Collins, "My Father," track 3 on Judy Collins, *Who Knows Where the Time Goes*, Elektra Records, 1968, album.

46 *"You're still young"*: Cat Stevens, "Father and Son," track 10 on Cat Stevens, *Tea For the Tillerman*, Island/A&M Records, 1970, album.

46 *"You are a man, you understand"*: Neil Young, "I Am a Child," track 9 on Buffalo Springfield, *Last Time Around*, Atco Records, 1968, album.

47 *"The child we once were"*: W. Hugh Missildine, *Your Inner Child of the Past* (New York: Simon & Schuster, 1963), p. 43.

48 *"warm fuzzies"*: Alvin Freed, *T.A. for Teens and Other Important People: Transactional Analysis Series*, vol. 5 (Jalmar Press, 1976), p. 58.

48 *"the kids read"*: Webster Schott, "Children's Books: What Do YA's Read?" *New York Times*, May 7, 1972.

49 *"awareness . . . living in the here and now"*: Eric Berne, *Games People Play: The Psychology of Human Relationships* (New York: Grove Press, 1964), p. 158.

52 *"I looked like a pregnant boy,"*: Booker T. Jones, *Time Is Tight: My Life, Note by Note* (Little, Brown and Company, 2019), p. 33.

52 *"I began to absorb all sound,":* Jones, *Time Is Tight*, p. 33.

53 *"I am the goddam blues,":* Bill Withers, "Just As I Am," video documentary included in DualDisc reissue, 2005.

55 *"When you are traveling on the road":* Bill Adler, "The Innervisions of Stevie Wonder," *Ann Arbor Sun*, October 4, 1974.

56 *"The unique link":* Yaffe, *Reckless Daughter*, p. 22.

57 *"It was mystical to come back from that disease":* Jim Irvin, "Joni Mitchell," *Word*, March 2005.

57 *"We were struck down by polio":* Vic Garbarini, "Joni Mitchell Is a Nervy Broad," *Musician*, January 1983.

57 *"I already have a cane collection":* Iain Blair, "Poetry and Paint Brushes," *Rock Express*, May 1988.

58 *"a life almost like [people on] the Russian tundra":* Timothy White, "Joni Mitchell—A Portrait of the Artist," *Billboard*, December 9, 1995.

58 *"'You look like a woman today'":* White, "Joni Mitchell."

58 *"With nothing but hobbled movement":* Mercer, *Will You Take Me As I Am*, p. 61.

59 *"The terrible suffering":* Marc Shell, *Polio and Its Aftermath: The Paralysis of Culture* (Cambridge: Harvard University Press, 2005), p. 36.

60 *"You always ask me why":* Sheila Weller, "Why Is No One Talking About Polio," *Air Mail*, May 23, 2020.

60 *"I run my own kind of marathon":* Peg Kehret, *Small Steps: The Year I Got Polio* (Morton Grove, Ill.: Albert Whitman, 1996), p. 155.

61 *"extremely bigoted":* John Einarson, "Cranky Joni Mitchell a Reminder of Winnipeg Shortcoming," John Einarson, *Winnepeg Free Press*, August 1, 2013.

Chapter 2: The Humming of the Wheels

Chapter 2 draws on original interviews with Tom Rush, Judy Collins, David Crosby, and Bobby Ingram in 2018 and 2019.

70 *"a satire on the Beats":* Nancy M. Grace, "Detecting Jack Kerouac and Joni Mitchell: A Literary/Legal Investigation in Search for Influence," *Kerouac on Record: A Literary Soundtrack* (London: Bloomsbury Academic, 2018), p. 231.

70 *"brothels":* William Ruhlmann, "From Blue to Indigo," *Goldmine*, February 17, 1995.

70 *"I gravitated to the best dance halls":* Ruhlmann, "From Blue to Indigo."

72 *"The reason painters live":* Susan Whitall, *Joni on Joni: Interviews and Encounters with Joni Mitchell* (Chicago: Chicago Review Press, 2018), p. 183.

73 *"a riot of batiks":* *Daily Variety*, January 6, 1960.

73 *"kicked wide the door":* Sheila Weller, *Girls Like Us: Carole King, Joni Mitchell, Carly Simon and the Journey of a Generation* (New York: Washington Square Press, 2008), p. 157.

74– 75 *"While audiences assure":* Peter Mathews, "Folk Singer: Two Career Girl," *Calgary Albertan*, December 4, 1963.

75 *"It was stuck between auto mechanics":* Ruhlmann, "From Blue to Indigo."

75 *"The thing about performing":* Les Irvin, "A Conversation with John Uren," JoniMitchell.com, August 29, 2005.

76 *"a portal from simple folk to new possibilities":* Steve Boisson, "The Story Behind Davey Graham's 1960s-Era Fingerstyle Classic 'Anji,'" *Acoustic Guitar Magazine*, February 18, 2016.

76 *"my Beatles"*: Joe Smith, *Off the Record: An Oral History of Popular Music* (New York: Warner Books, 1986).

76 *"I went straight to the Cotten picking"*: Jeffrey Pepper Rodgers, "My Secret Place," *Acoustic Guitar Magazine*, August 1996.

78 *"The moment I began to write"*: Ruhlmann, "From Blue to Indigo."

82 *"we were not communicating"*: Brian D. Johnson, "Joni's Secret: Mother and Child Reunion," *Maclean's*, April 21, 1997.

83 *"Joni exuded charisma"*: Weller, *Girls Like Us*, p. 149.

86 *"one month into the marriage"*: Bill Higgins, "Both Sides at Last," *Los Angeles Times*, April 8, 1997.

86 *"Two Single Acts Survive a Marriage"*: A. L. McClain, "Two Single Acts Survive a Marriage," *Detroit News*, February 6, 1966.

88 *"Visually, Miss Mitchell was the epitome"*: M.S., "Moments of Beauty from Joni Mitchell," Toronto *Globe and Mail*, November 9, 1966.

89 *"She came down to the Gaslight"*: Anne Hershoran, "Profile: Joni Mitchell," *Hoot*, September 1966.

89 *"I saw Joni Mitchell, wearing that little red"*: "Bonnie Raitt's Blues," New England Public Radio, November 9, 2015.

94 *"For the first time"*: Sylvie Simmons. *I'm Your Man: The Life of Leonard Cohen* (Toronto: McLelland & Stewart, 2012), p. 174.

94 *Les Brown, calls Mitchell "Leonard Cohen's 'Suzanne'"*: Les Brown, "Joni Mitchell," *Rolling Stone*, July 6, 1968.

107 *"Back then it was just us"*: David Crosby and Carl Gottlieb, *Long Time Gone: The Autobiography of David Crosby* (David Crosby & Carl Gottlieb, 2007), p. 61.

109 *"of people being guided by your music"*: David Yaffe, *Reckless Daughter* (New York: Sarah Crichton Books/FSG, 2017), p. 66.

110 *"Absolutely amazing, sailing through"*: Crosby, *Long Time Gone*, p. 61.

Chapter 3: The Boys

Chapter 3 draws on original interviews with David Crosby, Graham Nash, Michelle Phillips and Leah Kunkel conducted in 2018 and 2019.

113 *"Listen, I'm fucking a Byrd"*: James McDonough, *Shakey: Neil Young's Biography* (Random House, 2002), p. 245.

114 *"love her madly"*: Robby Krieger and Jim Morrison, "Love Her Madly," track 2 on The Doors, *L.A. Woman*, Elektra Records, 1971, album.

114 *"a squirming dog"*: Mick Jagger and Keith Richards, "Under My Thumb," track 4 on the Rolling Stones, *Aftermath*, Decca/London, 1966, album.

114 *"please don't let on"*: Bob Dylan, "Just Like a Woman," track 8 on Dylan, *Blonde on Blonde*, Columbia, 1966, album.

115 *"Just sit there and look groovy"*: Susan Gordon Lydon, "In Her House, Love," *New York Times*, April 20, 1969.

115 *"My house is a very free house"*: Jerry Hopkins, "The *Rolling Stone* Interview: Cass Elliot," *Rolling Stone*, October 26, 1968.

116 *"Joni Mitchell has written many songs sitting in my living room"*: Hopkins, "The *Rolling Stone* Interview: Cass Elliot."

118 *"mascot"*: David Browne, *Crosby, Stills, Nash and Young: The Definitive Saga of Rock's Greatest Supergroup* (New York: Hachette Books, 2019), p. 175.

119 *"the feeling of that was, man"*: Ben Fong-Torres, "David Crosby: The *Rolling Stone* Interview," *Rolling Stone*, July 23, 1970.

120 *"would have picked up a basketball and shot hoops"*: Sheila Weller, *Girls Like Us*, p. 354.

120 *"The feeling between them was very high"*: Dave Zimmer, *Crosby, Stills & Nash: The Biography* (Da Capo Lifelong Books, 2008), p. 74.

120 *"What isn't a boys' club besides needlepoint and nursery school?"*: Lacey Paige, "Interview: Jovanka Vuckovic in Honour of Women in Horror Month," *Cinema Head Cheese* (blog), February 2011.

121 *"On one side you've got"*: Fong-Torres, "David Crosby: The *Rolling Stone* Interview."

121 *"a kind of liberated zone"*: Alice Echols, "Thirty Years with a Portable Lover," *LA Weekly*, November 25, 1994.

122 *"I opened the door and let my rough-and-tumble self out"*: Diane di Prima, *Recollections of My Life as a Woman, the New York Years: A Memoir* (New York: Viking, 2001), p. 115.

122 *"the social organization which is most true of itself"*: Louis Menand, "Drive, He Wrote," *The New Yorker*, September 24, 2007.

123 *"At night when the cold air"*: Joyce Johnson, *Minor Characters: A Beat Memoir* (New York: Penguin, 1999), p. 133.

124 *"I know some very good women musicians"*: Julie C. Dunbar, *Women, Music, Culture: An Introduction* (Abingdon: Taylor & Francis, 2010), p. 133.

124 *"When one of the boys needed"*: Anita O'Day, *High Times Hard Times* (New York: Applause, 1981), p. 116.

124 *"Mary Travers, 1953"*: Diane di Prima, *Recollections of My Life as a Woman*, p. 119.

124 *"We lived outside, as if"*: Hettie Jones, *How I Became Hettie Jones* (New York: Grove Atlantic, 1990), p. 81.

125 *"I learned myself"*: Johnson, *Minor Characters*, p. 56.

125 *"I didn't feel like a woman"*: Stuart Werbin, "Carly Simon: The Rolling Stone Interview," April 26, 1973.

126 *"I've always enjoyed being a sideman"*: Carole King, *A Natural Woman* (New York: Grand Central Publishing, 2012), p. 314.

137 *"We female folksingers"*: Sheila Weller, "The Year That Upended Women's Fashion—and Nearly Everything Else," *Vanity Fair*, March 2, 2017.

140 *"Soup and salad and that was it"*: Graham Nash, *Wild Tales: A Rock & Roll Life* (New York: Three Rivers Press, 2013), p. 131.

142 *"If you hold sand too tightly in your hand, it will run through your fingers"*: Nash, *Wild Tales*, p. 185.

142 *"Why is Joni Mitchell the token female musician"*: Lindsay Zoladz, "Joni Mitchell: Fear of a Female Genius," *The Ringer*, October 16, 2017.

142 *"I wasn't in the same league as Aretha Franklin, Joni Mitchell"*: King, *A Natural Woman*, p. 208.

143 *"you had to have double the guts and 20 times the talent"*: Barbara Rowes, "Woman's Sound Knocks the Double Standard," *Los Angeles Times*, July 15, 1973.

143 *"not being a bossy chick"*: Barbara Rowes, *Los Angeles Times*, 1973.

143 *"I'd have to be stupid to take them up on it"*: Barbara Rowes, *Los Angeles Times*, 1973.

143 avoiding *"male groupies"*: Barbara Rowes, *Los Angeles Times*, 1973.

144 *"life has been constantly filled with interruptions"*: Ben Fong-Torres, "Joni Mitchell," *Rolling Stone*, May 17, 1969.

145 *"Los Angeles is a relaxed and relaxing city"*: Jerry Hopkins, "Inside the Los Angeles Scene," *Rolling Stone*, June 22, 1968.

146 the magazine named Mitchell *"Old Lady of the Year"*: "Random Notes," *Rolling Stone*, February 4, 1971.

147 *"Bust of the Year" for a police incident*: *Rolling Stone*, February 4, 1971.

147 *"Couple of the Year"*: *Rolling Stone*, February 4, 1971.

147 *"While it may never be my favorite album"*: Lenny Kaye, "'Deja Vu': Album Review," *Rolling Stone*, July 22, 1971.

148 *"a penny yellow blonde with a vanilla voice"*: Les Brown, "Joni Mitchell," *Rolling Stone*, July 6, 1968.

148 *"Joni Mitchell's developed the ability to express"*: Jon Landau, "Jon Landau's Year-End Wrap-Up," *Rolling Stone*, December 2, 1970.

148 *"totally lacks . . . the poetry and vision of Joni Mitchell"*: Gary von Tersch, "Album Review: 'Whales & Nightingales,' Judy Collins," *Rolling Stone*, February 4, 1971.

148– *"the first great pop album of 1974"*: Jon Landau, "Review: Joni Mitchell Strikes
149 a Delicate Balance on 'Court and Spark,'" *Rolling Stone*, February 28, 1974.

149 *"contains more fun than profundity"*: Jon Landau, "Album Review: 'Hotcakes,'" *Rolling Stone*, June 6, 1974.

149 *"sexy, sexual or just plain sex"*: Ben Fong-Torres, "An Evening with Linda Ronstadt," *Rolling Stone*, March 18, 1971.

150 *"Joni Mitchell is 90% Virgin"*: Rock and Roll Hall of Fame Library & Archives.

150 *"funny" lady who's "fussy about advertising copy"*: correspondence, Mo Ostin Collection, Rock and Roll Hall of Fame Library & Archives.

150 *"It was in no way my intent to embarrass you"*: correspondence, February 11, 1969, Stan Cornyn, Mo Ostin Collection, Rock and Roll Hall of Fame Library & Archives.

151 *"Joni, as you probably know"*: correspondence, 1978, Warner Bros. label manager to associate. Mo Ostin Collection, Rock and Roll Hall of Fame Library & Archives.

152 *"Once, I heard her playing"*: Nash, *Wild Tales*, p. 147.

153 *"a very turbulent girl"*: Mark Bego, *Joni Mitchell* (Taylor Trade Publishing, 2005), p. 64.

155 *"Henry Lewy and I have had a working relationship"*: Malka Marom, *Joni Mitchell: In Her Own Words* (Toronto: ECW Press, 2014), p. 150.

159 *"the biggest batch of gypsies you ever saw"*: David Crosby to Dick Cavett, *The Dick Cavett Show*, August 19, 1969.

159 *"She played it for us before we even got settled"*: Nash, *Wild Tales*, p. 168.

Chapter 4: The Sorrow

Chapter 4 draws on original interviews with Dr. Alice Echols, James Taylor, and Russ Kunkel from 2018 and 2019.

165 *"I have trouble with* as it was": Joan Didion, *Play It As It Lays,* (New York: Farrar Straus & Giroux, 1970), p. 8.

167 *"This above all, to refuse to be a victim":* Margaret Atwood, *Surfacing* (Toronto: McClelland and Stewart, 1972), p. 229.

168 *"It was in these women that I first began":* Betty Friedan, *The Feminine Mystique* (New York: W.W. Norton, 1960), p. 336.

168 *"an outright betrayal of our best and bravest":* Geoffrey Clark and DeWitt Henry, "An Interview with Richard Yates," *Ploughshares,* Winter 1972.

168 *"We had more in our lives than just men":* Erica Jong, *Fear of Flying* (New York: Holt, Rinehart and Winston, 1973), p. 148.

170 *"Just watch as I crucify myself":* Olivia Rodrigo and Dan Nigro, "love is embarrassing," track 9 on Olivia Rodrigo, *Guts,* Geffen Records, 2023, album.

172 *"Ethiopia!":* David Yaffe, *Reckless Daughter* (Sarah Crichton Books/FSG, 2017), p. 312.

174 "outside Chicago/outside Detroit/outside Houston": Ntozake Shange, "Dark Phases," *for colored girls who have considered suicide/when the rainbow is enuf* (choreopoem, 1976), (New York: Scribner, 1997), p. 5.

174 *"I had convinced myself colored girls":* Ntozake Shange, "Pyramid," *for colored girls who have considered suicide,* p. 39.

174 *"If you are sad, then you should feel sad":* "Into the Pain of the Heart," *Time,* April 4, 1969.

175 *"It oscillates and vacillates":* Anne Hilker, "Dreams and False Alarms: Melancholy in the Work of Joni Mitchell," *Joni Mitchell: New Critical Readings* (Bloomsbury Academic, 2019), p. 89.

178 *a woman perfected is marble-white, dead:* Sylvia Plath, "Edge," *Ariel* (London: Faber and Faber, 1965), p. 84.

179 *"The* Blue *album, there's hardly a dishonest note"*: Cameron Crowe, "Joni Mitchell Defends Herself," *Rolling Stone,* July 26, 1979.

180 *"I can't listen to Joni Mitchell in a room with other people":* Zadie Smith, "Some Notes on Attunement," *The New Yorker,* December 9, 2012.

181 *"Joni also resents being reduced to a musical memoirist":* Michelle Mercer, *Will You Take Me As I Am: Joni Mitchell's Blue Period* (New York: Free Press, 2009), p. 17.

181 *"On* Blue,*" Mercer writes, "Mitchell began":* Mercer, *Will You Take Me As I Am,* p. 104.

182 *"Miles was the first subject of a* Playboy *interview":* Gary Giddins, *Visions of Jazz: The First Century* (Oxford: Oxford University Press, 1998), p. 342.

183 *"all about pruning away excess and distilling emotion."* Ashley Kahn, "Blue Heaven," *The Guardian,* March 9, 2001.

183 "Kind of Blue *was not so much a revolution as a realization":* Darius Brubeck, "1959: The Beginning of Beyond," *The Cambridge Companion to Jazz* (Cambridge: Cambridge University Press, 2003), p. 197.

183 *"There is a Japanese visual art":* Bill Evans, "Improvisation in Jazz," liner notes for Miles Davis, *Kind of Blue,* Columbia Records, 1959.

186 *"Though James and Joni are singing on separate mics":* Carole King, *A Natural Woman* (New York: Grand Central Publishing, 2012), p. 321.

186 *"In Tucumcari, Joni knitted the vest James now wears":* Susan Braudy, "James Taylor, a New Troubadour," *New York Times Sunday Magazine,* February 21, 1971.

188 *"How do you know?":* Kenneth Tynan, liner notes for Miles Davis, *Tallest Trees*, Prestige Records, 1972.

189 *a long trail of themes and variations, each line:* David Ake, *Jazz Cultures* (University of California Press, 2022), p. 83.

190 *"There was such an unusual harmony":* Joel Dinerstein, *The Origins of Cool in Post-War America*. (Chicago: University of Chicago Press, 2017), p. 4.

Chapter 5: Freedom Through Fusion

Chapter 5 draws on original interviews with Randy Brecker, Larry Carlton, and Peter Asher from 2019 and 2022.

193 *"lead a kind of 'Heidi' existence":* Penny Valentine, "Joni Mitchell Interview," *Sounds Magazine*, June 3, 1972.

197 *"Some people thought I was trying to do jazz":* Robert Hilburn, "Joni Mitchell: The *MOJO* Interview," February 2008.

199 *"the broken middle":* Kevin Fellezs, *Birds of Fire* (Durham: Duke University Press, 2011), p. 8.

200 *"As in quantum physics":* Greg Tate "The Song of the Body Electric: Jazz-Rock," in Yuval Taylor, ed., *The Future of Jazz* (Chicago, Ill.: A Capella Press, 2002), p. 62.

200 *"what it would be like if John Coltrane met George Harrison":* Richie Unterberger, liner notes for The Free Spirits, *Out of Sight and Sound* reissue, Sunbeam Records, 2006.

205 *"I was floored":* Barbara Charone, "Lost Innocence with a Rock and Roll Band," *New Musical Express*, February 9, 1974.

207 *"An unintentional travesty":* Stephen Holden, "Fantasy," *Rolling Stone*, August 2, 1973.

211 *"I think that he's like a musical genius, I really do":* Malka Marom, "The Entertainer's Interview," CBC-AM, February 3, 1974.

212 *"It doesn't matter what color you are":* Mary Campbell, "Stevie Wonder on Tour," *The Atlanta Constitution*, June 17, 1972.

212 *"I know that Stevie Wonder was using Moog and stuff":* Malka Marom, *Joni Mitchell: In Her Own Words* (Toronto: ECW Press, 2014), p. 133.

213 *"unbaggable. What he writes and sings":* Phil Casey, "Glad to Have It All, Glad to Have It," *The Washington Post, Times Herald*, August 29, 1972.

215 *Wonder, spiritual jazz pioneer Alice Coltrane and Led Zeppelin:* Earl Calloway, "Rufus Comes Home with Stevie: STARDOM," *Chicago Defender* (daily edition), October 28, 1974.

215 *"Being a black pop singer isn't easy,":* Vince Aletti, "Dionne Warwick," *Rolling Stone*, February 17, 1972.

217 *"little things and gadgets":* Jojo, "Airto Moreira," *Talking Drums*, August 22, 2018.

218 *"ethnic illegibility":* K. E. Goldschmitt, *Bossa Mundo: Brazilian Music in Transnational Media Industries* (Oxford: Oxford University Press, 2019), p. 78.

219 *"almost constant companion":* Robert Hilburn, "Frosting on Geffen's Cake," *Los Angeles Times*, February 23, 1974.

220 *"It's the ultimate extension of her effort":* Sean Nelson, *Joni Mitchell's* Court and Spark (Bloomsbury Publishing, 2006), p. 51.

222 *"The crowd was the prime fascination"*: Joyce Haber, "A-M Will Play the White House," *Los Angeles Times*, May 5, 1975.

222 *"How would you define the stomping"*: Leonard Feather, "A Year of Selling Out," *DownBeat 16th Annual Yearbook*, 1971, 10.

223 *"So many expert artists are playing money music"*: Leonard Feather, "The L.A. Express at Donte's," *Los Angeles Times*, April 9, 1975.

223 *"Fusion, in the main"*: Amiri and Amina Baraka, *The Music: Reflections on Jazz and Blues* (New York: Morrow, 1987).

226 *"total work"*: Joni Mitchell, liner notes for *The Hissing of Summer Lawns*, Asylum Records, 1975.

226 *"This really is the 'total work' she tells us it is"*: John Rockwell, "The Pop Life," *New York Times*, November 28, 1975.

226 *"It was a premature experiment; people thought I'd lost my marbles"*: Mitchell on Dutch National TV, May 28, 1988.

227 *"Let's go to Washington Square Park"*: Marom, *Joni Mitchell: In Her Own Words*, p. 246.

229 *"fluid pluralism"*: Anne Karppinen, *The Songs of Joni Mitchell: Gender, Performance and Agency* (Taylor and Francis, 2016), p. 10.

229– *"human bodies as made of rhythms"*: Anne Karppinen, *The Songs of Joni Mitchell*, **230** p. 13.

230 *"very alert and very sensual and very unwritten."*: Leonard Feather, "Joni Mitchell Makes Mingus Sing," *Downbeat*, September 6, 1979.

233 *"I really dig Joni but she's not a jazz musician"*: Spottswood Erving, "Jaco Pastorius: The Eccentric from the Everglades," *Musician*, May 1983.

Chapter 6: Hejira Means Pilgrimage

237 *"She didn't have anything to do"*: Steven V. Roberts, "Ode to a Freeway," *New York Times*, April 15, 1973.

239– *"She confesses she doesn't like to travel"*: Stephen Davis, *More Room in a Bro-* **240** *ken Heart: The True Adventures of Carly Simon* (New York: Gotham Books), p. 140.

241 *"zipless fuck"*: Erica Jong, *Fear of Flying* (New York: Holt, Rinehart and Winston, 1973), p. 8.

245 *"Ambivalence is a characteristic of neurotic states"*: David Shumway, *Rock Star: The Making of Musical Icons from Elvis to Springsteen* (Baltimore: Johns Hopkins University Press, 2014), p. 166.

247 *"An artist needs a certain amount of turmoil"*: Marci McDonald, "Joni Mitchell Emerges From Her Retreat," *Toronto Star*, February 9, 1974.

248 *"Americans were confronted with an 'imponderable dilemma of choice'"*: Jessica Grogan, *Encountering America: Humanistic Psychology, Sixties Culture, and the Shaping of the Modern Self* (New York: Harper Perennial, 2012), p. 219.

248 *"I'm a person who's been in therapy"*: Patrick Goldstein, "David Geffen: The *Rolling Stone* Interview," *Rolling Stone*, April 29, 1993.

250 *"her sui generis musical genre"*: Martin Kasindorf, "Dory Previn Sings Her Demon into the Open," *Los Angeles Times*, August 2, 1970.

253 *"I left his office and for three days"*: "Heart of a Prairie Girl," in Susan Whitall, ed., *Joni on Joni: Interviews and Encounters with Joni Mitchell* (Chicago: Chicago Review Press, 2018), p. 279.

253 *"I can't quit analyzing; I'm an artist"*: Dmitri Ehrlich, "Joni Mitchell," *Interview*, April 1991.

253 *"Third World"*: Angela LaGreca, "The Making of the *Don Juan's Reckless Daughter* Cover," *Rock Photo*, June 1985.

253 *"My intention was in a way to go"*: Anthony Fawcett, "Joni Mitchell: A Search for Clarity," *California Rock, California Sound* (Reed Books, 1978).

256 *"Mitchell decided, mid-session"*: Wesley Struck, "Joni Mitchell Meets Don Juan's Reckless Daughter," Circus, March 2, 1978.

256 *"pow-wow sound"*: Joni Mitchell, liner notes for *Love Has Many Faces: A Quartet, a Ballet, Waiting to Be Danced*, Rhino Records, 2014.

261 *"habitual non-expert"*: Ariel Swartley, "Hejira," *Rolling Stone*, February 10, 1977.

261 *"He was preparing to die"*: Ben Sidran, "The Underdog Meets Joni Mitchell," *Rolling Stone*, December 28, 1978.

262 *"the angry man of jazz"*: Nichole Rustin-Paschal, *The Kind of Man I Am: Jazzmasculinity and the World of Charles Mingus Jr.* (Middletown, CT: Wesleyan University Press, 2017), p. 3.

262 *"wide emotional spectrum"*: Sidran, "The Underdog Meets Joni Mitchell."

263 *"Synopsis: White woman does justice to Black men on record"*: Tom Reed, "Music Records and Reviews," *Los Angeles Sentinel*, July 5, 1979.

Chapter 7: For Art's Sake

Chapter 7 draws on an original interview with Miles Grier conducted in 2022.

265 *"Joan Black"*: Lee Hedgepath, "How an Alabama Winn-Dixie Changed Joni Mitchell," CBS42.com, August 10, 2022.

267 *"walked with a New York diddy-bop kind of step"*: Phil Sutcliffe, "Joni Mitchell," *Q Magazine*, May 1988.

267 *"I went into a sleazy menswear [shop]"*: Sutcliffe, "Joni Mitchell."

268 *published in the* Village Voice: Adrian Piper, *The Mythic Being*, *Village Voice* Ads (1973–75). Museum of Modern Art, June 2010–September 2011.

268 *"on the subject of love"*: Charles Schreger, "A Feminine Omnibus: Film Has Nine 'Loves,'" *Los Angeles Times*, December 5, 1980.

269 *"white or white-dominated city"*: Eric Lott, "Tar Baby and the Great White Wonder: Joni Mitchell's Pimp Game," *Black Mirror: The Cultural Contradictions of American Racism* (Cambridge, Mass.: Harvard University Press, 2017), p. 144.

269 *"I was the only black man at the party"*: Katherine Monk, *Joni: The Creative Odyssey of Joni Mitchell* (Vancouver, Toronto, and Berkeley: Greystone Books, 2012), p. 4.

269– *"It not only spoke to Mitchell's increasing distance"*: Fellezs, *Birds of Fire*,
270 p. 165.

270 *"It's as though the best you could do"*: Lott, Black Mirror, p. 152.

271 *"she deeply believes"*: David DeVoss, "Rock 'n' Roll's Leading Lady," *Time*, December 16, 1974.

272 *"the sense of a person at war with a mask"*: Janet Maslin, "'Renaldo and Clara,' Film by Bob Dylan: Rolling Thunder," *New York Times*, January 26, 1978.

272 *"Sahibs are always tied"*: Rudyard Kipling, *Kim*, edited by Cedric Watts. (Ware, England: Wordsworth Editions), p. 135.

273 *"Joni the Drag King"*: Michael Snyder, "A New Wave of Rock Fever," *Berkeley Barb*, January 20, 1978.

273 *"a pimply-looking negro":* Tom Reed, "Music Records and Reviews," *Los Angeles Sentinel*, March 16, 1978.

273 *Alias . . . worried some might assume the pimpish figure was based on him:* Sheila Weller, *Girls Like Us*, p. 428.

274 *"he lunged towards me":* David Yaffe, *Reckless Daughter* (New York: Sarah Crichton Books/FSG, 2017), p. 334.

274 *"smacked her up":* Karen Bliss, "Both Sides Now: Joni Mitchell's Biographer Tells His Stories," *Billboard Canada*, October 30, 2017.

275 *"all the way":* Weller, *Girls Like Us*, p. 529.

276 *"Don't ask me about those people":* David Rensins, "Jackson Browne: Such a Clever Innocence," *Crawdaddy*, January 1974.

276 *"naturally, unaffectedly, black":* Tim Crouse, "Music," *Rolling Stone*, January 20, 1972.

277 *"In the song, Don Juan":* Angela La Greca, "The Making of the *Don Juan's Reckless Daughter* Album Cover," *Rock Photo*, June, 1985.

278 *"You have teeth":* Carl Swanson, "Joni Mitchell, Unyielding," *New York*, February 8, 2015.

278 *"Joni Mitchell is so black":* Greg Tate, "How Black Is Joni Mitchell," Joni Mitchell Symposium, McGill University, October 22, 2004.

278– *"everything but the burden":* Greg Tate, ed., *Everything but the Burden: What White*
279 *People Are Taking from Black Culture* (New York: Harlem Moon/Broadway Books, 2003).

279 *"Mitchell's 'best Negro' riposte":* Miles Grier, "The Only Black Man at the Party: Joni Mitchell Enters the Rock Canon," *Genders* 56, September 22, 2012.

280 *I read their books:* Daphne A. Brooks, *Liner Notes for the Revolution: The Intellectual Life of Black Feminist Sound* (Cambridge, Mass.: Harvard University Press, 2021); Maureen Mahon, *Black Diamond Queens: African American Women and Rock and Roll* (Durham: Duke University Press, 2020); Kim Mack, *Fictional Blues: Narrative Self-Invention from Bessie Smith to Jack White* (Amherst: University of Massachusetts Press, 2020); Francesca T. Royster, *Black Country Music: Listening for Revolutions* (Austin: University of Texas Press, 2022).

283 *"It was because you are a singer":* Daniel Levitin, "A Conversation with Joni Mitchell," *Grammy Magazine*, March 1997.

Chapter 8: The Marriage

Chapter 8 draws on an original interview via email correspondence with Larry Klein from 2023.

292 *"fearless, futurist auteur":* Annie Zaleski, "Joni Mitchell's 80s: How the Canadian Songwriter Became a Fearless, Futurist Auteur," *The Guardian*, September 27, 2022.

292 *"I seem to be out of sync with the times in this decade":* Kristine McKenna, "Chalking It Up to Experience," *Los Angeles Times*, March 27, 1988.

295 *"I wanted to learn to use the studio as an instrument":* E.E. Bradman, "Joni Mitchell's Bass Desires," *Bass Magazine*, December 22, 2021.

299 *"He's twenty-five and he's come up in an era":* Vic Garbarini, "Joni Mitchell Is a Nervy Broad," *Musician Magazine*, January 1983.

301 *"Dreaming on a dime, she listens":* John Milward, "Wild Things Run Fast," *Rolling Stone*, November 25, 1982.

302 *"The ultimate erotic challenge, in fact":* George Leonard, "The End of Sex," *Esquire*, December 1, 1982.

302 *"The thing the writer said that sticks in my mind"*: Ben Fong-Torres, "Joni Rocks Again," *Chatelaine*, June 1998.

302 *"cocooning"*: Beth Ann Krier, "The Essence of Cocooning," *Los Angeles Times*, August 7, 1987.

303 *"The media are having a swell time telling us"*: Faludi, *Backlash*, p. 94.

304 *"a symbol of the bourgeoisie and the right wing generally"*: Barney Hoskyns, *Waiting for the Sun: A Rock 'n' Roll History of Los Angeles* (Lanham: Backbeat Books, 1996), p. 334.

305 *"There's no one really cutting it"*: Sean O'Hagan, "Idol Talk," *New Musical Express*, June 4, 1988.

309 *"should have put a disclaimer"*: Robert Hilburn, "Q&A with Joni Mitchell: Your Life Should Affect Your Direction," *Los Angeles Times*, October 27, 1994.

309 *"all about carrying a torch"*: Al Brumley, "Artist Slashes Back After Joni Mitchell's Cutting Lyrics in 'Blame,'" *Dallas Morning News*, September 23, 1997, p. 2C.

311 *"ridiculously good-looking, "*: Tony Hale, "Rock Master Class: A Music and Interview Program," Capitol Radio 95.8, December 29, 1985.

312 *"semi-war"*: Bill Flanagan, "Secret Places," *Musician Magazine*, May 1988.

317 *"I don't want to be interior-decorated out of my own music"*: Iain Blair, "Lucky Girl," *Los Angeles Herald*, March 9, 1986.

317 *"People think Klein took me over"*: Malka Marom, *Joni Mitchell: In Her Own Words* (Toronto: ECW Press, 2014), p. 269.

320 *"This country is going very conservative"*: Mick Brown, "The Travailer's Tale," *London Times*, November 10, 1985.

321 *"Caine Mutiny"*: David Yaffe, *Reckless Daughter* (New York: Sarah Crichton Books/FSG, 2017), p. 321.

323 *"God dog, Jesus dog, you know"*: Joni Mitchell, KCSA-FM interview, October 25, 1994.

326 *"I cast voices just like I would cast faces for a film"*: Chris DaFoe, "Mitchell's Not a Prophet but a 'Witness to My Times,'" *Toronto Globe and Mail*, March 25, 1988.

327 *"detachment"*: John Alton, "What We Talk about When We Talk about Literature: An Interview with Raymond Carver" (Chicago: Chicago Review), Issue 36:02, Autumn 1988.

330 *"Night Ride Home is her umpteenth comeback"*: Dave Marsh, "The Queen of Singers Returns," 1991.

330– *"It simply sounds like the distilled essence of everything that's come before"*: Linda Sand-
331 ers, "Night Ride Home," *Entertainment Weekly*, March 1, 1991.

331 *"Our studio was in a leg of the house"*: Larry Klein to E. E. Bradman, "Joni Mitchell's Bass Desires." *Bass Magazine*, December 21, 2021.

332 *"One starts to wonder where the poetry can come from, "* Bradman, "Joni Mitchell's Bass Desires."

332 *"grand, sweeping curves"*: Lloyd Whitesell, *The Music of Joni Mitchell* (Oxford: Oxford University Press, 2008) p. 189.

333 *"middle age"*: Chris Willman, "Album Review: Joni Mitchell, 'Night Ride Home,'" *Los Angeles Times*, February 24, 1991.

Chapter 9: Weaving Garlands

340 *she'd just won two Grammys: Turbulent Indigo* won a Grammy Award for Best Recording Package as well as Best Pop Album.

341 *"I have so much respect for her that I'm willing"*: Neil Strauss, "The Hissing of a Living Legend," *New York Times*. October 4, 1998.

342 *"a chancey commercial prospect":* Ken Tucker, "'Biograph' Reveals Dylan the Singer," *Philadelphia Inquirer*, November 24, 1985.

342 *"I've never really known what this thing is supposed to be":* Mikal Gilmore, "Behind the Glasses, Dylan at 44 Looking Scruffy But Ready," *Chicago Tribune*, November 10, 1985.

344 *"Execs have realized that if they have the back catalog, they don't need the aging artist.":* Dave Simpson, "'I'm Quitting This Corrupt Cesspool': Why Joni Mitchell Has Had It with the Music Business," *The Guardian*, November 21, 2002.

344 *"Rather than thinking of me as a bitter old fogey":* Dave DiMartino, "The Unfiltered Joni Mitchell," *MOJO*, August 1998.

345 *"Being a writer herself, we were very careful":* Nigel Williamson, "Both Sides Now," *Uncut*, December 2020.

347 *"At a certain point it's all in the phrasing":* James Reginato, "The Diva's Last Stand," *W Magazine*, December 2002.

349 *"I like the life that it has":* David Wild, "A Conversation with Joni Mitchell," *Rolling Stone*, May 30, 1991.

349 *"She separated the self from the art":* Claire Dederer, *Monsters: A Fan's Dilemma* (New York: Alfred. A. Knopf, 2023), p. 200.

353 *"a blaze of media attention":* Brian D. Johnson, "Joni Mitchell's Secret," Maclean's, April 21, 1997.

354 *"Our relationship is beautiful":* James Reginato, "The Diva's Last Stand."

354 *"I was recording some music with Wayne Shorter":* Greg Kot, "Joni's Jazzed," *Chicago Tribune*, September 9, 1998.

354 *"This is about you":* Jody Denberg, "Joni's Jazz," *The Austin Chronicle*, October 9, 1998.

355 *"the highest melody I've ever heard":* Robert L. Doerschuk, "Embrace the Tiger," *Musician Magazine*, December 1998.

357 *"God knows I can't play like Joni":* J. D. Considine, "Touring Down the Road to Fame, Fortune," *The Baltimore Sun*, July 14, 1995.

357 *"She took the clay and molded it in a way we hadn't seen before":* Tori Amos, undated radio interview, transcribed at jonimitchell.com.

358 *"Joni's songs spoke to me in an intimate, personal way":* "Janet Jackson Returns with a Hit Album and a New Look," *Jet*, November 1997, p. 60.

360 *"came out of a pimp's tradition":* Barney Hoskyns, "Joni Mitchell in conversation with Barney Hoskyns," *MOJO*, September 14, 1994.

360 *"a look and the willingness to cooperate":* James Reginato, "The Diva's Last Stand."

360 *"raceless and genderless":* Robin Eggar, "Both Sides Now," *Word*, April 2007.

362 *"My body is like Afghanistan":* John Mackie, "On War, Peace, Memories, and Dance," CanWest News Service, January 15, 2010.

362 *"Yes, you can call me a recluse":* Richard Ouzounian, "Joni Mitchell Opens Up to the *Star* After Years Away from Spotlight," *Toronto Star,* June 11, 2013.

366 *"If you can't say anything nice, say nothing at all":* Cameron Crowe, "Joni Mitchell: 'I'm a Fool for Love. I Make the Same Mistake Over and Over,'" *The Guardian*, October 27, 2020.

Chapter 10: Emissaries

Chapter 10 draws on original interviews with Brian Blade, John Kelly, Jon Cowherd, and Brandi Carlile conducted in 2019.

369 *"the noble art of accommodation.":* Tom Moon, "A Southern Gentleman Courts the Future's Spark," *JAZZIZ*, December 1998.

376 *"mute storyteller"*: Dan Callahan, "'Artists Are Warriors': An Interview with John Kelly, a Performer Outside of Time," *Village Voice*, February 26, 2018.

376 *"What does it mean to be a man?"*: John Kelly, *John Kelly* (New York: 2wice Arts Foundation/Aperture, 2001).

383 *"'Right on, man!'"*: Jonathan Bernstein, "Brandi Carlile to Perform Joni Mitchell's 'Blue' in Its Entirety," *Rolling Stone*, April 9, 2019.

385 *"Joni shook me"*: Michael Rietmulder, "Brandi Carlile Opens Up About Overcoming Insecurities, Her Latest Grammy Win and Her Memoir," *Seattle Times*, April 2, 2021.

391 *"shine theory"*: Ann Friedman, "Shine Theory: Why Powerful Women Make the Greatest Friends," *The Cut*, May 31, 2013.

392 *"Oh, that's gone"*: Cameron Crowe, "Joni Mitchell Opens Up to Cameron Crowe About Singing Again, Lost Loves and 50 Years of 'Blue,'" *Los Angeles Times*, June 20, 2021.

393 *"Then Herbie Hancock walks in"*: Patrick Doyle, "Musicians on Musicians: Bonnie Raitt & Brandi Carlile," *Rolling Stone*, November 2, 2019.

398 *"weeping profusely"*: Kaley Lane Eaton (@kaleylaneeaton), "I cannot handle this double whammy between weeping profusely at the brilliance of Joni at Newport and now Beyoncé absolutely serving pure genius," Tweet, July 30, 2022.

398 *"watching Joni Mitchell at Newport folk clips at a coffee shop"*: Lucas Mann (@lucaswmann), "lil thrill of watching joni mitchell at newport folk clips at a coffee shop daring myself not to cry in public," Tweet, July 28, 2022.

398 *"the videos of Joni at Newport"*: FrankleyMyDear (@shfrank), "Hear me out-the videos of Joni at Newport make me feel like there's a knitted blanket around my brain," Tweet, July 26, 2022.

398 *"Joni Mitchell showing up"*: Los Angeles Times (@latimes), "Just when you're Googling 'most affordable and isolated mountaintops,' @jonimitchell shows up," Tweet, July 26, 2022, quoting Mary MacNamara, "Once Again, Joni Mitchell Gives Us All a Reason to Live," Los Angeles Times, July 26, 2022.

398 *"Joni Mitchell at Newport Folk Fest I think"*: Harvey Creasey (@harvsofficial), "Joni Mitchell at Newport Folk Fest I think just changed my life," Tweet, July 24, 2022.

Viva: A Moving Conclusion

402 *"the dissecting, skewering gaze*: Michelle Mercer, "Take Me As I Am: Asking All the Wrong Questions About Joni Mitchell's Comeback," *Call & Response* at substack .com, June 16, 2023.

402 *"the freedom to be cruel is one of journalism's uncontested privileges,"*: Janet Malcolm, *The Silent Woman: Sylvia Plath and Ted Hughes* (New York: Vintage Books, 1993), p. 41.

403 *"Viva la old age!"*: Steve Baltin, "Joni Mitchell Returns with Epic All-Star Celebration at the Gorge," *Rolling Stone*, June 11, 2023.

INDEX

About the Author

Ann Powers is widely acknowledged as one of the most influential music writers working today. Her books include *Good Booty: Love and Sex, Black and White, Body and Soul in American Music; Weird Like Us: My Bohemian America*; and, with the artist, the *New York Times* bestseller *Tori Amos: Piece by Piece*. With Evelyn McDonnell, she also coedited the groundbreaking anthology *Rock She Wrote: Women Write About Pop, Rock, and Rap*. She has been a pop critic at the *New York Times*, the *Los Angeles Times*, and the *Village Voice* and a curator at Seattle's Museum of Popular Culture. Since 2011 she has been the critic and correspondent at NPR Music. Her articles have been widely anthologized in publications including *The Faber Book of Pop*, the Library of America's *Shake It Up: Great Pop Writing from Elvis to Jay Z, The World of Bob Dylan, Women Who Rock,* and six consecutive years of the Da Capo *Best Music Writing* series. She won the ASCAP-Deems Taylor Award for excellence in music writing in 2010. In 2017 Powers cofounded NPR's Turning the Tables, an ongoing project to recenter the popular music canon to be more inclusive of marginalized, under-estimated and forgotten voices. The first season of the series won a Gracie Award from the Alliance for Women in Media. She lives in Nashville.